THE INDEX

If you aren't sure what topic to select from the main menu, index at the back of the book. For instance, if you don't kr of whether to use *imply* or *infer* (it's a word-choice proble *imply, infer* in the index at the back, and you will find the ar

THE GLOSSARY OF USAGE

If you are not sure about how to use a particular word (for example, *accept* or *except*, or *imply* or infer, or *phenomenon* or *phenomena)*, you can flip to "Glossary of Usage" (p. 561) and seek the answer in the alphabetical glossary provided for that purpose. The glossary may also direct you to a fuller explanation of the term located somewhere else in the book.

THE DIRECTORIES TO DOCUMENTATION MODELS

No one ever remembers all the details about how to document a research paper. That's what reference guides like these are for. Chapters 5 through 8 detail the various documentation styles: Modern Language Association (MLA), American Psychological Association (APA), *Chicago Manual of Style* (Chicago), Council of Science Editors (formerly the Council of Biology Editors/CBE), and Columbia Online Style (COS). The chapter dividers make it easy for you to locate explanations and examples of the style you need to use for a particular assignment.

IF ENGLISH IS NOT YOUR FIRST LANGUAGE

If your first language is not English, most of the advice you seek will appear in Chapter 15 ("ELL"). Other ELL advice occurs throughout the text and is flagged with a special icon. You can also find ELL advice by looking up *ELL* in the index at the back of the book.

CORRECTION SYMBOLS

A list of standard correction symbols is provided at the back of the book. (Note, however, that some instructors use their own codes for correction.)

CHECKLISTS

You can download many of the checklists and boxes in this book from the CourseMate website at **http://www.checkmate3e.nelson.com**. This makes it easy for you to refer to guidelines such as the Structural Revision Checklist in Chapter 1 or the Things to Do to Avoid Plagiarism list from Chapter 4 as you write your papers and essays.

Checkmate

A WRITING REFERENCE FOR CANADIANS

THIRD EDITION

Joanne Buckley

NELSON EDUCATION

NELSON EDUCATION

Checkmate: A Writing Reference for Canadians, Third Edition

by Joanne Buckley

Vice President, Editorial Director:
Anne Williams

Executive Editor:
Laura Macleod

Senior Marketing Manager:
Amanda Henry

Managing Developmental Editor:
Sandy Matos

Photo Researcher and Permissions Coordinator:
Cindy Howard

Senior Content Production Manager:
Natalia Denesiuk Harris

Copy Editor:
Emily Dockrill Jones

Proofreader:
Maria Jelinek

Indexer:
Gillian Watts

Senior Production Coordinator:
Ferial Suleman

Design Director:
Ken Phipps

Managing Designer:
Franca Amore

Interior Design:
Greg Devitt Design

Cover Design:
Greg Devitt Design

Compositor:
Greg Devitt Design

Printer:
RR Donnelley

Library and Archives Canada Cataloguing in Publication Data

Buckley, Joanne, 1953–
      Checkmate : a writing reference for Canadians / Joanne Buckley. — 3rd ed.

Includes index.
ISBN 978-0-17-650256-0

      1. English language—Rhetoric— Handbooks, manuals, etc. 2. English language—Grammar—Handbooks, manuals, etc. I. Title.

PE1408.B818 2012   808'.042
C2011-907319-6

ISBN-13: 978-0-17-650256-0
ISBN-10: 0-17-650256-4

Design Images:
Abstract blue/green symbol: Anna Tyukhmeneva/Shutterstock; back of man: drbimages/iStockphoto; binoculars: jeffreeee/iStockphoto; blank whiteboard: mbbirdy/iStockphoto; checkmark/X buttons: iQoncept/Shutterstock; computer: jsemeniuk/iStockphoto; computer mouse: zoom-zoom/iStockphoto; daily planner: unalozmen/iStockphoto; dictionary: DNY59/iStockphoto; laptop: andersphoto/Shutterstock.com; notepad: blackred/iStockphoto; sticky note: stockcam/iStockphoto; stopwatch: Bibigon/iStockphoto; TV: Maliketh/iStockphoto; wrench with keyboard: mmaxer/Shutterstock

BRIEF TABLE OF CONTENTS

TO THE STUDENT

Or, what can a handbook do for me as a writer?

Handbooks are often among the most unread of books—a distinction they share with bestsellers such as physicist Stephen Hawking's *A Brief History of Time*, which has been called the most popular unread book of all time.

This book is designed not to be read in detail from cover to cover, but to be used as a reference to answer specific questions. Its unique layout will allow you to find answers quickly and easily and in as much or as little detail as you require. The use of columns separates guiding examples from explanatory text. Often, an example speaks volumes: you can see immediately how to resolve a problem without necessarily needing a fuller analysis. When you do need more detail, the second column will provide it. This separation of abstract principles and concrete examples allows you to learn at your own pace and find answers as you need them. Banner headings that cross columns will keep you on track.

In addition, the book includes tips, strategies, student samples from a variety of disciplines, information about the use of technology, and checklists to help you assess your work as you go through the writing process. There is also advice for English Language Learners, both in a specific chapter and at appropriate points throughout the book. Disability Awareness tips help you find resources and technology that may make writing a more accessible task.

Having easy access to the kinds of information this book provides can raise your grades—about 10 percent, generally

kaarsten/iStockphoto

speaking, since that is approximately how much is usually deductible for errors of correctness or style in any discipline. Obviously, though, the improvement may go further than that, because writing instructors in particular tend to mark impressionistically—with a certain regard for "artistic impression," a quality easily affected by a minor error or confusing sentence.

Why lose 10 percent of your grade if you don't have to? Students today are encouraged to write and revise a number of drafts of papers, rather than completing them in one shot; your instructor may well allow you to—or demand that you—hand in an outline of your assignment or a working draft before you hand in the finished product. This is a great opportunity for you to mine the resources in this guide.

If, for example, you know that you have a weak understanding of research processes or source documentation, you can review the sections on these topics briefly, then keep the model essays and sample bibliographic entries nearby as you write your papers. You may never internalize all the details of a particular documentation style, but you will know where to find the answers.

If you have identified problems with grammar or spelling in your work, this book will give you a tool to check your drafts with and protect your investment in your work. Hang on to this handbook and consult it whenever you have a question. Essays will seem easier to write as a result, and odds are that your grades will be higher, too.

TO THE INSTRUCTOR

This clear, easy-to-use guide for students from all disciplines presents grammar and punctuation, style and usage—and detailed documentation—in an often funny, always readable way. It is a truly Canadian handbook, rather than merely Canadianized, as will be seen in much of its content and many of its examples. The book is designed to help students refer easily to areas of difficulty as they go through the writing process in different disciplines. It provides advice for students for whom English is not a first language, and it provides help for students with disabilities.

It provides a visual format that gives students the opportunity to see examples separate from explanations, to tailor the level of detail to the needs of the students.

track5/iStockphoto

Beginning the Writing Process

Revised to include strategies to help students modify their writing process to make it more suitable to the demands of higher education, this guide provides examples of student writing and tips on how to write and revise their work from the whole to the parts. Structured with the writing process in mind, the book takes a friendly, lighthearted approach to what can be a dry subject.

What's New in the Third Edition?

Organization

The third edition of *Checkmate* has been reorganized in columns to improve the flow of information. Examples are typically provided in one column, where readers can find them quickly and see models of correct style, grammar, and punctuation, as well as longer samples of student writing. Explanations and analysis of the conventions of academic writing appear in an adjacent column to provide a greater level of detail for further exploration and understanding.

Boxes now summarize strategies, tips, and useful checklists to help writers assess and improve their own work as they go through the writing process. This level of self-assessment makes it easier for students to understand their own writing needs and goals and to understand the grades they receive. Five kinds of colour-coded tabs link similarly themed chapters:

- Writing Purpose (Chapters 1–2)
- Research and Documentation (Chapters 3–8)
- Writing Tools (Chapters 9–11)
- Editing Tools (Chapters 12–14)
- ELL (Chapter 15)

The third edition includes more discussion of rhetoric in the first two chapters. Research and documention has been updated to include the latest information on MLA, APA, Chicago, CSE, and CGOS.

Chapter 1—Composing an Essay

This chapter has been revised to include more information on rhetorical strategies to help students understand the purpose and audience of given assignments. It includes more samples, checklists, and advice on how to use technology appropriately. It also includes a new sample student essay that shows the elements of writing a critique.

Chapter 2—Reading and Writing in an Academic Setting

This chapter has been added to help students with study skills and to sharpen their ability to create good thesis statements and arguments. There are sections on how to recognize logical fallacies and on how to use visuals to enhance writing.

Chapters 3 to 8—Research and Documentation

Chapter 3 now presents updated information on how to use electronic databases and more visual aids on Internet resources.

Chapter 4 stresses academic integrity in plain language with clear examples of what to do and what not to do to avoid plagiarism.

Chapter 5 covers the Modern Language Association (MLA) style of documentation.

Chapter 6 covers covers the American Psychological Association (APA) style.

Chapter 7 covers *The Chicago Manual of Style* (Chicago).

Chapter 8 covers the Council of Science Editors (CSE) and the Columbia Online Style (COS) manuals.

The chapters have been closely revised and updated to reflect the latest versions of these guides, including the 16th edition of *The Chicago Manual of Style* (2010), the 7th edition of *Scientific Style and Format: The CSE Manual for Authors, Editors, and Publishers* (2006), and the 2nd edition of *The Columbia Guide to Online Style* (2006). More prominence is given to online documentation in each of these chapters, and new dedicated essay examples are provided for the MLA, APA, and Chicago chapters. Sample bibliographies are provided for CSE and CGOS styles.

Chapters 9 to 11—Grammar, Common Sentence Errors, and Punctuation

The overall approach of these chapters has been geared toward the new theme, "Writing Tools." These are chapters students need to master before and during the writing of their essays. Special efforts have been made to ensure that topics are dealt with in the most logical chapter.

Chapters 12 to 14—Sentence Structure and Style, Usage, and Mechanics and Spelling

These chapters have been revised with the new theme "Editing Tools" in mind. They are chapters that students should consult in preparing a final draft. Some material from the old "Common Sentence Errors" chapters has been moved to "Sentence Structure and Style."

Chapter 15—ELL (English Language Learners)

This chapter has been renamed ELL (English Language Learners) to reflect the reality that English is often not a second language, but another language for international students. This section has more detailed information on grammar than previous editions. ELL boxes throughout the text stress issues useful to English language learners at appropriate points in the book.

ANCILLARIES

CourseMate for *Checkmate*, Third Edition

Nelson Education's CourseMate for *Checkmate*, Third Edition, brings course concepts to life with interactive learning and exam preparation tools that integrate with the printed textbook. Students activate their knowledge through quizzes, games, and flashcards, among many other tools.

CourseMate provides immediate feedback that enables students to connect results to the work they have just produced, increasing their learning efficiency. It encourages contact between students and faculty: You can choose to monitor your students' level of engagement with CourseMate, correlating their efforts to their outcomes. You can even use CourseMate's quizzes to practise "Just in Time" teaching by tracking results in the Engagement Tracker and customizing your lesson plans to address their learning needs.

Watch student comprehension and engagement soar as your class engages with CourseMate. Ask your Nelson representative for a demo today.

Nelson Education Teaching Advantage (NETA)

The Nelson Education Teaching Advantage (NETA) program delivers research-based instructor resources that promote student engagement and higher-order thinking to enable the success of Canadian students and educators.

Instructors today face many challenges. Resources are limited, time is scarce, and a new kind of student has emerged: one who is juggling school with work, has gaps in his or her basic knowledge, and is immersed in technology in a way that has led to a completely new style of learning. In response, Nelson Education has gathered a group of dedicated instructors to advise us on the creation of richer and more flexible ancillaries that respond to the needs of today's teaching environments.

Instructor's Ancillaries

Key instructor ancillaries are provided on the Instructor's Faculty website (www.checkmate3e.nelson.com/instructor), giving instructors the ultimate tool for customizing lectures and presentations. The instructor ancillaries include

- **NETA Engagement:** The Enriched Instructor's Manual was written by Heather Barfoot, Niagara College. It is organized according to the textbook chapters and addresses key educational concerns, such as typical stumbling blocks student face and how to address them.
- **NETA Presentation:** Microsoft® PowerPoint® lecture slides for every chapter have been created by Heather Barfoot, Niagara College. NETA principles of clear design and engaging content have been incorporated throughout.

INFORMATIONAL DESIGN

To ensure students can easily read and locate information, the visual look of *Checkmate* has been significantly revised. Colour has been added to make material more appealing and to reinforce some rules and examples. Blue type and a green checkmark icon have been used to highlight correct or recommended examples, while red type and a red X icon signal examples that are erroneous or in need of improvement.

The new layout is geared toward visual learners in the electronic age. The use of columns allows readers to scan for quick information, whether concrete examples or more detailed explanations. This way, readers can access what they need to know when they need to know it. Banner headings keep readers oriented. Boxes that summarize information provide advice on technology, checklists for editing, strategies for approaching writing tasks, and tips for all learners, including those learning English and those who have disabilities that may make writing more difficult.

Pedagogy

Disability Awareness

DISABILITY AWARENESS

Create a draft using the spoken word. Using a word-processor with voice-recognition software will give you the chance to say your ideas rather than write them; the words you repeat will then

The Disability Awareness box is a feature for individuals with special needs that includes tips on what software can be used and how to use it.

Definitions

DEFINITIONS

Appeals in argument
Logos
the appeal of logic or reason and the construction of argument

Definitions of words used in the instructions are presented in the text.

ELL Note

Watch out for certain common suffixes (or endings) on nouns. These endings are often a clue that the word in question is a noun. These endings include *-ance*, *-ence*, *-ness*, *-ion*, and *-ty*.

The English Language Learners (ELL) box gives helpful tips to individuals whose first language isn't English.

Get Online

GET ONLINE

How Reliable Is the Internet?
Information on the Internet is public and free. It also changes quickly, so

This feature presents popular and academic websites that make online research faster.

Get Organized

GET ORGANIZED

How to Revise: A Collaborative Activity
Here is a checklist that may help you read others' material as part of peer review:

In the Get Organized boxes, students will find helpful checklists that will keep them focused on their writing assignments.

Strategies

The Strategies box outlines key points to keep in mind when writing.

Technology Toolbox

These helpful screen-captures show students how their writing assignments should be researched, formatted, and prepared in various programs.

Word-Processing Tips

WORD-PROCESSING TIPS

Creating Correct Margins and Formatting in Microsoft Word

The Word-Processing Tips feature gives students quick, easy shortcuts for working in Microsoft Word.

Quick Tip

Make sure to avoid ambiguity when citing publishers.

These helpful tips appear throughout the text as reminders to students.

Other Special Features

For guidelines on formatting a bibliog-raphy see 7-3. A sample bibliography is also included in 7-5.

This special icon directs students to related sections within the text that offer additional information.

Helpful Menus, Tabs, and Index

This resource is designed to help students without a firm knowledge of grammar terminology find quick answers to their questions. It will be useful to students not only before submitting a paper but also after it is returned, as they respond to their instructor's comments. The index and tabs make it easy for users of this book to find the information they need to check their work.

Teaching by Example

Numerous sample research papers and writing formats have been added to *Checkmate*. More illustrations are included—for example, new Statistics Canada figures and tables to illustrate proper documentation style and new screenshots to illustrate online library research tools. One important innovation is that following examples of effective writing by well-known authors, bibliographic details are now supplied. Instead of appending just the author's name and the item title, *Checkmate* includes the author's name, the poem or article name, the book name, and the place, publisher, and year of publication. This level of detail is supplied to indicate *Checkmate*'s emphasis on the seriousness of proper documentation.

Addressing ELL Issues

Chapter 15 alerts students to special problems with English. There are also ELL notes throughout the text to indicate areas of special concern for those learners for whom English is not the first language.

Glossary of Usage

The glossary of usage is now found at the end of the text. The glossary includes words that may cause confusion, and they are clarified with examples on how the word is to be used in a sentence.

ACKNOWLEDGMENTS

I extend my thanks to Mary Buckley, Ethel Weick, and Carol Hartung for their kind support throughout my writing process, and thanks to Sandy Matos, Managing Developmental Editor, who was so helpful to me during the development. Her positive attitude was very reassuring. Thanks also go to Anne Williams, Editorial Director and Vice-President; Laura Macleod, Executive Editor; Amanda Henry, Senior Marketing Manager; Natalia Denesiuk Harris, Senior Content Production Manager; Ferial Suleman, Senior Production Coordinator; Greg Devitt, Designer; Cindy Howard, Permissions Researcher; Emily Dockrill Jones, Copy Editor; Elizabeth Phinney, Cold Reader; and Maria Jelinek, Proofreader, for all their hard work through the editing and production of this publication.

I would like to thank Desmond Pouyat for helping me make this book possible. I would also like to thank Dustin Manley, who helped me find examples and details to immensely enrich this handbook. Other student authors who graciously agreed to allow me to use their work include April Beresford, Joel Castelli, Zarena Cassar, Alyssa Lai, Daniel Rosefield, Melissa Seaborg, and Kamran Shaik. Their work adds immeasurably to the depth and authenticity of this handbook.

I would like to express my thanks to Shannon MacRae of Niagara College, who wrote a weekly journal of suggestions for the new edition. Her dedication and feedback is greatly appreciated.

The reviewers, who took time to read and help me revise, are also responsible for the improvements and innovations in this edition of *Checkmate*. I would like to thank all of these people for their efforts:

Daniel Burgoyne, Vancouver Island University

Grant Coleman, Mohawk College

Jill Jackson, University of Windsor

Nina Pyne, Sault College of Applied Arts

David Quiring, University of Saskatchewan

Scott Straker, Queen's University

Trevor Tucker, University of Ottawa

Yuri_Arcurs/iStockphoto

Good Writing
is a kind of
skating which carries off
the performer where
he would not go.

— *Ralph Waldo Emerson*

Composing an Essay

1

Writing in Our Time

Writing has expanded the scope of its technology beyond pen and pencil to embrace software and streaming.

Writing is often done in groups, rather than strictly by individuals.

Writing is more immediate and can reach many people at once.

Writing has a public face on the Web that demands a different attitude toward tone and toward the boundaries of self-expression.

Writing is global and demands understanding that transcends one language group.

Writing is often accompanied by visuals, and the image as well as the word tells the story.

Writing today involves thinking about the medium in which we write. Once a private, slow process, writing has become immediate and global in its influence, depending on the medium of its transmission.

As a result of this breadth of impact, our purpose and our audience matter more than they ever have before. Although writing should begin with self-expression, the process of writing should consider the audience more than ever before, if only because now writers can reach such a wide audience with such ease.

For many of us, starting to write is a challenge. Like learning, starting to write demands some tolerance of uncertainty. Feeling lost is common. Even if you start by feeling lost, try to live with the uncertainty and trust the process. You find your way by writing. Standing in front of a blank canvas, we are faced with overwhelming choices, if not about the subject matter of our work, which may have been assigned, then about its style, its tone, its wording, and the general approach we should take. The best advice is to learn to "divide and conquer." The best—and calmest—writers start with the large issues (subject matter, important ideas, research methods) and move to the smaller yet significant issues as the work proceeds. We can't get caught up in the details at the early stage. We need to allow ourselves room for mistakes—and for creativity. That way, we say something we want to say, as well as something that fits the occasion for which we are writing.

The problem of invention is not new. Aristotle divised some topics for invention that, with some revision, are still useful starting points today. You begin by asking yourself questions about the topic you have chosen. Not all of them will apply, of course, but those that do will help you determine the focus and direction of the work you will do.

Getting Yourself Ready to Write

Ask yourself these questions to figure out your working style:

- ❏ Where do you work best?
- ❏ At what time of day do you work best?
- ❏ Do you write best alone or with others?
- ❏ How do you approach your purpose in a given assignment?
- ❏ How do you approach your intended audience?
- ❏ What brainstorming methods work for you?
- ❏ What outlining methods work for you?
- ❏ What is your typical approach when writing a first draft?
- ❏ How do you go about revising your work?
- ❏ What works best for you in your own version of the writing process?
- ❏ What works least well for you for in the writing process?
- ❏ What are your problem areas in writing?

Monitoring your own writing process is a helpful way to understand the psychology of your own method of composition. Knowing what works for you and what does not will help you make the best use of this book and give you a chance to practice techniques that will make the process simpler and the product more effective.

Checklist to Stimulate Invention

The following classical breakdown of the approaches to invention may give you some insight into the direction of your work:

Definition
- ❏ How can you define key words in the topic?
- ❏ Where do the terms originate?
- ❏ How has the meaning of the words changed?
- ❏ How can the topic be divided into parts?
- ❏ What is sometimes mis-understood about the topic or key words in it?
- ❏ What are some concrete examples of the topic?

Comparison
- ❏ What is the topic like?
- ❏ What is it different from?
- ❏ How is it better or worse than something else?
- ❏ What can you contrast it with?

Cause, Motive, or Purpose
- ❏ What are the causes of the topic?
- ❏ What is the purpose of the topic?
- ❏ Why does it happen?
- ❏ What is the consequence of it?
- ❏ What precedes or follows it?

Testimony
- ❏ What do I already know about the topic?
- ❏ What do people say about the topic?
- ❏ What statistics or facts are available about the topic?
- ❏ What information on the topic is available in popular culture?
- ❏ What do the experts say on the topic?

Context
- ❏ Is the topic possible?
- ❏ If it is possible, is it desirable?
- ❏ When did it happen previously?
- ❏ Who has done or experienced it?
- ❏ Who can do it?
- ❏ If this topic started, what would end it?
- ❏ What conditions would produce this topic now?
- ❏ What might stop It from happening?

This approach, topical invention, can help you break your topic into approachable categories by asking questions about it.

Note that topical invention can be used to broaden your topic—to help you consider a range of possibilities—and to narrow it down by helping you select an aspect of the topic that you wish to pursue in more detail.

1-1 PLANNING

For most writers, even professional ones, reaching the ultimate goal of a persuasive, polished document demands a complex writing process. The process varies among writers but generally includes the following three major stages.

These stages often overlap as you develop and polish a piece of writing.

Figure 1.1 Three Stages of Writing

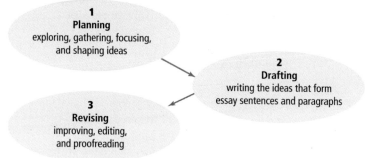

1
Planning
exploring, gathering, focusing, and shaping ideas

2
Drafting
writing the ideas that form essay sentences and paragraphs

3
Revising
improving, editing, and proofreading

MEETING THE DEMANDS OF AN ASSIGNMENT

What does the assignment want you to do?

What information do you need to read to do it?

What do you find intriguing about the topic, and how can you use that interest?

What approach might you take to set your work apart from the run-of-the-mill responses?

Do you understand the purpose of the assignment? Why does it make sense in the context of your course?

What specifics do you need to keep in mind? These might include page length, hints about organizing material, or rubrics that show you the emphases that are most important for grading.

Who will read the paper besides the implicit reader who will be grading the assignment?

© Justin Horrocks/
iStockphoto.com

The first step when planning any written document—and one that many fledgling writers neglect—is figuring out what is required. Assessing the scope and requirements of the assignment or the goals of the finished document will help make the writing task manageable—even pleasurable—and, all-importantly, it will ensure that you satisfy your audience's expectations. Here are a few criteria and questions to consider as you analyze a writing task.

SUBJECT/TOPIC

The **subject** is what you are writing about. The **topic** is the specific aspect of the subject you will focus on in your writing.

- Has the topic been assigned, or are you free to choose your own topic?
- Why is this topic worth writing about? Why would you want to spend your time researching it and writing about it? And, why would a reader want to spend his or her time reading about it?
- How do your own experiences, interests, and knowledge relate to the topic? What do you bring to the writing table?
- Does the topic need to be narrowed down to make it clearer and the writing task manageable?

PURPOSE

The **purpose** is what you are trying to accomplish in your writing.

- What is your writing purpose? To inform? Explain? Persuade? Express? Entertain? Or something else?
- Is it a combination of the above?
- If the writing topic has been assigned, what key words indicate the writing purposes (e.g., inform, summarize, outline)?

AUDIENCE

The **audience** is whom you are writing for. It's important to understand your audience members' backgrounds, knowledge, interests, attitudes, sensibilities, and expectations—you can't persuade your readers if you don't take the time to analyze who they are.

- Are you writing for a very specific audience, such as your instructor, or a wider audience, which could include your classmates or others?
- What might this audience already know about the topic?
- What is it important to tell them?
- How will you capture and maintain this particular audience's undivided attention and interest?
- How will you tell them about the important topic ideas and information? (It's not too early to start thinking about such writing considerations as tone and formality of language)
- What writing features and techniques will most effectively communicate essential ideas and information to this specific audience?

DOCUMENT LENGTH

- How long is the essay required to be?
- If it's up to you to determine the length, what length would be appropriate, given the breadth of your topic and how deeply you intend to explore it? (Translation: Don't try to write the history of religion in 500 words.)

DEADLINES

- When is the essay due? In large measure, this will determine the breadth and depth of content you can cover effectively. The deadline will also help you determine how much time to spend on each essential stage in the writing process.

DOCUMENT STYLE AND DESIGN

- Which document style and design does your school and/ or instructor require or prefer? ASK! Some subject instructors prefer the Modern Language Association (MLA) style, others the American Psychological Association (APA) or the Chicago Manual of Style (Chicago) style.
- Where do you find out about the instructor's preferred style and design specifications once he or she has identified them? Stay tuned. Chapters 2, 10, and 11 of this guide are good places to start.

SPECIFIC REQUIREMENTS
These are the considerations that help you make decisions about writing content, the way you spend your time, and even the appearance of your completed work.

INFORMATION SOURCES

You're making headway. It's just about time to turn yourself loose on the topic.

- What kind of information will you need? Perhaps a literary work and critical commentary on that work; reports, text, or visuals from an Internet site; or your own experiences, observations, and insights.
- How should you acknowledge these information sources? Again, this book provides complete information. Maybe it's time to begin your research by scanning the book to find out what it offers and how it can meet your academic writing needs.

1-1B GENERATING AND EXPLORING IDEAS

For any writer, just getting started can be intimidating. Accomplished writers often have a repertoire of strategies for generating and exploring ideas and, in some cases, starting to shape and connect thoughts to create new ideas.

You are encouraged to try or at least consider all of them. Then, choose the strategy or strategies that work best for you.

The idea-generating strategies outlined here include
- brainstorming and listing
- clustering and branching
- free-writing
- asking questions
- writing journal entries

DISABILITY AWARENESS

Help make websites accessible:
Use the "Contact Us" button when you find a website that you cannot easily access. Developers need to know that their websites cannot reach all the users.

Here is a brainstorm list on working dogs.

Working Dogs

- history of dogs
- breed characteristics
- hazardous situations
- avalanche rescue dogs
- fire protection dogs
- amazing sense of smell
- they hear extremely well, too
- dogs that sniff suitcases at airports
- pet visitation dogs at hospitals
- human-animal bond

ELL Note

If English is not your first language, consider brainstorming in your native language. Such a practice may improve the speed and spontaneity of your thinking as you develop your topic.

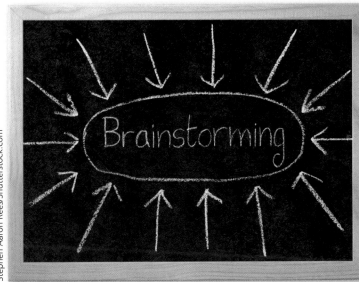

Stephen Aaron Rees/Shutterstock.com

BRAINSTORMING AND LISTING

You might think of brainstorming as a group activity, but it can also be used while working alone to generate ideas for writing. It is similar to free-writing (see below), but it differs from free-writing in that what is written down is generally a list of phrases or, sometimes, just words.

If your writing topic has been established for you, start with it; or, if you can choose your topic, begin with a subject that interests you. Give yourself a set amount of time in which to list freely *all* the ideas relating to the subject that come into your mind. Don't try to censor or criticize any of the list items. At this point, your goal is quantity, not quality.

When the time you have given yourself is up, and only then, take a critical look at your brainstormed list. Reject weak or irrelevant ideas, add any new ideas that occur to you, and start looking for idea patterns and linkages. This kind of shaping and organizing is a preliminary step to the writing outline.

CLUSTERING AND BRANCHING

The goal of clustering and branching is not just to put ideas on paper or on the screen, but to start showing possible relationships between ideas. To start clustering, put a key subject word at the top or centre of a blank page. Look for ideas related to the key word and connect them to it, and to other ideas, using circles and lines. Let your mind explore all possible associations freely. Here is a sample cluster to generate ideas for an essay on "People I Admire."

Note that the person who generated this cluster used different shapes to designate different types of ideas. Someone else might use colour-coding to group ideas and show the relationships between them.

Branching is another strategy for generating ideas and showing how they are linked. To create a branch diagram, put your topic at the top of a blank page, with your main ideas branching from it. Next, write in any supporting ideas and details on branches below each main idea. Extend the branching options as far as you think necessary.

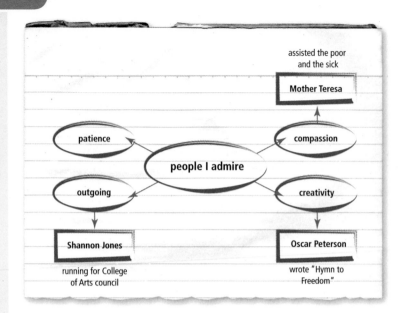

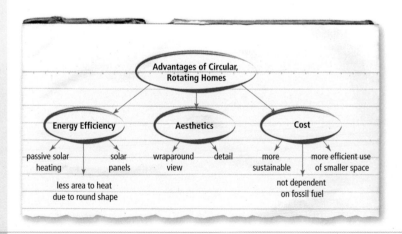

SAMPLE FREE-WRITING

Free-writing can be enhanced by using intermittent explorations of the same topic, something called "looping." To do this here, you would take the main idea that developed in the first free-writing session and make it the central focus of the next free-writing session.

Notice how each of these paragraphs spins off from the central theme of the one previous to it.

Or, a similar cluster could be done on the theme of revolutionizing homes.

Hope as part of counselling. People bring hope with them into counselling, and sometimes hope, by itself, can make people better. Hope is the mystery component. Hope is organic, something grown, planted from seed, starts small, may grow or not depending on conditions. Hope needs to be nurtured like a small seed in order to develop into the goals that a client has.

Conditions that may help or hinder growth include the relationship with the therapist, the family situation that a client finds himself or herself in, and the state of mind of the client when the therapy begins.

The relationship with the therapist is one of the main sources of hope in therapy. The nurturing relationship allows the client to express needs and goals in an atmosphere where one does not need to fear judgment.

FREE-WRITING

Free-writing is writing freely for a set period of time—say, five to ten minutes—or in a given amount of space—say, part of a page or a whole page—about a very general subject. Ideas should flow out uncensored and without concern for spelling, grammar, or punctuation. The important goals are to keep going and to be open to a process of discovery. Then, after you've met your time or space quota, review what you've written and try to see any patterns, topics, or ideas that look interesting enough to develop in a piece of writing. You can free-write in longhand on paper or by typing into a computer. It's best to use the writing mode in which you are most proficient so you can keep the ideas flowing. One-fingered, incompetent typing defeats the purpose of rapid free-writing. If you're happy with the keyboard, though, typing can ensure that your ideas are saved and secure.

ASKING QUESTIONS

At this initial stage of the writing process, it's a good idea to think like a journalist. Reporters are known for probing subjects by asking the 5 Ws and H, which is short for *who, what, where, when, why,* and *how.* Suppose you're writing an explanatory essay for an environmental studies course on a new, energy-efficient, circular, rotating home.

RTimages/Shutterstock.com

Following are some questions you might ask:
- Who designed this revolutionary home?
- What are the environmental advantages of the new design?
- Where would the home be most energy efficient?
- When will it be available to the general public?
- Why was it designed?
- How does it work?

Your first set of questions can easily lead to other questions that will help you identify even more ideas.

Often, academic disciplines have special questions that are asked consistently by researchers and analysts in these fields. For example, in English Literature, you might be asked "What is the central theme of the work?" Try to identify key questions in any discipline you're studying. They come in handy when generating ideas for papers in that discipline.

For instance, another *who* question might be this one: Who will need the new product?

Good questions to help you critique something that you need to explore in more detail are these:
- What? What is this about?
- How? How does it work?
- How well? How well does it work to convince me?
- So what? How am I going to use what I have learned by reading this?

Entries might record

- your observations
- interesting ideas and facts learned from reading
- your reactions to course content
- connections you've made between ideas

These are just a few possibilities. Keeping a journal has many advantages:

1. It gives you practice articulating your thoughts.
2. It strengthens your powers of observation and memory.
3. It provides you with a record of ideas when you need them for writing assignments.

You may wish to experiment with ideas in your journal before you try incorporating them into a formal draft.

Oct 10. The girl in biology I have a crush on said she was a real Robert Ludlum fan. I said I had a copy of his latest book that I could lend her. Of course, I didn't. I must have gone to every bookstore in Victoria looking for a copy. They were all sold out. Finally, I got one in the local Shoppers Drug Mart. I dog-eared it so it looked like I'd read it about six times. When I gave the book to her, she was pretty cold. Suddenly, I understood what James Joyce meant in "Araby" when he said, "I saw myself as a creature driven and derided by vanity." I now have a pretty good sense of what "epiphany" means, too.

Sven Hoppe/Shutterstock.com

JOURNAL WRITING

Journal writing is similar to free-writing in that it gives you complete latitude to express yourself. The key goal is to get those ideas down on paper. The main difference is that your journal entries are made on a regular basis.

WORK DIARY

A work diary may include notes of what you are reading in preparation for writing. It is intended to catalogue the accumulated sources you delve into and your insights into them as you go along. Keeping a work diary increases your awareness of how the things you are writing fit together into a whole.

After thinking broadly to collect as many ideas related to your writing topic as you can, it's time to begin focusing your thoughts to frame a controlling idea called a **thesis**. A **thesis statement** alerts your reader to the main argument of the essay and prepares him or her, in a general way, for the content that is to follow. A good thesis statement states your case as clearly as it can in a sentence or so. In an academic essay, a thesis statement should be just that—a statement—and not a question. It provides the answer, generally, to the questions you had in mind as you explored the topic. It presents your educated opinion on the topic and, ideally, has a controversial edge.

Let's look at a few examples of essay thesis statements:

Genetically modified foods need to be labelled in order to protect Canada's population from potential long-term dangers to health and to the environment.

Yann Martel's *Life of Pi* demonstrates how magic realism has become a literary form that transcends cultural boundaries and the limits of contemporary time and place by reducing us to our limited humanity in the face of nature.

The self-fulfilling prophecy helps shape social reality often through a combination of stereotypes and expectations based on ability in school.

CHARACTERISTICS OF A GOOD THESIS STATEMENT

A thesis is effective if it has these characteristics:
- appealing to its potential audience
- specific in what it claims and suited to the word length of the paper
- able to be supported by evidence such as reasons, statistics, examples, or testimony from authorities
- single-minded and clear in its position

- Does your thesis statement provide an **assertion** in which you state clearly your topic and your position on the topic?
- Is your thesis statement specific enough to be defended by clear, relevant evidence?
- Does your thesis statement give a sense of your purpose (to persuade, explain, describe, entertain)?
- Does your thesis statement give the reader a sense of how you will organize and present your argument?
- Does your thesis statement relate to the themes and overall direction of the course materials assigned? In other words, does it fit the context of the course? Does it engage in the themes of the course?
- Does your thesis statement go beyond the facts to present an argument based on your educated opinion about the facts?

Your thesis statement should help to settle a question—perhaps not definitively, but to the best of your ability. An essay typically presents evidence to support your thesis statement. Hence, the thesis statement is an educated opinion about the facts, or the evidence, that you have found in your research and your thinking on the subject. The thesis will hold the entire essay together, so it needs to be a forcefully defended statement of your findings on a subject.

As you progressively hone your outline and more precisely focus your ideas, you will probably need to refine your thesis statement.

PRELIMINARY THESIS STATEMENT
Circular, rotating homes offer users many advantages.

MORE REFINED THESIS STATEMENT
Circular, rotating homes offer significant advantages in terms of energy efficiency, building costs, and the aesthetics of design.

This can be seen in the following introduction from David Adams Richards's "My Old Newcastle."

> In Newcastle, New Brunswick, which I call home, we all played on the ice floes in the spring, spearing tommy-cod with stolen forks tied to sticks. More than one of us almost met our end slipping off the ice.

—David Adams Richards, "My Old Newcastle,"
in *A Lad from Brantford and Other Essays* (Fredericton, NB: Broken Jaw Press, 1994).

Notice that the words *significant* and *in terms of* limit the topic and focus it more precisely. To a large extent, a thesis statement frames the choices you make about content. The thesis statement usually comes within the first paragraph, in the final sentence or sentences.

In certain writing situations, such as essays with a non-academic purpose, a thesis statement may be too confining, and writers may need more latitude to introduce a theme or spark a reader's interest.

For example, most writers of essays published in newspapers have a thesis, but theirs may not follow the rigours of clarity demanded in an academic or business setting. In journalism, the reader is more apt to be voluntary rather than captive, and more willing to sort out meaning. Hence, you may find a great deal more latitude in published essays of a non-academic type. Unlike students, these writers may more freely use questions, broad implications, or sweeping statements to serve as the thesis or purpose statement in their writing.

When generating your preliminary thesis statement, you might consider these points, though you may not be able to satisfy all of these requirements.

It's important to remember that you're engaged in a writing *process*. Good thesis statements don't just drop out of the sky. They're the result of ongoing revision and refinement.

DISABILITY AWARENESS

Knowing Your Audience

Effective writers learn as much as possible about their readers so that they can find ways to build common ground. For example, there are over 100,000 students currently enrolled in post-secondary education who have disabilities, and only 1/4–1/2 of them regularly receive disability-related services.

http://www.adaptech.org/cfichten/abCanadianpostsecondarystudentswithdisabilities.pdf

🔀 How does regionalism affect Canadian politics?

~~I believe~~ that regionalism contributes positively to Canadian identity.

🔀 Regionalism in Canada contributes to Canadian identity but sometimes interferes with Canada's ability to act as a unit in world affairs.

A good thesis statement

- makes a contract with the readers and meets their expectations
- makes a statement that clarifies your approach to the topic
- appears early in the essay, usually after some background has been established
- addresses the subject rather than the act of writing the essay (hence, you can avoid phrases like "I believe," "It is my view that," "I am writing to demonstrate," etc.)

THESIS:
Independent-study high schools provide a better education because they prepare students for university by combining freedom with responsibility.

Disadvantages

- Immature students may take advantage of the greater freedom.
- Students forfeit many opportunities for discussions and group projects.
- The social element of the educational experience is limited.

Advantages

- Students who have had educational difficulties are removed from the classroom context of failure.
- Scheduling flexibility accommodates mature students or those who have had medical difficulties.
- Students are better prepared for the university experience, where they will be largely unsupervised.
- Students are allowed to take complete responsibility for their own learning.

PRELIMINARY ORGANIZATIONAL PLAN

Now that you've generated writing ideas and a thesis statement to define your topic, you may want to create a preliminary outline to frame a general structure for ideas. In this first, tentative outline, organize your ideas into categories under your thesis statement.

QUICK TIP

When preparing to do research, remember your evidence can take four forms: expert opinion, statistics, examples, and reasons.

FORMAL WRITING OUTLINE

The formal outline differs from the preliminary outline in its level of detail. The formal outline should be flexible enough so as not to be too limiting, but it should show clearly the logical flow of your ideas or arguments. Like informal outlines, formal outlines are generally created in the planning stage of the writing process, but they can be created while drafting or even revising if you sense your writing is losing focus or logical flow.

Here is a formal outline for a very short persuasive essay on xenotransplantation (the use of animal organs in human transplants).

Thesis: Transplanting organs from animals to humans is acceptable because it saves human lives, it is safe, and it is ethical.

I. Saving Human Lives
   A. People die waiting for transplants every day.
   B. Transplantation can be done humanely.

II. Little Risk of Disease Spreading from Animals to Humans
   A. Insulin from sheep has been used for over seventy-five years without presenting any immunological problems.
   B. We already use pig valves in heart-valve replacements.
   C. We have overcome diseases spread from animals before (swine flu, bird flu, rabies).

III. Ethical Issues
   A. We already use animals to serve human needs (clothing, food) and save human lives (medical research and testing).
   B. It would be unethical to deny people who are suffering from medical problems such as diabetes or liver disease the possibility of improving their quality of life and, in some cases, saving their lives.

To generate a formal outline, do the following:

1. Begin your outline by writing your thesis statement at the top of the page.
2. Next, write the Roman numerals I, II, and III, spread apart, down the left side of the page.
3. Beside each Roman numeral, write one main idea that you have about your topic, or a main point that you want to make.
   a) If you are trying to persuade, you will want to write your best arguments.
   b) If you are trying to explain a process, you will want to write the steps to follow. (You will probably need to group these into categories. If you have trouble doing this, try using Beginning, Middle, and End.)

c) If you are trying to inform, you may want to write the major categories into which your information can be divided.

For more detail on types of organization, see 1-3c.

4. Under each Roman numeral, write *A*, *B*, and *C* down the left side of the page.
5. Next to each letter, write the fact or piece of information that relates to the main idea. Note that the information used may either support or refute the thesis, since the writer must manage all information, pro and con, related to the argument.
6. If you are adding more minor levels of ideas and information to the outline (under the alphabet letters), write numbers, and under these, use lowercase letters.

The traditional outline follows this pattern:

I. Introduction to classification of headaches
II. Kinds of headaches
   A. Vascular
      1. Migraines
      2. Cluster headaches
      3. High-blood-pressure headaches
   B. Myogenic
      1. Tension headaches
      2. Muscle aches of the neck or head
   C. Headaches from specific causes
      1. Ictal headaches
        a. seizure-related
        b. usually affect one side of the head
          (1) easily misdiagnosed
          (2) often mistaken as psychotic symptom
            (a) detected with EEG
            (b) treated with anticonvulsants

Here are a few guidelines:

- Each outline level should have more than one entry.
- Entries should be grammatically parallel if phrases are used.
- Outlines should remain flexible. Remember, you're still in the *planning* process, and plans often have to be adjusted. The outline does not have to be followed rigidly.

1-2 DRAFTING THE DOCUMENT: CREATING A STRUCTURE

The drafting stage is where all your planning pays off, because many of your critical writing decisions have been made, freeing you to think, write, and discover. **Drafting** is putting your ideas on paper in logically connected, coherent paragraphs composed of clear sentences.

But don't put too much pressure on yourself at this point. This part is called a **rough draft** for a reason. Once the rough draft is complete, you still have the revision stage to improve, edit, and proofread—in essence, to craft the rough draft into a finely polished piece of writing.

As you sit down to begin drafting (or stand, if you're Ernest Hemingway), ensure your writing resources are arranged meaningfully at your workstation. Resources might include these items:

- outlines
- index cards
- quotations with accompanying citations
- visuals such as diagrams and graphs

Writing quickly and maintaining a good momentum are important when drafting, and nothing can interrupt the flow of ideas more than having to stop to hunt for a scrap of paper on which you have noted a key supporting idea.

Generally, there are three major parts, or elements, to a piece of academic writing:

1. An **introduction** that engages the reader and introduces the controlling idea
2. A **body** that develops ideas logically and coherently and incorporates convincing supporting evidence
3. A **conclusion** that follows logically from the introduction and body and presents a summary or generalization

The introduction should have these main goals:

1. To engage the reader, generating interest that will make him or her want to read further
2. To describe your topic, your point of view, and the main points you will cover in the body of your document

To engage or hook the reader, you might consider using one of the following in your introduction:

- an anecdote, illustration, or incident
- an apparent contradiction or ironic statement
- background historical information
- a shocking or unusual fact or statistic
- a rhetorical question
- a quotation
- humour
- a description
- an analogy

In the following introductions, see if you can identify the hooks used by the writers. Ask yourself how well these hooks work to establish interest in what will follow. *(The thesis statement of each introduction appears in italics.)*

> A central feature of Alice Munro's literary technique is her use of paradox. Paradox may be understood as "an apparently self-contradictory statement which, on closer inspection, is found to contain a truth reconciling opposites."[1] In "Dulse" Munro contrasts romantic and empirical perspectives as embodied in Mr. Stanley and the telephone workers, respectively. Lydia moves to the realization that, exclusively, neither of these contradictory outlooks sufficiently defines the complexity of experience. *By examining in "Dulse" the relationship of style, point of view, structure, and imagery to paradox, one achieves an appreciation of how these technical features sustain Alice Munro's thematic insistence on the doubleness of reality.*
>
> —Carla Thorneloe

The introduction is your opening paragraph, which usually ranges between 100 and 150 words.

Writers use a thesis statement to describe their topic, their point of view, and the main points they will cover. Generally, a thesis statement is the last sentence in the introduction, though that is not a rigid rule.

In North America, the thesis is generally stated early in the paper, though some cultures may consider that approach awkward. Be as direct as you can in the statement of your thesis.

QUALITIES OF A COMPELLING THESIS STATEMENT

In the thesis statement, you should present a generalization about your topic. While it is a generalization, it should not be too broad, and the statement must be focused enough to avoid vagueness.

It's important to remember that generating a thesis statement is a recursive process: you must expect to go back and forth between the drafting and revising stages a number of times. For example, the writer of the last, improved thesis statement may have revised his thesis statement to reflect his content more accurately, or he may have shaped his content better to reflect the controlling idea of his thesis statement—or maybe he did both.

Once you've crafted a workable, focused thesis statement, there should be a seamless, logical transition into the body of your essay.

Avoid making thesis statements that are

- too factual or statistical
- too broad
- too vague

A thesis statement that is too factual cannot be argued, and it fails to give your reader an indication of the direction your content will take.

Too Factual: At eighteen, Ty Tryon is the youngest full-time member in the history of the PGA tour.

Improvement: Allowing teenagers to participate full-time in professional sports cannot be justified psychologically, educationally, and, above all, morally.

Don't make your thesis or purpose statement too broad; otherwise, you will be expected to deliver on all your writing promises, and this will not be possible given deadline and assignment-length requirements.

Too Broad: Recreational running has countless benefits.

Improvement: Recent research indicates that regular recreational running has demonstrable physiological, psychological, and social benefits.

- ⊘ **Too Vague:** Robertson Davies develops a universal human theme in his novel *Fifth Business*.

- ✔ **Improvement:** In Robertson Davies's *Fifth Business*, the opposition of imagination and "practicality" is dramatized through the worlds of the theatre and small-town Ontario. The paper will examine the tension between these two forces by examining the career of Paul Dempster/Magnus Eisengrim, the conflicts within the character of Dunstan Ramsay, and the narrator's description of the contrast between the theatre and the small town of Deptford.

DRAFTING THE BODY   1-2B

You might approach drafting the body in two stages:

1. First, concentrate on developing the paragraphs so they provide enough evidence and detail to support each key point. At this stage, follow the focus and direction of your outline, but be open to in-process writing discoveries that might lead to even better key points and, hence, different paragraphs.
2. After this initial rough drafting of the body, take a step back from your work and assess how well blocks of paragraphs work together as a unit and how well transitions between paragraphs are made. Then, make any changes needed to achieve greater unity and balance.

If this were a painting, it would mean sketching the broad figures and general composition of your work, then using a fine paintbrush to give better definition to the figures of your composition.

As you draft the body, review your thesis statement and the formal outline, if you are using one. Every body paragraph should be related either directly or indirectly to the intention outlined in your thesis statement.

If the document is very short, you might cover each lettered topic in one well-organized paragraph. Or, if you have the luxury of more space, you might break a main point down and cover it in a series of closely related paragraphs.

Your final paragraph should be concise and echo what you have just told your readers, while drawing a logical conclusion that relates to your thesis.

Never introduce new facts, ideas, or arguments in the conclusion. Also avoid hesitancy and uncertainty about the ideas expressed in your conclusion. To make a musical analogy, you've structured your ideas and arguments to a crescendo and raised reader expectations, so don't let them down by ending with a barely audible peep. Rather, offer a conclusion that is confident, strong, and, above all, positive.

STRATEGIES

Strategies for Creating a Strong Conclusion
- Indicate how all your main points strongly—even inevitably—point to your central thesis.
- Propose a solution to a problem.
- Offer a call to action.
- Refer to an anecdote or quotation you used in your introduction.
- Use a poetic turn of phrase.
- Provide a summary of the main arguments.
- Offer a commentary on the argument.
- Restate the thesis, usually in different words.

Remember that the conclusion answers the question, "So what?" Tell the reader how the point you have argued will make a difference.

SAMPLE STUDENT CONCLUSION

The use of animal organs in human transplants is justified by the humane conditions used, the low risk of complications, and the improvements to quality of human life that will result. To deny the use of this technology to the human race would be to subject them to unnecessary suffering and loss of life.

These paragraphs must

- have unity
- be fully and well developed
- have appropriate and logical organization
- be coherent
- have appropriate and easily digestible length (perhaps five to twelve sentences)

Structuring Your Paragraphs

At a minimum, paragraphs typically contain

- a topic sentence
- some elaboration of the point being made
- some supporting evidence for the point, perhaps an example or some testimony from an authority
- some elaboration of the example since examples do not speak for themselves!

Let's focus on how to compose the very important paragraphs that make up the body of your document. They are different in purpose than the special-function paragraphs that introduce and conclude your essay or report. (See 1-2a and 1-2c on the functions of introductory and concluding paragraphs.) Paragraphs in the body contain arguments, ideas, and information to develop and support the main points of the essay or report.

QUICK TIP

Make sure that you use your evidence to make your point. Don't quote an expert or give an example and assume the point is made. Explain why the quotation or the example is there.

You achieve unity within a paragraph by ensuring that all sentences within the paragraph relate to its central idea or main point.

STATING THE MAIN POINT IN THE TOPIC SENTENCE

Just as your entire essay is framed by a thesis statement or statement of purpose, each paragraph within the body should have a **topic sentence.** The topic sentence is usually the first sentence of the paragraph. It states the main point or controlling idea of the paragraph and prepares the reader for what follows in the rest of the paragraph.

Topic sentences can be placed at other positions within the paragraph, such as the end, or they might even be implied. And sometimes they are not needed—for instance, when the unity of sentences within the paragraph is already so remarkable that a topic sentence would only state the obvious and interrupt the flow of ideas.

Here is a unified paragraph from a piece celebrating the life of the late Pierre Elliott Trudeau. The topic sentence appears in italics.

> *He was no neuter.* It is one of the grandest things we will say of his memory that, at times, he antagonized as much as he inspired; our affection for Pierre Trudeau was turbulent and always interesting. If citizens of this day lament that leadership is a game of polls and cozy focus groups there will always be the example of this man to remind us that convictions can be set in bedrock, and that adherence to principles is the most enduring charisma.
>
> —Rex Murphy, "Pierre Trudeau: He Has Gone to His Grace,"
> http://www.cbc.ca/national/rex/rex20000928.html, September 28, 2000.

PARAGRAPH DEVELOPMENT: TRI (TOPIC-RESTRICTION-ILLUSTRATION)

- Use the topic sentence to provide early focus for the reader.
- Include sentences that restrict the focus and make the topic less general.
- Use sentences to illustrate your point by examples.

STUDENT SAMPLE USING TRI

—One strategy to prevent famine in Sub-Saharan Africa involves the use of Famine Early Warning Systems (FEWS). FEWS is a system that monitors certain trends over time, such as chlorophyll production for plants as well as measurements of food availability and price in a specific area (Baro and Deubal, 2006: 531). The FEWS strategy combines elements of social science and physical science through analysis of the economy and ecological data in order to predict whether or not a famine is likely to occur (Brown, 2008: vii). This strategy is especially effective for larger-scale areas on a regional and national level (Chaiken et al., 2009: 52). Some argue that aside from quantitative measurements, anthropologists should also analyze survey input to acquire more information on a more qualitative level (Chaiken et al., 2009: 51). Assuming there is adequate funding and humanitarian support, data from surveys are indicative of the opinions of the majority (Chaiken et al., 2009: 52). These surveys combined with quantitative measurements provide a strong bank of information to identify whether or not a famine may occur in Sub-Saharan Africa.

Courtesy of Kamran Shaikh.

The first sentence states the topic. The second sentence defines or explains the topic and thus narrows it for the reader. The last part of the paragraph gives an example to show how the topic relates in the context of the larger essay.

In the paragraph below, the sentence in italics clearly does not support the topic sentence, nor does it relate meaningfully to other sentences in the paragraph.

While the Nanaimo Estuary is important to the forest industry, it is equally vital to the local fisheries. The estuary accounts for 25 percent of the catch in Georgia Strait fishing. It is one of the vital links in the life cycle of Nanaimo River salmon. *Recently, a firm selling bungee jumping experiences opened for business in a canyon along the Nanaimo River.* The estuary, then, is instrumental in the maintenance of fish which support commercial fishing, freshwater sport fishing, tidal sport fishing, and the Native food industry.

KEEPING TO THE MAIN POINT IN EACH PARAGRAPH

Any sentence within a paragraph that does not relate to the topic sentence undermines the paragraph's unity and focus, and should be deleted. The sentence may need to be shifted elsewhere, or it might become the basis of a new essential point and demand a separate paragraph.

Once you've drafted a paragraph, these writing questions arise:

- What is the optimum length?
- How much is too much?
- How much is not enough?

The length of your paragraph and, consequently, the development that is required may vary depending on these important considerations:

- **Audience:** A very young audience may require less supporting detail, whereas an older or unsympathetic audience may require a great deal of evidence to persuade it of the merit of your topic sentence's main point.
- **Purpose:** If your purpose is to persuade, an argument may need considerable development to convince your reader.
- **Form:** If you are writing for a newspaper, paragraphs are generally short; if you are writing for an academic or professional journal, paragraphs tend to be longer.

After drafting paragraphs, it's important to assess whether or not they are adequately developed. Let's consider a sample writing situation. In an article taken from a Canadian journal, Dr. Arlene McLaren writes about the need to consider how parents protect their children in the face of increasingly dangerous traffic.

For such a topic, audience, purpose, and form, the following paragraph—which Dr. McLaren did not write—would be inadequately developed.

LACKS ADEQUATE PARAGRAPH DEVELOPMENT

Parental safety rules for their children need further study. There are fewer accidents over the past decades, even though there are more cars and there is more travel, but, despite this apparent improvement, roads have not become safer.

This summary is sketchy and undeveloped. It does not explain that roads are unsafe for children because traffic safety is focused on moving vehicles quickly and smoothly and not on the safety of pedestrians, particularly children. It also does not explain that parents themselves have acted to protect their children by taking steps to eliminate traffic risks they might encounter. Now consider the following paragraph, which Dr. McLaren did write, and which reflects good paragraph development.

GOOD PARAGRAPH DEVELOPMENT

In North American urban environments, children's spatial mobility largely takes place within an automobility system dominated by the private motor vehicle. From the inception of the automobile, traffic safety regimes have sought to protect children by removing them from streets with the purpose of promoting the speed and movement of motor vehicle traffic over the rights of pedestrians (Norton 2008). Though death and injury rates on the roads have generally declined in westernized countries during the past few decades as car ownership and kilometres traveled have risen, the fact remains that road traffic is inherently dangerous (Wegman 2007). According to Adams (1993), roads have not become safer; instead, because parents recognize them as so dangerous, they compensate on behalf of their children by removing them from traffic risks. Despite this insight, scholars have paid remarkably little attention to parents' everyday traffic safety practices.

—Arlene McLaren, "Parents and Traffic Safety: Unequal Risks and Responsibilities En Route to School," *Canadian Journal of Sociology*, Volume 36 (2), p.161–184.

A good way to test whether or not your paragraph is adequately developed is to have someone who fits the profile of the intended audience read the paragraph and provide feedback on how well it is developed. Another good strategy is to ask someone to read your work for you and let you know where what you have written does not make sense.

In addition to adequately developing each paragraph, you need to organize ideas within paragraphs appropriately. Choosing a particular structure will help you keep your focus clear in your mind. The paragraph organization should be consistent with the overall purpose of your writing assignment. For example, if your assigned or chosen writing task is to create a piece in which you describe the landscape of Cape Breton, then paragraphs within your document should follow a *descriptive* pattern or **method of development.**

In the following pages, you will see some of the more common paragraph organization patterns:

- narration
- description
- definition
- classification and division
- process analysis
- comparison and contrast
- cause and effect
- examples and illustrations
- analogy
- argumentation or persuasion

NARRATION

Narration is storytelling. In a narrative paragraph, the writer tells all or part of a story, usually following the order in which events occurred (chronological order).

In the following paragraph, an acclaimed Canadian poet narrates a story about her mother's working life.

> When I was eight Mom found a job at the outdoor swimming pool, lifting heavy baskets stuffed with shoes and clothing to their numbered place on the four-tiered shelves, lifting them down again when the swimmers plunked their metal tags on the counter and claimed their belongings to get dressed. It was hard and menial work, but it was a paying job, and she finally had money of her own. She also did "day work," the name then given to cleaning other people's houses, and in the winter she sold tickets at the Bronco hockey games. After her first paycheck, I don't think she ever asked my father for grocery money again.
>
> —Lorna Crozier, "What Stays in the Family,"
> in *Dropped Threads: An Anthology of Women's Writing,* edited by
> Marjorie Anderson and Carol Shields (Toronto: Vintage Canada, 2000).

In the paragraph below, writer Andrew Ward describes the devastating effects of an oil spill on bird life along the North American west coast.

> But even the hardiest birds were languishing. You can tell if a bird is dehydrated by the protrusion of its keel, and if it's anemic the inside of its beak turns bright orange. Some of the sickest birds lay apart from the huddled groups with their oily wings outstretched. You noticed them blinking their eyes more slowly, or holding their beaks open as if gulping for air. Some grasped feebly at the fish that was offered and then shook their heads, as if politely declining. They bunched together in the corners of the pens: some of them, I think, to keep warm, or maybe they had just followed the plane of a plywood wall, trying to escape.
>
> —Andrew Ward, "Oil and Water,"
> in *Out Here: A Newcomer's Notes from the Great Northwest*
> (Harmondsworth, UK: Penguin, 1991).

The paragraph below serves to define for the reader exactly how the writer will use a term within the context of her entire essay.

> The word "addiction" is often used loosely and wryly in conversation. People will refer to themselves as "mystery book addicts" or "cookie addicts." E.B. White writes of his annual surge of interest in gardening: "We are hooked and are making an attempt to kick the habit." Yet nobody really believes that reading mysteries or ordering seeds by catalogue is serious enough to be compared with addictions to heroin or alcohol. The word "addiction" is here used jokingly to denote a tendency to overindulge in some pleasurable activity.
>
> —Marie Winn, "Television Addiction,"
> in *The Plug-in Drug: Television, Computers, and Family Life*
> (New York: Viking, 1977).

DESCRIPTION

In a descriptive paragraph, the writer uses words evocatively to create a picture of a place, person, event, thing, or possibly a mood or idea. Details within the paragraph often appeal to the reader's senses.

DEFINITION

At certain points within an essay or report, you may need to define or clarify key words or terms in your composition. Often, this can be done in a few sentences, but occasionally it will require an entire paragraph.

CLASSIFICATION AND DIVISION

Classification involves grouping items such as ideas, people, facts, or things according to some system of classification, known as the **basis of classification**.

In the paragraphs below, the basis for the classification is loneliness.

Lonely Places are the places that don't fit in; the places that have no seat at our international dinner tables; the places that fall between the cracks on our tidy acronyms (EEC and OPEC, OAS and NATO). Cuba is the island that no one thinks of as West Indian; Iceland is the one that isn't really part of Europe.

Australia is the odd place that no one knows whether to call an island or a continent; North Korea is the one that gives the lie to every generality about East Asian vitality and growth. Lonely Places are the exceptions that prove every rule: they are ascetics, castaways, and secessionists; prisoners, anchorites, and solipsists.

—Pico Iyer,
Falling Off the Map: Some Lonely Places of the World
(New York: Vintage Departures, 1993).

In the division method of paragraph organization, the writer separates something into its elements to better understand the entity.

Choral music is performed by groups of singers, called a choir or chorus, in which there is more than one voice to a part. A group with only one voice to a part is called an ensemble. A choir may consist of women only, men only (or boys and men) or may be mixed, with both women and men. The voice parts in a mixed choir are usually soprano, alto, tenor, and bass. There is choral music for 8-part (or more) mixed choirs where the sections are subdivided into first and second soprano, first and second alto, first and second tenor, baritone and bass. The voices with the higher tessitura are designated by the term "first." Sometimes a descant (an ornamental line usually higher than the soprano) is added, most often to the harmony to enhance the sound but not to cover the voices.

—Isabelle Mills, "Choral Music,"
in *The Canadian Encyclopedia*. The Historica Foundation of Canada. 2006.
http://www.thecanadianencyclopedia.com

In this paragraph, the writer describes how to cook spinach:

> The trick with spinach, I know, is to cook it as little as possible. Just grab a handful, chop off the heaviest stems, run cold water over what you have left and, without shaking it dry, pop it into a saucepan, jam the lid on and cook on high for *one minute*—Northern Dancer's time for five furlongs. Want to get fancy? Squeeze half a lemon over the spinach before you start to steam it. Want to get *really really* fancy? Plop a dash of sour cream on top as you bring your spinach to the table. With either or neither or both, it's wonderful.

> —"And the Best Damn Stew-Maker Too,"
> from *Selected Columns from* Canadian Living by Peter Gzowski © 1993.
> Published by McClelland & Stewart Ltd. Used with permission of the publisher.

In the following paragraph, the writer uses the block comparison method to present his response to changes in how we use phones.

> It's the cell phone, of course, that's putting the pay phone out of business. The pay phone is to the cell phone as the troubled and difficult older sibling is to the cherished newborn. People even treat their cell phones like babies, cradling them in their palms and beaming down upon them lovingly as they dial. You sometimes hear people yelling on their cell phones, but almost never yelling at them. Cell phones are toylike, nearly magic, and we get a huge kick out of them, as often happens with technological advances until the new wears off. Somehow I don't believe people had a similar honeymoon period with pay phones back in their early days, and they certainly have no such enthusiasm for them now. When I see the cell-phone user gently push the little antenna and fit the phone back into its brushed-vinyl carrying case and tuck the case inside his jacket beside his heart, I feel sorry for the beat-up pay phone standing in the rain.

> —Ian Frazier, "Dearly Disconnected,"
> *Mother Jones* (January–February 2000),
> http://www.motherjones.com/news/feature/2000/01/disconnected.html

PROCESS ANALYSIS

In a process analysis paragraph, the writer analyzes and explains how something works or how to do or make something. The paragraph pattern closely follows the chronological pattern in the process being described. Put one essential step out of sequence, or miss a step, and the reader can be in big trouble.

COMPARISON AND CONTRAST

When you make comparisons, you usually examine similarities, although the dictionary meaning of compare also includes consideration of differences. When you contrast two entities, you focus exclusively on their differences. Juggling comparisons between two things you are writing about can be challenging.

There are two major approaches to organizing comparison-and-contrast paragraphs effectively. In the first method, sometimes called the block method, you deal first with one subject and then the other.

In the second method, the point-by-point method, the elements of the two items being compared are dealt with at the same time, point by point.

Fred Flintstone of *The Flintstones* and Ralph Kramden of *The Honeymooners* are remarkably similar. The first of these similarities is their appearance. Both have black hair and five o'clock shadows; in addition, both have large paunches and wear loud, baggy clothes. Their personalities are also similar. Both have large appetites, boisterous personalities, and a tendency to act before they think. Moreover, they both have best friends who play second fiddle to them, Barney Rubble for Fred and Ed Norton for Ralph. Additionally, both Fred's and Ralph's favourite activity on a Friday night is to go out bowling with the guys. Finally, when Fred and Ralph put down their bowling balls, they earn their living by working remarkably similar jobs. Fred drives a truck in a gravel pit, and Ralph drives a city bus. In spite of the difference in the two shows' settings, the main characters share a number of similarities.

From ROBITAILLE/BUNYAN. *Canadian Writer's Resource Now*, 2E.
© 2012 Nelson Education Ltd. Reproduced by permission.
www.cengage.com/permissions

In the paragraph below, the author details the cause-and-effect relationship between the sinking of the *Titanic* and the development of radio. Although the sinking of the *Titanic* did not cause radio to develop, the disaster made it possible to showcase the power of radio and thus influenced its development.

> The *Titanic* disaster also had a profound influence on the rise to prominence of the medium of radio. It was the first occasion that news of the catastrophe reached the public over airwaves. Guglielmo Marconi, the Italian inventor who developed wireless and who had bought a ticket for the *Titanic's* April 20th return voyage to England, was able to dramatically exploit the usefulness of the medium. Within a few years, radio would become the most powerful mass medium in the world, even supplanting film as the most pervasive of all media, a position usurped by television some 25 years later.
>
> —Derek Boles, "Titanic as Popular Culture,"
> in *Deconstructing the Titanic: A Teaching Unit for Middle & Secondary Students*
> (Media Awareness Network, http://www.media-awareness.ca/english/
> resources/educational/teachable_moments/deconstructing_titanic_5.cfm).

CAUSE AND EFFECT
In a cause-and-effect paragraph, the writer shows the relationship between ideas and events. The cause is often presented in the topic sentences, and the effect of that cause is explored in the rest of the paragraph.

EXAMPLES AND ILLUSTRATIONS

An example serves to support the generalization presented in the paragraph's topic sentence.

In the paragraph below, the topic sentence generalization is this: "Living in Canada as I do, I've seen plenty of examples of hockey fan stupidity." The remainder of the paragraph provides an example to support that generalization.

> Living in Canada as I do, I've seen plenty of examples of hockey fan stupidity. Indeed, Toronto probably has more dumb hockey fans per capita than any city in the world. The proof comes every year when the die-hards continue to sell out Maple Leafs games despite the team not having a hope in hell of winning the cup. I also remember walking down the street as a kid wearing a hand-me-down Montreal Canadiens T-shirt, which was apparently enough to motivate some complete stranger to roll down their window and yell "f----!" as they drove by. What a lovely thing to say to a child.
>
> —Peter Nowak, "It's time for some science on sports riots,"
> *Canadian Business*. June 20 2011.

In some instances, an example is extended to provide an illustration, as psychoanalyst Erich Fromm does in the following paragraph.

> Different from these "symbol dialects" is the fact that many symbols have more than one meaning in accordance with the various kinds of experiences which can be connected with one and the same natural phenomenon. Let us take the symbol fire again. If we watch fire in the fireplace, which is a source of pleasure and comfort, it is expressive of a mood of aliveness, warmth, and pleasure. But if we see a building or forest on fire, it conveys to us an experience of threat and terror, of the powerlessness of man against the elements of nature. Fire, then, can be the symbolic representation of inner aliveness and happiness as well as of fear, powerlessness, or of one's own destructive tendencies. The same holds true of the symbol of water. Water can be a most destructive force when it is whipped up by a storm or when a swollen river floods its banks. Therefore, it can be the symbolic expression of horror and chaos as well as of comfort and peace.
>
> —Erich Fromm, "Symbolic Language of Dreams,"
> in *Language: An Inquiry into Meaning and Function*,
> edited by Ruth Nanda Anshen (New York: Harper & Row, 1957).

In the following paragraph, the author uses an analogy to a previous situation to warn of the potential dangers of cutting funding to the aerospace industry.

> The Avro Arrow program cancellation in 1959 immediately made over 14,000 Canadians unemployed and affected the aerospace and space systems sectors for decades. Many of Canada's brightest science and technology minds of the day left the country for the United States. Canada's loss was the U.S.'s gain. The stimulus money the government has provided to the CSA will run out by 2012. The Canadian Space Agency is a fundamental driver for science and technology development in Canada through its partnerships with Industry. Having planted the seed to help push industry along one can only hope that the government of the day will see that continued investments in the Canadian space sector will further benefit the economy and Canadians. The government should keep that in mind as it prepares the 2011-2012 budget and future budgets.
>
> —Marc Boucher, "The Space Shuttle Retirement and the Avro Analogy," SpaceRef Canada, October 22, 2010. http://spaceref.ca/editorial/the-space-shuttle-retirement-and-avro-analogy.html.

Volunteering one's time is an important part of education. Giving one's time to a cause—whether it be helping out at a homeless shelter, raising money for a good cause, reading to people who are visually impaired, or making visits at a local hospital—is a valuable way of developing altruism in one's character and ensuring that the future is better for everyone. The good effects work two ways: they improve conditions for others, and they leave us more satisfied with ourselves.

ANALOGY

Writers can use a type of comparison called an analogy to help the reader understand a difficult concept by relating that concept to something with which the reader is familiar.

ARGUMENTATION OR PERSUASION

Persuasive writing or argumentation needs to establish its point strongly and marshal the reasons for it.

Coherence is the quality of writing by which the parts of a composition relate to each other closely, clearly, and logically. Good writing is coherent on the sentence and paragraph levels—ideas flow smoothly from one to the next. There are a number of thoughtful strategies for strengthening the connections, and hence the coherence, between paragraphs and within them.

Achieving Coherence in Your Paragraphs

Coherence in paragraph writing is created by strong connections between the points you make. To create coherence, make sure that you use these elements wisely:

- pronouns to link your ideas together
- lexical ties (that is, words that restate the meaning with slight variations, like synonyms)
- parallel phrasing to emphasize points you make and present them clearly and memorably

LINKING IDEAS CLEARLY

While drafting a paragraph, you may find that ideas are occurring to you so quickly that you just want to get them down on paper. At this stage, ideas within the draft paragraph, as expressed in individual sentences, may not be strongly related or well linked.

The Interactive Behaviour Therapy (IBT) model fosters group cohesion, enabling each group member to better relate to one another. Although in my personal practice I will not be running group therapy, there are many elements of IBT that I intend to execute during my weekly documentary meetings. Given that I work with high-functioning adults who are on the autism spectrum, my team-mates tend to be egocentric and struggle to relate to one another's

As a result

perspectives.^Often my team-mates "tune-out" when someone else is talking at team meetings and only remain engaged in conversation when their own ideas are explored. Having learned about IBT, going forward I have greater insight as to how I can help encourage my group to work more effectively.

Expand by writing a kind of umbrella sentence here showing how, in general, this will apply.

In the role of a discriminating reader, ask these questions:

- What is the main idea of this paragraph as communicated in its topic sentence?
- Does each paragraph sentence, either directly or indirectly, link to the main idea?
- Do paragraphs typically move from information that the reader already knows to new information, thus enabling understanding?

Then, as a writer, ask yourself these questions:

- Which sentences do not relate directly or indirectly to the main point of the paragraph (the topic sentence) and thus impair coherence?
- Can these poorly linked sentences be revised, or do they need to be moved elsewhere within the document or deleted to improve paragraph coherence?

Paragraph coherence example:

In the first quatrain of "God's Grandeur," Hopkins uses **alliteration** to create an image associated with **power**. In the first line of the poem he mentions that "the world is charged with God's Grandeur," where "charged" is related to electricity, a force typically associated with **power** and energy (Hopkins 1). The **alliteration** and imagery show God's **power** as if it were striking and fearsome, allowing Him to enforce complete control over His creations. By using the alliterative phrase "shining from shook foil," Hopkins leads the reader to imagine the visceral lightning both visually and audibly, connecting the fear of lightning to the fear of God (2). In the **following** line, Hopkins again uses **alliteration** with the phrase "gathers to a greatness," and compares it to the "ooze of oil" (3). Hopkins uses the repetition of "G" in "God," "grandeur" and "greatness" to enhance the association of those terms. The word "ooze" is a better term in this situation than "leak" because it creates **alliteration**, which causes the reader to spend more time focusing on the image of the oil. **Moreover**, "ooze" is indicative of overwhelming volume that cannot be contained, which is compared to God's power. In "God's Grandeur" **alliteration** is used to enhance imagery, which produces a feeling of power that Hopkins attributes to God.

ASSESSING COHERENCE AT THE PARAGRAPH LEVEL
Once an entire draft is complete, it is important to review each paragraph carefully, assuming the perspective of a highly critical reader who knows little or nothing about the subject.

To create coherence in a paragraph,
1. use pronouns
2. use repetition
3. use parallel structure
4. use transitions

On occasion, you may sense that a paragraph lacks coherence but may not be able to pinpoint which sentence or sentences are creating problems. In such instances, you may need to perform a more in-depth analysis on paragraph content. One strategy is to rank each sentence within the paragraph according to how closely it links to the topic sentence. For example, suppose in an early draft of the paragraph, Darwin included sentences that related only weakly—or not at all—to the topic sentence.

As you compose, you might insert these designations at the end of each paragraph sentence. Once all sentences have been classified, ideas should flow in a logical hierarchy from **T** to **D**'s to **I**'s. Any sentences designated **W** or **N** should be revised or eliminated. So, for example, if Darwin's first paragraph had included a sentence such as "Gardeners often spread dung on the soil to improve its nutrient quality" (N), it would be eliminated from the paragraph because it is not linked to the topic sentence and it interrupts the flow of ideas. In short, the sentence detracts from the paragraph's coherence.

Ask the questions listed on page 39 about the following paragraph written by naturalist Charles Darwin.

> Worms prepare the ground in an excellent manner for the growth of fibrous-rooted plants and for seedlings of all kinds. They periodically expose the mould to the air, and sift it so that no stone larger than the particles which they can swallow are left in it. They mingle the whole intimately together, like a gardener who prepares fine soil for his choicest plants. In this state it is well fitted to retain moisture and to absorb all soluble substances, as well as for the process of nitrification. The bones of dead animals, the harder parts of insects, the shells of land-molluscs, leaves, twigs, etc., are before long all buried beneath the accumulated castings of worms, and are thus brought in more or less decayed state within reach of the roots of plants. Worms likewise drag an infinite number of dead leaves and other parts of plants into their burrows, partly for the sake of plugging them up and partly as food.

—Charles Darwin, "The Formation of Vegetable Mould through the Action of Worms" (London: John Murray, 1881).

You probably noted that in this very coherent paragraph, each sentence links to the main idea expressed in the topic sentence.

Each draft sentence could be classified as follows:

T	the *topic* sentence
D	*directly* related/linked to the topic sentence
I	*indirectly* related/linked to the topic sentence
W	*weakly* related/linked to the topic sentence
N	*not* related/linked to the topic sentence

Examine the relationship between the following thesis statement and topic sentences that have been excerpted from an essay.

THESIS STATEMENT
There is no doubt that the Web is reconnecting us with a civilization based on the written word.

TOPIC SENTENCE OF FIRST BODY PARAGRAPH
The Net is not a threat.

TOPIC SENTENCE OF SECOND BODY PARAGRAPH
Never has so much been written in such a short period of time as since the introduction of the Internet.

TOPIC SENTENCE OF THIRD BODY PARAGRAPH
And if you want to write well and acquire a functional vocabulary, you have to read, whether it's on a screen or on the printed page.

By reviewing these elements of the essay, you can obtain a clear sense of how information in the body paragraphs supports the argument presented in the thesis statement.

ASSESSING COHERENCE AT THE DOCUMENT LEVEL
You will also need to assess how well paragraphs are linked as a whole and how smoothly ideas flow from one paragraph to the next. Again, assume the role of an ultra-critical reader when evaluating your work for coherence. In most cases, the reader should be able to scan your thesis or purpose statement in the introduction and supporting topic sentences in each body paragraph and get a clear sense of how the paragraphs support the main point.

REPEATING KEY WORDS

By repeating key words, you can strengthen coherence in your paragraphs. However, too much repetition can create a highly undesirable, mechanical, "chiming" effect.

Skilled writers achieve coherence and avoid exact repetition of key words by using

- variations of key words (*run, runner, running*)
- pronouns referring to the word (*the atom bomb … it*)
- synonyms for the key word (*boat, craft, ship, liner*)

In the following paragraph, the author uses a synonym phrase, a pronoun, and direct repetition to enhance paragraph coherence. These elements appear in italics.

> The "*third man in the ring*," usually anonymous so far as the crowd is concerned, appears to many observers no more than an observer *himself*, even an intruder; a ghostly presence as fluid in motion and quick-footed as the boxers themselves (indeed, *he* is frequently an ex-boxer). But so central to the drama of boxing is *the referee* that the spectacle of two men fighting each other unsupervised in an elevated ring would seem hellish, if not obscene—life rather than art. *The referee* makes boxing possible.
>
> —Joyce Carol Oates, from *On Boxing*
> (New York: Doubleday, 1987).

Below, in a paragraph by Nobel Peace Prize winner Elie Wiesel, two sentences begin with the "It is so much easier" structure. Parallel grammatical structures such as these help to link related ideas and information within paragraphs more strongly. Here, Wiesel employs parallel structure to create a similar effect to that of refrains in poems; the "It is so much easier" repetition is like an echo of conscience.

> Of course, indifference can be tempting—more than that, seductive. It is so much easier to look away from victims. It is so much easier to avoid such rude interruptions to our work, our dreams, our hopes. It is, after all, awkward, troublesome, to be involved in another person's pain and despair. Yet, for the person who is indifferent, his or her neighbours are of no consequence. And, therefore, their lives are meaningless. Their hidden or even visible anguish is of no interest. Indifference reduces the other to an abstraction.

> —Elie Wiesel, "The Perils of Indifference"
> (speech given at the White House, April 12, 1999;
> see http://www.historyplace.com/speeches/wiesel.htm).

Notice how well the author uses transitions in the following paragraph. The transitions appear in **blue**.

> We do a lot of complaining about the lack of "community" in modern societies, **but** few have noted the absence of public and participatory festivities can, however briefly, unite total strangers in ecstatic communion. Emile Durkheim calls this experience "collective effervescence," which he discerned in the ritual dance of Australian aborigines and postulated to be the emotional basis of all religion. A few religious denominations—Pentecostalism, for example—still offer a collective ecstatic experience, **as** did rock culture at its height. **But** the ecstatic religions tend to be marginal, **and** rock has been tamed for commercial consumption or driven into clubs and "raves." **Hence**, perhaps, the attempts by fans to transform sports events into an occasion for communal festivities—where else, in a culture of cubicles and class, can you lose yourself so completely in a transient community of a like-minded other?

> —Barbara Ehrenreich, "Where the Wild Things Are."
> Reprinted by permission of International Creative Management, Inc.
> Copyright © 2000 by Barbara Ehrenreich.

USING RHETORICAL DEVICES

Think about the structures you use as you write. You can make a point more persuasively by presenting it with flourish.

USING TRANSITIONS

Subtle and purposeful use of transitions can significantly improve coherence in paragraphs and in the document as a whole. Transitions are words or phrases that link ideas, sentences, or paragraphs, making it easier for the reader to perceive how these parts are related. Some of the more commonly used transitions are listed to the right. Use these words cautiously, and think about the directions they give the reader. They have a crucial effect on the logic of your writing.

It is important to use transitional words precisely; for example, don't use *if* when *consequently* is more accurate.

This list is by no means exhaustive. As you read the works of other writers, it's a good idea to note which transitions they use and how they use them. Then, you can incorporate these transitions into your own writing. Sometimes, of course, coherence may be accomplished simply through careful sequencing. Transition words are not always a necessary component in creating coherence in written work.

Commonly Used Transitions

To Show Time
after, as, before, next, during, eventually, later, finally, meanwhile, then, when, while, immediately, soon, subsequently, next, today, tomorrow, yesterday

To Show Direction or Place
above, around, below, beyond, beside, farther on, nearby, opposite to, close, to the right, elsewhere, here, there

To Show Addition
additionally, and, again, also, too, at the same time, besides, equally important, finally, further, furthermore, in addition, lastly, moreover, next

To Compare
also, similarly, likewise, compare, by way of comparison, in the same way

To Contrast
but, however, at the same time, on the contrary, in contrast, yet, on the other hand, nevertheless, in spite of, conversely, still, although, even though, instead, though, despite

To Give Examples
for instance, for example, specifically, to illustrate, in fact, indeed, that is, in particular, namely, thus

To Show Logical Relationship
consequently, thus, as a result, if, so, therefore, hence, accordingly, because, otherwise, then, to this end, first, second

To Concede
of course, naturally, granted, although, certainly, even though, with the exception of

To Conclude or Summarize
altogether, in brief, in conclusion, in other words, in short, in summary, to summarize, to sum up, therefore, that is, in general, finally

STRATEGIES

Tips to Decide Paragraph Length

1. Pace: If material will be read quickly, your paragraphs should be short, sometimes less than 100 words.
2. Layout: In the narrow columns used in newspapers and many reports, short paragraphs read more easily; in documents where type spans the page, paragraphs can be longer.
3. Instructor expectation: Paragraphs in student essays tend to be between 100 and 200 words, and instructors typically expect one or two paragraph breaks per page.

Combine paragraphs to
- eliminate the choppiness of too many short paragraphs
- link closely related ideas
- clarify structure

Break long paragraphs into shorter ones to
- indicate the shift to a new idea
- set off an idea, emphasizing its importance
- break up text that looks too intimidating
- signal a new speaker in story dialogues
- emphasize a contrast
- signal a place or time shift
- mark the end of your introduction or the beginning of your conclusion

How long should your paragraphs be? The answer, although it sounds evasive, is quite honestly this: as long as they need to be to make one coherent point. That said, there are a few considerations that will help you adjust your paragraphs to an appropriate length.

AUDIENCE

Your audience can have a great deal to do with determining optimal paragraph length. A scholarly audience would probably feel very comfortable reading paragraphs of over 200 words.

FUNCTION

As a general rule, special-function paragraphs such as the introductory and concluding paragraphs are shorter than those in the body.

Often, after reading your draft silently or aloud, you will discover that you need to adjust paragraph length. In an assignment, it's always a good idea to consider paragraph length if you see that you have more than two breaks on a page, or if you have no breaks on a page. Much depends on how the page looks. Paragraphs might also seem short and choppy and thus interrupt the flow of your ideas. Or, they might be long and tedious. To remedy these problems, you might combine paragraphs or break very long paragraphs into shorter ones.

QUICK TIP

Avoid one-sentence paragraphs in formal writing.

1-4) REVISING

To make the process of revising easier to do, start with the subjective elements. Ask yourself some basic questions about the paper you have written.

Revising is a crucial stage in the writing process. In fact, many experienced writers spend the greatest proportion of their time planning and revising. When revising, it is important to have a thought-provoking and efficient strategy. The best approach is to address large or prevalent problems first, then work your way down to the more minor ones. There's no point sweating over where to put a comma if in your next revision step you decide the paragraph in question has to go. Move from the whole to the parts.

The best plan of attack for revising follows this sequence:

1. The broad view
   - Focus: Does the piece of writing suit its audience and fulfill its purpose?
   - Structure: Are paragraphs and ideas organized in the best possible way?
   - Content: Is the topic covered adequately?
2. Sentence problems
   - How can sentences be improved to make them as clear as possible?
3. Grammar, spelling, punctuation, and mechanics
   - How can you catch any other problems to make sure the work you submit is free of errors?

Ask Yourself Reflective Questions to Guide Revision

Jot down responses to these questions to plan the work of revision:

What areas of the paper do you feel are strong? Why do they work well?

Which areas of the paper do you feel are weak? Are there things you could do to strengthen them?

What was the simplest section to write? Why?

What was the most difficult section to write? Why?

Does your paper cover the expected scope of the assignment?

Is your support adequate for the point you are making?

Do you make the best use of the essay form to reinforce your ideas?

After you satisfy yourself in a preliminary revision, apply some of the principles of rhetoric to your essay to see if it will meet the needs of your audience.

The main focus is the whole of the paper, in terms of audience, purpose, and context.

Revising with the Rhetorical Context in Mind

Purpose
Does your draft do your ideas justice?

Does your paper explain the significance of the subject?

Does your paper take into account the perspectives of others on the subject?

Does your paper direct the audience toward a specific thought or action?

Audience
Does the draft take into account what your audience already knows about the subject?

Does your language create credibility with your audience?

Does your paper take the reader's reactions into account?

Timeliness
Is your treatment of the topic in the paper current?

Does your paper address something significant for the time?

How will the timing of your paper affect its reception by readers?

1-4A MAKING STRUCTURAL REVISIONS

At the broad level of revision, your emphasis should be on the major writing concerns: focus, structure, and content.

To make revisions, attend to focus first. You need to make sure that the reader can see your main point.

Next, look at structure. How do you conceive of headings or, alternatively, topic sentences as leading through your argument? Last, look at content. Is everything there that needs to be? Is there extraneous content?

Structural revisions, since they are often major, can be dramatic. They might entail any of these operations:

- **adding** material if you decide content coverage is incomplete or needs clarification or amplification
- **deleting** material that is off topic or redundant
- **replacing** material that doesn't work with a revised paragraph or paragraphs
- **reordering** paragraphs to improve the logical organization and flow of material

There are a number of useful strategies to help you decide whether or not structural revisions are needed in your draft.

- Budget time before the deadline so you can set the draft aside for a few days. By doing so, you can look at the draft from a fresh, objective perspective.
- Read your draft through once from beginning to end. As you read, note in the margin your general impressions relating to possible focus, structure, or content problems. Then, on subsequent readings, concentrate on any problems you flagged. Are they indeed problems? What causes the problems? How do you fix them?
- Have a neutral person read the draft. Make sure it is someone whose judgment you trust, someone who is honest and objective and will provide constructive, critical feedback.
- Use or generate a checklist that forces you to examine potential structural problems. Consult the following structural revision checklist for ideas. As with any writing checklist, remember that you can use a word-processing program to personalize the list for your particular writing needs.

Structural Revision Checklist

Focus
- My topic is sufficiently narrow for a document of this length.
- My thesis or purpose statement clearly states my topic, focus, and purpose.
- My document displays an awareness of my reading audience—their background knowledge, interests, and expectations.
- My document keeps to the controlling idea of my thesis statement or statement of purpose.

Structure
- My document is organized logically. The arrangement of ideas makes sense.
- Information within paragraphs is organized logically.
- Ideas are well linked between and within paragraphs.
- My conclusion follows naturally from the body and relates well to the thesis or purpose statement in my introduction.

Content
- Enough information is provided to develop and support ideas adequately. All parts are well developed.
- Material that is not related to my topic has been cut.
- As a reader, I can say the author has answered all of my questions about the topic.
- No content needs to be revised or improved.
- I have given adequate emphasis to the really important ideas related to my topic.
- The material is interesting. My intended audience should find it engaging and compelling.

Many of the following pages in this handbook deal with

- writing clear, powerful sentences
- sentence grammar
- punctuating sentences correctly
- making sure your sentences are free of spelling and mechanical errors
- revising to improve conciseness

Information within these pages will be especially valuable when revising your sentences. Skim the table of contents and the index, and flip through the tabbed sections relating to sentences. You'll find a wealth of information at your fingertips.

When revising and editing, it's best to indicate your changes on hard-copy draft pages. Just from glancing at the revision, you can tell wording has been tightened. Generally, changes are made for these reasons:

- to follow the conventions (rules) of English
- to improve clarity
- to improve economy

GET ORGANIZED

How to Revise: A Collaborative Activity

Here is a checklist that may help you read others' material as part of peer review:

❏ Remember to edit from the whole to the parts.

❏ What are your thoughts on the overall argument?
  What is clear? What is confusing?
  What is strong? What is weak?

❏ Does the essay meet the requirements of the assignment?

❏ Is the introduction effective and interesting?

❏ Is the thesis clear? Does the writer keep the promises made in the introduction?

❏ How does the essay treat its audience?

❏ Where does the writer stand? How clearly is that position stated?

❏ Can you list the main points made?

❏ Does the argument follow logically and easily?

❏ What was most or least interesting? What paragraphs contributed best to the argument?

❏ Were there issues with grammar or mechanics? Sentence structure or variety?

❏ Is word choice accurate and effective?

❏ Are tone and level of language appropriate for the intended audience?

❏ Is the conclusion effective? Does it summarize or echo the main point? Does it indicate future directions or broader implications?

BEFORE SENTENCE REVISION

Raising public awareness will be undertaken through a variety of broad

comma splice

strategies and activities, however, due to the extensive nature of this strategy, only the focused components encompassing public relations and communications will be detailed in this organizational consulting project. The emphasis of this project will be on understanding current

not a sentence

members. Also focusing on getting potential new members, marketing trends, and recruitment concepts. Once this research is distilled and

awkward pronoun use

analyzed, it will culminate in a broad strategy that will include repositioning, methods for attracting members and sponsors, and other methods for generating ongoing revenue streams. Research acquired

wordy

can ultimately be used as a template for best practices in the areas of non-profit management for public relations and communications management.

AFTER SENTENCE REVISION

An extensive variety of strategies and activities will be undertaken to raise public awareness; this project will detail only the public relations and communications components. The project emphasis will be on understanding current members, recruiting new members, and developing marketing trends. Drawing from project research analysis, the report will offer a strategy that includes repositioning, attracting members and sponsors, and generating continuous revenue streams. The research can also be used as a template of best practices for non-profit public relations and communications management.

Some of the changes are not open to debate; for instance, non-sentences must be turned into sentences or otherwise made grammatically correct. Other changes are optional, however, and more a matter of style, such as changing *ongoing* to *continuous*. In fact, as you will see in the remainder of this book, there are often several possibilities from which to choose when considering any revision or improvement.

Proofreading is the final stage of the writing process. It refers to correction of errors in language or layout.

As a fluent reader, you probably read text quickly, skipping over words and phrases because you know what they will be, based on your knowledge of language patterns. This problem is exacerbated when you are reading your own material, particularly if you haven't allowed it to get "cold" before checking it through. Proofreading is painstaking. It demands slow, careful, and methodical reading so you can identify any errors in the final draft.

SOME PROOFREADING CONCERNS

- grammar
- usage
- punctuation
- spelling
- capitalization
- typography
- missing words or letters
- layout problems
- any other mechanical or writing convention problems

ELL Note

Review your draft with a friend. To improve your grasp of English, have a friend read your paper aloud and make suggestions before you submit it. That way, you will pick up idiomatic expressions and get advice on small issues that may affect your writing.

QUICK TIP

Be especially careful of headings when you proofread. The eye sometimes skips them, with embarrassing results.

- Read slowly, examining each word separately; consider using a ruler so that you focus on one line at a time.
- Make a list of your most common grammar, punctuation, spelling, and mechanical errors, and then check your draft thoroughly for any occurrences of these errors.
- Use a proofreading checklist to check for errors systematically; better yet, create your own individualized checklist, or adapt an existing checklist to suit your particular writing needs.
- Proofread aloud, emphasizing each part of a word as you read.
- Proofread your sentences in reverse order (this will take your attention off meaning so you can focus on words, letters, and punctuation).
- Read "against copy"; this means comparing your final draft one sentence at a time against the edited draft to ensure that all editorial changes have been implemented.
- Use computer spell-checkers and grammar-checkers, but never rely on them exclusively. All such tools have limitations and should only be employed as part of your extensive proofreading repertoire.
- Have a classmate proofread your work (but never rely totally on this step).

DISABILITY AWARENESS

Spelling

While some English spellings may be a challenge for all of us, spelling is a source of severe difficulty for those who have learning disabilities. Some technologies can help, including "talking pens" that read words aloud when they are scanned (Smartpen) or voice-recognition computer programs that transcribe dictated text (Dragon).

PROOFREADING STRATEGIES

Here are a few proofreading strategies. Since proofreading requires checking and re-checking your work, you might consider combining strategies or experimenting with a series of strategies to reach your goal: an error-free manuscript.

Finally, don't underestimate the importance of proofreading. Submitting an error-free manuscript makes two clear statements about your relationship with the reader:

1. I care about my work.
2. I respect you as a reader.

Submitting a manuscript riddled with errors undermines a writer's credibility; it suggests that perhaps the writer didn't bother to check supporting facts either, or even think too rigorously about large ideas. In the working world, employers have been known to reject job applications containing a single spelling or punctuation error that should have been caught by careful proofreading.

As you've probably discovered, writing is a process of exploring, experimenting, changing, and improving. With its capabilities for easily adding, deleting, revising, replacing, reordering, and checking text, the computer is a dynamic tool to help you in the writing process.

However, it must be kept in mind that word-processing software is only a tool for writing; you are the ultimate decision-maker and must take complete responsibility for what appears on the page.

Here is some advice to help you work with Microsoft Word, the most popular word-processing program. There may, of course, be variations, depending on which version of Word you use.

WORD-PROCESSING TIPS

Hints for Working with Microsoft Word

To add page numbers	Insert menu > Page numbers
To avoid numbering your first page	File menu > Page Setup > Layout; select "Different first page"
To single-space	Control key + 1
To double-space	Control key + 2
To add a header for each page	View menu > Header and Footer; type your header in the box
To set a hanging indent (e.g., for a Works Cited page)	Format menu > Paragraph > Indents and Spacing > Special: select "Hanging"
To find and replace a word	Edit menu > Find; type the word; then select "Replace" and type the change you want to make
To prevent unwanted text colour (links to websites, for example)	Format menu > Font > Color; select black instead of automatic colour (alternatively, right-click on hyperlinked text and select "Edit Hyperlink" > Remove Hyperlink)

2011 / november

Sunday	Monday	Tuesday	Wednesday	Thursday	Friday	Saturday
		Research essay topics ①	②	③	Dinner with Jim ④	Work 9 to 5pm ⑤
Study group 1pm ⑥	⑦	⑧	⑨	⑩	Study group 1pm ⑪	Work 9 to 5pm ⑫
Write essay ⑬	STUDY ⑭	Quiz ⑮	⑯	Revise Essay ⑰	⑱	Work 9 to 5pm ⑲
⑳	㉑	Essay Due! ㉒	㉓	㉔	㉕	Work 9 to 5pm ㉖
㉗	㉘	㉙	Work 6 to 10pm ㉚			

visualhunter/Shutterstock.com

SCHEDULING

Some word-processing programs, or other computer programs, have time- or project-management components. These tools can help you break the entire writing process down into manageable tasks and establish target dates for task completion so you meet the deadline. They will also allow you to flag specific tasks that you need to follow up on.

These are just some of the ways the word processor and other computer productivity programs can help you in the planning stage of writing.

Adrian Hughes/Shutterstock.com

OUTLINING

This is an outline for a formal essay, taking advantage of the hierarchical headings of Microsoft Word.

Outline

Outline begins with thesis and uses standard format.

Thesis: Forster uses the British and Indian characters of Chandrapore in *A Passage to India* to demonstrate the inherent flaws in the philosophy of "the white man's burden."

Sentences are parallel throughout.

I. "The white man's burden" was the unspoken philosophy of the League of Nations Covenant in 1919 and became the underlying principle of British Imperialism in the 1920s.
   1. A novelist of conscience, Forster shows the British intent to interact with the Indians rather than force rule upon them.
   2. Liberal humanism, as Forster refers to it, depends on Indian assimilation of laws imposed on Indians by British Imperialists.
   3. The trial in *A Passage to India* tests the ideology of "the white man's burden" as a means of justifying racial subordination.
   4. Said's notion of Orientalism is shown in the polarization between the British and the Indians in the novel.

II. The novel shows the "burden" will create a permanent superior role for the British and not the enlightened "civilizing" force originally intended.
   1. All the British characters feel superior to the Indians.
   2. Mrs. Moore and Fielding, though sympathetic, see the Empire as essential.
   3. Adela's relationship to Indians shows some change, but not progress.
   4. Forster shows through the trial the failure of this "civilizing force" ideologically and legally.

TRACKING CHANGES

Note that many documents these days may need a great deal of collaborative editing, something which may be done by tracking changes—that is, by inserting or deleting material or adding comments in another person's electronic document using different colours and/or fonts. This allows people to work together on a single document with ease.

Remember to regularly save and back up anything you create on a computer. And don't forget the computer's capability for printing. Often, it's beneficial to make a hard copy of the entire draft and spread it out on a table to obtain an overall picture of how ideas flow and are related. A serious limitation of using a computer to write is that you can see only what's on the screen. You can't see, for example, how well the wording of the thesis statement in the introduction relates to the concluding sentence of your twelfth paragraph.

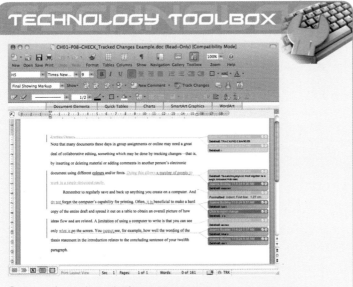

TECHNOLOGY TOOLBOX

● Microsoft Word's Track Changes Feature

It can be helpful to edit documents, especially those that are a product of collboration.

When reviewing Track Changes, you can choose to incorporate marked-up text changes one by one or accept them all at once.

Track Changes is especially helpful for collaborative work because you can see a variety of options identified by the person who made them and by the time they were made.

USING SPELLING AND GRAMMAR CHECKERS

These word-processing features can alert you to possible errors. However, these tools should never be trusted absolutely. Many spell-checkers will recommend American spellings as the default, even though in some you can select Canadian English as an option from the Language menu. Grammar checkers often miss errors or offer misleading advice. For example, they will often highlight passive constructions, which usually should be avoided but in a few instances are required. *You* must decide which sentence construction is most useful for your communication purpose.

SEARCHING FOR PARTICULAR PROBLEMS

Most word-processing programs have a search function. So, if you spell an author's name incorrectly or use a word incorrectly and discover your mistake when proofreading, you can use the search function to correct the error throughout the document. Often you can make needed changes through a global search and replace,

QUICK TIP *for good revision:*

1. Read aloud.
2. Edit on paper, not just on screen.
3. Keep a list of your common errors for reference.
4. Ask a friend to do a peer review.

QUICK TIP

The paramedic method below (originally developed by Richard Lanham in Revising Prose) can help make your writing concise.

Use the paramedic method for style revision. This method of editing will make your work less static and more dynamic by emphasizing verbs rather than nouns and will help improve clarity and interest.

1. Mark prepositional phrases.
2. Circle static verbs, such as *to be*.
3. De-emphasize nouns in favour of verbs.
4. Use simple verbs.
5. Make sentences active.
6. Avoid long introductory phrases.
7. Keep the subject close to the verb.
8. Vary sentence length.

Read for the variety of sounds.

Dustin Manley   *Need title.*

When I told people during the 2010 Vancouver Winter Olympics that my 26-year-old cousin, Graeme Murray, plays defence for Canada's National Sledge Hockey Team, they asked what sledge hockey ... s even were. When Olympic season ends, even more ... ware of the Paralympics or Canada's National Sledge ... ple may be assuming that the Paralympics are not as athletic or competitive; however, the main reason could be a lack of sufficient media coverage on the event.

The 2010 Vancouver Olympic Games cost $1.76 billion dollars to operate (*The Tyee*) and were broadcast worldwide to hundreds of millions of viewers. Canadians and the rest of the world were ripe with "Olympic fever", and our nation cheered its athletes on to win 26 medals—14 of which were gold—in ... events. However, after the closing ceremonies of the Olympics, ... world, including Canada, left Vancouver just as the Paralympics ... Paralympics may be shorter than the Olympics, with only a ... events, but there are still Olympic-level athletes competing. The ... Paralympics are not based on a policy of sport equity that allows people with disabilities to compete after the 'real' Olympic Games are finished. Canada displayed an enormous amount of national pride during the Olympic Games; why did the fire burn out for our Paralympic athletes?

Governed by the International Paralympic Committee (IPC), the Paralympic games originated from a small group of British WWII veterans in 1948. It is now the second-largest international sport ... 39 countries represented by 506 athletes as of the 2010 ... There are Winter and Summer Paralympics held immed ... where athletes with physical disabilities inc... ... tions, blindness, and Cerebral Palsy compete. The five winter ... he skiing, biathlon, cross-country skiing, wheelchair curling, ... ckey. Despite being the second-largest international sporting

The student changed this to reflect that "compound" adjectives that precede the noun take a hyphen.

The student made this less wordy by starting with the subject and verb and by searching for redundant wording.

This student made this sentence clearer and more sensitive by putting "people" first.

The student inserted this paragraph to explain the background of the games.

Courtesy of Dustin Manley

though you must use such features with caution. Remember that the computer is not context-sensitive and cannot intuit your meaning.

Another way to guard against misspellings is to use the automatic correction feature in many programs, where common words are automatically corrected when mistyped. Again, you must be careful that the program doesn't introduce its own errors as it "corrects" your work.

MAINTAINING WRITING RESOURCE FILES

Consider setting up and maintaining computer files containing information to help you revise. For example, you might include in one file a list of strategic transition words and phrases you've encountered in your reading. When it comes time to revise a draft, you can draw from this list to improve writing unity.

GENERATING REVISION CHECKLISTS

Input a checklist that covers such revision concerns as sentence structure, word choice, grammar, punctuation, and mechanics. Boldface checklist items that have posed problems for you in previous writing assignments. Pay particular attention to these items when you revise and proofread. Add new checklist items as additional repeated problems emerge in your writing. Delete checklist items as you master writing skills. As a bonus, your checklist revisions become a measure of your personal writing growth.

When what you think is the final manuscript comes out of the printer, resist the temptation to believe that because it looks neat, it's perfect. Allow time to set the draft aside, and then check it again.

event, there is a wide funding gap between the Olympic and Paralympic Games, a leading cause of the lack of media presence at the Paralympics.

Television broadcasts of the Paralympics began in 1976; however, the Paralympic Games have had difficulty maintaining a consistent international media presence until the 2000 Paralympics in Sydney, which were broadcast to 300 million people (Cashman). Desp improvement of global media exposure, my family still had to Graeme and Team Canada win the gold medal streamed online via the Paralympic Sport TV website (paralympicsport.tv).

> The student's changes made here reduce foggy language and wordiness.

During the 2008 IPC Ice Sledge Hockey World Championships held at the lacklustre New England Sports Centre in Marlborough, Massachusetts, media coverage and awareness of the sledge hockey event was clearly lacking. There were 200 athletes from 10 countries participating in this event, and although it was the world championships, the audience was mostly family and friends of the athletes. Footage for *Sled Head*, winner of Best Documentary at the DeREEL Independent Film Festival (SledHeadMovie.com), was shot here to highlight Canada's National Sledge Hockey Team and its members, among many others. The biggest highlight of the footage was when Canada scored the winning goal with 10 seconds left in the final period, and all of the Canadian audience ran onto the ice to celebrate the victory.

In 2010, Canadian Paralympic media exposure grew immensely. Instead of having to watch games streamed over the IPC website, we could now watch games broadcast by Canada's Olympic Broadcast Media Consortium, a joint venture between CTVglobemedia and Rogers Media (CTVOlympics.ca). CTV planned a record of 50 hours of television coverage, including a 90-minute daily highlight program, as well as live coverage of Canada's sledge hockey games and the gold medal game (which Canada was unfortunately not participating in).

> The student caught a dangling modifier here.

Outside of the games, the Paralympics have raised tremendous awareness for disabled persons in the public. A 2010 study of the Olympic Global

Impact (OGI) of the Paralympic Winter Games, conducted by the University of British Columbia (UBC), showed that of approximately 1,600 Canadians surveyed, 41 to 50 percent believed that the Games "triggered additional accessibility of buildings, sidewalks and public spaces. . . [and] 23 percent of employers said the Games had increased their willingness to hire people with disabilities" (University of British Columbia). While accessibility of public spaces and hiring of disabled people shouldn't be increased solely because of the Paralympic Games being in town, this rising awareness is a tremendous sign of success.

Awareness of the Paralympic games has grown—the fact that I was able to watch my cousin play with Team Canada live on CTV, while four years previously the family was huddled around a computer screen, is proof of this. Fifty hours of coverage is a huge improvement, but this coverage and media awareness need to continue growing. I hope that with the dramatic rise in awareness and media coverage of the Paralympics over the past decade, come 2014, I won't get blank faces when I tell people that my cousin, Graeme Murray, is number 29 on Canada's National Sledge Hockey Team because they will be cheering on Canada's Paralympic athletes as well.

The student adjusted the wording of the quotation to make it clearer by adding square brackets to add his own words.

The student caught a subject and verb agreement problem here.

The student eliminated "hopefully" because it is a dangling modifier.

Start list on a new page.

Still need Tyee reference.

Works Cited

Cashman, Richard and Simon Darcy. *Benchmark Games: The Sydney 2000 Paralympic Games*. Petersham, Australia: Walla Walla Press, 2008. Print.

Sledhead. Web. 10 June 2010. *Need URL.*

"Record hours of coverage for Paralympic Games". CTVOlympics.ca. June 16, 2009. Web. 14 February 2010.

Thomson, Hilary. "Paralympics a Force for Change « UBC Public Affairs." *UBC Public Affairs*. 4 Mar. 2010. Web. 20 May 2011.

Student made changes to conform to MLA format.

NOTE: The spacing looks a bit wonky. It should be just double spaced throughout.

Planning Stage

Topic: a critique of Abella and Troper's *None Is Too Many*
Audience: scholarly audience who have read the book
Thesis development: Abella and Troper's work assesses Canada's immigration policy in World War II and reveals its anti-Semitism.

Outline Stage

Title: Something provocative
Introduction: What is the purpose of Abella and Troper's book?

Body:

Point 1: Abella and Troper show that the Holocaust was preventable.
- Jews trying to leave Germany were rejected.
- Those that were accepted were hidden away.

Point 2: Abella and Troper criticize Canada's refugee record in World War II.
- Canada's record for accepting refugees at the time was the worst in the world.
- Canada, despite the evidence of mass murder, chose to disregard cries for help.
- The title of the book is a quip from Canada's head of immigration at the time.

Point 3: Abella and Troper offer insights for future immigration to Canada.
- Canada should play a key role in aid to refugees.
- Politicians need to act morally, not politically.

Conclusion: Summarizes the argument and explains its contribution

Why Were None Too Many?

A Review of Irving Abella and Harold Troper's *None Is Too Many*

Daniel Rosenfield

Jewish History 3ZZ3

March 31, 2010

ESSAY: "A Review of Irving Abella and Harold Troper's *None Is Too Many*" by Daniel Rosenfield (student)

The first part of the critique explains WHAT the point of the book is.

The first paragraph of a review introduces what the purpose of the book was. The first three paragraphs set the stage for the critique.

This paragraph provides a clear map of the arguments that follow.

The second section of the critique explains HOW the main point of the book is made.

Why Were None Too Many?:
A Review of Irving Abella and Harold Troper's *None Is Too Many*

In *None Is Too Many: Canada and the Jews of Europe 1933–1948*, Irving Abella and Harold Troper offer a scathing glance at Canada's immigration policy during the period surrounding and including World War II. Abella and Troper's publication takes the reader into the deepest areas of government and fully depicts Canada's rejection of nearly all Jewish immigrants. Canada's blatant anti-Semitism during this period is exposed, and Canadian readers are ashamed to be Canadian after reading about such bigoted and racist policy toward immigrants, both Jewish and not.

Written with a visible Jewish bias, Abella and Troper's book systematically examines Canada's foreign policy and exposes the racist tendencies of nearly all government officials. From paperwork-processing clerks to Prime Minister Mackenzie King, nobody is immune from criticism in this caustic yet gripping book. The book employs a linear time frame, following the struggle of European Jews from the beginnings of Nazi oppression, through their extermination in the gas chambers, to the exodus of the few survivors from Europe. The constant rejection that the Jews suffered throughout this time period is elucidated and expounded brilliantly as a recurring theme.

While not explicitly stated, the underlying reasons for writing *None Is Too Many* are to remind the world that the Holocaust was preventable, to chastise Canada for its terrible refugee record, and to offer insights for the future of immigration.

Abella and Troper begin the book with an anecdote about a Jewish family in 1938, who wanted to join their relatives in Canada to escape Nazi persecution.

To the oppressed Jews, Canada "represented life, luxury and salvation; it was a Garden of Eden in Hell" (Abella and Troper, p. 4). Unfortunately, Canada was also unattainable. The family is shown to exhaust every possible diplomatic route in a vain attempt to secure entrance visas. All attempts fail, and the story does not have a Hollywood ending; rather, the family perishes in Auschwitz. This story is quickly followed by another short anecdote of a family who tries a similar route; however, they tell immigration officials that they are Christians. After they transferred large sums of money to Canada, the entrance visas were approved and these people survived, at the expense of their culture.

> Use details from the text to make your point specifically.

These anecdotes were placed at the beginning to illustrate the simple point that Jews were not welcome in Europe, Canada, or elsewhere, and that any attempts to escape were futile. Included is a quote by famed Zionist Chaim Weizmann, who said, "The world seemed to be divided into two parts—those places where the Jew could not live, and those where they could not enter" (p. 5). This is immediately followed by a brief, albeit poignant, explanation of Canada's immigration policy. The Canadian policy had always been highly selective, and only when it was economically self-serving would they accept non-American or non-British people. Jews, Orientals, and Blacks were at the bottom of the "desirable" list, and "were acceptable as long as they were out of sight, risking life and limb in the mines and smelters of the west and north, holed up in lumber camps deep in the forest, or farming the more marginal areas of western wheat frontier" (p. 6). The Jews were designated as "city" people, and thus they were at the very bottom of acceptable immigrants. This section is followed by a brief description of Canada at the time—the world's second-largest nation in terms of land mass, with a population of just over eight million.

> Note how the topic sentence here shows what the rest of the paragraph is about.

These points were made to emphasize the racism and bigotry underlying the immigration policy. Under the guise of protecting the national interests of Canadians, head of immigration F.C. Blair and Prime Minister Mackenzie King refused to open the door of immigration for Jews, or any other minority attempting to escape Nazi oppression. Abella and Troper fortify their point that unbridled racism was behind the immigration policy by illustrating that Canada would have benefited immensely from Jews, and that all the reasons given to Canadian Jews for the barring of their European brethren were obvious fabrications. The most poignant example of this is the 1939 cross-Atlantic voyage of the *St. Louis*, a ship filled with Jews fleeing Nazi persecution. After no country would allow them entrance, they arrived at Canada, where they were promptly turned away and eventually sent to their deaths in Germany. This was in direct contrast to other immigrant ships of Ukrainian and British refugees, which were welcomed with "open arms" (p. 64).

Abella and Troper make it clear that expulsion was the first idea that the Nazis had to rid themselves of their Jewish population, not genocide. This reality is emphasized in order to show that had Canada accepted some Jews, there is a good chance that they would not have been slaughtered by the Nazis. The authors do not try to blame Canada entirely for the ultimate fate of the European Jews; however, Canada's record for accepting refugees at this time was the worst in the world. Even countries with much more limited resources, such as Argentina, Chile, and Bolivia, found room for many more Jews than Canada did. The underlying point is that had Canada accepted more Jews, not only would those Jews have been saved, but its policy may have led other countries to increase their quotas as well. Given the fact that Canada's refugee record was so poor, regardless of internal attempts to take in refugees, it is no surprise that Abella and Troper chastise, berate and attack the government's policies relentlessly throughout the book.

One of the strengths of *None Is Too Many* is its unremitting critique of racist and bigoted immigration policies. The authors leave no stone unturned and no politician untouched in their investigation as to how Canada watched idly as six million Jews and countless others were massacred by the Nazis. One recurring myth that defenders of the Canadian government use is the idea that Canadian politicians were unaware of the Nazi war crimes. Abella and Troper unequivocally dispel this rumor, and state that "it is clear that by the summer of 1943, at the *latest*, some two years before the German surrender, Canadian officials had available to them not only authenticated accounts of Nazi barbarism, but also evidence that this barbarism was part of a systematic and scientific program of mass murder of Jews" (p. 185). Included in *None Is Too Many* are many primary documents graphically and explicitly portraying the Nazi slaughter of Jews, and by providing a cornucopia of evidence that the politicians chose to ignore, trivialize or discard, Abella and Troper prove that the Canadian government's behaviour around this time period was reprehensible at best, and horrific at worst. Throughout the book, the authors repeatedly show that Canada could have—but consciously chose not to—help refugees. It is shown, beyond a shadow of a doubt, that Canada's moral conscience was invisible during this period, and that, even after the war, they accepted refugees only because it was seen to be economically beneficial.

Nowhere is this viewpoint more evident than in the conclusion, where the authors illustrate that the Jewish problem was nothing more than a mere

> The third section of the paper, ending here, is about HOW WELL the writer is convinced by the arguments made in the work being critiqued.

> Note how the topic sentence here is a kind of "umbrella statement" for what follows in the paragraph.

"nuisance" to politicians. By diminishing the annihilation of nearly an entire nation, the authors illustrate that Canadian politicians were not only rude and insensitive, but heartless and callous, due to their staunch refusal to assuage the refugee problem even to the smallest degree, as the title makes clear—reportedly a quip from Frederick Charles Blair, head of immigration in Mackenzie King's government. While exposing the insensitivity of the Canadian administration was successfully accomplished, it was not the primary goal of *None Is Too Many*.

Historical books are rarely written solely to chastise or comment on the events of the past, but rather, as is the case with *None Is Too Many*, to offer insight into the future. While the authors show that Canada could have and should have done more to help refugees, they also show that the viewpoints of the politicians reflected the viewpoints of the general public; Jews and other non-white minorities were not welcome in Canada. The social commentary is essentially that it was not any one individual's fault for the fate of European Jewry, but rather a collective guilt placed upon the world. Canada was guilty of watching idly as millions were massacred—an experience that Abella and Troper hope will never be repeated.

Since the Holocaust, immigration restrictions have been greatly loosened, and today Canada is known for its celebration of racial diversity. In this sense, Canada has learned from its errors, but nevertheless there are ongoing crises in developing nations that, according to the authors, need to be addressed in a prompt and orderly fashion. In these cases, Canada should play a key role in the aid and absorption of refugees. While this not was explicitly stated, given the intonations and implications of the book, it was a key implication of the text.

In addition, another implicit message underlying Abella and Troper's writing is that politicians should abide by their moral values, as opposed to letting political motivations cloud their judgment. The authors emphasize that it was not politically expedient to open the doors of immigration to Canada for Jews, as Mackenzie King could have potentially lost many votes. In this case, Abella and Troper implicitly argue that Mackenzie King's moral conscience should have superceded his quest to maintain peace and harmony in government. In essence, he should have sacrificed potential votes for the sake of humanity. Modern leaders can heed the advice of the authors, and in cases where it may not be politically beneficial to adopt a certain policy (i.e., aiding refugees), they should act morally and accept the refugees, regardless of the political consequences.

None Is Too Many is an insightful, fact-filled account of Canada's refugee policy in the time surrounding World War II. It is eloquently written with biting undertones, and the authors offer a rarely heard perspective on the plight of the Jews—that they could have been saved, but were not. The book was written with three intents in mind. First and foremost, the authors show that the slaughter of Jews was preventable, because the vast majority of European Jewry would have gladly fled Europe had there been a nation willing to accept them. Canada accepted nearly no Jews, and the authors chastise Canadian policy-makers, government officials, and the Canadian public for their lack of empathy. Finally, Abella and Troper offer advice for the future, indicating that when making moral decisions, policy-makers should follow their conscience and not only what they believe will gain them the most popularity amongst their constituents. *None Is Too Many*, while written nearly 40 years after the Holocaust ended, tells a chilling story that few are aware of, and I commend Abella and Troper for bringing it to light.

The last paragraph provides a summary of the main points of the text.

The last part of a critique typically answers the question SO WHAT. That is, it explains the perceived contribution of the piece being critiqued.

Note that the focus of a book review is not appreciation, though that may come into it, but an analysis of what arguments the text makes.

References

Abella, I., & Troper, H. (1982). *None is too many: Canada and the Jews of Europe 1933–1948.* Toronto: Lester & Orpen Dennys.

Those who *write* CLEARLY have readers; those who *write* obscurely have commentators.

—Albert Camus

Reading and Writing in an Academic Setting

GET ORGANIZED

How to Actively Read a Textbook

- ❑ Survey: Skim the material to be covered.
- ❑ Question: Consider your questions about the material and imagine what the instructor might ask you.
- ❑ Read: Select appropriate amounts of reading for your attention span; break large readings into chunks.
- ❑ Record: Keep notes of those areas that you believe you will need to learn in greater depth.
- ❑ Recite: Take time to practise reciting information that you will need to know by heart.
- ❑ Relate: Arrange time to visit with a partner or study group to discuss reading materials.
- ❑ Review: Revisit the material often for best results in learning.

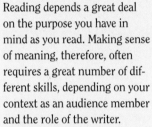

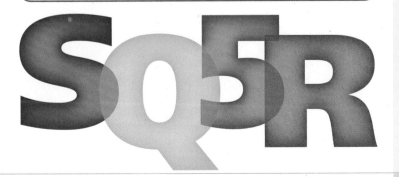

Reading depends a great deal on the purpose you have in mind as you read. Making sense of meaning, therefore, often requires a great number of different skills, depending on your context as an audience member and the role of the writer.

Reading a textbook demands a very different set of skills from those that are needed to read novels. To make the most sense of academic reading, become actively engaged in the reading. Ask questions as you read, make predictions about the reading, and articulate your disagreements and confusions.

SURVEYING THE TEXT

Often readers neglect to survey a text, anxious to get on with the thorough reading that is almost always expected in academic circles.

But to know where you are going, you need to look at the text in front of you as if it were a map. You can gather a great deal of information painlessly by surveying some of the general features of the book. Starting a thorough reading without orienting yourself first will result in lost information. You will not be able to see the forest for the trees.

While you survey the text, form questions about it and anticipate questions the instructor might ask. Your questions will form the groundwork for your future interactions with the reading. If they indicate that you are lost, you will need to seek help to make sure that you find your way again since much of the information you will read may be cumulative.

GET ORGANIZED

How to Survey an Academic Text

❏ Note the title.

❏ Look at the table of contents.

❏ Look at the illustrations and graphics.

❏ Read the preface, introductory blurb, or abstract to get the gist of the reading.

❏ Consider how the reading fits with what you already know.

❏ Ask yourself why you are reading this text in the context of your course work.

❏ Write a reflective summary of what you have read for your eyes only.

❏ Ask yourself what you will need to learn from this text.

Debbie Yea/Nelson Education Ltd.

GET ORGANIZED

How to Do a Critique

❑ Answer these questions:
- What (is the reading about)?
- How (does the author approach the subject)?
- How well (does the author make his or her case)?
- So what (Why is this important in the context of the course, to the audience, and to the topic itself)?

❑ Determine the author's main question or claim.

❑ Find the key points that the author considers.

❑ Find the key words used to discuss this issue and make sure you can define them in your own words.

Rogers's view of necessary and sufficient conditions for therapy

1   Genuineness of therapist
2   Unconditional positive regard
3   Empathy

– profoundly influential article
– adopted into most therapies

To assess whether you are reading critically and have successfully learned from what you are reading, subject the piece you are reading to questions designed to summarize the writer's ideas and to analyze how he or she arrived at them.

After reading, you should be in a position to respond to what you have read.

Summarizing will help you make sense of the claims made in the reading. You should then be able to find the main points made in support of that claim.

The summary will help you grapple with a writer's ideas. If you can summarize the main points in a reading, you have demonstrated your understanding of the concepts.

Analyzing something means breaking it into its main parts to show how they connect. Analysis of the readings you do will give you insight into how the author organized information and to what purpose.

Analyzing a piece of writing involves dealing with its structure and helps to determine how the author approached the material.

Consider the nature of evidence in the academic readings that you do. They will influence the academic writing that you do as well.

The key question when you read something critically is whether it persuades you. Then you need to determine how the author has succeeded in persuading you, or not, as the case may be.

Critical reading presents not just facts and opinions, but organized arguments in support of a particular perspective.

How to Analyze an Author's Argument
- ❏ Examine how the reading is organized.
- ❏ Examine its assumptions about the audience.
- ❏ Examine the kinds of evidence the author presents: the statistics, the authorities, the examples, and the reasons.
- ❏ Examine the reliability of the author's sources for evidence.
- ❏ Examine the author's stance toward the material. Is it objective, subjective, biased?
- ❏ Pay attention to issues of style.
- ❏ Pay attention to the role the author plays in his or her own writing.

How to Evaluate an Author's Argument
- ❏ Find out if the evidence is accurate and accepted by others.
- ❏ Examine the credibility of the source.
- ❏ Ask if there is enough evidence to convince you of the point the author is making.
- ❏ Ask if the evidence presents a fair statement of the facts.
- ❏ Consider what assumptions the author is making.
- ❏ Assess which of the author's assumptions might be challenged.

DEFINITIONS

Appeals in Argument

Logos
the appeal of logic or reason and the construction of argument

Pathos
the appeal to the emotions of the audience

Ethos
the appeal to the ethical response of the reader (his or her sense of identification with the author, awareness of the author's authority, or respect for the author's tone in dealing with the subject).

GET ORGANIZED

How to Determine the Rhetorical Stance

❏ Discover when and where the text was written.

❏ Assess the values of the author in terms of its context, purpose, and audience.

❏ Try to see the writing as it fits into the larger framework of similar documents you have read.

Checklist for topic choices:

❏ Pick something you know is debatable.

❏ Pick something that feels important to you.

❏ Pick something you can manage to deal with in the space allotted for the assignment.

To become a better judge of the various appeals that can be made in an argument, you need to look at the author's logos, pathos, and ethos.

Beyond this ancient categorization of the appeals pertinent to argument, you need to consider the context.

Keep in mind the author's rhetorical stance. He or she is writing with a specific purpose, for an assumed audience, and in a particular time and place.

Critical reading is dependent on an awareness of rhetorical stance. Good readers do not read in a vacuum; they frame what they are reading and assess it in that context.

REFLECTIONS DURING AND AFTER READING

Most of us do not remember everything we read. Our memories improve with more exposures and with more engagement.

A reading journal—even in brief point form—will allow you not just to record notes about what you read, but what you thought about the reading.

Highlighting text is one approach that readers use to keep track of important ideas in their reading. Make sure to keep highlighting significant words so that it becomes a useful guide for you later.

Supplement highlighting with notes. These should be in point form and include page numbers so that you can refer back to the text in question for clarification.

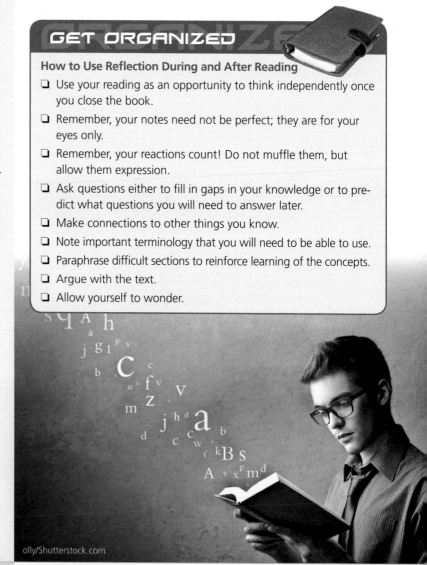

GET ORGANIZED

How to Use Reflection During and After Reading

❑ Use your reading as an opportunity to think independently once you close the book.

❑ Remember, your notes need not be perfect; they are for your eyes only.

❑ Remember, your reactions count! Do not muffle them, but allow them expression.

❑ Ask questions either to fill in gaps in your knowledge or to predict what questions you will need to answer later.

❑ Make connections to other things you know.

❑ Note important terminology that you will need to be able to use.

❑ Paraphrase difficult sections to reinforce learning of the concepts.

❑ Argue with the text.

❑ Allow yourself to wonder.

olly/Shutterstock.com

Most academic writing aims to persuade the reader by marshalling evidence in support of a claim. Depending on the discipline, different kinds of evidence may come into play.

In some respects, academic writing is rooted in opinion. This does not mean that academic writers found their thinking on their emotional responses to something, but that they ground them in facts that are specific and that can be demonstrated.

ARRIVING AT A WORKING THESIS STATEMENT 2-2A

Unsuitable thesis statements:

- Canada's population growth would be negative were it not for its immigration policy. (just a fact; not an opinion)

- The next prime minister of Canada will be female. (based on faith; not testable)

- Alice Munro is an award-winning writer of short stories. (based on fact; does not interpret anything or make any claim)

Better thesis statements:

- Canada needs to combat America's current protectionist trade policy because it will do harm to our business and our status in the world.

- Canada's next prime minister must embrace new technology to ensure that copyright law and broadcasting rights do not hinder creativity.

- Alice Munro's work shows that mastery of the short story depends on, among other things, attention to detail in setting.

The opinions that good academic writers hold are based on fact, but go beyond fact. They involve the author's interpretation of the meaning of the facts. They are not responses based on gut feeling or faith; they are opinions that can be tested in research situations.

In this sense, your thesis statement when you write an essay is also an opinion, supported by facts as you interpret them.

A good topic for an essay is one that is controversial in some respects. An essay will attempt to make sense of a great

Jirsak/Shutterstock.com

deal of information in order to settle the issue according to your evaluation of the current facts. This does not mean that you will prove anything definitely, merely that you will show good reasons why you have taken the position you did.

A topic is not a thesis statement. Although instructors frequently assign topics, they rarely tell you what focus you should take with regard to a particular topic. That is dependent on your thinking and your research.

A good starting point for arriving at a thesis statement is the following formula:

X is good because …

Or

X is bad because …

Or

Something needs to change because …

Not only do you need to determine what evidence will support your argument but you need to contend with those arguments that can be mounted against you.

GET ORGANIZED

How to Develop a Working Thesis

❏ A thesis statement needs to be significant to you.
❏ A thesis statement needs to find support from sources beyond you.
❏ A thesis statement is specific and limited to a workable discussion of the topic.
❏ A thesis statement should take a stand and avoid suspense.
❏ A working thesis should be adaptable in the face of incoming evidence.

Examples

Reducing use of water bottles is good for the environment because it reduces our reliance on non-biodegradable items.

The tendency toward political correctness today is bad because it runs the risk of covering up discrimination, rather than confronting it.

The tenure system needs to change to accommodate the role of teaching as well as research in academia.

Despite being told that leisure hours are increasing, Canadians are finding that they are busier than ever before because of encroaching technology and the loss of the conventional family unit.

To ensure equitable vote counting across Canada, ridings need to be changed to indicate changes in population growth.

FALLACIES

Fallacies are flaws in the structure of arguments.

RECOGNIZING FALLACIES

AD HOMINEM:

Of course the prime minister would defend the raise for members of parliament. After all, he is the prime minister.

AD POPULUM:

I will certainly buy that new CD. It has already sold ten million copies.

House M.D. is the best show on television; it has a high number of viewers every week.

AD VERICUNDIAM:

The Americans had no business in Vietnam, just as Mohammed Ali said.

As Karen Kain says, the National Ballet of Canada is the best in the world.

AD IGNORANTIAM:

There is no good reason to quit smoking marijuana; therefore, I intend to continue to do so.

No one has proven that marijuana is dangerous to our health; therefore, I see no reason to outlaw it.

APPEAL TO TRADITION:

The school has always been affiliated with the church, so it should continue in that tradition.

Year-round schooling has never been necessary in the past, so why should we start now?

Recognizing fallacies will make you better able to analyze what you read and what you write. Be careful to learn and use the following list of fallacies judiciously; they are complex and dependent on the rhetorical situation.

FALLACIES IN ARGUMENT

Ad hominem: Argument that attempts to discredit the person making the argument rather than dealing with the argument itself

Ad populum: Argument that suggests that something is true or false because many people agree

Ad vericundiam: Argument that something is true because someone significant says so

Ad ignorantiam: Argument that there is nothing against this position; therefore, it is true

Appeal to tradition: Argument that something has always been so; therefore, it should continue as it is

Appeal to novelty:
Argument that something is new; therefore, it is the best evidence

APPEAL TO NOVELTY:
New research shows that multiple sclerosis may be related to the circulation of the blood.

This new diet advocates different diets for different blood types, and that approach changes the way we think about food choices.

Post hoc, ergo propter hoc: Argument that mistakenly assumes cause and effect simply because one thing followed another

POST HOC, ERGO PROPTER HOC:
Every time I eat pizza I gain weight, so pizza must be fattening.

Internet usage must lead to climate change; they began to occur around the same time.

Weak analogy: Argument that compares two things that are not necessarily logically connected

WEAK ANALOGY:
Children are like pets: they will behave well if they are trained well.

A good teacher is like a good parent: they take responsibility for a student's well-being.

Straw man: Argument that minimizes or distorts the opponent's argument and defends against it without really dealing with the important issues

STRAW MAN:
The feminist hatred of men will lead to the dissolution of marriage as we know it.

Though kindergarten stresses play-based learning, students need to learn the value of hard work.

Equivocation: Argument that uses words in two different ways

EQUIVOCATION:
Man-eating sharks are no danger to women or children.

Thank you for your essay. I shall lose no time in reading it.

False dichotomy: Argument that creates an either/or situation that does not reflect the truth of the situation

FALSE DICHOTOMY:
Either we ban cross-border shopping, or we damage the Canadian fashion trade.

Either we go on strike today, or we lose our rights forever.

RED HERRING:

Let's reduce the workload in the course. There is less likelihood of problems in class if students are treated fairly.

Let's invite all the employees to a party. That will improve morale after the pay cuts.

HASTY GENERALIZATION:

People in Quebec don't know how to drive. I was there for just a couple of days when I was hit by a careless driver.

Don't young people realize that texting behind the wheel is dangerous?

GUILT BY ASSOCIATION:

You shouldn't believe in astrology. Only crazy people like Hitler believe in astrology.

I would never vote for Bob Rae as the Liberal leader because he used to be the head of the NDP.

SLIPPERY SLOPE:

Drinking alcohol leads to uninhibited behaviour and dangerous risk-taking.

Getting a C on the test tomorrow will affect my chances of admission to graduate school in a few years.

CIRCULAR ARGUMENT:

Studying literature is morally rewarding because reading can make you a better person.

Going to university can broaden your social network because you will meet many people.

BEGGING THE QUESTION:

Same-sex marriage must be wrong because it is illegal.

Red herring: Argument that rests on a tangential point rather than something significant to the issue

Hasty generalization: Argument that claims something based on very limited evidence

Guilt by association: Argument that claims that one thing is tainted by its relationship to another thing

Slippery slope: Argument that something will inevitably lead to something even worse

Circular argument: Argument that essentially restates the premises in the conclusion

Begging the question: Argument that lacks important information

VISUAL RHETORIC

Thinking about visuals has become more and more important in our time. Persuasion is often more related to the presentation of a visual than it is to any textual argument; hence, readers of images need to become conscious of what images are intended to do. Whether you are watching television, surfing the Internet, or browsing through a magazine, you need to pay attention to the demands that visuals make on you and the ways in which they operate to persuade you.

To analyze a visual, you need to think of the rhetorical situation, just as you do textual information. You need to consider the purpose, the audience, and the context in which an image appears to determine what its role is rhetorically.

GET ORGANIZED

How to Analyze Visuals

Answer these questions:

❏ What draws you to the image and how does that make you react to it?

❏ How does the structure of the image relate to its point? Examine the location of the image and its distance from you. What is in the background or in the foreground? How do these things affect your reaction?

❏ How is colour used in the image? Why do you think these colours were chosen to make this image in this rhetorical situation?

❏ What is the relationship between the words, if any, that accompany the image and the image itself? Why are words included or left out?

❏ What impression does the image make? How does it appeal to you in terms of logos, pathos, and ethos?

❏ How effective is the image in accomplishing its purpose where you are concerned?

Visuals include the following text features:
- charts
- graphs
- tables
- diagrams
- illustrations
- maps

There are two key decisions to make when considering visuals.

1. Which visuals are most appropriate for the ideas and information you want to communicate?

2. Where is the most effective place to position each visual within your document?

Visuals can communicate ideas and information quickly and succinctly. They can add to, clarify, or enhance the meaning of the print text. In many instances visuals are the most efficient way to describe, explain, or compare concepts, patterns, and trends.

You can use visuals from other sources in your report as long as you correctly acknowledge where the information was obtained (see 4-1). You can also create your own visuals using such tools as graphics software programs. All visuals should have a title that clearly and concisely indicates what the visual is about.

USING CHARTS, GRAPHS, TABLES, AND DIAGRAMS

Each type of visual serves a different purpose or purposes. You must decide which visual is most suitable for your communication purpose.

Look at this bar graph. It is a good example of a visual because it uses clear labelling to indicate what the reader is meant to see. Note that charts, graphs, tables, and diagrams depend on titles and labels to make their point.

Figure 2.1 Example of a Bar Graph

Retention of Information

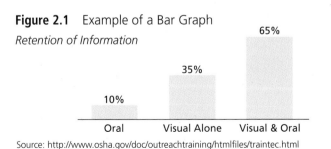

Source: http://www.osha.gov/doc/outreachtraining/htmlfiles/traintec.html

Charts

Charts are good for showing the relationships between ideas and data. A **flow chart** illustrates a process for the reader, showing how parts of the process are related. See Figure 2.2.

A **pie chart** is a circular graph that is appropriate for showing readers how a part of something relates to the whole. Information must be in percentages since the whole is represented as 100 percent.

Figure 2.2 Example of a Flow Chart

Sources of Income

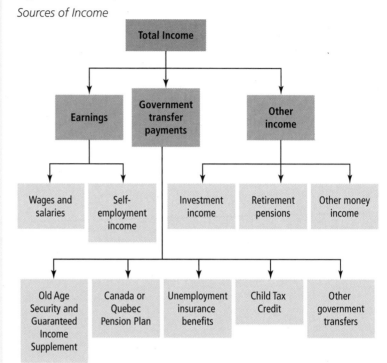

Source: "Sources of Income," adapted from Statistics Canada Website, Learning Resources, Teachers, Teacher's Kit, *1996 Census Results Teacher's Kit*, Income, Activity 7, page 6, http://www.statcan.gc.ca/kits-trousses/pdf/edu04_0048c-eng.pdf.

Figure 2.3 Example of a Line Graph

Number of Marriages and Divorces in Canada, 1921–2002

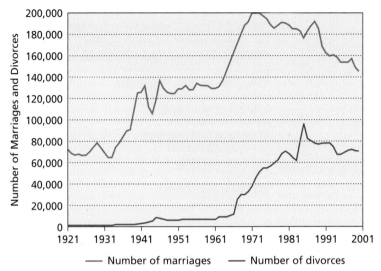

Source: "Number of marriages and divorces in Canada, 1921–2002," adapted from Statistics Canada publication *The Daily*, May 4, 2004, http://www.statcan.gc.ca/daily-quotidien/040504/dq040504a-eng.htm.

Graphs

Graphs are suitable for presenting statistical information in ways that make it easy to understand.

A **line graph** is useful when illustrating trends over time or comparing data for a relatively small number of entities. See Figure 2.3.

A **bar graph** is suitable when you want to compare statistical information for a large number of entities. The reader can quickly see which variable is greatest, which is smallest, and how each entity compares with any other on the graph. See Figure 2.4.

Figure 2.4   Example of a Bar Graph

Hourly Wages by Educational Attainment for Men and Women, Canada, 2003

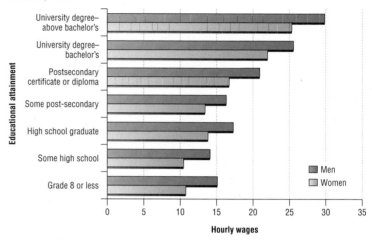

Source: Adapted from Statistics Canada, 2003, "The Canadian Labour Market at a Glance," Catalogue 71-222. Retrieved November 17, 2004 (http://www.statcan.ca/english/freepub/-XIE2004000.htm).

Table 2.1 Example of a Table

Television Viewing by Type of Program, Fall 2003
Total, all persons two years and older

	Total % of viewing time	Canadian programs	Foreign programs
All programs	100.0	40.2	59.8
News and public affairs	26.2	19.8	6.4
Drama	24.9	4.9	20.1
Variety and games	12.9	4.5	8.4
Comedy	11.3	1.3	10.1
Sports	8.2	5.1	3.1
Other television programs	16.3	4.8	11.6

Source: "Television viewing by type of program, Fall 2003," adapted from Statistics Canada publication *Canada at Glance 2006*, Catalogue 12-581-XIE2005001, http://www.statcan.gc.ca/pub/12-581-x/12-581-x2005001-eng.pdf.

Tables

A table allows you to summarize large amounts of information, which is usually in statistical form. Since tables are set up in columns, they are also useful for comparing information. See Table 2.1.

Remember that visuals give the reader concrete evidence of something that you refer to—and explain—in the text of your paper. Don't make the mistake of thinking that the visuals will speak for you. You need to tell the reader what the findings mean to your study or how they relate to your thesis.

Diagrams

A diagram is a concise visual representation of an idea or object. It often allows you to explain a complex idea or describe an intricate object much more economically than you could with words. Sometimes diagrams are the only way to visualize and understand scientific phenomena, unless of course you have access to sophisticated technology such as electron microscopes.

Figure 2.5 Example of a Diagram

Diagram of the Process of Hydroelectric Power Generation

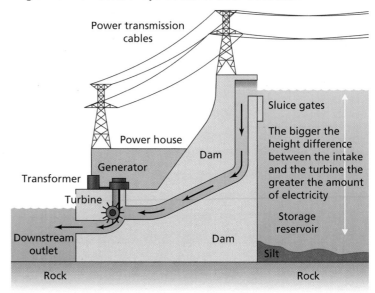

Source: Canada. Environment Canada. "Freshwater: Instream uses—Hydroelectric power generation." (Ottawa, 1999); reproduced in Natural Resources Canada, *The Atlas of Canada.* Reproduced with the permission of the Minister of Public Works and Government Services Canada, 2011.

GET ORGANIZED

How to Place Visuals

A visual can be placed in one of two places within the document:

❏ in or near the print text to which the visual relates

❏ in an appendix to the document, where the visual should be labelled (the visual should be referenced within the text)

If you are placing a visual within the main text of the document, place the visual as near to the print text to which it relates as possible. Some software programs allow you to run text around the visual. You may need to position the visual later in the relevant print text discussion, or after it. Often it is easiest to place a visual at the bottom of the page, where space can be set aside. Put the title above the visual and place complete source information below it. Source information must include the name of the visual's creator and the place and date of publication. Ensure that any visual you use is readable and appropriately sized for the page. The visual should be large enough to understand but must still fit within the margins of the page.

● The photos above illustrate how to place a photo in a block format. The photos below illustrate how to place a photo in the main text so that the text flows around the photo.

PORTRAIT VERSUS LANDSCAPE

Of course, if a visual needs to be wider than a typical page, you could format it as a "landscape page" to be read horizontally rather than vertically.

● A photo can be placed vertically (portrait) or horizontally (landscape), as illustrated here.

Marta Paniti/Shutterstock.com

The discipline of the writer is to learn to be still and listen to what his subject has to tell him.

— Rachel Carson

Research Papers

KEY TASKS IN THE RESEARCH PROCESS

Before entering a library or going online to conduct research,

- identify a worthwhile research-paper topic from good research questions
- focus the topic to make it manageable in scope
- identify good potential information sources about that topic
- generate workable research strategies

At the research library and online,

- locate sources
- evaluate sources to ensure that the information they provide is credible, is reliable, and meets research-topic needs
- read to gather information
- take useful research notes
- ethically, completely, and correctly document and acknowledge all sources consulted and used in the paper

Writing research papers is an essential part of your post-secondary education and, quite possibly, of your occupation. Many of the skills and techniques you apply in writing a paper draw heavily on what you learned about writing essays in Chapter 1, "Composing an Essay." However, an essential difference between the short essay and the research paper is that, in the latter, the majority of the information you present comes from other sources. Often you will need to use other people's information and ideas to formulate your own conclusions. This does not mean that you can blithely reproduce verbatim what others have said and written. Rather, you must analyze, evaluate, and synthesize your research findings and organize them to develop and support your own views and positions.

Before even entering a library or going online to start your research, you will need to do considerable planning to ensure that your research time is spent efficiently and productively. Any research project you choose will demand a research strategy, a careful and systematic assessment of your findings, and the ability to write down your findings in a way that will enable others to learn from and benefit from your work.

Start with your own questions or the ones central to your discipline.

For example, in English courses, you might hear these questions:

- How does the author use images to make us aware of the theme?
- How does the author use dialogue to show the relationship between the characters?

GET ORGANIZED

How to Organize Your Research Project

- ❑ Allow time for topic development and preliminary research.
- ❑ Allow time for focused research with a working thesis.
- ❑ Allow time for writing a first draft with rough documentation.
- ❑ Allow time for rewriting and polishing notes and bibliography.
- ❑ Assume that each step will take longer than you expect.
- ❑ Keep track of steps in a log or journal for ease of revision and as backup for documentation.
- ❑ Ask for help when you need it: from librarians, peers, and/or instructors.

SAMPLE RESEARCH LOG

- Jan. 27 Today I started my paper on a disorder studied in Abnormal Psychology. I am considering working on bipolar disorder. The paper is due on Mar. 3.

- Jan. 29 Couldn't narrow down my focus on bipolar disorder after looking at library database, but came across BPD, pediatric bipolar disorder, so asked the prof if I could use that as my topic, to which he agreed.

- Jan 31 Found some articles on BPD and did a Google search that found some newspaper articles as well.

- Feb. 2 Decided that the main controversy related to BPD is whether it is a valid diagnosis, given the young age group, sometimes as young as three.

- Feb. 4 Did more reading and decided that BPD seems largely to be a North American phenomenon.

In discussions or readings in political history courses, you will frequently hear or see variations of questions such as these:

- How does (such and such contemporary source) account for the causes of the conflict/war?
- What factors might explain the success/failure of the treaty/policy decision?

GET ORGANIZED

How to Approach a Research Assignment

❏ Keep the constraints of the research assignment in mind.

Check to see if you know the answers to these questions:

❏ Does your instructor demand a specific number of sources?
❏ Are there limits on the kind of sources you can use, for example, Internet sources or full-length books?
❏ Are you working independently or in collaboration with other students?
❏ What kind of documentation style should the paper have?

How does Faulkner use images in "A Rose for Emily"?

How would John Stuart Mill see censorship issues on the Internet based on his themes in "On Liberty"?

What are the controversies surrounding autism-spectrum disorder?

In most academic disciplines, certain questions or types of questions appear again and again.

As you plan your research for a paper, keep in mind those questions central to your discipline. The goal of most academic research is to answer a question. This question may be stated explicitly in your research paper, or it may be implicit. Often, a definitive answer cannot be found, but new light can be shed on important and complex issues and ideas.

A manageable research question is the fundamental starting point of the research process. A good question provides a solid framework and a clear direction for your research.

As with writing a short essay, the first challenge in writing a research paper is getting ideas—here, research questions—on paper. Your instructor may have given you a specific research question or topic. Often, however, you will be given the freedom to frame your own research question.

By consulting general and course resources and opening your mind to free association, you can generate research questions that can either frame your research or lead you to other questions that could serve as the starting point for your research paper. This kind of research question gives your search and the work you finally produce a focus. Seek questions that are open to discussion, provocative, and unlikely to be answered definitively. Your work is thus intended to persuade the reader of the best possible answer, given the evidence you uncover.

There are a number of sources you might call on for help in developing ideas for research questions in any subject:

- *Your own interests:* Jot down questions that have sparked your interest and aroused curiosity during your studies.
- *Core questions in your discipline:* Good research questions can come from your recollections of class discussions or lectures, or from your course notes.
- *Course materials:* Reviewing your textbooks can help give you a sense of important questions and issues. These might even be suggested by section or chapter headings.
- *Print or broadcast media:* Reliable and credible media can offer leads to research questions on more current topics. Sources can include popular magazines or academic journals, depending on the subject.
- *Discussion with experts:* From this source you can often get leads on what sources to consult next, such as books or other experts who could answer questions.
- *The Web:* Enter a general topic related to your discipline in an Internet search engine, and then review article annotations. Sometimes posted research papers suggest issues and questions for further study.

You may also find it helpful to apply some of the idea-generating techniques outlined in 1-1b, such as brainstorming and free-writing.

At this stage of your research, take a realistic look at

- the time you can afford to spend on researching and writing
- the research resources available on your topic

GET ORGANIZED

How to Schedule Your Research Paper

❑ Allow time for each activity and schedule deadlines at important points in the project.

❑ Choose a topic and examine the demands of the assignment.

❑ Narrow your topic and come up with a working thesis.

❑ Examine general sources and develop a search strategy.

❑ Keep notes on the progress of your research thinking.

❑ Do background reading and make further adjustments to your thesis.

❑ Keep a list of sources used as you go along.

❑ Develop a working thesis and a tentative outline of the direction of your paper.

❑ Read and critique sources, taking one page of notes per source.

❑ Do research critiques by asking these questions of sources: What? How? How well? So what? Put the emphasis on the last two to develop your thinking about them in your own words.

❑ Add to research as appropriate: do you need interviews, surveys, questionnaires, visuals?

❑ Write a detailed outline based on your thinking thus far.

❑ Write a rough draft for your eyes only.

❑ Edit your rough draft with an eye to correcting typical errors, remembering to edit from the whole to the parts, beginning with the argument and moving through to grammar, mechanics, and documentation.

❑ Ask others to read and critique your draft.

❑ Revise your paper, incorporating changes that come to light.

❑ Proofread carefully.

Initial ideas for research questions will probably be based on your existing knowledge of the topic and reflect your own particular interests. Next, you will need to explore general resources to obtain a better understanding of the topic. As you become more knowledgeable, you will want to focus your guiding research question more precisely.

Time invested in narrowing your focus will make your research task ultimately much more manageable and less frustrating.

It's a good idea to make an exploratory trip to the library, then limit your research question based on available library resources.

Record your findings as you go along.

- Indicate author, title, and publication information for each source you read along the way. List the date you found it if it is an online source. Even if you don't wind up using it, it is easier to keep track of ideas this way.
- Note ideas in your own words as you gather them.
- Note any quotations that you find appealing or useful in quotation marks attached to the source information.

Use a text file or an index card to keep this information handy.

Explore your resources.

- Check the library's website to see if subject research guides have been set up. Some libraries list subject headings (e.g., Art) followed by the major encyclopedias, dictionaries, bibliographies, and online databases on that subject, plus any major reference works (online and printed materials). For an example, see http://main.library.utoronto.ca/eir/articlesbytopic.cfm?subject=10.
- Visit the library and ask for any printed material the library has produced for research guides.
- Visit or email the subject librarian.
- Attend information sessions by librarians on the reference tools for a particular subject.
- Scan headings of online university catalogues to get a sense of topics and sub-topics related to your general research question.
- Browse online or hard-copy periodical listings to obtain a sense of important research questions.
- Look up key words in the indexes of subject encyclopedias, such as the *Encyclopedia of Psychology* or the *Encyclopedia of Science and Technology*. These key words may lead to more specific sub-topics related to a general topic. Online encyclopedias, while not always indexed, may offer subject groups that can lead to sub-topics, as well.
- Read articles in a general information source such as the current edition of *The Canadian Encyclopedia*. Ideas and information in a general article might spark ideas for more focused questions that will frame a precise context for further research.
- Look up articles of interest in online encyclopedias, such as *Encarta* at http://encarta.msn.com, *Brittanica* at www.brittanica.com, or *Bartleby* at www.bartleby.com.
- Note any relevant encyclopedia articles or further readings at the end of general articles. These resources could lead you to a more refined research question.

Here are some general questions you might consider as you formulate your research strategy:

- What do I already know about the topic?
- What kinds of information will I need for a research paper of this nature?
- What kinds of sources should I consult to find this needed information?
- In what order should I find and evaluate these sources?
- Where can I obtain these sources of information (e.g., at a university or reference library, at a community library, in a personal library, on the Web)?
- What skills, resources, technologies, and research resource people will help me tap into the information I need?

STRATEGIES

A Strategy for Finding Information
1. Start with the general and move to the specific.
2. Start with what you know. Look for articles and suggestions from your instructor, your textbook, and class discussons.
3. Generate a list of key words and test them in a search engine such as Google Glossary.

A research strategy is an organized, systematic plan for tracking down and assembling sources of information for your research. By creating such a plan, you give direction to the research process, and you will find that you locate the information you need more efficiently.

RESEARCH STRATEGY
A successful plan will take into consideration the requirements of the topic, your own background knowledge about the topic, the library resources available, and the time available to conduct the research. Research work requires that you locate and evaluate many more sources than you eventually use in your paper.

While an intelligent research strategy must be systematic, it should not be treated as lockstep. Research should be a process of discovery, so you must be open to ideas and information that will take you in directions you did not anticipate.

Any research process can be recursive; this means that once you think you've completed one stage, you could find ideas or information that require you to revisit and repeat steps.

If you need to base your research on primary sources, such as interviews and surveys, it will take longer to collect the required information. And if you use secondary sources, or work from other investigators and researchers, you will need to be systematic and meticulous in recording and ethically acknowledging the work of others.

FROM GENERAL TO SPECIFIC

The best way to structure your strategy is from the general to the specific. For example, when working on a humanities research paper, in the early stages of research, you should read very general articles about the topic, such as those found in encyclopedias. As you become more knowledgeable about the topic, locate and read more specialized articles, such as those found in journals. Often you will find that by reading article abstracts, you can decide if it is worth your time and effort to read an entire article.

Types of Primary (field) Research

Interviews

Observations

Surveys

Experiments

DEFINITIONS

What Kind of Research Are You Doing?

Secondary sources
the commonest research, looking at the work of others in the library and on the Internet as well as in other media.

Primary sources
research where you find new information using experiments, surveys, interviews, or observations. Primary sources may also include historical documents that you examine for your study.

STRATEGIES

Types of Source Material for Research Papers
1. Scholarly books for detailed coverage of your topic
2. Scholarly periodicals for current findings on specific areas of your topic
3. Trade journals for current information on specific areas or products
4. Popular magazines for current information on trends in areas of popular interest
5. Newspapers for information and varying perspectives in different locations
6. Government publications for statistics, studies, and reports
7. Other sources such as video or audio programs, graphics, maps, and documentaries

As you articulate your search strategy on paper, you will probably find that sources start to cluster. For instance, some sources are general and available at the university or college library, so these libraries will be a logical place to start your research. Other sources might be more highly specialized and stored in special collections, so you would pursue this information later in the research process.

QUICK TIP

Distinguish between popular and scholarly research.
- Scholarly works are usually available in libraries on library databases, include abstracts, and cite detailed sources. They have few advertisements and are explicit about authors' credentials.

- Be cautious about use of popular works that may be more general and less credible.

KEEPING A RESEARCH LOG

Keep a list of the sources you examine, both physical and virtual, either in a notebook or in an electronic file.

- Mark down titles and location of materials according to the documentation system you intend to use (APA, MLA, Chicago, or otherwise). These will constitute your working bibliography.
- Summarize briefly in your own words what you found that was useful in a given resource, and keep track of details and quotations that might be pertinent later.
- Keep notes about your thinking as you peruse these resources.

Bloom Bissonette, Melissa. "Teaching the Monster: Frankenstein and Critical Thinking." College Literature 37.3 (2010): 106-120. Print.

This article explains the importance of maintaining the perspective of the monster as a monster and argues that this approach can be helpful in dealing with alienation as a theme in other works as well.

FINDING RESEARCH MATERIALS

Many people find libraries intimidating, but they are very helpful resources, either in person or electronically. There are many online resources published by colleges and universities that provide step-by-step guides to using the resources available, regardless of your discipline. Your college or university likely has helpful online resources, all aimed at making the process easier. You may feel that your questions seem stupid, but in

http://www.libdex.com/

QUICK TIP

Databases like WorldCat and First-Search allow access to library materials on a global scale.

When you have a research question that you think is a good one, review it by asking these questions:

- Can I research and write about this topic in the time and space allowed?
- Does the topic satisfy all of the research assignment criteria?
- Am I interested enough in the topic to spend my time and energy researching it and writing about it?

If you answered yes to all three questions, you're ready to formulate a good search strategy and then start researching.

Figure 3.1 Sample Cluster Diagram

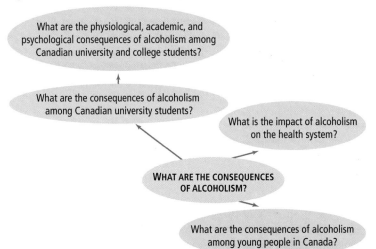

The diagram illustrates how one student focused a very general and unmanageable research question about the consequences of alcoholism. Depending on assignment requirements, the student might want to narrow his or her research even more precisely, for example, by focusing exclusively on physiological or psychological consequences.

Eventually, as you move into the writing stage, you will need to develop your research question into a good thesis statement. A thesis statement is a sentence that explicitly identifies the main point of the paper and perhaps previews its main ideas. (See 1-1c.)

fact, because resources change daily, your questions will often make good sense. Ask a librarian how to go about gaining access—both in person and online—to library materials.

These days, a great many resources are available online. With a username and password from the educational institution in which you are enrolled, you will find you have instant access, even when you are at home, to thousands of resources, often in full-text form. Publicly available resources on the Internet are only a small part of the story. The online resources available in your school library allow you access to many authoritative resources that have been purchased for your use—up-to-date and across all disciplines. That said, the library is a great place to start, in person as well as online.

TESTING YOUR RESEARCH QUESTION: TOO BROAD OR TOO NARROW?

You can test whether your overriding research question is too narrow or too broad by using key words within the question as search terms in a library's catalogue system, periodical indexes, or Internet search engines. Generally, if you are finding too much material, it may indicate that your research question is too broad. If you are finding too little material, it may indicate that you need to broaden the scope of your research question.

In most cases, avoid research questions that are too current, as a significant body of research information may not yet be available. As well, avoid topics that are too obscure—say, nightlife on the Falkland Islands—as it may be highly frustrating trying to find good information on a very specialized topic.

Because a great deal of information is available in electronic format or must be located through computerized catalogues, databases, or search engines, you must ensure that your online research skills are up-to-date. When you go to the library at the institution where you work or go to school, make sure you know how to find materials by title, by author, and by subject key word. Can you quickly find out about resources and technology tools to help you efficiently locate needed information? Also, keep your library skills current: make sure you can find shelf numbers that you need; investigate databases you may use

Locate key words.

Library of Congress

● The Library of Congress page will help you define proper key words to find what you are looking for.

Avoid too many hits.

Courtesy McMaster University Library

● A search for Freud gets too many hits.

Narrow your hits by adding other key words.

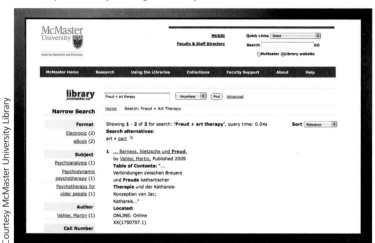

● A search for Freud and "art therapy" reduces the number of hits.

The types of information you will probably use can be grouped into five broad categories.

3. Books from the library's general collection

4. Other sources within the library

2. Periodicals

5. Information outside the library

1. Reference resources

for a project; and make sure you can find and use an index or other general reference work when you need to. Don't overlook the actual (as opposed to virtual) library—books and other printed materials are good sources of information. And if you get stuck at any stage of your research strategy, don't forget that one of your most reliable resources is "non–technology based": in other words, ask the librarian.

RESEARCHING: INSIDE AND OUTSIDE THE LIBRARY

College or university libraries offer storehouses of information. The library will probably be the focus of most of your search efforts. What resources you use will depend on your specific assignment, and the resources available at your particular college or university will vary. As well, what is available in libraries and how information is presented and accessed have changed dramatically in recent years: what used to be offered only in hard-copy format now appears in electronic, often online, formats. Becoming familiar with the library's website is also key to knowing where access tools such as the catalogue and the research databases are and how they are organized.

Learning how to find and retrieve needed information efficiently is a key part of your postsecondary education. Early in the academic year, you should thoroughly familiarize yourself with the college or university's library or libraries. It is your responsibility to find out what is available in the library, where that information is located, and whom to ask if you need help. Many universities provide free handouts on research skills; this information may be on their website as well. These resources can be as specific as "How to Research and Write a History Paper." Since so many university and college libraries allow you to access information through the computer, it is a good idea to learn how to use information-location technology before you need to use it for a particular research assignment. By doing so, you will avoid frustration and save precious research time.

Check out the library:
- Browse library resources.
- Talk to reference librarians when you need help.
- Survey the library website.
- Take advantage of any opportunities to learn how to use library resources, such as classes or workshops.

Use the library website to perform these searches:
- author search, usually last name first (e.g., Keats, John)
- title search, starting with first word, but leaving out "a," "an," or "the"
- keyword search (e.g., John Keats, which will bring up titles by and about this author)

Stephen Coburn/Shutterstock.com

Assessing Sources

You need to survey source material quickly to decide if it will be useful to you as you write your research paper. To avoid reading too many sources needlessly, focus on these items:

Abstracts

These give summaries and brief findings for books and periodical articles to save you time and help you select appropriately.

Preface or Foreword

These parts of larger works help you identify the author's purpose and see if it aligns with your own.

Headings

Skimming through the headings in a book or article will help you determine what parts of a source will be most valuable.

Conclusion

Summaries of findings and overviews of material covered will enable you to determine whether a source meets your needs.

QUICK TIP

Good resources for finding out about the various general reference books available are Guide to Reference, 12th ed., under the leadership of Robert H. Kieft, and Introduction to Reference Work, 8th ed. by William A. Katz and available at http://www.mhhe.com/socscience/katz/.

A library website may also offer a brief introduction to reference works both in print and online, and librarians are good resources for finding the reference works related to a project.

Reference Resources

Reference resources are good sources for factual information such as quick facts, subject overviews, and definitions. Many (e.g., *The Canadian Encyclopedia*) are available in both print and electronic form. Some library websites have a page for reference resources by subject.

Reference resources in print form are usually found in a specific reference section of the library. Most often, you should use them only for preliminary research, to obtain an overall understanding of your topic. Never rely exclusively on general reference resources; you will need to investigate further by exploring sources offering more specific information. Usually, printed reference resources do not circulate; that is, they must be used within the library.

Make sure to look at reference books independent of the Internet. These books provide a touchstone for the reader, a place to start. They give a basis of common, accepted knowledge in a particular discipline and often provide you with respected secondary sources that you should be aware of.

Reference books, when up-to-date, are a guaranteed source of agreed-upon expert knowledge in any given field, whereas the Internet may give a basic common knowledge. Go to the field experts first, and get a good grounding in the subject before you let yourself loose on the Internet, where things are more disorganized and some contributors are self-appointed experts.

Reference resources can be located through the library's computer cataloguing system. Often they are labelled REF, for reference books. The following are some major types of reference resources and examples of each type.

Explore reference works:

- almanacs, news digests, yearbooks to find facts and figures
- atlases to find maps and statistical data
- biographical guides to find out about specific individuals
- chronologies or timelines to get a historical perspective
- concordances to find how particular words are used in context (e.g., in the Bible or in Shakespeare)
- dictionaries to find words listed alphabetically with help to pronounce, use, and understand their origins, often in specialized fields
- directories to make contact with institutions such as organizations, universities, and foundations
- encyclopedias to find short articles arranged alphabetically
- quotation books to find quotations on specific topics
- reference guides or indexes to locate materials in particular subject areas

ELL Note

Note that in North America, academics expect to see sources identified explicitly. Make sure to follow the expectations of your instructor when you quote, paraphrase, or summarize materials from other sources to avoid plagiarism.

Encyclopedias: Note that encyclopedias give information on a breadth of topics, and they usually provide extensive bibliographies that can serve as the basis for your own research. Whether online or in the library, encyclopedias are a wealth of general, if not absolutely current, information. If an entry on your topic is not available, try other key words.

The Canadian Encyclopedia

Encyclopedia Britannica

Encyclopedia of Human Rights

International Encyclopedia of Statistics

The Bulfinch Guide to Art History

Dictionary of Mathematics

FP Markets: Canadian Demographics

Courtesy of The Historica Foundation

ITP Nelson Canadian Dictionary

Oxford English Dictionary

Oxford Dictionary of Philosophy

Dictionary of Plant Sciences

Dictionary of Archaeology

The Encyclopedia of the Biological Sciences

McGraw-Hill Encyclopedia of Science and Technology

Encyclopedia of Associations

Dictionary of Current Biography

Dictionary of Canadian Biography

Dictionary of National Biography
(British)

Harvard Concise Dictionary of
Music and Musicians

Biographical Dictionary of American Sports

Biograpical Dictionary of Modern World Leaders 1900–1991

Canadian News Facts

Canada Year Book

Demographic Yearbook

World Almanac and Book of Facts

Facts on File: News Digest

Historical Atlas of Canada

Atlas of Canada

Times Atlas of the World

Dorling Kindersley World Reference Atlas

Zondervan NIV Atlas of the Bible

Word or Phrase Dictionaries: These works define words or terms. Use abridged dictionaries to limit the number of words, and use unabridged to find the wealth of words in a given language or discipline. Besides general dictionaries, remember that there are dictionaries that address individual disciplines.

Biographical Dictionaries: These dictionaries tell you basic information about the lives of people that may help you to trace important events in a particular person's life. Ask for the volume appropriate to your research.

Almanacs and Yearbooks: These are compendiums of facts in a variety of subject areas, published both in print and online. They often provide good summaries of a year's events in areas as diverse as technology, sports, government, and science.

Atlases: These works compile maps of our planet and even of other planets.

Gazetteers: These volumes contain geographical information, such as climate, population, resources, and topographical features.

Gazetteer of Canada

Canada Gazetteer Atlas

Columbia Gazetteer of the World

Bibliographic Guides and Reference Indexes: These guides help you get a broad overview of your discipline. In these works, you can get short descriptions of resources that are available to you.

World Painting Index

Popular Song Index

Guide to Reference Materials in Political Science: A Selective Bibliography

Halliwell's Film and Video Guide

Periodicals and Newspapers: Periodicals are publications, such as magazines and academic journals, that are issued on a regular basis but less frequently than daily. They differ widely in content, readership, and frequency of publication. Newspapers and periodicals can offer good sources of opinion and current information.

The Globe and Mail

Maclean's

English Studies in Canada

Do not overlook special reference works for subject areas, such as the following:

History	*Cambridge Ancient History*
Literature	*Literary History of Canada*
Drama	*The Oxford Companion to the Theatre*
Philosophy	*The Encyclopedia of Philosophy*
Mythology	*Larousse World Mythology*
Music	*Grove's Dictionary of Music and Musicians*
Science	*The Encyclopedia of the Biological Sciences*
Technology	*McGraw-Hill Encyclopedia of Science and Technology*
Books of Quotations	*Bartlett's Familiar Quotations*

Within libraries, recent issues are often displayed, while back issues are available from storage, or are bound and placed in the general stacks. Some back issues of newspapers and magazines may be accessible online or on microfiche. Some are available only as e-journals.

Periodicals and newspapers, along with books, may be found in electronic databases as well as in the physical library. Note that databases may be convenient, but they also have their limitations, one of which is their focus on recent events. Often a periodical online will not include early references, so print sources are still a must. Coverage of online journals may go back only to the 1990s. If you need to refer to things less current, print may be the only answer.

Databases: A database is a collection of information on a particular subject, usually acquired by a college or a university to allow users to search for information in a particular field. User fees may apply, so your registration in a particular institution may grant you access to materials not readily available to the general public. Databases may be accessed online or by CD-ROM, and there are two major types:

1. *Reference* databases indicate books or other print sources of information. These provide bibliographical material, such as title, author, date of publication, and publisher or periodical, depending on whether the material is a book or an article. You may also find an abstract, or summary, of the article to help you ascertain whether it will be useful to you.

2. *Source* databases provide the information itself, which may include complete articles, statistics, and surveys. Some give full text of articles or allow you to look up the article on microfiche. Sometimes these databases allow you

GET ONLINE

Databases

Libraries purchase access to databases from database publishers such as EBSCOhost, Gale, and Lexis-Nexis. Databases may provide bibliographical (reference) information or full-text (source) articles.

Interdisciplinary Indexes and Databases

Biography Index

ERIC (Educational Resources Information Center)

FirstSearch

JSTOR

LexisNexis Academic Universe

Project Muse

Some Specialized Indexes and Databases

Humanities

Art Index

Arts and Humanities Citation Index

International Index to Music Periodicals

Humanities Index

Literature Online

MLA International Bibliography

Music Index Online

Philosopher's Index

Proquest

Science

BIOSIS

General Science Abstracts

Medline

PubMed

OVID

Web of Science

Social Sciences

Business Periodicals Index

Canadian Business and Current Affairs

EconLit

Education Index

PsychINFO

PAIS (Public Affairs Information Services)

Social Science Abstracts

Social Sciences Citation Index

Sociological Abstracts

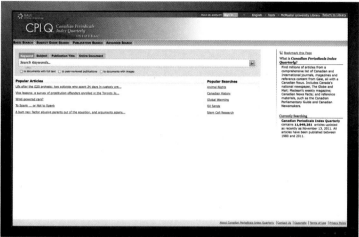

From Gale. Screenshot (*Canadian Periodicals Index Quarterly*). © Gale, a part of Cengage Learning, Inc. Reproduced by permission. www.cengage.com/permissions

to purchase articles in full. Ask a librarian for advice on which electronic databases pertinent to your topic are available in your library and how to access them.

Locating a Particular Periodical Article: The best resource to use for locating particular periodical articles is a periodicals index. *The Readers' Guide to Periodical Literature* covers most American and some Canadian magazines, while the *Canadian Periodicals Index* focuses on Canadian magazines. Indexes can be available online or in print form. Sometimes they are a combination, with more recent references indexed online and earlier references available in print-form indexes. Often, these indexes are available in print form in the reference section of a library, but increasingly libraries are offering these indexes in electronic databases. Computer databases make searching for particular entries easier, but you must know how to search the database using author, title, subject, or key word search terms.

Many journal and newspaper articles are now accessible through electronic indexes and abstracts such as CBCA, Current Events, and Canadian Newsstand, or services such as Factiva. Generally, these are organized by subject matter. Article sources may also be found under "reference databases" or "article databases" on a library website. For specific instruction on how to find articles and journals relevant to your topic through the library website, ask your librarian.

Books

Books within the library's main collection will probably be one of the principal sources of information for your research report. At the majority of modern college and university libraries, books can be accessed through a computer catalogue system. As illustrated in the screen capture in Figure 3.2, you can search for a particular book through four major routes:

- by subject
- by title
- by author
- by a combination of key words

Use whatever is most suitable in your circumstances.

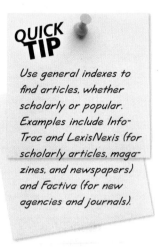

QUICK TIP

Use general indexes to find articles, whether scholarly or popular. Examples include Info-Trac and LexisNexis (for scholarly articles, magazines, and newspapers) and Factiva (for new agencies and journals).

Figure 3.2 Points of Entry for Online Library Searches

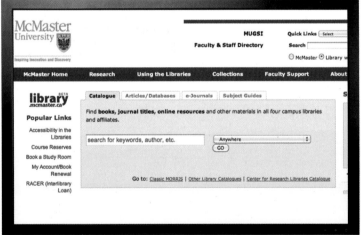

● Here is an example of a university library Web page that allows you to search for a variety of options.

QUICK TIP

Database portals typically allow you to narrow down the materials you choose by date as well as by key words.

GET ORGANIZED

How to Do Quick Web and Database Searches

When you get too many results,

❏ make your search more specific by using different key words

❏ use two search terms separated by AND

❏ put quotation marks around a group of words that will appear together

❏ use NOT to indicate terms you do not want to use

❏ take your cue from a good article that you already have. Its key words should help you narrow your search appropriately

If a search produces too few results,

❏ check your spelling

❏ use OR between two search terms to broaden the search

❏ try different key words

❏ try a different database or search engine

Note that many books are now available electronically; a library catalogue will indicate whether a specific title is available in both hard-copy and electronic formats. The library catalogue may also direct you to publications that exist only in electronic format on the Web, as is the case with some Canadian government publications.

Suppose you were creating a research paper on regulating drinking water quality in Canada. You might enter the search term *drinking water quality*, and the computer might provide a variety of entries.

If your key word search terms calls up too many entries, you could narrow the search down by entering *drinking water quality* AND *Canadian* AND *regulations*.

From the list of possible entries, you would select one that looked promising.

Finally, you would record the information you need to locate the book in the stacks, such as its call number, title, and author. Some libraries allow you to print out this display page.

OTHER SOURCES WITHIN THE LIBRARY

Any college or university library may include a host of other resources that are extremely useful for research purposes.

Special Collections: These could include rare books, unpublished manuscripts, or the papers of writers or other people who have made contributions in their field.

Information or Vertical Files: Information stored in library filing cabinets could include newspaper or magazine clippings, visuals, and pamphlets from governments, companies, professional groups, universities, or special-interest groups.

Media: Audiovisual materials might include records, tapes, CDs, DVDs, films, videos, visuals, and multimedia. Usually this material cannot be borrowed, so you will have to use it at the library.

Use AND to search for two key words simultaneously and thereby narrow the results. For example, a search on Dickens may yield thousand of results, but a search for Dickens AND caricature may be significantly limited.

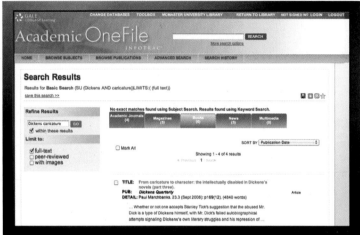

From screenshot, *Academic OneFile*. © Cengage Learning

● Academic OneFile, an electronic database, displays one result of four for Dickens AND caricature.

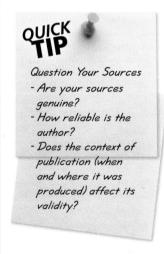

QUICK TIP

Question Your Sources
- *Are your sources genuine?*
- *How reliable is the author?*
- *Does the context of publication (when and where it was produced) affect its validity?*

QUANTITATIVE AND QUALITATIVE SOURCES

A great deal of academic research is quantitative and involves proceeding in a scientific manner. The process is deductive, and researchers attempt to test the truth of theories.

- Qualitative research, by contrast, is interpretive. Researchers interpret reality, and research is done by observing and asking others how they interpret reality.
- In some disciplines, your instructors will ask you to do field research that involves conducting observations, interviewing others, or taking surveys of opinion.
- Observations demand a thoughtful purpose, an open-minded attitude about findings, attention to the difficulties and permissions involved in observation, and good note-taking skills that capture both what you see and what you conclude about it.
- Interviews require good preparation: You must ask for permission to use materials or to record them, and you need to be careful of your demands on others' time. You need prepared, open-ended questions and good note-taking skills, perhaps supplemented by recording devices. Remember to thank those who gave their time to allow you to interview them for your research.

GET ONLINE

Some Government Resources

1-800-OCANADA: federal government information

Statistics Canada: www.statcan.ca

Contact your government: http://canada.gc.ca/
    directories-repertoires/direct-eng.html

SOURCES BEYOND YOUR COLLEGE OR UNIVERSITY LIBRARY

Interlibrary Loan:
Occasionally, a book that you need will not be available at your college or university, but could be available through interlibrary loan. Check with your reference librarian about lending procedures for this service. Also ask how long it will take to obtain the needed resources. This could be crucial if your research paper has a very tight deadline.

Government Departments:
Many federal, provincial, and local government departments provide a wealth of useful research information that could be relevant for reports in a range of college and university disciplines. Your library website may have created a pathfinder document on various federal and international government access points. Government department phone numbers are listed in the blue pages of the telephone book.

PRIMARY SOURCES

Research can include information generated from your own interviews, surveys, and experiments. Communication technology such as email allows you to interview a person who may live a great distance away. Other primary source information can be obtained from attending a play or concert, or visiting a museum. If you use this kind of information in a research report, allow adequate time to prepare and collect information.

THE INTERNET AND OTHER ELECTRONIC SOURCES

On the Internet, there is no research librarian available to assist you, and all information obtained from these sources must be carefully evaluated for reliability and credibility. Publicly accessible websites, such as those you find through Google, may not always be authoritative; don't restrict yourself to the Web alone.

Make sure to use library-based resources too. Libraries provide access to a wealth of peer-reviewed full-text articles and information without your needing to leave your house. Although there is a profusion of resources on the Internet, such as websites from the

PRIMARY AND SECONDARY SOURCES

PRIMARY SOURCES

- Documents from archives: check libraries, museums and similar organizations for original printed documents.
- Search digital archives.
- Consider oral histories from interviews as a source of information about events.

SECONDARY SOURCES

- Examine original secondary sources written by people living at the time of events.
- Consider subsidiary sources written by researchers.

STRATEGIES

How Reliable Is the Internet?
Information on the Internet is public and free. It also changes quickly, so

1. note where you found it
2. check to see if it is accurate by comparing it to information from other peer-reviewed sources
3. make sure the source is credible

QUICK TIP

Using Google Efficiently

1. *Search for phrases whenever possible, enclosed by quotation marks to narrow the findings.*

2. *Check related searches at the bottom of the page of your first results for other typical searches.*

United Nations and Statistics Canada, many sites are not easy to search. Library resources are apt to be searchable and, hence, more readily accessible and organized.

Here are some URLs for possible search engines:

- www.google.ca
- www.yahoo.ca
- www.altavista.com
- www.excite.com
- www.webcrawler.com
- www.go.com
- www.hotbot.com

Some Internet search engines, such as Google, are well suited to academic use. Here are some other subject directories and search engines that may be useful:

Librarians' Internet Index: http://www.itc.nl/Pub/Home/library/Library-general-information/more-info-databases/lii_info.html

Infomine: http://infomine.ucr.edu/

The Internet Public Library: www.ipl.org

BUBL LINK: http://bubl.ac.uk/

Learning to Search the Web

Online research on controversial topics can be very successful, since the Web, by its very nature, is a democratic and fluid medium. The Web is often the best source for current news and material on popular culture. No matter what you are looking for, however, it is best to have a grounding in typical library sources before you turn to the Web. Some good websites to start with are Internet Public Library (http://www.ipl.org/div/subject/browse/ref32.00.00/), Librarians' Internet Index (http://lii.org/), and Alcove 9 (www.loc.gov/rr/main/alcove9/). Also useful is Voice of the Shuttle, found at http://vos.ucsb.edu/; this site is a good compendium of up-to-date materials, particularly those with a technological bent.

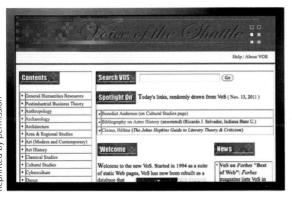

Dmitry Strizhakov/Shutterstock.com

Reprinted by permission

Using Search Techniques in Databases or on the Web

Often, you will need to tailor your search by using options such as "all the words" or "the exact phrase." Although search engines vary (both in what they find and in their exact instructions for searching), all of them have *Help* files that may be accessed to narrow down a search to a manageable size.

Use Boolean logic to combine different fields in a catalogue or database to produce more accurate results. Remember, you can go beyond using simple key words by combining or excluding catalogue and database fields (e.g., enter hobbit in the Title field and Tolkien in the Author field).

USING BOOLEAN SEARCHES

Be aware that some search engines can do Boolean searches, which use certain standard commands to narrow the search criteria:

- If you type "Internet AND copyright," you get materials with both terms in that order.
- If you type "Internet OR copyright," you get a broader search of either term separately.
- If you type "Internet AND copyright NOT Napster," you get a search that eliminates documents with the word *Napster* in them.
- If you type "Internet copyright," the search will be confined to those words grouped together. The words will be found in that order in the documents selected.
- If you type "Internet NEAR copyright," you will get (on some engines, like AltaVista) documents where the two words are within ten words of each other.
- If you type parentheses ( ) to group words together, you will find Internet articles that include both terms, as with quotation marks. "(Internet copyright) AND (intellectual property)" will find articles about both issues together.

Tip: Wildcards

A wildcard search (*) allows you to look for forms of a word with different endings.

For example, you might try advertis* to find advertising, advertisement, or advertised. Write theat* to get both theatre and theater. Wildcards are useful when there are alternate spellings.

WEB RESOURCES

Roget's Thesaurus: http://www.thesaurus.com

Encyclopedia Britannica: http://www.britannica.com

The Voice of the Shuttle "Web Site for Humanities Research": http://vos.ucsb.edu/

Bartleby Library: http://www.bartleby.com

These sites (and many associated links) provide invaluable resource materials—without charge.

Broadband use in Canada is not as strong as it should be, and there are few government initiatives to offset the cost. Canada has an estimated 500 000 households that can't afford broadband, which is not necessarily a case of whether telecom companies are charging too much for the service, but rather a simple fact of poverty. The Canadian government's record in all things broadband, meanwhile, is dismal, particularly in comparison with our G8 partners. Along with the U.S., every other country that counts has taken definitive steps to get all of its citizens connected.

"Canadian broadband: the time for complaining is over" by Peter Nowak, *Maclean's*, Friday, November 11, 2011.

Keeping Track of Valuable Information

Keep track of reference sites that may be important to you in your writing. Record the websites listed to the right in your *Bookmarks* or *Favourites* (or on your personal website, if you have one) for easy reference.

Saving Materials You Find

It is often a good idea to download material from a website onto a CD or memory stick. Websites often change from day to day, and the material you find today may not be accessible tomorrow. Keep a log to tell you when you accessed the websites you use.

Using Another Font for Materials from Websites

To avoid charges of plagiarism, it is often a good idea to use another font when taking "notes" by copying and pasting from a website you visit. That way, it is easy to tell where your words stop and another's words begin.

Documenting Web Sources

This is often a difficult matter, but the same rules apply as for written sources.

When documenting websites, list author's name (if given), title of website, date of your access, publication information (if given), and dates (if given). APA style requires a DOI or URL (if DOI is not available). MLA style does not require URL, but check with your instructor to be sure.

For more information on how to document Web sources, see section 3-1d, p. 124.

Assessing Websites for Credibility

It is absolutely essential to evaluate your sources, especially when they are taken from the Internet. While the Internet is often the most up-to-date and reliable source imaginable, it is hampered by the fact that it is possible (indeed, easy) to publish something on it that is inaccurate, misleading, or biased. You must make sure that the sources you have chosen for evidence are impeccable.

To summarize, a good website for research material will possess these qualities:

- accuracy
- authority
- objectivity
- currency
- coverage

EVALUATING WEBSITES

- **Consider the source.** Note the extension on the address: a site that ends in .gc.ca comes from the Canadian government; one that ends in .gov comes from the American government; one that ends in .com may well be a commercial site, which, while informative, may also be trying to sell you something; .edu is an extension that denotes an educational institution. Can you trust the authority of the source?
- **Consider the authorship.** Who wrote the material on the website, if an author is named? Is that person a recognized authority on the subject?
- **Consider the date of posting.** Has the site been recently updated? (This information is often at the bottom of the home page.) Is it current?
- **Consider the evidence.** What kind of support is included for the information? Are there facts, interviews, and statistics that may be verified? Is the evidence convincing to you? Is it accurate? Can it be checked? Does it cover issues responsibly?
- **Consider bias and motivation.** Can you trace bias in the author's point of view? Does the site aim to sell you something instead of just provide information? Is it objective, and does it cover all sides of the story?
- **Consider commercial influences.** Do banners and ads clutter up the website? Do they affect the objectivity of the research?

- *Consider readability and ease of navigation.* Like books, Web pages are visual as well as textual. A Web page should be aesthetically appealing and easy to read. In a professional (and, thus, likely more credible) website, information will be presented in a satisfactory way appropriate to the subject matter. Does the visual quality help or hinder your sense of the site's authority?
- *Consider Web resources for assessment.* Investigate these websites for guidelines on how to assess online materials:
  - Evaluating Web Pages: Techniques to Apply and Questions to Ask at http://www.lib.berkeley.edu/TeachingLib/Guides/Internet/Evaluate.html
  - Five Criteria for Evaluating Web Pages at http://www.library.cornell.edu/olinuris/ref/webcrit.html
  - Evaluating Website Content at http://www.studygs.net/evaluate.htm
  - Criteria for Evaluating Web Sites at http://www.library.dal.ca/How/Guides/Criteria/

Ask yourself if the material fits these criteria. Checking out websites' sources, motives, and links should help you decide whether you can trust the findings or not.

On-screen text used by permission of McMaster University Library

RADIO AND TELEVISION

Radio and television programs, especially those produced by the CBC or PBS, can provide worthwhile research information. You will need to check print or Internet broadcasting schedules to identify programs that relate to your research needs.

BE DISCRIMINATING

You will probably find that your research yields more sources than you can possibly read. Often, when looking at a computer entry on a library's catalogue screen, you will have to decide whether the source is worth locating and reading.

MAINTAIN A WORKING BIBLIOGRAPHY

The working bibliography is the information you record about your research sources. It should include all the information you will later need to create a list of works cited or a complete bibliography.

As you locate and consider sources through the library's computer catalogue or via the Internet, it is important that you accurately record documentation information for potentially useful books, periodicals, websites, or other materials.

Although such detailed recording may seem time-consuming at this stage of the research process, it will save time later. The consequence of not recording complete source

Criteria you might use to evaluate a potential research source include the following:

- Is the information relevant to my research question?
- Is the information current, if it needs to be (e.g., the latest development in water-testing technology)?
- Does the material come from a credible, reliable author?
- Does the material reflect any bias?

HAMLET PAPER DUE
NOV. 10, 2011
- START RESEARCHING
  AT LIBRARY AND
  ONLINE

OCT. 3, 2011

Books about Hamlet at
the library to get:

1. PR 2807.G62 (1926)
2. PR 2807.K59 (1973)
3. PR 2807.L (1959)

Web searches:
1. Shakespeare Resource
   Centre
   www.bardweb.net

(notebook) Blackbirds/Shutterstoc

Check your facts!

information will be that you will need to make several trips to the library to obtain missing bibliographic details. Accurately recording each resource's call number will allow you to find the resource easily if you need to do any fact-checking or obtain more information.

SAMPLE DOCUMENTATION STYLES

- *MLA Handbook for Writers of Research Papers*, 7th ed. (New York: MLA, 2009)
- *Publication Manual of the American Psychological Association*, 6th ed. (Washington, D.C.: American Psychological Association, 2010)
- *The Chicago Manual of Style*, 16th ed. (Chicago: U of Chicago P, 2010)
- *The Columbia Guide to Online Style*, 2nd ed. (New York: Columbia UP, 2008)
- *Scientific Style and Format: The CSE Manual for Authors, Editors and Publishers*, 7th ed. (Reston, VA: Council of Science Editors, 2006)

CHECK YOUR INSTRUCTOR'S PREFERRED DOCUMENTATION STYLE

Review this handbook's examples of bibliographical entries following that documentation style (Chapters 5 through 8).

Scan the relevant documentation style to identify the details required to write a complete bibliographic citation for

- a book
- a periodical (journal or magazine) or newspaper
- an online source, such as a website
- any other type of source you plan to use in your research report

Now you can be sure you are recording all the information needed to create a complete entry for a list of works cited or a bibliography.

Check with your instructor about the documentation style he or she prefers before you start your research.

WHAT TO RECORD AND HOW TO RECORD IT

There are a number of ways to record entries and maintain your working research bibliography. Traditionally, researchers have often recorded entries on 7.5 × 13 cm (3 × 5 in.) note cards. A separate card is used for each source. The advantage of cards is that they allow you to manipulate entries. For example, as your collection of cards grows, you could alphabetize cards by authors' last names, organize the cards by source type (e.g., books, periodicals), or separate out any sources you consulted but did not cite within your paper.

Do not throw away cards. In a complete bibliography, you will list all resources you consulted in your research, while in a list of works cited, you will only list the works you referred to in your paper. Other options for maintaining a working bibliography include keeping a journal of resources or compiling a computer file of bibliographic information. You can also highlight, copy, and paste copies of electronic information and store the data yourself. Use the working-bibliography strategy that works best for you.

INFORMATION NEEDED FOR RESEARCH NOTES

BOOKS
Call number
Author/editor
Title in full
Place of publication
Publisher
Year published
Any additional information

PARTS OF BOOKS
Call number
Author of part
Title of part
Author/editor of book
Title of book in full
Place of publication
Publisher
Year published
Inclusive page numbers for the part you read

ARTICLES
Call number of journal or DOI of article
Authors
Title of journal
Volume number
Issue number
Date
Inclusive page numbers

ELECTRONIC SOURCES
Author, if given
Title of document
Title of website
Editor of site
Publication information for print version, if any
Date of publication
Date you accessed the information
URL or DOI

Figure 3.3 Card with Book Information

> Author: Dallaire, Roméo A.
> Call number: Call No UB 416 D36 2010
> *They Fight like Soldiers, They Die like Children: The Global*
> *Quest to Eradicate the Use of Child Soldiers.* Toronto:
> Random House Canada, 2010

Figure 3.4 Card with Periodical Information

> Poster, Mark
> "McLuhan and the Cultural Theory of Media"
> *MediaTropes*, 2010, Vol. 2 Issue 2, pp. 1–18

The following information will help you complete a working-bibliography entry for a book, a periodical, or an online source.

Book

Record the following information for a book:

- all authors, and any editors or translators
- title and subtitle
- edition (if not the first edition)
- publication information, including the city, country, publisher, and date of publication
- call number

Periodical

Record the following information for a periodical article, such as one from an academic journal or a magazine:

- all authors of the article
- title and subtitle of the article
- title of the magazine or journal
- date and page numbers (inclusive)
- volume and issue number, if relevant

Newspaper

Record the same information as for periodicals, plus the following:

- the section of the newspaper in which the article appears
- all article page numbers, especially if the article does not appear on consecutive pages
- the edition, if any (e.g., *western ed.*, *nat'l. ed.*, *afternoon ed.*)

If the information is from an editorial, letter, or review, you should make a note of this as well.

Online Source

Record the following information for any website you use in your research:

- any authors or site sponsors
- title and subtitle of the document
- title of longer works to which the document belongs
- document date (or date last modified)
- date you accessed the site
- address of the site or its network path

Figure 3.5   Card with Newspaper Information

> Straziuso, Jason. "UN Food Program Will Restart Aid Effort to Southern Somali Famine Zone." *The Globe and Mail* A1.

Figure 3.6   Card with Online Source Information

> Canadian Drinking Water Guidelines July 26, 2011
> - Health Canada. June 24, 2011
> - http://www.hc-sc.gc.ca/ewh-semt/water-eau/drink-potab/guide/index-eng.php

STRATEGIES

Try Cornell Note-Taking:

1. Make notes from a lecture or textbook reading on one side of your notebook, leaving the other side blank.
2. After completing notes, take a break.
3. Upon returning to your notes, spend 10 minutes reviewing them.
4. On the blank side, list questions that you have about the material.
5. Then, list questions that you might be expected to answer in your paper.
6. Use these review notes as guides for further research and to review your materials quickly.

MAKE A WORKING ANNOTATED BIBLIOGRAPHY

- After reading an article or a section of a book, write a short summary of it.
- Describe what the reading is about.
- Analyze the quality of the source to determine its relevance to your topic.
- Record how the reading is useful to you.

Jiang, H. J., Friedman, B., & Begun, J. W. (2006). "Sustaining and improving hospital performance: The effects of organizational and market factors." *Health Care Management Review*, 31(3), 188-196.

- In this paper, the relationship between hospital operation costs and quality of care is explored through a comparison of "cost/quality" measures, using a framework that proposes that when environmental changes occur, organizations initiate strategic changes in order to ensure survival.
- This paper is concerned with the effects of changes in policy on the cost/quality relationship, not how differences in quality of care or organizational characteristics affect costs incurred.

Taking notes is essential for using source material in a research paper. Note-taking should never be merely collecting and copying information; rather, it should involve active thinking as you select, organize, analyze, and synthesize information and ideas to develop and support your thesis. Slavish copying of material will not make your case for you.

The point of good note-taking is that it helps you get ready for your first draft by helping you find your own words and form your own educated opinions in light of the evidence you uncover. Efficient note-taking does not depend on the quantity of your notes but on their quality. Indeed, gathering too many notes without discriminating between what is essential to your research purpose and what is not can make organizing your secondary source material completely overwhelming.

USING NOTE CARDS

Many researchers find that recording research information on cards is a handy and systematic way of taking notes. Note cards can be the same size as those used for compiling a working bibliography (7.5 × 13 cm, or 3 × 5 in.). When you locate a piece of information that you consider important, record it on a separate card. In the upper right-hand corner, place the author's name and the title of the work. In the upper left-hand corner, record the subject. You might do this in pencil, since you may later wish to reclassify information as you organize ideas. Sample note cards appear throughout this section.

There are several advantages to using cards for note-taking, such as their portability—you can take the cards wherever you must work. But perhaps most importantly, cards allow you to manipulate the information you locate. For instance, you can sort information into important and less important ideas, then organize the information into an overall report or even a paragraph structure. This makes essay-writing much easier.

GET ORGANIZED

How to Make Note Cards for Your Bibliography

Information to note for a book:
- ❏ Author
- ❏ Title: Subtitle
- ❏ Place of publication
- ❏ Publisher
- ❏ Date
- ❏ Inclusive page numbers if you use only a part of a book

Information to note for a scholarly article:
- ❏ Author of article
- ❏ Title of article
- ❏ Name of journal
- ❏ Volume and issue number
- ❏ Date of issue
- ❏ Inclusive page numbers for the article

If the article is online, you need to include the digital object identifier (DOI) required to reference the article in APA format.

If there is no DOI, you need to include the URL to help the reader locate the article.

Africa Studio/Shutterstock.com

ORIGINAL SOURCE

More than $2 billion worth of products and agricultural commodities from Canada's farms and fisheries is exported to developing countries each year. The developing countries, for most of the 1980s, purchased more manufactured goods from Canada than did either Japan or all members of the European Community combined.

Canadian diplomatic, trade, and consular representatives are resident in developing countries in every region of the world. Ottawa is host to one of the world's largest resident foreign diplomatic corps: 105 embassies and high commissions, of which 73 are from developing countries. Canada's political independence and territorial integrity depend heavily upon the juridical recognition that these countries extend to Canada, as well as their adherence to the United Nations Charter.

Make sure to keep impeccable notes from your sources so that you can explicitly identify where materials came from. North American postsecondary institutions demand careful attribution of sources and value research papers for students' skills at assembling relevant research rather than for demonstrations of their knowledge.

RECORDING NOTES

The materials you employ to record information are not as important as how you record your notes. You may find electronic notes handier than paper and just as easy to take, especially if you have a notebook computer to work with in a library. Very generally, there are three ways you can record the secondary research ideas and information you locate:

- summarizing
- paraphrasing
- quoting directly

Whether you decide to summarize, paraphrase, or quote directly will depend on the nature of the information you locate and how you plan to use that information in your research paper.

Summarizing

A summary of source material captures in your own words, and in a highly condensed form, the very essential ideas of a passage. Since the summary contains only major points, it is much shorter than the original text.

To create a summary, first identify the main points of the source information, then express them very economically in your own words without losing the essential meaning of the original. If you must use any words or phrases from the original, place this material within quotation marks. Within the summary itself, do not attempt to interpret the author's work. If you wish to record your thoughts, use a pencil and write in any white space on the note card.

Generally it is best to use a summary when you want to record the central idea of a longer passage. This passage could be a longer explanation, an argument, or background information.

GET ORGANIZED

How to Summarize Material

- ❑ Identify the main points you need from the source in question.
- ❑ Include only essential information related to the main points from the original source.
- ❑ Make an effort to use your own words. If you do include any exact wording, put it in quotation marks.
- ❑ Keep track of the author's name, a shortened title, and a page number for future reference.
- ❑ Include the source in your working bibliography.

Figure 3.7 Card Showing Summarized Material

Importance of developing nations
Head, "Hinge of History"

Canada does a significant amount of trade in fishing and farming with developing nations ("more than $2 billion" a year). Canada has diplomatic representation in most areas of the developing world, and developing nations in turn have significant representation in Ottawa. Recognition by these countries in part defines Canada as a nation. (p. D5)

GET ORGANIZED

How to Paraphrase Material

❏ Read your source carefully to make sure you understand the main ideas and significant details.

❏ Jot down the main ideas you wish to note, being careful to vary your wording as you go along.

❏ Reread the source to make sure you have done the original idea justice in your notes.

❏ Include any exact phrasing in quotation marks.

❏ Include the author's name, a shortened title of the work, and a page number for future reference.

❏ Make sure to include the source of the paraphrase in your working bibliography.

Figure 3.8 Cards Showing Paraphrased Material

Importance of developing nations
    Head, "Hinge of History"

Canada does a great deal of yearly trade with developing nations. Ivan Head, the former president of the International Development Centre, says the figure is "more than $2-billion worth" in sectors such as fisheries and farming. From 1980 to 1989, our trade with developing nations exceeded that with Japan and all the countries of the European Community.

Canada has diplomatic and trade representatives stationed in most developing nations, or at least in the regions where these countries are located. Many developing countries have representatives stationed in Ottawa. According to Head, of the 105 embassies and high commissions in Ottawa, 73 are from developing countries. Developing countries also play a significant role in defining Canada's unique identity. This is done through their legal recognition of Canada, and the fact that they follow the UN charter. (pD5)

Paraphrasing

In a paraphrase, you restate information in your own words instead of quoting the source directly. Unlike a summary, which is a short version containing only essential information from the original source, the paraphrase is often the same length as the original, and it may be longer. A paraphrase should closely parallel the presentation of ideas in the original, including particular points of emphasis. However, the paraphrase should not use the same words, phrases, or sentence structure as the original, since this would constitute plagiarism.

Paraphrasing demands that you think about the ideas in an original source and clearly understand them. Use your own words, phrasing, and sentence structure to restate the message of the original. If you need to quote directly, make sure this material is framed within quotation marks. Reproduce the order of ideas in the original and retain any points of emphasis.

Note: It is very easy to slip inadvertently into plagiarism when paraphrasing. To avoid plagiarism, do not look at the original source when you paraphrase. Then, when you complete the paraphrase, check to ensure you have kept the general meaning of the original but not the author's exact words.

Use paraphrasing for important information or ideas relevant to your research. Since a paraphrase is often as long as the original source material, do not try to paraphrase whole pages or chapters. Paraphrases are most useful when you want to present an author's general line of thought.

Original:

The fact that rival construals of a single occurrence can trigger an extravagant court case tells us that the nature of reality does not dictate the way that reality is represented in people's minds. The language of thought allows us to frame a situation in different and incompatible ways. The unfolding of history on the morning of September 11 in New York can be thought of as one event or two events depending on what we choose to focus on and what we choose to ignore. And the ability to frame an event in alternative ways is not just a reason to go to court but also the source of the richness of human intellectual life. As we shall see, it provides the materials for scientific and literary creativity, for humor and wordplay, and for the dramas of social life. And it sets the stage in countless arenas of human disputation.

In the past decade prominent linguists have been advising American Democrats on how the Republican Party has outframed them in recent elections and on how they might regain control of the semantics of political debate by reframing, for example, taxes as membership fees and activist judges as freedom judges.

Paraphrase:

Steven Pinker theorizes that language permits us to frame events in varying, sometimes opposing, ways, depending on what we concentrate on and on what we leave out. This framing of situations is the source of disputes, but also the foundation for human diversity and creativity. Over the past ten years in America, linguistic experts have consulted with the Democrats to help them reassert semantic power "by reframing, for example, taxes as membership fees and activist judges as freedom judges" (Pinker, 2007, p. 5).

Figure 3.9 Card Recording Direct Quotation and Related Information

Developing nations and Canadian identity
*   Head, "Hinge of History"*

According to Ivan Head, former president of the
International Development Research Centre, "Canada's
political independence and territorial integrity depend
heavily upon the juridical recognition that these countries
[developing nations] extend to Canada, as well as their
adherence to the United Nations Charter." (p. D5)

QUICK TIP

Making photocopies of
source material, such as
quotations or bibliographic
information, helps to
ensure that you record it
accurately.

Quoting Directly

When quoting a source directly, you copy the author's words exactly.

If you locate a passage that you think would make an interesting quotation, copy it down word for word, and enclose the material within quotation marks. When copying, make sure that you take down the exact wording, spelling, capitalization, and punctuation of the original. Proofread the quotation a number of times to ensure that it is accurate. If you need to add words for explanation or clarity, do so within square brackets. Whenever you leave anything out, indicate this with an ellipsis mark.

In literary essays, when you analyze stories, novels, poems, or plays, it is often necessary to quote extensively to provide evidence for your ideas. However, be selective when you use direct quotations in research papers. Here, direct quotations might be best employed to present an especially clear explanation from an expert, a colourfully or passionately stated idea, or another writer's key arguments.

OTHER WAYS OF TAKING NOTES

Computer

As an alternative to using note cards, some researchers prefer to input notes using a computer. Taking notes in this way allows you to easily rearrange ideas, print out material, and incorporate notes into research report drafts.

Guard against typos when using a computer to record direct quotations.

SOME SAMPLE NOTES TAKEN ON A LAPTOP DURING A CONFERENCE PRESENTATION

Results:
Passionate desire of the need for change
Frustration at the multitude of barriers faced daily
What we found
Attitudes were the barriers more often
Almost 60% identified attitudes as barriers
53% architectural
others together—47%

That means:
Over a million people in province experience attitudinal barriers—potentially discriminatory—when accessing goods and services.
—taken from presentation at conference given by Deborah Cohen, Performance Solutions Network,
—Title of presentation: Visible and Invisible Barriers: Research on Barrier Frequency, Importance and Impact, at University of Guelph Accessibility Conference, May 31 and June 1, 2011.

(notes) © Deborah Cohen

GET ORGANIZED

How to Quote Materials

❏ Make sure that you copy quotations exactly.

❏ Enclose quotations in quotation marks, even in your working copy.

❏ Use square brackets around any word or phrase that you add to the original.

❏ Use ellipses (… or …. if they occur at the end of a sentence) to indicate words omitted from a source.

❏ Identify the author, shortened title, and page number in your notes for future reference.

❏ Keep track of these sources in a working bibliography as you go along.

When should I quote materials?

❏ Quote when only the author's exact wording will do, perhaps because of its impact or level of detail.

❏ Quote if you intend to use the quotation in detail to explicate something in your paper.

❏ Avoid quoting when paraphrase or summary will do.

When drafting your research paper, avoid using too many quotations. Some style guides, such as the *Publication Manual of the American Psychological Association*, actively discourage quotations. Just because you collect a significant number of direct quotations on note cards does not mean that you must use them all in your research paper. Having too many quotations can interrupt the flow of ideas and give readers the impression you cannot think independently. A central purpose of the academic research paper is to show that you can analyze and synthesize information and make wise decisions about which evidence best supports your thesis.

When used appropriately and judiciously, though, direct quotations can be an extremely powerful way to make or reinforce a point. However, you must integrate quotations into your papers so that there is a smooth transition between your own ideas and any quoted materials.

Following are guidelines and techniques for integrating quotations smoothly and clearly into the text of your research paper.

USING SIGNAL PHRASES EFFECTIVELY

1. Use authors' names often to introduce quotations, rather than hiding them in parentheses at the end.
   Example:
   A study by Basu and de Jong (2010) provides clear evidence that income and geographical location are factors in the size of families that prefer sons to daughters.

2. Use verbs that indicate the author's stance.
   Example:
   Alice Munro in "Free Radicals" shows how a story may serve as expiation.

3-2A   USING SIGNAL PHRASES

Signal phrases are excellent for introducing information paraphrased from a source or direct quotations and integrating them into a research paper. A signal phrase alerts the reader that a quotation is about to begin. It can indicate who spoke or wrote the words and from what source the material comes.

Schaefle, Smaby, Packman, and Maddux (2007) concur that mastery among counsellors involves some combination of goal attainment and social influence. While achieving these goals is ambitious, Jennings and Skovholt insist on the importance of a "congruent life," as one of their respondents put it, so that personal and professional values match (p. 7).

NEVER INCLUDE A QUOTATION WITHOUT A CLEAR SIGNAL PHRASE

Without a signal phrase to integrate the quotation into the flow of your paper, quoted information can appear disjointed and confusing to the reader.

QUOTATION WITHOUT A CLEAR SIGNAL PHRASE

Some think Canada has an inferiority complex. "Sometimes it appears to me that Canada, even intact Canada, is not so much a country as a continental suburb, where Little Leaguers govern ineffectually, desperate for American approval" (Richler 147).

QUOTATION WITH A CLEAR SIGNAL PHRASE

Some think Canada has an inferiority complex. According to Mordecai Richler in *Oh Canada! Oh Quebec!*, "Sometimes it appears to me that Canada, even intact Canada, is not so much a country as a continental suburb, where Little Leaguers govern ineffectually, desperate for American approval" (147).

A few ideas for varied constructions include the following:

In *Amusing Ourselves to Death*, Postman argues ...
Jung describes the fire jumper's role graphically ...
... argues Naomi Wolf in *The Beauty Myth*.

Introducing an author and providing credentials:

Gabriel Garcia Marquez, winner of the Nobel Prize for Literature, ...
Mark Bittman, noted food writer for *The New York Times* and bestselling cookbook author, ...

VARY YOUR SIGNAL PHRASES

Just as you should use sentence variety in your general writing, so too should you employ variety in your use of signal phrases. If you require a number of direct quotations, don't use similar wording or structure in the signal phrases. For instance, using a phrase such as, "According to Mordecai Richler ..." or "Richler says ..." again and again makes the writing seem mechanical.

By including the author's name and the title of the work or the author's credentials in the signal phrase, you can introduce the quotation and at the same time emphasize the credibility of the source.

USE APPROPRIATE VERBS IN SIGNAL PHRASES

A key element of the signal phrase is the verb. Avoid using the same verbs, such as *says, notes, writes,* or *states,* again and again.

Through the judicious choice of verbs in your signal phrases, you can communicate the quoted writer's tone or intent and how the quotation relates to the flow of your own ideas. For example, the verb can indicate whether the quotation offers an observation, explanation, or argument.

WEAVE QUOTED FRAGMENTS OR PHRASES INTO YOUR TEXT

As an alternative to using a full-sentence quotation, you might quote only a fragment or fragments, which may be easier to integrate into your text and will often make a point just as convincingly. When using a phrase or fragment, make sure that it retains the source's original meaning.

To evaluate how well you have integrated quotations within your paper, try reading the text aloud. As well, you might focus on the integration of quotations at the editing stage of your writing process.

Table 3.1 Effective Verbs to Use in Signal Phrases

acknowledges	admits	agrees	argues	asserts
believes	claims	complains	concedes	concludes
concurs	confirms	contends	declares	disagrees
denies	disputes	emphasizes	grants	holds
implies	insists	laments	maintains	observes
points out	predicts	proposes	reasons	refutes
rejects	speculates	suggests	warns	illustrates

Orwell contends that the English language "becomes ugly and inaccurate" for the simple reason that people's thoughts can be foolish (370).

QUICK TIP

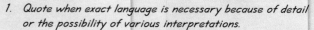

1. *Quote when exact language is necessary because of detail or the possibility of various interpretations.*
2. *Quote when you are referring to a well-known, respected authority.*
3. *Quote only when you are prepared to explain the significance of the quoted words to the reader.*
4. *Quote when the exact wording of a point from an expert is a valuable source of support.*
5. *Don't quote if you can reasonably paraphrase or summarize, and the other rules do not apply.*

E.D. Hirsch Jr. clearly defines in his preface what it means to be culturally literate:

> To be culturally literate is to possess the basic information needed to thrive in the modern world. The breadth of that information is great, extending over the major domains of human activity from sports to science. It is by no means confined to "culture" narrowly understood as an acquaintance with the arts. Nor is it confined to one social class. (xiii)

Punctuate long quotations correctly. In poetry, keep formatting similar to the original.

Hopkins uses alliteration repeatedly as a linking device in "God's Grandeur":

> THE WORLD is charged with the grandeur of God.
>   It will flame out, like shining from shook foil;
>   It gathers to a greatness, like the ooze of oil
> Crushed. Why do men then now not reck his rod? (1–4)

—from Gerard Manley Hopkins (1844–89). *Poems*. 1918.

In prose:

> For King and Hicks (2007), there is more to maturity than happiness; the other side is complexity. Happiness, they contend, may just be a side effect of maturity, at least as far as Erikson conceived of it. In their words,
>
> > Certainly, Erikson … did not include happiness as a criterion for personality development, but it is not difficult to imagine that a person who has attained trust, autonomy, initiative, industry, identity, intimacy, generativity, and integrity is going to be happier than the unfortunate soul who ended up on the other side of those psychosocial conflicts. (p. 628)

A long quotation in poetry is considered more than three lines, while in prose it is more than four lines. Indent the quoted material 2.5 cm (1 in.) from the left-hand margin. (See 11-5b.) The right-hand margin does not change. Double space the quoted material. You do not need to use quotation marks with a longer quotation because the convention of indenting indicates to the reader that the material comes from another source.

Direct quotations should be as succinct as possible. However, in some instances, such as to illustrate a writer's evocative description, a long quotation may be needed. When quoting material of more than two paragraphs in length, indent the first line of each new paragraph an additional 1.25 cm (0.5 in.).

Introduce the long quotation with a complete sentence that usually ends with a colon. The colon indicates that the introduction is closely related to the quotation that follows it.

The parenthetical citation for a longer quotation appears outside the punctuation of the last sentence.

Two useful types of punctuation for working with quotations are the ellipsis mark and brackets. The ellipsis is commonly used to shorten quotations, while brackets allow you to add words to quotations. Use both where appropriate to integrate quotations smoothly into your text.

ELLIPSIS MARK

The ellipsis mark indicates that you have omitted a word, phrase, sentence, or more from a quoted passage. This punctuation form communicates to the reader that a quotation does not completely reproduce the original. An ellipsis mark normally consists of three spaced periods. Leave a space before them and after them as well. However, when you have deleted something at the end of a sentence, use four spaced periods, thus.... In this case, there is no space before the first period because it is seen to be the period marking the end of the previous sentence.

© laurent Renault/iStockphoto.com

Ivan Head, the man behind the Earth Clock and nonstop generator of ideas about the realities behind the Doomsday equation, is leaving the research centre on an angry note after thirteen years as president. Mr. Head [...] cannot accept the indifference of the planet's North, the world's industrialized nations, to the Third World South. (D2)

The writer omitted the words "diplomat, lawyer, and foreign policy adviser"—perhaps because, in the context of the paper or the point being made, these roles were not relevant.

The use of the ellipsis mark with quotations is quite refined:

- Use **...** for any omission from the middle of a single sentence.
- Use **, ...** to show a jump from the middle of one sentence to the middle of another.
- In all other cases, use a period with the ellipsis mark, positioned to show if text is missing before **....** or after **....** the period.

Pheromones influence the onset of puberty in males and females.... They can act as an aphrodisiac and, by stimulating the sex hormones, augment the sex drive. (Smith, 2005, p. 61)

Ellipsis marks can be employed to keep a long quotation as short and to the point as possible. When using ellipsis marks to shorten quotations, follow two guiding principles:
1. Maintain the meaning of the original source in your shortened version.
2. Ensure that the briefer version is grammatically correct and consistent with the surrounding text.

> Full light showed her [Marilyn Bell] haggard and gaunt. Pain probed her arms and legs, her stomach throbbed. Her breathing and her stroke had lost their coordination, and she gulped unwanted water from the lake. She began to cry. Ryder extended liniment on the stick for her dragging legs (363).

> Like existential therapy, cognitive therapy aims at changing clients' interpretations of meaning, though it brings a more specific agenda to the task. Although cognitive therapy has the reputation of being aligned to positive thinking, Leahy (1996) argues that "cognitive therapy is the *power of realistic thinking, not the power of positive thinking* [emphasis added]" (p. 24).

Usually you do not use an ellipsis mark at the beginning or end of a quotation. Include one at the end of the quotation only if you have omitted words at the end of the final quoted sentence and it is important to indicate that the quotation ends mid-sentence.

BRACKETS
Brackets are sometimes called "square parentheses"; they allow you to insert words in quoted material. For instance, you might use square brackets within a quotation to enclose information clarifying a pronoun, to change the tense of a verb so that it fits grammatically with the surrounding text or to add or remove a capital letter. As with the ellipsis mark, your use of brackets should never distort the meaning of the original quotation.

Adam was the only man who, when he said a good thing, knew that nobody had said it before him.

—Mark Twain

Academic Integrity and Documentation Overview

4

Not all sources are alike.

Quote
- *if the wording is memorable and cannot be improved upon*
- *if you want to focus on the author whom you are quoting*
- *if you want to draw attention to the quoted words in detail*

Paraphrase
- *when the ideas in the sources are the focus and not the exact words themselves*
- *when you want to emphasize your understanding of a concept*

Summarize
- *when the details are not as important as the central idea*

ELL Note

Make sure to follow guidelines for academic integrity to the letter, and ask your instructor when in doubt.

In research writing, whenever you summarize, paraphrase, or directly quote another person's words, ideas, or thoughts, or use facts and statistics that are not commonly known, you must ethically acknowledge your source to avoid plagiarism (see 4-1) and properly document your source in accordance with one of the special documentation styles scholars require in their academic journals (see 4-2).

Plagiarism occurs when you use facts, words, or opinions that you obtained from someone else without identifying your source or acknowledging that they weren't originally yours. Plagiarism occurs when an author appropriates—steals— and passes off the ideas or words of another as her or his own without crediting the original author. Plagiarism can be a deliberate act, such as copying longer passages without proper acknowledgment, or an unintentional offence, such as neglecting to credit direct quotations and frame them in quotation marks.

Since the purpose of a research essay is research, you shouldn't be put off by the fact that something is not original. Just make sure to give credit where credit is due.

Keep accurate notes in which you document where you obtained information and exactly what ideas and words came directly from another author. Be systematic.

GET ORGANIZED

How to Avoid Plagiarism

❑ Develop a reliable note-taking system and working bibliography to keep track of sources and page numbers for quotations.

❑ Credit any ideas you found, whether in person or on the TV, radio, or Internet. If a friend gives you an idea, thank the person in a footnote or endnote. No citation is necessary.

❑ Be careful of the placement of citations. They normally should come at the end of the idea you are identifying as belonging to someone else.

❑ Look for ideas that you have heard about. Tracking them back to their origins is a good idea, though often challenging.

❑ Use quotation marks whenever you use exact wording. Page numbers are also needed in this case.

❑ Cite ideas that are like your own, even if you thought of them before you read the research. Originality is not really the purpose of the research essay; doing research is!

❑ Learn to paraphrase. Write your papers without borrowing wording from other sources. Even summaries and paraphrases must be acknowledged, however.

❑ Don't just copy and paste. Reword it or quote it exactly, remembering in both cases to include sources.

❑ Don't leave out information even if it is difficult to find. The sources you examined are a key to assessing the quality of your work.

❑ Don't hand in the same assignment in two different classes without prior approval.

❑ Protect your work from misuse by others.

❑ Don't hand over the essay to your sources. You are the writer; use the sources to make your own case. The sources provide the evidence and support for your opinions.

Plagiarism: Keeping Your Ideas Original

- Read for understanding of critical ideas.
- Take careful notes. Include author, title, year, publication information, and inclusive page numbers (for articles and parts of books). Make note of the URL or DOI for anything found on the Web.
- Separate your thoughts and interpretations from your descriptive notes about sources.
- Keep notes until after an assignment is returned as evidence of your research.

TAKING RESEARCH NOTES

Careless note-taking can easily result in inadvertent plagiarism—using someone else's ideas or wording without proper acknowledgment. Plagiarism carries severe academic consequences, and it is penalized by academic institutions whether it is intentional or unintentional. You, the writer, are responsible for the integrity of anything that appears on the page under your name.

These days, it is simple for an instructor to find your online sources, either through Google or a similar search engine or by using software like Turnitin (http://www.turnitin.com). Don't run the risk of severe academic penalties by putting off source acknowledgment.

One of the best ways to avoid problems with academic integrity is to use an accepted style of documentation to cite the sources for any phrases or ideas not completely your own.

original excerpt
Gladwell, Malcolm. *Blink: The Power of Thinking Without Thinking.*
New York: 2005.

MALCOLM GLADWELL WRITES IN *BLINK*:

I polled about half of the companies on the Fortune 500 list—the largest corporations in the United States—asking each company questions about its CEO. The heads of big companies are, as I'm sure comes as no surprise to anyone, overwhelmingly white men, which undoubtedly reflects some kind of implicit bias. But they are also virtually all tall: In my sample, I found that on average CEOs were just a shade under six feet. Given that the average American male is 5'9" that means that CEOs, as a group, have about three inches on the rest of their sex. But this statistic actually understates matters. In the U.S. population, about 14.5 percent of all men are six feet or over. Among CEOs of Fortune 500 companies, that number is 58 percent. Even more strikingly, in the general American population, 3.9 percent of adult men are 6'2" or taller. Among my CEO sample, 30 percent were 6'2" or taller.

MY SUMMARY:

Gladwell (2005) shows in his poll that male CEOS on the Fortune 500 list are roughly three inches taller than the average American man.

When are in-text citations appropriate?

- when you are using the exact words of others, making sure to place those words within quotation marks
- when you are using facts or ideas obtained from other sources
- when you are expressing the words or ideas of others in your own words, as in summaries and paraphrases

When are citations not required?

- when you are using your own ideas
- when you are presenting common knowledge (e.g., the Magna Carta was signed in 1215)

There are a number of acceptable academic styles for citing sources in your paper. Always ask your instructor which documentation style he or she prefers. One of the most common documentation styles is that of the Modern Language Association (MLA); see 4-2a and Chapter 5.

The citations follow these rules:

1. If you have introduced the information from another source with a signal phrase clearly identifying the author, then only the page reference is needed in parentheses, so long as the reference clearly refers to the work of the author you mention.

According to James Joyce biographer Richard Ellmann, the great Irish writer "sometimes used *Ulysses* to demonstrate that even English, that best of languages, was inadequate" (397).

2. Otherwise, the citation should include the author's last name and a page reference for the source work.

It may be true that Joyce "sometimes used *Ulysses* to demonstrate that even English, that best of languages, was inadequate" (Ellmann 397).

3. In a list of works cited, at the end of the research paper, the name of the author, title of the work, and other publishing information about the source are provided.

Ellmann, Richard. *James Joyce*. New York: Oxford UP, 1983.

For more details on MLA documentation style, see 4-2a, where you will also find guidelines on APA style for in-text citations and instructions on using footnotes.

HOW TO HANDLE ONLINE SOURCES

- Don't take words or ideas from a website without noting where you found them.
- Highlight or use a different font to make sure that information you glean from online sources is attributed correctly to its source. Whenever you gather material, get into the habit of acknowledging where it comes from immediately so that you don't lose track and face embarrassment or accusation later.

(screen) andersphoto/Shutterstock.com

MLA note: Gladwell (2005) shows in his poll that male CEOS on the Fortune 500 list are roughly three inches taller than the average American man.

MLA Works Cited entry: Gladwell, Malcolm. *Blink: The Power of Thinking Without Thinking*. New York: Little, 2005. Print.

In MLA style, you acknowledge your sources with brief parenthetical citations in your text; these correspond to an alphabetical list of works cited, which appears at the end of the paper.

QUOTING SOURCES ACCURATELY   4-1B

GET ORGANIZED

How to Take Notes from Sources
To avoid unintentional plagiarism, take notes that reflect how you have been influenced by what you are reading:

❏ Cite quotations and borrowed ideas.
❏ Enclose borrowed language within quotation marks.
❏ Write summaries and paraphrases completely in your own words.

In academic research writing, whenever a writer draws on another's work, he or she must acknowledge that intellectual indebtedness by precisely specifying what was borrowed (a fact, an opinion, the writer's own words) and from where it was borrowed.

It is possible to commit plagiarism inadvertently, either by not clearly distinguishing between your own thoughts and material you gathered from others, or through ignorance of what constitutes unethical use of another writer's work.

WHAT YOU MUST CITE

1. Any direct quotation
2. Any idea, opinion, fact, or resource borrowed from another source, including the following:
   a) paraphrases of sentences
   b) summaries of sentences or chapters
   c) statistics and little-known facts
   d) visual information such as tables, graphs, diagrams, and illustrations, including photographs and screen shots from the Internet

CITE QUOTATIONS AND BORROWED IDEAS

You should have a good idea of what to cite and what not to cite. Here are a few guidelines.

Sometimes it can be a challenge to decide whether factual information is common knowledge or not. Generally, if you see the information in a number of sources, treat it as common knowledge in your paper. If you are not sure, you might ask an expert. Cite any factual information that is controversial. If you are still in doubt, it is wise to be cautious and cite the source.

ENCLOSE BORROWED LANGUAGE WITHIN QUOTATION MARKS

If, in the text of your research paper, you are using the exact words of another author, you must clearly indicate this to the reader by enclosing the borrowed material within quotation marks. It is not adequate to use the author's words and merely provide a citation at the end of the quoted sentence. Failure to use quotation marks qualifies as plagiarism. The only exception to this rule is if you are quoting a longer passage and using indentation, as opposed to quotation marks, to indicate that the quoted material contains the exact words of the author. (See 3-2b.)

WHAT YOU DO NOT NEED TO CITE

1. Proverbs like "A stitch in time saves nine" or "Money doesn't grow on trees"
2. Common knowledge, or information that can be found easily in a variety of sources, such as the knowledge that Shakespeare wrote *Hamlet* or that the Bible is Christianity's holy book
3. Things you discover in conversation or in a classroom setting
4. Visuals that you create independently

The following examples indicate how a researcher could commit and correct plagiarism.

ORIGINAL SOURCE MATERIAL

> In India, which invented family planning, but has made a mockery of it, it seems unlikely that the government will be able to fix the population crisis without first fixing itself.
>
> —John Stackhouse, "Okay, You Can Take Her," p. A1.

Plagiarism

According to John Stackhouse, in India, which invented family planning, but has made a mockery of it, it seems unlikely that the government will be able to fix the population crisis without first fixing itself (A1).

The researcher has not used quotation marks to set off exact words from John Stackhouse's article. The impression is given that the researcher generated the content and structure of the comment on India, which is not true.

Correcting Plagiarism with Quotation Marks

According to John Stackhouse, "In India, which invented family planning, but has made a mockery of it, it seems unlikely that the government will be able to fix the population crisis without first fixing itself" (A1).

It is now abundantly clear that the opinion as well as the words and sentence structure used to express that opinion are exclusively attributable to John Stackhouse.

ORIGINAL SOURCE MATERIAL

> The mass of men serve the state thus, not as men mainly,
> but as machines, with their bodies.
>
> —Henry David Thoreau, *Civil Disobedience*, p. 361.

Plagiarism due to Borrowing Phrases

Rather than working for their country as men, the mass of men work
for it as machines, with their bodies (Thoreau 361).

Plagiarism due to Borrowing Sentence Structure

The preponderance of men serve the country, not as men mainly, rather
as machines, using their physical labour (Thoreau 361).

Acceptable Paraphrase

During Thoreau's time, workers were not considered individuals;
instead, they were only valued for the physical work they could provide
(Thoreau 361).

Neither words, phrases, nor sentence structure are used in the acceptable paraphrase. The information from Thoreau illustrates a fundamental research choice you may have to make:

> Is it better to use a paraphrase or, because the thought is so
> succinctly and eloquently expressed by the author, quote the
> original directly and place the author's exact words within
> quotation marks?

WRITE SUMMARIES AND PARAPHRASES COMPLETELY IN YOUR OWN WORDS

It is very easy to lapse into plagiarism when summarizing or paraphrasing the work of others. You must acknowledge not only another writer's ideas and facts, but also the writer's language and form—the exact words and sentence structures he or she uses to present those ideas and facts. Therefore, anything directly borrowed must appear within quotation marks. A borrowed sentence structure must be recast so it is truly your own.

To avoid any accusation of plagiarism, ensure that you use your own words and sentence structures when summarizing and paraphrasing. Then, of course, cite the source.

Paraphrasing and Summarizing

To avoid inadvertent plagiarism when summarizing or paraphrasing, follow these steps:

1. Close the book containing the original source material. Since you must rely on your own understanding and memory of the original content, this should prevent copying.
2. Write a summary or paraphrase according to your understanding of the concepts you are explaining.
3. Once you have completed the summary or paraphrase, check it against the original to ensure that you are not indebted to the author for any word, phrase, or sentence structure.

4-2) DOCUMENTATION OVERVIEW

You must also think about your final product—the research paper. There are a number of acceptable report presentation and documentation styles. The most common ones are covered in this handbook. One of your first tasks should be to ask your instructor which style he or she wants you to follow.

Once you identify the style you are to follow, review the relevant section. Then, as you conduct your research, you will know the source information needed.

Helder Almeida/Shutterstock.com

For detailed descriptions of the major styles, see Chapters 5 (MLA), 6 (APA), 7 (Chicago), and 8 (CSE and Columbia Online).

MODERN LANGUAGE ASSOCIATION (MLA) STYLE

Manuscript format and documentation guidelines presented in the *MLA Handbook for Writers of Research Papers* are often followed in English and humanities courses. Chapter 5 outlines essential style guidelines from the *MLA Handbook* (7th ed., 2009) and concludes with a model research paper following the MLA format and documentation style.

Example:
Cameron, Julia. *The Sound of Paper: Starting from Scratch*. New York: Penguin, 2004.

AMERICAN PSYCHOLOGICAL ASSOCIATION (APA) STYLE

Manuscript format and documentation guidelines presented in the *Publication Manual of the American Psychological Association* are often followed in social science courses such as psychology, anthropology, business, economics, and sociology. Chapter 6 outlines essential style guidelines from the *APA Manual* (6th ed., 2010) and

Example:
McConnell, J. (1974). *Understanding human behavior: An introduction to psychology.* New York: Holt, Rinehart, & Winston.

concludes with a model research paper following the APA format and documentation style.

UNIVERSITY OF CHICAGO (CHICAGO) STYLE

Manuscript format and documentation guidelines presented in *The Chicago Manual of Style* are often followed in history and other humanities courses. Chapter 7 outlines the basic style guidelines from *The Chicago Manual of Style* (16th ed., 2010) and concludes with a model research paper following Chicago format and documentation style.

Example:

Eagleton, Terry. *Marxism and Literary Criticism.* London: Methuen, 1976.

COUNCIL OF SCIENCE EDITORS (CSE) STYLE

The style guidelines of the Council of Science Editors are followed in many branches of science. Documentation guidelines presented in *Scientific Style and Format: The CSE Manual for Authors, Editors, and Publishers* (7th ed., 2006) are outlined in 8-1.

Example:

Hawking SW. 2001. The universe in a nutshell. New York: Bantam. 216 p.

Humanities Style:

National Association of Photoshop
Professionals. NAPP. 2006.
http://www.photoshopuser.com/
(6 Nov. 2006).

Scientific Style:

National Biodiesel Board. (2006). Biodiesel.
http://www.biodiesel.org/ (8 Nov. 2006).

the
columbia
guide
to
online
style

janice r. walker
and
todd taylor

second edition

COLUMBIA ONLINE STYLE

COS style, which has been endorsed by the Alliance for Computers and Writing, has variations for humanities and scientific disciplines and can be useful for citing electronic sources no matter which specific style of documentation you are required to use. Documentation guidelines presented in *The Columbia Guide to Online Style* (2nd ed., 2006) are outlined in 8-2.

OTHER STYLES AND STYLE GUIDES

Institute of Electrical and Electronics Engineers

IEEE provides a comprehensive website for research and documentation that allows access to thousands of articles in abstract or in full text and makes standards of documentation clear on its website at http://www.ieee.org/index.html.

In some disciplines, such as physics and geology, you may be asked to follow documentation guidelines produced by an association related to the discipline. A list of specialized style guides, organized by discipline, is provided here.

As well, many academic institutions—and departments—produce style guides. These published guidelines are often available at your college or university library.

BIOLOGY AND OTHER SCIENCES

Huth, Edward J. *Scientific Style and Format: The CSE Manual for Authors, Editors, and Publishers.* 7th ed. New York: Cambridge UP, 2006, http://www.councilscienceeditors.org.

CHEMISTRY

Coghill, Anne M., and Lorrin R. Garson, eds. *The ACS Style Guide: Effective Communication of Scientific Information.* 3rd ed. Washington, DC: American Chemical Society, 2006, http://pubs.acs.org.

ENGLISH AND THE HUMANITIES

The Canadian Style: A Guide to Writing and Editing. Rev. ed. Toronto: Dundurn Press and Public Works and Government Services Canada Translation Bureau, 2004.

The Chicago Manual of Style. 15th ed. Chicago: University of Chicago Press, 2003, http://www.chicagomanualofstyle.org.

Dodds, Jack, and Judi Jewinski. *The Ready Reference Handbook: Writing, Revising, Editing.* 5th Canadian ed. Scarborough: Allyn and Bacon Canada, 2009.

Gibaldi, Joseph. *MLA Handbook for Writers of Research Papers.* 7th ed. New York: MLA, 2009, http://www.mla.org.

Gibaldi, Joseph. *MLA Style Manual and Guide to Scholarly Publishing.* 3rd ed. New York: MLA, 2008.

Strunk, William Jr., and E.B. White. *The Elements of Style Fiftieth Anniversary Edition.* New York: Longman, 2009.

Turabian, Kate L. *A Manual for Writers of Term Papers, Theses, and Dissertations.* 7th ed. Chicago: University of Chicago Press, 2007.

JOURNALISM

Goldstein, Norm, ed. *The Associated Press Stylebook*. New York: Basic Books, 2004.

Tasko, Patti, ed. *The Canadian Press Stylebook: A Guide for Writers and Editors.* 15th ed. Toronto: Canadian Press, 2008.

McFarlane, J.A., and Warren Clements. *The Globe and Mail Style Book*. 9th ed. Toronto: McClelland & Stewart, 2003.

LAW

Yogis, John A., et al. *Legal Writing and Research Manual*. 6th ed. Toronto: Butterworths Canada, 2004.

LINGUISTICS

Linguistic Society of America. "Language Style Sheet." Published each year in the December issue of the *LSA Bulletin* and available online at http://www.lsadc.org/info/pubs-lang-style.cfm.

MATHEMATICS

Swanson, Ellen. *Mathematics into Type*. Updated ed. Providence, RI: American Mathematical Society, 1999, http://www.ams.org.

MEDICINE

American Medical Association. *American Medical Association Manual of Style*. 10th ed. Baltimore: Williams and Wilkins, 2007. Updates are available at http://www.amamanualofstyle.com/oso/public/index.html.

MUSIC

Holoman, D. Kern. *Writing about Music: A Style Sheet*. 2nd ed. Berkeley: University of California Press, 2008.

PHYSICS

American Institute of Physics. *AIP Style Manual.* 4th ed. New York: AIP, 1990. Available online at http://www.aip.org/pubservs/style.html.

POLITICAL SCIENCE

American Political Science Association. *Style Manual for Political Science.* Rev. ed. Washington, DC: American Political Science Association, 2006, www.ipsonet.org/data/files/APSAStyleManual2006.pdf.

PSYCHOLOGY AND THE SOCIAL SCIENCES

American Psychological Association. *Publication Manual of the American Psychological Association.* 6th ed. Washington: APA, 2010, http://www.apastyle.org.

SCIENCE AND TECHNICAL WRITING

Rubens, Philip, ed. *Science and Technical Writing: A Manual of Style.* 2nd ed. New York: Routledge, 2001.

CROM/Shutterstock.com

MLA Style of
Documentation

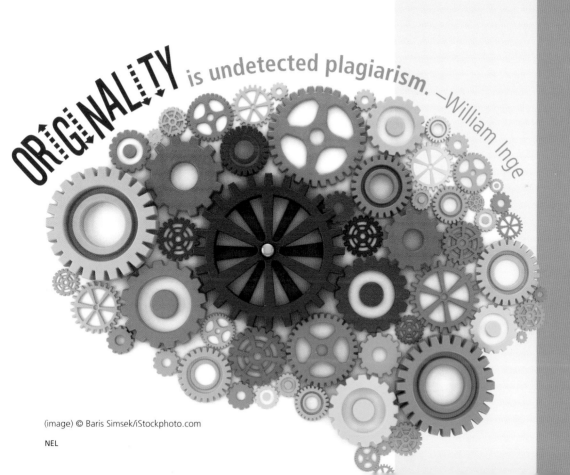

ORIGINALITY is undetected plagiarism. –William Inge

(image) © Baris Simsek/iStockphoto.com

MLA Style of Documentation

MLA FORMAT: SOME GUIDELINES FOR ESSAY WRITING

1. Use standard letter-size paper.
2. Double space in a readable font, such as Times New Roman in 12 pt.
3. Set margins to 2.5 cm (1 in.) on all sides.
4. Identify your paper with your last name and the page number in the upper right-hand corner.
5. Use no title page, unless suggested by your instructor.
6. Indent paragraphs 1.25 cm (0.5 in.) and indent long quotations of more than four lines, or 2.5 cm (1 in.).
7. List works cited at the end of your paper, on a separate page.
8. Leave only one space after periods or other end punctuation.
9. Use italics for titles of long published works, rather than underlining; use quotation marks for names of shorter published works.
10. See model MLA essay for more detailed information.

TEXT CITATION

Note that MLA uses parenthetical references to sources in the body of your essay. These correspond to the alphabetically listed *Works Cited* at the end of your paper.

To make it simple for readers to find sources, you must make sure your parenthetical references and Works Cited listings correspond. This is done by matching the signal words, usually the author's last name but sometimes a shortened version of the title of the work in question.

Writers in the arts and humanities, particularly in English, foreign languages, and literature, generally follow the Modern Language Association (MLA) guidelines for formatting research papers and documenting sources. This chapter summarizes MLA style guidelines published in the *MLA Handbook for Writers of Research Papers*, 7th ed. (New York: MLA, 2009) and concludes with a model research paper following MLA format and documentation style.

If a reader, such as your instructor, wants to check any source you used for words, facts, or ideas, he or she needs complete information about your sources. When following MLA style, you document your sources in two ways:

1. Within the body of the paper, using **in-text citations**
2. At the end of the paper, in a **list of works cited** (see page 210)

The citation briefly cites the author and page in parentheses within the essay, and each of these parenthetical citations has a matching entry giving complete publication information in the *Works Cited* list on a separate page at the end of the essay.

Use both the first and last names of authors the first time you mention them in a paper.

> Lorna Crozier's "Packing for the Future: Instructions" and Dionne Brand's "Blues Spiritual for Mammy Prater" are two free verse poems that relay a narrative about time, looking at the future and the past respectively.

Include page numbers when you cite from a source. Note that there is no comma between the author's name and the page number.

> In "Girl," when the daughter speaks, she does so in an anxious and defensive manner; "but I don't sing benna on Sundays at all…" (Kincaid 307).

5-1) IN-TEXT CITATIONS

An in-text citation consists of a **parenthetical reference** that gives the minimum information necessary to identify a source and locate the relevant material within it. Most often, this is the author's last name (unless the signal phrase mentions the author's name) and a page number or numbers. Full information on the source

Make sure quotations are accurately copied.

If you notice errors in grammar or spelling that are not your own, indicate them with the Latin word *sic*, meaning "thus" or "so" to let readers know that you are aware of the error but are reproducing the quotation correctly.

> In a press release, the CEO said the company would "do everything possible to accompany [*sic*] the strikers' demands" (Smith A2).

Put end punctuation after the citation with short quotations.

> There is a sense of worry in the daughter's voice when she says
> "…but what if the baker won't let me feel the bread?" and the
> reader is left to decide if she will become "the kind of woman who
> the baker won't let near the bread" (Kincaid 308).

Put question marks or exclamation marks inside quotation marks.

> An individual has not begun to live until he can rise
> above the narrow horizons of his particular individualistic
> concerns to the broader concerns of all humanity. Every
> person must decide, at some point, whether they will
> walk in the light of creative altruism or in the darkness of
> destructive selfishness. This is the judgment. Life's most
> persistent and urgent question is, "What are you doing
> for others?" (King 1957).

Dr. Martin Luther King, August 11, 1957; Source(s): http://crc.ohio.gov/pdf/2009MLK.pdf

Put a slash surrounded by spaces to indicate the end of a line of poetry.

> "There are strange things done in the midnight sun / By the men
> who moil for gold" (Service, lines 1–2).

is supplied in the list of works cited. The goal is to be as brief as possible while enabling the reader to locate the source in the *Works Cited* list accurately.

SHORT QUOTATIONS

Aim to make short quotations fit smoothly into your sentences, using quotation marks to indicate where the quoted words begin and end. Place the citation close to the quotation at the end of the sentence and place punctuation after the parenthesis, not inside the quotation mark.

LONG QUOTATIONS

If a quotation is more than four lines long, indent it 2.5 cm (1 in.) and double space it, just like the rest of the paper. Note that the punctuation comes at the end before the parenthesis. Leave one space between the quotation and the parenthesis.

Indent long quotations after an appropriate introduction.

> For King and Hicks (2007), there is more to maturity than happiness; the other side is complexity. Happiness, they contend, may just be a side effect of maturity, at least as far as Erikson conceived of it. In their words,
>
>> Certainly, Erikson … did not include *happiness* as a criterion for personality development, but it is not difficult to imagine that a person who has attained *trust, autonomy, initiative, industry, identity, intimacy, generativity*, and *integrity* is going to be happier than the unfortunate soul who ended up on the other side of those psychosocial conflicts. (628)

5-1A IN-TEXT REFERENCES TO AUTHORS

AUTHOR MENTIONED IN A SIGNAL PHRASE

A signal phrase indicates that something taken from a source—for example, a quotation, summary, or paraphrase—is about to be used. When you mention the author's name in a signal phrase, give only the page reference within the parentheses. Note that the parentheses are inside the end punctuation.

> Peter Schrag observes that America is "divided between affluence and poverty, between slums and suburbs" (118).

One commentator notes that America is "divided between affluence and poverty, between slums and suburbs" (Schrag 118).

QUICK
TIP

Always remember to source, especially if you use multiple works by the same author.

In *Lament for a Nation*, George Grant claims that "modern civilization makes all local cultures anachronistic" (54).

George Grant claims that "modern civilization makes all local cultures anachronistic" (*Lament* 54).

AUTHOR NOT MENTIONED IN A SIGNAL PHRASE

If the author's name is not mentioned in a signal phrase, it must appear in parentheses along with the page reference. No punctuation is required between the author's name and the page reference.

TWO OR MORE WORKS BY THE SAME AUTHOR

When you use two or more works by the same author in a research paper, you will have multiple entries for that author in your list of works cited. Your in-text citation must direct the reader to the correct entry in the *Works Cited* list. You can do this in one of three ways:

1. If you have provided the author's name and the title of the work in the signal phrase, include only the page number(s) in parentheses.
2. If only the author's name is given in the signal phrase, include the title of the work (abbreviated if the title is long and you have cited it in full at least once) within the parenthetical reference.

3. If there is no signal phrase, the parenthetical reference should include the author's last name, the title or a shortened version of it, and the page number(s). Use a comma to separate the author's name and the title.

> Some propose that "modern civilization makes all local cultures anachronistic" (Grant, *Lament* 54).

TWO OR THREE AUTHORS

You can include the names of the authors in the signal phrase or place them within the parenthetical reference.

> According to Clarkson and McCall, even late in the decade of the Quiet Revolution, "Trudeau saw the constitutional question as only one facet of his general mandate for the Justice Department" (258).

> Even late in the decade of the Quiet Revolution, "Trudeau saw the constitutional question as only one facet of his general mandate for the Justice Department" (Clarkson and McCall 258).

With three authors, use a serial comma in the reference:

> (Wynkin, Blynkin, and Nodd viii)

MORE THAN THREE AUTHORS

If the work you are citing has more than three authors, you have two options:

1. Name only the first author and use *et al.* (Latin abbreviation for "and others").
2. Give all names in full.

Note that *al.* takes a period (it is an abbreviation), but *et* does not.

> One position is that "in cultures whose religion, unlike Christianity, offers no promise of an afterlife, a name that will live on after one's death serves as the closest substitute for immortality" (Abrams et al. 3).

> The former Council of Biology Editors states in the previous edition of the style manual that "any coordinate system must be based upon a known reference point" (241).

> The previous edition of the manual states that "any coordinate system must be based upon a known reference point" (Council 241).

This example illustrates a reference to a magazine article, with the shortened title enclosed in quotation marks.

> The incidence of deep vein thrombosis, the so-called Economy Class Syndrome, has been associated with a genetic predisposition to this type of blood clotting ("Flying" 8).

> Some have claimed that "the terms 'black' and 'white' ultimately acquire meaning only in opposition to each other" (L. Hill 208).

In a signal phrase, give the full name.

> When considering mixed-race issues in Canada, Lawrence Hill contends "the terms 'black' and 'white' ultimately acquire meaning only in opposition to each other" (208).

The method you choose should match the one you use in the *Works Cited* list.

CORPORATE AUTHOR

A corporate author is a company, an agency, or an institution that is credited with authorship of a work and is treated like an individual author. Since long references tend to be disruptive, put long names in a signal phrase if possible. For long names in parentheses, shorten terms that are commonly abbreviated.

NO AUTHOR

If there is no author named, the parenthetical citation should give the full title (if brief) or a shortened version, unless the title appears in a signal phrase.

AUTHORS WITH THE SAME LAST NAME

If two of your sources have authors with the same last name, add the first initial in a parenthetical citation. If the initial is also shared, give the full first name.

MULTI-VOLUME WORK

If you cite specific material from a multi-volume work, include the volume number followed by a colon, a space, and then the page reference in the parenthetical citation. Do not include the words *volume* or *page* or their abbreviations.

If you are referring to an entire volume of a multi-volume work, however, it is not necessary to cite the page(s). The author's name is followed by a comma and the abbreviation *vol.* (Abrams et al., vol. 1). Note that if such a reference is included in a signal phrase, *volume* should be spelled out.

LITERARY WORK

Since literary works are often available in different editions and therefore have different page numbering, you should refer to a particular chapter, act, scene, or line using appropriate abbreviations.

Abrams et al. state that "the period of more than four hundred years that followed the Norman Conquest presents a much more diversified picture than the Old English period" (1: 5).

The contribution of 19th century essayists and poets to our contemporary understanding of Shakespeare can be seen in anthologies such as *Great Shakespeareans* (Poole, ed. vol. 4).

Tischenko Irina/Shutterstock.com

In Atwood's *The Robber Bride*, Tony reveals a distorted picture of Zenia: "She has thought of Zenia as tearless, more tearless even than herself. And now there are not only tears but many tears, rolling fluently down Zenia's strangely immobile face, which always looks made-up even when it isn't" (190; ch. 25).

In *Civil Elegies*, Lee describes Canadians' relationship with the rugged land:

> We lie on occupied soil.
> Across the barren Shield, immortal scrubland and our own,
> where near the beginning the spasm of lava
> settled to bedrock schist,
> barbaric land, initial, our
> own, scoured bare under
> crush of glacial recessions (3.40–46)

Shakespeare establishes the dark mood of *Macbeth* in the second witch's response to the first witch's query on when they should meet again: "When the battle's lost and won" (1.1.3).

Novel

When citing a passage from a novel, the parenthetical reference should give the page number followed by a semicolon and other identifying information.

Poetry

When citing lines from poems and verse plays, omit page numbers and cite the division (e.g., act, scene, book, or part), and then the line, using periods (without spaces) to separate the numbers.

Drama

Include the act, scene, and line numbers in the parenthetical citation. Use Arabic numerals unless instructed otherwise.

THE BIBLE OR A SACRED BOOK

When citing a passage from the Bible, include—either in the signal phrase or the parenthetical reference—the book, chapter, and verse. Books of the Bible may be abbreviated in a parenthetical reference if you wish. Similarly, cite a sacred book like the Vedas, the Koran, or the Talmud, without italicizing the title.

The Bible refers specifically to the importance of love to accompany action (1 Cor. 13.1).

Rev. 20.2

The highest form of wisdom is kindness. (Talmud Brakhot 17a)

WORK IN AN ANTHOLOGY

If you are referencing a particular part of an anthology—for example, an essay or a story—name the author of that piece rather than the editor of the anthology. The *Works Cited* list gives additional information about the anthology and the editor (see 5-2).

Robert Budde argues that postcolonialism is no longer an appropriate term to use for the disparate forms of Canadian Literature.

Budde, Robert. "After Postcolonialism: Migrant Lines and the Politics of Form in Fred Wah, M. Nourbese Philip, and Roy Miki." *Is Canada Postcolonial? Unsettling Canadian Literature*. Ed. Laura Moss. Waterloo: Wilfrid Laurier UP, 2003. 282-94. Print.

INDIRECT SOURCE

Although you should try to use original sources, if your only option is an indirect source, begin the citation in the parenthetical reference with the abbreviation *qtd. in* ("quoted in").

To Woody Allen, the successful monologue is a matter of attitude: "I can only surmise that you have to give the material a fair shake at the time and you have to deliver it with confidence" (qtd. in Lax 134).

In *The Second Sex*, Simone de Beauvoir brilliantly argues her position on women's inequality.

In *Barney's Version*, director Richard J. Lewis tells the picaresque story of the title character in a rambling but lively way.

An understanding of the business cycle is fundamental to successful investing (Gardner 69; Lasch 125).

ENTIRE WORK

When citing an entire work, it is preferable to provide the author's name in a signal phrase rather than a parenthetical reference. No page reference is required. The corresponding entry in the *Works Cited* list provides publication information. This also applies to works with no page numbers, such as a film or television program.

MORE THAN ONE WORK IN A SINGLE CITATION

Cite each work as you normally would, using semicolons to separate the citations.

ELECTRONIC SOURCES 5-1C

STRATEGIES

To cite electronic sources in your paper, follow these guidelines:

1. Include in your citation the first word that will appear in your *Works Cited* list. If your citation has an author, that will be the author's last name. If it does not, that will be the article name (or a shortened version of it) or the website name or film name.
2. Do not include page numbers or paragraph numbers unless they are explicitly included in the source.
3. Do not include the URL for the source in your essay's text. Occasionally, you may refer to the domain name, such as CBC.ca, rather than the complete URL.

The MLA guidelines for in-text citations of electronic sources are the same as those for print sources. However, many online sources do not include a page numbering system. You should not take page numbers from a printout, as pagination may vary in different printouts. Some electronic sources use alternate systems, numbering text by paragraph, section, or screen, but others do not. Here are some guidelines for situations you may encounter when citing electronic sources.

ELECTRONIC SOURCE WITH AN AUTHOR AND FIXED PAGE NUMBER(S)

Give both the author's name and the page numbers, with the author's name either in the signal phrase or the parenthetical reference.

According to Caroline Spurgeon, "The main image in *Othello* is that of animals in action, preying upon one another, mischievous, lascivious, cruel or suffering, and throughout the general sense of pain and unpleasantness is much increased and kept constantly before us" (2).

ELECTRONIC SOURCE WITH AN AUTHOR BUT NO PAGE NUMBER(S)

If the electronic source uses an alternate numbering system, use it to cite a specific location in the source, abbreviating *paragraph(s)* as *par.* or *pars.* and *section* as *sec.*, or using the full word *screen(s)*.

Fackrell asserts the accommodation for animals is adequate: "We have lodgings for up to 12 dogs at a time in our indoor/outdoor runs" (par. 9).

ELECTRONIC SOURCE WITH NO NUMBERING SYSTEM

Give the author's name where possible and cite the entire work in the *Works Cited* list.

Human rights violations are said to be decreasing as a result of foreign aid initiatives in the region (Danko).

According to the web page sponsored by Children Now, an American organization that provides support for children and families, "52% of girls and 53% of boys say there are enough good role models for girls in television, although more girls (44%) than boys (36%) say there are too few" ("Reflections in Media").

If the author of the electronic source is not known, either use the complete title in the signal phrase or use a shortened form of the title in the parenthetical reference.

LIST OF WORKS CITED 5-2

Works Cited   McLean 12

Banting, Pamela. *Body, Inc.: A Theory of Translation Poetics.* Winnipeg: Turnstone, 1995. Print.

---. "The Undersigned: Ethnicity and Signature-Effects in Fred Wah's Poetry." *West Coast Line 2* (1990): 83–94. Print.

Beauregard, Guy. *Asian Canadian Literature: Diasporic Interventions in the Work of Sky Lee, Joy Kogawa, Hiromi Goto, and Fred Wah.* Diss. U of Alberta, 2000. Print.

---. "The Emergence of 'Asian Canadian Literature': Can Lit's Obscene Supplement?" *Essays on Canadian Writing 67* (1999): 53–75. Print.

When you are following the MLA documentation style, a list of works cited should appear on a separate page at the end of your paper. The list provides essential publication information for each of the sources cited in your paper and simplifies documentation by allowing you to make only brief references to these works in the text.

Include in your list of works cited only the sources from which you quoted, para-phrased, or summarized infor-mation. Do not include sources that you consulted but did not refer to in your paper, unless instructors require it.

TITLE AND PLACEMENT

Start the list of works cited on a new page at the end of your research paper. Title the listing *Works Cited*, and centre the title at the top of the page. The title word *Works* allows you to include books and articles, as well as films, recordings, websites, television programs, and other non-print sources.

MLA WORKS CITED: SOME GUIDELINES

1. *Works Cited* appears at the end of your essay on a separate page.
2. *Works Cited* should appear as the title, centered at the top but without underlining or italics.
3. All entries should be double spaced.
4. All entries should have hanging indents, with the second and following lines indented five spaces. This can be easily done in the Format menu of Word. Simply select Paragraph, then Special, and finally, Hanging.
5. List inclusive page numbers for articles or sections in books.
6. Include medium of publication, such as CD-ROM, DVD, Web, Print.
7. Do not include a URL for electronic sources unless your instructor insists or if the source would be difficult to find without it. When you include a URL, enclose it in angle brackets and end with a period. Remember to break long URLs after a slash to format them smoothly.
8. If you retrieve a source from an electronic database (such as ERIC), type the database's name in italics. Web sources must also include the date you accessed them.
9. Use headline style for titles; that is, do not capitalize small words except for the first word in the title or subtitle.
10. No longer use underlining for long published works; use italics instead.

See MLA model essay for an example of a complete Works Cited list.

Works Cited   Beresford 16

Wendell, Susan. *The Rejected Body: Feminist Philosophical Reflections on Disability*. New York: Routledge, 1996. Print.

Baughman, James L. *The Republic of Mass Culture*. Baltimore: Johns Hopkins UP, 2006. Print.

Ramey, Carl R. *Mass Media Unleashed*. Lanham: Rowman & Littlefield, 2007. Print.

Note that two entries by the same author would appear the following way in your *Works Cited* page.

Yalom, Irvin, D. *The Gift of Therapy: An Open Letter to a New Generation of Therapists and Their Patients*. New York: HarperPerennial, 2002. Print.

---. *Staring at the Sun: Overcoming the Terror of Death*. San Francisco: Jossey, 2008. Print.

Pearson, Keith Ansell, and Duncan Large, eds. *The Nietzsche Reader*. Malden, MA: Blackwell, 2006.

Prinzi, Travis. "The Future: Centaurs in Sorcerer's Stone." *The Hog's Head* 7 Jan. 2006. 9 Oct. 2007 <http://thehogshead.org/the-future-centaurs-in-sorcerers-stone-69/>.

PAGINATION

Continue the page numbering of the text throughout the *Works Cited* list; for example, if the last page of your research paper is 15, the first page of *Works Cited* would be 16. Position page numbers in the upper right-hand corner.

SPACING

Double space within and between entries.

INDENTATION

Begin each entry at the left margin; if an entry runs more than one line, indent the subsequent line or lines 1.25 cm (0.5 in.) from the left margin.

ARRANGEMENT OF ENTRIES

Alphabetize entries in the *Works Cited* list by the last name of the author. For entries with more than one author that begin with the same author name, alphabetize according to the last names of the second authors listed. If a source has no author or editor, alphabetize by the title, ignoring any initial articles (*A*, *An*, or *The*).

For a sample *Works Cited* list, refer to the model essay provided at the end of this chapter.

EXAMPLES OF *WORKS CITED*

Examples of citations follow. If you encounter sources that are not covered here, consult the *MLA Handbook for Writers of Research Papers*, 7th ed. (New York: MLA, 2010).

Rowling, J[oanne] K[athleen]. *Harry Potter and the Chamber of Secrets*. New York: Scholastic, 1999.

---. *Harry Potter and the Deathly Hallows*. New York: Scholastic, 2007.

---. *Harry Potter and the Goblet of Fire*. New York: Scholastic, 2000.

---. *Harry Potter and the Half-Blood Prince*. New York: Scholastic, 2005.

5-2B   BOOKS

There are three main units of information in a book entry. They are (1) author's name, (2) book title, and (3) publication information.

Author's name   Book title

Seabrook, John Nobrow. *The Culture of Marketing—The Marketing of Culture*. New York: Knopf, 2000. Print.

Publication information

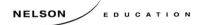

NELSON EDUCATION

Checkmate: A Writing Reference for Canadians, Third Edition
by Joanne Buckley

**Vice President,
Editorial Director:**
Anne Williams

Executive Editor:
Laura Macleod

Senior Marketing Manager:
Amanda Henry

Managing Developmental Editor:
Sandy Matos

**Photo Researcher and Permissions
Coordinator:**
Cindy Howard

Senior Content Production Manager:
Natalia Denesiuk Harris

Copy Editor:
Emily Dockrill Jones

Proofreader:
Maria Jelinek

Indexer:
Gillian Watts

Senior Production Coordinator:
Ferial Suleman

Design Director:
Ken Phipps

Managing Designer:
Franca Amore

Interior Design:
Greg Devitt Design

Cover Design:
Greg Devitt Design

Compositor:
Greg Devitt Design

Printer:
RR Donnelley

**Library and Archives Canada Cataloguing in
Publication Data**

Buckley, Joanne, 1953–
    Checkmate : a writing reference for
Canadians / Joanne Buckley. — 3rd ed.

Includes index.
ISBN 978-0-17-650256-0

    1. English language—Rhetoric—
Handbooks, manuals, etc. 2. English
language—Grammar—Handbooks, manuals,
etc. I. Title.

PE1408.B818 2012   808'.042
C2011-907319-6

ISBN-13: 978-0-17-650256-0
ISBN-10: 0-17-650256-4

The publication details for a book are found on the **title page** and on the reverse side of the title page, which is known as the **copyright page**. A very few books have publication information at the back of the book. When writing an entry, use information from the source itself as opposed to information from a bibliography or library catalogue. This will reduce the chance of errors in your entry.

Thompson, Judith. *Palace of the End.* Toronto: Playwrights Canada, 2007. Print.

AUTHOR'S NAME

Put the last name first, followed by a comma and a space, and then the first name and initials, if any are included on the title page. Leave a space between two initials. Put a period after the complete name.

BOOK TITLE

Provide the full name of the book, including any subtitles. The entire title, but not the period following it, should be italicized. Capitalize important words within the title (see 14-3c). If there is a subtitle, separate it from the main title with a colon and one space. Always capitalize the first and last words in any subtitle. End the title with a period and leave one space before the publication information.

PUBLICATION INFORMATION

Place of Publication: If several cities are listed on title or copyright pages, use only the first. Place a colon and one space between the place of publication and the name of the publisher. For cities outside the United States that may be unfamiliar or ambiguous, add a comma and the province or country in abbreviated form. For example, if London, Ontario, is meant rather than London, England, write

TITLE WITHIN A TITLE

- If a title within an italicized title would normally be italicized, do not italicize it nor place it in quotation marks.

> White, E. B. *Writings from* The New Yorker *1927–1976*. Ed.
> Rebecca M. Dale. New York: HarperPerennial, 1991. Print.

- If a title within an italicized title would normally be in quotation marks, keep them. Note that the period is inside the quotation mark.

> Card, James Van Dyck. *An Anatomy of "Penelope."* Rutherford:
> Farleigh Dickinson UP, 1984. Print.

For information on whether to italicize or use quotation marks for titles, see page 157.

> Burt, Stephen, and David Mikics. *The Art of the Sonnet*.
> Cambridge, MA: Harvard UP, 2010. Print.

QUICK TIP

Make sure to avoid ambiguity when citing publishers.

QUICK TIP

Use an appropriately shortened version of the publisher's name.

Bissoondath, Neil. *The Soul of All Great Designs*. Toronto: Cormorant, 2009. Print.

Nietzsche, Friedrich. *Beyond Good and Evil*. 1886. Trans. Marion Faber. Oxford: Oxford UP, 1998. Print.

QUICK TIP

Use only the name of the press. It is not necessary to include the word press.

Bergen, David. *The Retreat*. Toronto: McClelland, 2009. Print.

Use only the first name if the publisher has two names (i.e., *McClelland*, rather than *McClelland & Stewart*).

London, ON. For a foreign city, you may substitute the English name or add a translation in brackets.

Publisher: You do not need to use the complete name of the publisher; simply give enough information to enable your reader to find the source easily. Omit any articles (*A, An, The*), common abbreviations (*Inc., Co.,* and *Ltd.*), and descriptive words (*Books, House, Press,* and *Publishers*). However, for university presses always include the abbreviations *U* and *P* or *UP* as the case may be (e.g., *Oxford UP* or *U of Chicago P*) because the university itself may publish independently of its press. If the publishing company includes the name of one person, cite the surname alone (*Norton* rather than *W. W. Norton*). If it includes two names, cite the first surname only (*McGraw* rather than *McGraw-Hill*). Place a comma between the name of the publisher and the year of publication.

COPYRIGHT © 2013, 2008
by Nelson Education Ltd.

Printed and bound in the United States
1 2 3 4 15 14 13 12

ALL RIGHTS RESERVED. No pa
work covered by the copyrigh
be reproduced, transcribed, o
form or by any means—graph
or mechanical, including pho
recording taping Web dist

SINGLE AUTHOR

A book by a single author is likely to be one of the items you will most frequently include in your *Works Cited* list. Follow the guidelines regarding the author's name, book title, and publication information as described above.

Cameron, Julia. *The Sound of Paper: Starting from Scratch.*
New York: Penguin, 2004. Print.

TWO OR THREE AUTHORS

Give the authors' names in the same order as they appear on the title page, which may not be in alphabetical order. Reverse the name of the first author only, add a comma, and give the other name(s) in normal order. Use *and* rather than an ampersand (&) before the last name in the list. Place a period after the last name.

Dickerson, Matthew, and David O'Hara. *From Homer to Harry Potter: A Handbook on Myth and Fantasy*. Grand Rapids, MI: Brazos, 2006. Print.

MORE THAN THREE AUTHORS

For more than three authors, either list all names as described above or give the first name followed by a comma and the abbreviation *et al.*

Newman, Garfield, et al. *Canada: A Nation Unfolding*. Toronto: McGraw, 2000. Print.

Downie, Mary Alice, and Barbara Robertson, eds. *Early Voices: Canadian Portraits by Women Writers 1639–1914*. Calgary: Red Deer, 2009. Print.

EDITOR(S)

If you are citing an edited collection, follow the same guidelines as for authors, adding a comma and the lowercase abbreviation *ed.* or *eds.*

Brontë, Charlotte. *Jane Eyre*. Ed. Susan Cockcroft. Cambridge: Cambridge UP, 1996. Print.

Davies, Robertson. *Selected Works on the Art of Writing*. Ed. Jennifer Surridge. Toronto: Penguin Canada, 2009. Print.

AUTHOR WITH AN EDITOR

If a work was prepared for publication by an editor, start the entry with the name of the author and the title; then use the abbreviation *Ed.* or *Eds.* followed by the name(s) of the editor(s), with no comma in between.

Apuleius. *The Golden Ass*. Trans. Jack Lindsay. Bloomington: Indiana UP, 1962. Print.

Tremblay, Michel. *The Red Notebook*. Trans. Sheila Fischman. Vancouver: Talonbooks, 2009. Print.

TRANSLATION

The translator of a work is listed after the title of the work. Use the abbreviation *Trans.*

PriceWaterhouseCoopers Inc. *Technology Forecast: 2000*. Menlo Park: PriceWaterhouseCoopers Technology Center, 2000. Print.

CORPORATE AUTHOR

A corporate author could be a company, institution, association, or agency that is credited with authorship of a publication. This name should begin the entry. Omit any initial article (*A, An, The*).

ANONYMOUS WORK

Begin the entry with the title and alphabetize it by the title, ignoring any initial article (*A*, *An*, *The*). In this example, *Second* would be the word used to alphabetize.

"The Second Shepherds' Pageant." *Everyman and Medieval Miracle Plays*. Ed. A. C. Cawley. New York: Dutton, 1959. Print.

TWO OR MORE WORKS BY THE SAME AUTHOR

Give the name of the author in the first entry only. In succeeding entries, type three hyphens followed by a period in place of the author's name. Then provide the title and publication information. If the author served as an editor, translator, or compiler on a work cited, follow the hyphens with a comma followed by *ed.* or *trans.* or *comp.* Alphabetize by title.

Roth, Philip. *The Human Stain*. Boston: Houghton, 2000. Print.

---. *Patrimony: A True Story*. New York: Simon, 1991. Print.

Toews, Miriam. *A Complicated Kindness*. Toronto: Knopf, 2004. Print.

---. *The Flying Troutmans*. Toronto: Knopf, 2009. Print.

Brym, Robert J. *Sociology as a Life or Death Issue*. 2nd ed. Toronto: Nelson Education, 2012. Print.

Brym, Robert J., and John Lie. *SOC+*. Toronto: Nelson Education, 2012. Print.

QUICK TIP

If an author is the co-author of a second entry, do not use three hyphens; begin the second entry with the author's full name.

SECOND OR SUBSEQUENT EDITION

The edition number or name is shown on the title page. If there is none, the work is probably a first edition. Identify later editions by placing the number or name and the abbreviation *ed.* after the title—for example,

Strunk, William, Jr., and E. B. White. *The Elements of Style*. 3rd ed. New York: Macmillan, 1979. Print.

2nd ed., Rev. ed. (for Revised edition), *Abr. ed.* (for "Abridged edition) or *1994 ed.*

MULTI-VOLUME WORK

Cite the number of volumes after the title (and editor or edition, if any) and before the publication information, using the abbreviation *vols.* Do not indicate any specific volume or page number(s) here; rather, supply these in the parenthetical reference in the text.

If you used only one of the volumes, give the volume number and publication information for that volume alone. In this case, give only page numbers in the parenthetical citation. You may add the total number of volumes at the end of the entry.

ENCYCLOPEDIA, DICTIONARY, OR OTHER REFERENCE WORK

If the articles in the source are arranged alphabetically, you do not need to provide the volume and page numbers. If the reference is familiar, you may also omit publication information.

If the articles are not alphabetically arranged, provide the page number. If the resource is not well known, provide complete publication information.

QUICK TIP

This is the correct way to cite this entry if you are using the entire multi-volume work.

Wasserman, Jerry, ed. *Modern Canadian Plays.* 3rd ed. 2 vols.
    Vancouver: Talonbooks, 2000. Print.

Wasserman, Jerry. ed. *Modern Canadian Plays.* 3rd. ed. Vol 1.
    Vancouver: Talonbooks, 1994. Print. 2 vols.

STRATEGIES

Reference works may be listed in a shortened form as follows:

1. Author of the article (if known)
2. Title of the article, in quotation marks
3. Title of the source, italicized
4. Edition (if stated)
5. Year of publication

Boles, Glen. "Mount Assiniboine." *The Canadian Encyclopedia.*
    2000 ed. 1999. Print.

WORK IN AN ANTHOLOGY

If you cite a short story, poem, essay, or other work that is published in an anthology, provide this information, placing a period after each major unit of information as shown in the example.

If you wish to indicate that a work other than a scholarly article was previously published, give the year of original publication after the title, followed by a period.

SAMPLE WORK IN AN ANTHOLOGY

For a previously published scholarly article, give all information for the earlier publication immediately after the selection title (or after the selection translator, if any). Add *Rpt. in* (for "Reprinted in") followed by the title of the collection, the new publication facts, and inclusive page numbers.

If the article was first published under another title, give the new title and publication facts first, followed by *Rpt. of* and the original title and publication information.

1. For the selection:
   a) author's name, reversed
   b) title, enclosed in quotation marks (unless the work was previously published as a single work, in which case the title is italicized)
   c) translator (if any)
2. For the anthology:
   a) title, italicized
   b) editor, translator, or compiler (if any)
   c) publication information (place of publication, publisher, and publication date)
3. Inclusive page numbers for the selection (not just the material you used); do not use the abbreviations *p.* or *pp.*

McFadden, David W. "Slow Black Dog." *Why Are You So Sad?: Selected Poems by David W. McFadden*. Ed. Stuart Ross. Toronto: Insomniac, 2007. 115. Rpt. *The 2008 Griffin Poetry Prize Anthology: A Selection of the Shortlist*. Ed. George Bowering. Toronto: Anansi, 2008. 92. Print.

Lewis, C. S. "Viewpoints: C. S. Lewis." *Twentieth-Century Interpretations* of Sir Gawain and the Green Knight. Ed. Denton Fox. Englewood Cliffs: Prentice, 1968. 100–01. Rpt. "The Anthropological Approach." *English and Medieval Studies Presented to J. R. R. Tolkien on the Occasion of His Seventieth Birthday*. Ed. Norman Davis and C. L. Wrenn. London: Allen, 1962. 219–23. Print.

1. Create a complete entry for the anthology.

Fetherling, George, ed. *The Vintage Book of Canadian Memoirs.*
Toronto: Random, 2001. Print.

2. Create a separate entry for each piece in the anthology, giving the author and title. Then cross-reference to the anthology by giving the last name(s) of the anthology editor(s) and the inclusive page numbers for the piece. The following are examples of cross-references to the anthology entry shown above.

Ignatieff, Michael. "The Russian Album." Fetherling 315–46. Print.

Wright, Eric. "Always Give a Penny to a Blind Man." Fetherling
407–53. Print.

Green, Richard. Introduction. *The Consolation of Philosophy*. By
Boethius. Trans. Green. Indianapolis: Bobbs, 1962. ix–xxiii.
Print.

Wilde, Oscar. Preface. *The Picture of Dorian Gray.* By Wilde. Ed.
Norman Page. Peterborough, ON: Broadview, 1995. 1–3. Print.

TWO OR MORE WORKS IN A SINGLE ANTHOLOGY

If you are using two or more works from the same anthology, you may create a complete entry for the anthology and cross-reference individual pieces to the entry.

INTRODUCTION, PREFACE, FOREWORD, OR AFTERWORD

Include the following:

1. Author of the element
2. Name of the element
3. Book title
4. Author of the book preceded by *By* (If the book author is different from the element author, cite the full name in normal order. If there is only one author, give only the last name.)
5. Book editor or translator (if any)
6. Publication information
7. Inclusive page numbers for the element

BOOK IN A SERIES

Give the author name(s), the title of the work, and the publication information, followed by the series name and number. The series name has neither underlining nor quotation marks and uses common abbreviations.

Lecker, Robert, Jack David, and Ellen Quigley. *Bissoondath, Clarke, Kogawa, Mistry, Skvorecky.* Toronto: ECW, 1996. Print. Can. Writers and Their Works 11.

REPUBLISHED BOOK

Place the original publication date after the title and then give the republishing information. When the republication includes new material, such as an afterword, include the information after the original publication date.

Moodie, Susanna. *Roughing It in the Bush.* 1852. Afterword Susan Glickman. Toronto: McClelland, 1989. Print.

PUBLISHER'S IMPRINT

If a publisher groups some of its books under imprints, this information appears on the title page along with the publisher's name. After the place of publication, give the name of the imprint followed by a hyphen and then the name of the publisher.

Munro, Alice. *Friend of My Youth.* Toronto: A Douglas Gibson Book-McClelland, 1990. Print.

Bass, George F. "Golden Age Treasures." *National Geographic.*
    Mar. 2002: 102–17. Print.

Saltzman, Marc. "Hot Games & Gadgets for Gamers." *Movie
    Entertainment.* Nov. 2011. 32–33. Print.

Henheffer, Tom. "The $150 Robot Revolution: How Microsoft's
    Affordable Kinect Video Game System Is Changing the World
    of Advanced Robotics." *Maclean's.* 14 Nov. 2011. 74+. Print.

Fillion, Kate. "The Youth Pill: Science Writer David Stipp in
    Conversation with Kate Fillion." *Maclean's* 26 July 2010: 13–15.
    Print.

Strain, Laurel A. "Seniors' Centres: Who Cares?" *Canadian
    Journal of Aging* 20 (2001): 471–91. Print.

ARTICLE IN A MONTHLY MAGAZINE

Give the author's name followed by a period, the name of the article in quotation marks with a period inside, and the name of the magazine, italicized and followed by the month and year and then a colon and space. With the exception of May, June, and July, abbreviate the months. Volume and issue number should not be included. Lastly, give the inclusive page numbers for the entire article, followed by a period. If the article is not printed on consecutive pages, give only the first page number and a plus sign.

ARTICLE IN A WEEKLY MAGAZINE

Follow the same general pattern as for a monthly magazine, but add the day of publication before the month.

ARTICLE IN A JOURNAL PAGINATED BY VOLUME

Some journals use continuous pagination, with all issues published in a single year composing one volume. The pages in these volumes are usually numbered in continuous sequence, beginning again at 1 in the next volume. To cite an article in a volume with continuous pagination, give the journal title, volume number, issue number when available, and year of publication in parentheses followed by a colon, a space, and inclusive page numbers.

ARTICLE IN A JOURNAL PAGINATED BY ISSUE

If the journal begins each issue as page 1, you must, of course, give the issue number to locate the source. Give the volume number followed by a period and no space and then the issue number, followed by the year and inclusive page numbers.

ARTICLE IN A DAILY NEWSPAPER

Give the author's name followed by the title of the article in quotation marks and then the name of the newspaper. Omit any introductory article (*the*). If the city is not included in the newspaper's name, add it in square brackets after the name, unless it is a nationally published newspaper (for example, *The Globe and Mail*). Then, give the full date (day, month, and year), abbreviating

McKenzie, Jonathon. "How to Mind Your Own Business: Thoreau on Political Indifference." *The New England Quarterly* 84.3 (2011): 422–43. Print.

Frickle, Michele. "In This Pure Land." *Surface Design Journal* 25.3 (2002): 26–29. Print.

Alphonso, Caroline. "Studies cast doubt on hotly debated MS treatment." *Globe and Mail* 4 Aug. 2010: A1+. Print.

Decker, Brian. "Liberal arts building poses questions: Enrolment, campus space at centre of university planning." *The Silhouette* [Hamilton] 7 July 2011: 1+. Print.

the names of all months except May, June, and July. This information is followed by a colon, a space, and the page number preceded by the section in which the article appears. Use a plus sign (+) after the initial page number if the article is not printed on consecutive pages. If the section is identified not by letter but by number, follow the pattern of the example given.

Some newspapers produce multiple editions of the same issue, and these contain different material. If the edition is specified on the newspaper masthead, add a comma after the date and then give the edition (e.g., *western ed., natl. ed., afternoon ed.*) followed by a colon and the page numbers.

Smith, David. "Britain Leads the Way as Markets Start to Recover." *Sunday Times* 3 Mar. 2002, internatl. ed., sec. 3: 1. Print.

"Northern Rockies Whopper." *Beautiful British Columbia* Spring 1998: 46. Print.

ANONYMOUS ARTICLE

If no author is given, begin the citation with the title. Include any initial article (*A, An,* or *The*), but alphabetize by the following word.

EDITORIAL

Add the word *Editorial* after the title, followed by a period. For unsigned editorials, begin with the title.

"Government that listens?" Editorial. *Globe and Mail* 4 Aug. 2010: A18. Print.

LETTER TO THE EDITOR

Give the writer's name followed by a period; then add the word *Letter* followed by a period and the publication information.

Kennedy, Paul. Letter. *Harper's* Sept. 2010: 4. Print.

REVIEW

Book Reviews

List the reviewer's name and the title of the review, if there is one, followed by *Rev. of* (for "Review of") and the title of the work reviewed. The title is followed by a comma and the word *by* and the name of the author. Then, include publication information for the source containing the review.

Gartner, Zsuzsi. "In Search of a Vanished Zeitgeist." Rev. of *The Doctor's House*, by Ann Beattie. *Globe and Mail* 2 March 2002: D3. Print.

Film Review

Use *dir.* (for "director" or "directed by").

Groen, Rick. "*Crazy, Stupid, Love*: Smart, Sweet, Funny." Rev. of *Crazy, Stupid, Love*, dir. Glenn Ficarra and John Requa. *Globe and Mail* 29 July 2011: D1. Print.

Ansen, David. "Brave Heart of Darkness." Rev. of *We Were Soldiers*,
    dir. Randall Wallace. *Newsweek* 11 March 2002: 63. Print.

Walker, Susan. "Spanish Dance Troupe Goes Wild in the Garden."
    Rev. of Senza Tempo dance/theatre troupe. Power of Place.
    Harbourfront Centre, Toronto. *Toronto Star* 29 June 2006:
    G6. Print.

Review of Live Performance

For a review of a performance such as theatre, dance, or music, add any significant details about the production.

WORKS CITED ON THE WEB 5-2D

To learn more about particular citation content and formats or to learn about electronic sources not covered in the following pages, consult these authoritative sources:

- *MLA Handbook for Writers of Research Papers* (7th ed., 2010)
- *MLA Style Manual and Guide to Scholarly Publishing* (3rd ed., 2008)

Bear in mind that documentation styles for electronic sources are still evolving and updates are sometimes posted online. For articles on documenting electronic sources, visit the MLA website at www.mla.org and follow the link to the Frequently Asked Questions page.

The list below indicates the information to include in a *Works Cited* entry for an online source. No source will require all items on the list. Choose those which are relevant and available, following the order shown below.

1. Name of the author (or editor, compiler, or translator), last name first, using appropriate abbreviations (for example, *ed.*).
2. Title of a poem, short story, article, or similar short work, placed in quotation marks and followed by a period. If the source is a posting to a discussion list or forum, take the title from the subject line and follow it with *Online posting* (not italicized) and a period.
3. Title of the overall website, italicized
4. Edition or version used: Name(s) of the editor, compiler, or translator cited earlier, preceded by *Ed.*, *Comp.*, or *Trans.*

Citations for works found on the Web serve the same purpose as do citations for print sources, and there are similarities in their formats. However, because standards for electronic media are less well established, you should save a copy of the Web sources to which you refer.

The documentation style described reflects that found in the most recent MLA guidelines.

5. Publisher or sponsor. If none is given, use *N.p.*
6. Date of publication (day, month, and year), depending on what is available. If none is given use *n.d.*
7. Medium of publication, in this case, *Web*
8. Date when you accessed the source

STRATEGIES

How to Find the Author of a Web Publication
To find an author's name, check the "Contact" or "About" section of the Web page or the bottom of the home page.

WORK ON THE WEB WITH PRINT PUBLICATION
You may decide to include print information if it is relevant to your work.

"Charles George Douglas Roberts." *UNB Electronic Text Centre.*
  2005–2006. U of New Brunswick Libraries. Web. 5 Mar. 2010.
Frost, Robert. "Mowing." *A Boy's Will.* New York: Henry Holt,
  1915. *Bartleby.com.* 1999. Columbia U. Web. 31 July 2010.

ENTIRE ONLINE SCHOLARLY PROJECT

The Complete Writings and Pictures of Dante Gabriel Rossetti:
  A Hypermedia Archive. Ed. Jerome McCann. 1993–2008.
  Institute for Advanced Technology in the Humanities, U of
  Virginia. Web. 10 Sept. 2010.

Rockwell, Geoffrey. Home page. 2004. 10 Sept. 2010 <http://www
.geoffreyrockwell.com/>.

QUICK TIP

Note that you may choose to include a URL in angle brackets, though it is not required.

PERSONAL WEBSITE

Epic Records. 2001. Sony Music Inc. Web. 18 Mar. 2010.

PROFESSIONAL WEBSITE

Keats, John. *Poetical Works.* London, 1884. *Bartleby.com: Great Books Online.* Web. 4 July 2010.

ONLINE BOOK

Dickens, Charles. *A Tale of Two Cities.* 1859. *Literature.org. The Online Literature Library.* Web. 3 July 2011.

ONLINE BOOK IN SCHOLARLY PROJECT OR REFERENCE DATABASE

Rist, Thomas. "Religion, Politics, Revenge: The Dead in Renaissance Drama." *Early Modern Literary Studies* 9.1 (2003): 20 pars. Web. 3 July 2011.

ARTICLE IN ONLINE SCHOLARLY JOURNAL

ARTICLE IN ONLINE MAGAZINE	Milgrom, Melissa. "Trigger Rides Again." *Salon.com*. 31 July 2010. Web. 3 Aug. 2010.
ARTICLE IN ONLINE NEWSPAPER	Yusuf, Nabeel, and Riaz Khan. "Floods in Pakistan Kill More than 800." *The Globe and Mail*. 31 July 2010. Web. 31 July 2010.
INTERNET SOURCE WITH NO AUTHOR	"Everything Postmodern." *Ebbflux*. Oct. 2004. Web. 31 July 2010.
EMAIL	Chamberlain, Tim. "Re: Credibility in Magazines." Message to the author. 12 Nov. 2010. Email.

5-2E   MISCELLANEOUS SOURCES

GOVERNMENT PUBLICATION WITHOUT AUTHOR'S NAME If you do not know the author of the work, give the name of the government followed by the name of the agency.	Ontario. Ontario Human Rights Commission. *Disability and the Duty to Accommodate*. Toronto: Ontario Human Rights Commission, 2006.
GOVERNMENT PUBLICATION WITH AUTHOR'S NAME If you know the author's name, you may put it either at the beginning of the entry or	Committee on the Status of Canadian Wildlife in Canada (COSEWIC). *COSEWIC status appraisal summary on the Dwarf Wedgemussel Alasmidonta heterodon in Canada*. By Janice L. Smith. Ottawa, 2009.

Canada. Canada Revenue Agency. *Registered Disability Savings Plan*. Ottawa: Canada Revenue Agency, 2009.

Haas, Arthur G. *Metternich, Reorganization and Nationality, 1813–1818*. Diss. U of Chicago, 1963. Knoxville: U of Tennessee P, 1964. Print.

Mercer, Todd. "Perspective, Point of View, and Perception: James Joyce and Fredric Jameson." Diss. U of Victoria, 1987. Print.

Cassidy, Frank, ed. *Proceedings of Land Claims in British Columbia Conference, February 21–22, 1990: Reaching Just Settlements*. Lantzville and Halifax: Oolichan and Inst. for Research on Public Policy, 1991. Print.

after the title, preceded by *By* or an abbreviation such as *Ed.* or *Comp.*

PAMPHLET
Use the same format as that of a book entry.

DISSERTATION
For a published dissertation, give the name of the author, the name of the dissertation (italicized and followed by a period), the abbreviation *Diss.*, the name of the institution that accepted the dissertation, the year it was accepted, and publishing information.

For an unpublished dissertation, the title appears in quotation marks rather than italicized.

PUBLISHED PROCEEDINGS OF A CONFERENCE
Treat as you would a book, but add any information about the conference.

LECTURE OR PUBLIC ADDRESS

Give the speaker's name, the title of the presentation in quotation marks, the name of the sponsoring organization, the location, and the date.

Hill, Larry. "Navigating the Void and Developing a Sense of Identity." Traill College, Trent University, Peterborough. 30 Jan. 2002. Lecture.

CD-ROM OR DVD ROM

Citations are similar to those for print sources, but state the publication medium.

The Rosetta Stone. Harrisburg, VA: Fairfield Language Technologies, 2010. CD-ROM.

MUSICAL COMPOSITION

Treat compositions as if they were books. Give the composer's name, then the title of the work. Add the date of composition after the title.

Beethoven, Ludwig van. *Symphony No. 7 in A, Op. 92.* 1811. New York: Dover, 1998. Print.

Mozart, Wolfgang Amadeus. *The Marriage of Figaro.* 1786.

QUICK TIP

Published scores are treated like books.

SOUND RECORDING

Which person you list first (composer, conductor, or performer) depends on what aspect of the recording you wish to emphasize. Give the title of a specific song in quotation marks and the title of the recording

The Band. "It Makes No Difference." *The Best of the Band.* Capitol, 1976. CD.

Verdi, Guiseppe. *Arias.* Perf. Simon Estes. New Philharmonic Orchestra. Cond. Gaetano Delogu. Philips, 1987. LP.

italicized. Next give the names of other artists. End with the manufacturer and year of issue, separated by a comma. Periods follow all other items. Place medium at the end of the note.

PERFORMANCE

Give the title, italicized, followed by the names of contributors such as the playwright, choreographer, director, or performers, preceded by *By*, *Chor.*, *Dir.*, or *Perf.* as appropriate. Then, give the site of the performance: usually the theatre name, followed by a comma, then the city, followed by a period. Conclude with the date of the performance.

FILM OR VIDEO

Give the title, italicized, followed by the name of the director, preceded by *Dir.* You may also name the writer, performers, narrator, or producer, preceded by the appropriate abbreviation. Then, give the distributor and year of release.

For a video recording, include the original release date if applicable. Then give the distributor's name and the year the video was released. Add the appropriate label or abbreviation, for example, *Videocassette* or *DVD*.

Richard III. By William Shakespeare. Dir. Miles Potter. Perf. Seana McKenna. Stratford Shakespeare Festival Theatre, Stratford, ON. 1 Aug. 2011. Performance.

Othello. Dir. Stuart Burge. Perf. Laurence Olivier, Maggie Smith, Joyce Redman, and Frank Finlay. Warner Bros., 1965. Film.

The Big Snit. Dir. Richard Condie. National Film Board of Canada, 1985. Videocassette.

Suspicion. Dir. Alfred Hitchcock. Perf. Cary Grant and Joan Fontaine. 1941. Turner, 1995. Laser disc.

RADIO OR TELEVISION PROGRAM

Give the title of the episode in quotation marks, then the title of the program, italicized. If applicable and relevant, give the name of the writer, narrator, producer, and/or performer(s) preceded by *By*, *Narr.*, *Prod.*, or *Perf.*, respectively. Give the series (if any) and the network; then list the call letters of the station and the city, separated by a comma. Finish with the date of the broadcast and the medium.

"Fasten Your Seatbeats." *The Fifth Estate*. CBC Newsworld. 9 Aug. 2010. Television.

"Inuit Odyssey." *The Nature of Things*. CBC News Network. 12 Aug. 2010. Television.

"Summertime and the Living Is Easy." Stuart McLean. *The Vinyl Café*. CBC. 1 Aug. 2010. Radio.

INTERVIEW

Give the name of the person interviewed followed by the title of the interview, if any, usually in quotation marks but italicized if it was published independently. If there is no title, use the label *Interview* after the name of the person interviewed, followed by the word *with* and the name of the interviewer, if relevant. Then give publication or broadcast information.

Bellow, Saul. "Treading on the Toes of Brahmans." *Endangered Species*. Cambridge, MA: De Capo, 2001: 1–60. Print.

Brumlik, Micha. Interview with Rick MacInnes-Rae. *The Current*. CBC Radio One. 5 July 2006. Radio.

PERSONAL INTERVIEW YOU CONDUCTED

Give the name of the person interviewed followed by a description such as *Personal interview*, *Telephone interview*, or *Email interview* and the date.

McAnuff, Des. Personal interview. 5 July 2010.

Hough, George. Personal interview. 10 Oct. 2010.

Weiland, Joyce. *Defendez la Terre*. Quilted wall mural. Science Library, Ottawa.

Chambers, Jack. *Victoria Hospital*. Painting. Art Gallery of Ontario, Toronto.

Moudakis, Theo. Cartoon. *Toronto Star* 4 July 2006: A14. Print.

Helm, Levon. Letter to the author. 5 July 2010. TS.

Great Britain/Scotland. Map. Paris: Michelin, 2001/2002. Print.

FINE ART

Give the artist's full name, then the title of the work, italicized. Then name the institution (or owner) and the city.

You may add the date of origin immediately after the title.

For a photograph of a work of art, follow the example to the left and add the publication information for the source containing the photograph.

CARTOON

Give the artist's name, the title of the cartoon or comic (if any) in quotation marks, the descriptive label *Cartoon* or *Comic strip*, and the publication information.

PERSONAL LETTER

Treat as a typescript. Give the letter-writer's name followed by *Letter to the author* and the date.

MAP OR CHART

Treat maps and charts as you would an anonymous book, adding the label *Map* or *Chart* as appropriate.

5-3) INFORMATION NOTES

Two types of optional information notes may be used with parenthetical documentation.

1. **Content notes** give the reader additional information that would have interrupted the flow of ideas in the text. They should be brief.
2. **Bibliographic notes** provide evaluative commentary on sources and may be used for references containing numerous citations.

To create an information note, place a superscript Arabic number at the appropriate place in the text and insert a matching numeral either at the bottom of the page (footnote) or on a separate page at the end of the paper before the *Works Cited* page (endnote).

Try to organize your sentence so the need for an information note falls at the end of the sentence. The raised (superscript) note number follows the end-of-sentence punctuation.

> Circumnavigation of any large land body in a kayak requires significant, time-consuming preparation.[1] The catastrophic effects of inadequate equipment or ill-prepared participants have been well documented in recent testimonials.[2]

Information notes should be numbered consecutively throughout the paper.

When writing a footnote or endnote, indent the first line, then follow the number with a period. Do not indent any line after the first one. Double space within and between notes.

> 1. For a full discussion of the preparation required, see Fenger 32.
>
> 2. Foremost among these are the stories of Smith and Patterson, the Ontario Kayak Club, and Michael Summers.

The following sections detail the current MLA specifications for formatting a research paper. Check with your instructor to find out if there are any additional or alternative requirements for a particular assignment.

MATERIALS AND TYPEFACE 5-4A

For academic writing, use good-quality, white, letter-size (8.5 × 11 in.) paper. Keep a spare copy of any paper you submit (ideally, both a hard copy and an electronic backup).

Ensure that your paper is easy to read by using one of the standard book typefaces, such as Times New Roman, and use 12-point font. Do not justify the text; it should be ragged right. Disable your word processor's hyphenation feature.

Zarena Cassar

Professor David Clark

English 4A43

15 December 2012

The Construction of Identity in Jamaica Kincaid's *My Brother*

Jamaica Kincaid's memoir, *My Brother*, is a poignant collection of memories of a brother who dies of HIV/AIDS. Although it appears at first that this book is, as the title indicates, primarily about her brother, Kincaid's story evolves into a commentary that reflects not only on the memories of a brother, but on a

Zarena Cassar

MLA requires no title page. Your name, your instructor's name, the course number, and the date appear at the top of the first page, flush with the left margin, and double-spaced. The title is centred two lines below the date. In the title, capitalize the first word, the last word, and all principal words, including those that follow hyphens, but not articles, prepositions, coordinating conjunctions, and the *to* in infinitives (see 14-3c). The title is not underlined or in quotation marks and is not followed by a period. Double space after the title and indent 1.25 cm (0.5 in.) at the beginning of the first line of the text.

For an example of the heading and title, see the sample essay on beginning on page 203.

Buckley   1

Joanne Buckley

Dr. Ross Woodman

English 600

March 26, 2011

Keats's Letters: The Relationship

between Immortality and Fame

WORD-PROCESSING TIPS

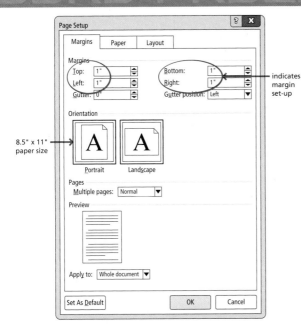

8.5" x 11" paper size

indicates margin set-up

Creating Correct Margins and Formatting in Microsoft Word

1. With your document open in Microsoft Word, select the Page Layout tab.
2. Select Page Setup.
3. Set margins on top, bottom, and both sides to 2.5 cm (1 in.) and Portrait orientation.
4. Check to see that Pages shows "Normal" and Preview > Apply to shows "Whole document."
5. Click OK.

Leave margins of 2.5 cm (1 in.) on the top, bottom, and both sides of the page unless your instructor requires a larger margin for marking purposes.

Double space everything in the paper, including quotations, notes, and the *Works Cited* list. Leave one space after a period or other punctuation mark, but do not space before or after a dash or between the two hyphens that compose a dash.

Indent the first line of each paragraph 1.25 cm (0.5 in.) from the left margin.

For quotations of more than four lines of prose and more than three lines of poetry, indent 2.5 cm (1 in.) from the left margin without adding quotation marks. Introduce the quotation with a colon.

(See page 204 and 11-5b for examples of quotations.)

Number all pages consecutively in the upper right-hand corner, 1.25 cm (0.5 in.) from the top of the page and flush with the right margin. Use only Arabic numerals and place your last name before every page number. You can use your word-processing program to create a header with your name and page number that will automatically appear on every page. Do not use the abbreviation *p.* or include hyphens or parentheses.

Castelli 1

Joel Castelli

Classics 201

Dr. T. Salmon

March 28, 2011

Heroism and the Ancient Greeks

As revealed in classical works like the *Iliad*, the ancient Greek heroes followed very different societal guidelines than modern heroes would. The Homeric heroes put all of their effort into the pursuit of personal glory, and violently killing the enemy was just as much of an act of heroism as saving an ally's life. As Homeric heroes were so important and admired, their social role in Greek society also played an important part. However, the Greek hero's natural place on the battlefield and set of moral codes manifested itself in their personal and social lives. Using the Trojan warrior Hector from Homer's *Iliad* as a prime example, this relationship between the hero's role as a warrior and the facets of their social life can be observed in both the role of the hero as a male and in the placement of *time* above family, personal happiness and even life itself.

Courtesy of Joel Castelli

NUMBERS IN MLA STYLE

Note that MLA expects you to spell out numbers of one or two words and to use numerals for numbers that are longer than two words.

Hyphenate numbers from twenty-one to ninety-nine. Count them as one word.

QUICK TIP

Use numbers according to MLA style:

three hundred

two million

nine

twenty-two (one word)

sixty-five thousand (two words)

HEADINGS   5-4E

MLA does not provide guidelines for headings and subheadings. In papers for English and the humanities, headings are not used as frequently as they are in business reports or research papers for social science disciplines.

QUICK TIP

If you wish to use headings, first check with your instructor to determine whether they are acceptable for a specific writing assignment.

If you need to use headings in your paper, follow the APA guidelines for headings described in 6-3g.

Visuals should be positioned as close as possible to the relevant text unless your instructor wants visuals placed together in an appendix at the end of the paper. MLA identifies two major types of visuals:

1. Tables
2. Figures (photographs, maps, drawings, graphs, and charts)

TABLES

A table should be given a label consisting of the word *Table* and an Arabic numeral (for example, *Table 1*). It should also have a caption, a brief description such as *Production Data for All Branches in 2006*. Both should be flush left above the table, double-spaced, and capitalized in headline style. The source and any information notes appear below the table, double-spaced.

FIGURES

Any illustration other than a table should be labelled *Fig.* with an Arabic numeral and should also be captioned. Both the label and caption appear below the illustration, double-spaced.

Fig. 1

Maslow's Hierarchy of Needs

Maslow believed we progress toward higher psychological needs once basic survival needs have been met.

Cassar 1

Zarena Cassar

Professor David Clark

English 4A43

15 December 2012

The Construction of Identity in Jamaica Kincaid's *My Brother*

Jamaica Kincaid's memoir, *My Brother*, is a poignant collection of memories of a brother who dies of HIV/AIDS. Although it appears at first that this book is, as the title indicates, primarily about her brother, Kincaid's story evolves into a commentary that reflects not only on the memories of a brother, but on a life complicated by what it means to be living with HIV/AIDS. Situated in a discerning context of family obligations and cultural differences, Kincaid's visceral memoir exemplifies how she comes to identify with her brother, her family, and most importantly, herself. In the act of writing *My Brother*, Jamaica Kincaid cultivates her own identity in response to how she remembers her brother's life, illustrating that identity itself is a construct and more so that HIV/AIDS fundamentally complicates how individuals come to identify not only with themselves but within their larger familial and cultural contexts. This is clearly demonstrated in Jamaica's realization of her own mortality, in the relationship she has with her mother, and the way in which she constructs her own memories within *My Brother*.

Although Jamaica is writing about her brother, this book becomes much more about herself than him. It is not until halfway through the book that she reveals her brother's name, Devon (Kincaid 99). Until then, he is always known as *brother* and consequently the reader only comes to identify with

Since there is no title page in MLA, list your name, the professor's name, the course number, and the date (in this format) here.

Centre title. Note that titles are not bolded, underlined, or italicized. Published works are italicized.

Use 12-point Times New Roman font throughout.

Courtesy of Zarena Cassar

Devon in his role as Jamaica's brother, and not simply as Devon. It is in this very possession of memories of her brother that Jamaica cultivates her own identity. Jamaica admits that she never really knew who her brother was, but more importantly that her brother was never able to develop his own identity:

> He had died without ever understanding or knowing, or being able to let the world in which he lived know, who he was; that who he really was—not a single sense of identity but all the complexities of who he was—he could not express fully: his fear of being laughed at, his fear of meeting with the scorn of the people he knew best were overwhelming and he could not live with all of it openly. (162)

The complexities of identity that Jamaica addresses in this passage are so much more complicated for her brother, because of his HIV/AIDS diagnosis. The implications of living with HIV/AIDS extend beyond the physical body, and profoundly shape and determine how individuals form an identity of self. In remembering her brother, Jamaica comes to the realization that the brother she remembers is not at all the same person whose name was Devon. Rather, Devon was a person unable to identify with his sexuality, and in his "fear of being laughed at" and of not being able to "live with all of it openly," Devon's identity became one of repression, as a result of cultural expectations and norms pertaining to homosexuality. Only in the act of reflecting on his death in this memoir is Jamaica able to learn about his life, not only how he died but how he lived.

My Brother is in many ways about how Jamaica explores her own identity as well. In her awareness and exploration of her brother's life and death, Jamaica's understanding of how HIV/AIDS factors into his identity also causes her to confront her own identity. She writes:

His reality was that he was dead but still alive; his reality was that

he had a disease called AIDS. And no matter what anyone says or for

that matter what anyone has discovered so far, it seems to me that

to be so intimately acquainted with the organism that is the HIV

virus is to be acquainted with death. (95-96)

In this revelation of what it means to live with AIDS, Jamaica confronts her own

understanding of being alive. Her brother's self becomes so defined by having

AIDS that Jamaica questions whether or not living with AIDS is really living at

all. Her brother's illness and eventual death sentence shaped the way he lived, the

person he was, and in appropriating memories of him, Jamaica begins to cultivate

her own identity in response to the life he was living. She notes:

Death was the thing that was going to happen to him, and yet every

time I got on an airplane to go and pay him a visit, I was quite afraid

that I would never come back: the plane would crash, or in some

way not at all explainable, I would never come back (92).

Her brother's diagnosis acts as a catalyst and forces Jamaica to examine

what it means to be alive in terms of her own life. In acknowledging that she

herself could die at any moment, Jamaica is confronting what it means to be

living with HIV/AIDS. Although she is not sick herself, she becomes aware

of how this illness not only determines whether a person lives or dies, but

imposes conditions on how one lives one's life. Jamaica's understanding of her

own life is facilitated by how she remembers her brother's life with HIV/AIDS.

This construction of identity, as prompted by Jamaica's revelations about

her brother's illness, is illustrated in the way that Jamaica identifies with

her mother, and how she identifies as a mother herself. Kincaid's memoir

is extremely distorted, and she consistently qualifies people as if they are possessions that belong to someone. For example, she often specifies which mother she is referring to when she talks about her own mother: "our mother – and sometimes I think of her as my mother only, and then sometimes she is the mother of my brothers also, and when she's our mother, she's another entity altogether" (115). In doing this, Jamaica constructs her mother as an identity, rather than as a person. This is extremely important, because it illustrates how Jamaica, and on a larger scale, society as a whole, view people based on only one of the many components that contribute to their identity. In the case of Devon, Jamaica identifies him as her brother who has HIV/ AIDS, and in doing so ignores the larger implications of who Devon is, and what makes him an individual. The crisis of identity that HIV/AIDS facilitates is demonstrated in the way people have to qualify individuals based on their illness, and only their illness.

This construction of a "mother" as an identity is further developed when Jamaica comes to see herself as a mother through the eyes of her son:

> He had not known or imagined that I, his own mother, could have in her life a someone about whom I felt the same way he felt about me. When he looks at me he does not see a person, he sees the sky blotted out, the horizon, too; there is no B.C.E or C.E, there is not present or future, there is no time at all; he sees his needs fulfilled, his needs unfulfilled, he sees satisfaction and disappointments. (63)

In admitting that her son does not see her as a person, but instead sees her as his mother, she becomes a constructed identity as well. Jamaica is much more than just a mother in this memoir; she is a daughter, a sister, a wife, a writer, an Antiguan person, an American person, and perhaps most importantly, she is an individual who is composed of far more than just one of these labels can signify. Having written this memoir from her own perspective, however, the reader comes to identify with other characters in the same way that Jamaica does. While the readers might be privy to a more complete understanding of Jamaica's identity, they only come to know Jamaica's relatives as Jamaica knows them, which is biased and based on the identities that Jamaica constructs for them. Smith and Beumel go so far as to argue that this approach to her brother's identity is in itself evidence of a postcolonial attitude on the part of the author. She constructs them; she does not really recognize their constructions of themselves. In a similar way, Jamaica also constructs the very memories that she revisits in her memoir.

Jamaica comes to know not only her family members, but herself through the act of remembering. Page argues that Kincaid sees her work as a way of preserving her country, like sending remittances home to protect her family—a way of preserving her home from beyond. This is problematic because Jamaica cultivates identity through these memories, which are clearly constructs themselves. This memoir is organized by a fragmented timeline that is not chronological; indicating that memory itself is not organized or logical, but rather that it is emotional, and selective. Kincaid writes:

> But the colour blue did not run through all my memories or my experiences; on the whole, every scene, every memory remained itself, just itself, and sometimes a certain colour might make memory more vivid and something again, not so at all, just not so at all; sometimes a memory is without colour, a dream is often like that, without colour, but the absence of colour does not mean the absence of truth, or truth in a way that one could understand as not a falsehood. (170)

Note that punctuation appears before parentheses in long quotations, though it appears after parentheses in other citations generally.

Use square brackets to make additions to quoted words.

Use ellipses to indicate words left out of a quotation.

Jamaica acknowledges that her own memories are heightened sometimes, and that they are extremely subjective. As Wallace comments, "Kincaid's persistent memory … arouses her mother's disdain [and] is indicative of her melancholic attachment to a past that still troubles and pains her" (110). Her memories belong to her; they are influenced by her perspective, and by her recollection of events. Colour is an important theme in how Jamaica remembers, especially the colour blue. When Jamaica remembers a mother at her son's funeral, she describes her outfit: "She was wearing a blue skirt, a blue that is the colour of seawater, Caribbean seawater when it is seen from far away; I cannot remember the colour of her blouse, and this must be why" (123). Jamaica then launches into a story about a lizard that distracted her from paying attention to the mother's blouse, illustrating the fallibility and unreliability of her own memory (123). Jamaica constructs identities in *My Brother* based on the memories she revisits, and if her memories are clearly constructed, then it only logically follows that these identities are constructed too. In the same way that the motif of the colour blue illustrates the interconnectedness of memory, this implies the equally complex and multifaceted construction of identity.

While Kincaid's memoir is emotionally provoking, in Bernard's words, "full of the messy complexities of life" (138), it highlights how Jamaica utilises memories of her brother to facilitate an examination of her own identity. As Gilmore comments, "Her brother's death is never far from a concern that defines her work: how writing can save your life" (119). Ultimately, it is her brother's HIV/AIDS diagnosis that forces Kincaid to explore both how her own and her brother's identities are contextualized by societal factors, familial relations, and the subjectivity of memory. In writing this memoir through a discourse of personal history, Kincaid speaks to the broader notion of how historical events and attitudes have come to shape present conceptions of the HIV/AIDS crisis, and the often-overlooked identities of those living with the disease.

Works Cited

Bernard, Louise. "Countermemory and Return: Reclamation of the (Post-
modern) Self in Jamaica Kincaid's *The Autobiography of My Mother and My
Brother*." *Modern Fiction Studies* 48.1 (2002): 113–38. Web. 19 May 2011.

Gilmore, Leigh. *The Limits of Autobiography*. Ithaca: Cornell UP. 2001. Print.

Kincaid, Jamaica. *My Brother*. New York: Farrar, 1998. Print.

Page, Kezia. "'What If He Did Not Have a Sister [Who Lived in the United
States]?': Jamaica Kincaid's *My Brother* as Remittance Text." *Jamaica
Kincaid*. Ed. Harold Bloom. New York: Infobase, 2008. 189–206. Print.

Smith, Deri, and Cliff Beumel. "My Other: Imperialism and Subjectivity in
Jamaica Kincaid's *My Brother*." *Jamaica Kincaid and Caribbean Double
Crossings*. Ed. Linda Lang-Peralta. Newark, NJ: U of Delaware P, 2006.
96–112. Print.

Wallace, Ann E. "'Look at This, Just Look at This': Melancholic Remains in
Jamaica Kincaid's *My Brother*." *Come Weep With Me: Loss and Mourning
in the Writings of Caribbean Women Writers*. Ed. Joyce C. Harte.
Newcastle upon Tyne: Cambridge Scholars, 2007. 110–27. Print.

Marginal notes:

List only works cited, on a separate page, double-spaced and alphabetically arranged.

Note that the medium of publication must appear in each entry. If the medium is the Internet, a date of access is also required.

The type of publication must be listed at the end of each reference.

APA Style of Documentation

> You could compile the worst book in the world entirely out of selected passages from the best writers in the world.
>
> —G. K. Chesterton

This book chapter is not a substitute for the *Publication Manual of the American Psychological Association* (*APA Publication Manual*) and is merely Nelson Education's supplement to the *APA Publication Manual*. We recommend that you consult the latest edition of the *APA Publication Manual* for the definitive APA Style.

Readers will find a number of resources at APAStyle.org to help them learn APA Style, including free tutorials, sample papers, FAQs, online courses, an APA Style blog, and background information on all aspects of scientific writing.

APA Style of Documentation

6

SOME BASIC REQUIREMENTS IN APA

1. Your paper should be double-spaced with 2.5 cm (1 in.) margins all around. Your font should be 12 points in Times New Roman.
2. Every page except the title page should include a page header in caps, usually a shortened version of the title, flush left.
3. Papers need a title page, a body usually divided by headings, and a *References* page. Some instructors may expect an abstract, a short summary of the paper's argument and findings. For a quick model of this format, see the sample essay at the end of this chapter.

The American Psychological Association (APA) produces a publication manual used to cite sources in the social sciences. This is an author-date system that emphasizes current publications, especially articles.

The most recent edition is the sixth edition of the *Publication Manual of the American Psychological Association* (2010).

IN-TEXT CITATIONS (6-1

CITING A SOURCE WITHIN YOUR PAPER

Rogers (1957) argued that unconditional positive regard was essential to the development of a therapeutic relationship in counselling.

Note that the past tense, whether simple past, as illustrated, or present perfect (*has argued*) is expected when signalling a source.

APA style uses the author-date method of citation, giving the author and date of publication in parentheses within the essay. Each of these parenthetical citations has a matching entry giving complete publication information in the *References* list on a separate page at the end of the essay. If a specific part of a source is paraphrased or quoted, the citation also includes the page number (or chapter, figure, table, or equation), as detailed below.

graja/Shutterstock.com

6-1A FORMAT OF CITATIONS FOR PRINT SOURCES

ONE AUTHOR

Give the name and the year of publication in parentheses, separated by a comma.

If the name of the author is given in a signal phrase, cite only the year of publication in parentheses.

If both the author and the year are given in a signal phrase, do not add parenthetical information.

One study (Woods, 2006) cast some doubt on the efficacy of the procedure.

As Bayly (2006) clearly demonstrates, the technical excellence of the procedure resulted in long wait times for patients.

Fawcett's seminal 2006 study showed that the data had been doctored to illustrate the desired result.

SPECIFIC PART OF A SOURCE

To cite quotations or paraphrased information taken from a precise location in a work, follow the guidelines above but also give a location reference such as the page number or the chapter, figure, table, or equation. Abbreviate "page" (p.) and "pages" (pp.), but not "chapter."

John English in *Just Watch Me* (2009, p. 157) observed of Trudeau, "His popularity rose to astonishing heights as he stared down the terrorists during the October Crisis, and memories persisted of Trudeaumania with its excitement, energy, and enthusiasm."

One biographer noted, "His popularity rose to astonishing heights as he stared down the terrorists during the October Crisis, and memories persisted of Trudeaumania with its excitement, energy, and enthusiasm" (English, 2009, p. 157).

Clarkson and McCall (1990) agree that Trudeau's writings during the early 1960s revealed him at the height of his powers as a writer and Quebec theoretician on federalism.

During the early 1960s, Trudeau was at the height of his powers as a writer and was viewed as the preeminent Quebec theoretician on federalism (Clarkson & McCall, 1990).

First Citation of the Source

Growing up Chinese in Canada is a complex process though ethnic identity appears to remain strong (Costigan, Su, & Hua, 2009).

Subsequent Citation of the Source

Parents play an important role in the development of their children's ethnic identity (Costigan et al., 2009).

Many assert that Canada's involvement in World War I was characterized by racism in some instances and by greed and corruption in others (Newman et al., 2000).

TWO AUTHORS
Cite both names along with the year of publication. If the names appear in a signal phrase, join them with *and*; in a parenthetical reference, use the ampersand (&).

THREE TO FIVE AUTHORS
Give the names of all the authors only in the first citation; remember to use the ampersand (&) instead of *and*. In subsequent citations, give only the first author's last name followed by the abbreviation *et al.* (not italicized and with a period only after *al*).

SIX OR MORE AUTHORS
For all citations of a work with six or more authors, use the first author's last name followed by *et al.*

NO AUTHOR

Cite the first few words of the title along with the year. Italicize titles of books, magazines, journals, and reports that appear in your paper. Use quotation marks around titles of articles or chapters.

CORPORATE AUTHOR

The name of a group author such as a corporation, organization, or agency is usually given in full. However, if the name is long and the abbreviation is readily understandable, you may first cite the source using the full name followed by the abbreviation in square brackets and then use the abbreviation and year in subsequent citations.

AUTHORS WITH THE SAME SURNAME

Include the initials in all text citations, even if the year of publication differs.

TWO OR MORE WORKS IN A SINGLE CITATION

Give the sources in alphabetical order by the authors' last names. Separate the citations with a semicolon.

One recent report ("UN Guns," 2006) suggests that the UN conference on the illicit gun trade ended in disarray, with weaker results than in 2001.

Example

Entry in Reference List: Assembly of First Nations. (2006).

First Citation: (Assembly of First Nations [AFN], 2006)

Subsequent Citations: (AFN, 2006)

A study by R. J. Jones (2006) indicates that….

It is a truism that children of immigrants acculturate more quickly compared to their parents, who appear to keep their ethnic culture to a greater degree (Kwak, 2003; Okagaki & Bojczyk, 2002).

Theories of ethnic identity and acculturation have advanced over the years (Phinney, 1992, 2003, 2006).

Studies determine degree of cultural adjustment by interviewing subjects about their Chinese identity. For example, one study asked mothers, fathers, and children to describe their sense of belonging to the Chinese group identity to compare their responses (Costigan & Dokis, 2006a, 2006b).

Two or more works by the same author(s) are arranged by year of publication with commas separating the years. If two or more works by the same author(s) have the same publication date, distinguish the works by adding *a*, *b*, *c*, and so on after the year.

Example

(Barthes, 1957/2007)

TRANSLATION

Cite both the original publication date and the date of the translation, separated by a virgule, also known as a forward slash (/).

J. Nadler (personal communication, November 12, 2011) indicated that the Russian mafia played a significant role in supplying protection for Budapest nightclub owners.

PERSONAL COMMUNICATION

For letters, memos, emails, interviews, and telephone conversations, give the initials and last name of the communicator and the date on which the communication took place. Because they are not verifiable, personal communications are not included in the reference list.

Follow the guidelines for print sources but add location information to direct the reader to a specific part of the source.

If an electronic resource does not list an author, use the title in a signal phrase or shorten the title and include it in parentheses.

If a resource has no date, use the abbreviation *n.d.* for "no date."

Queen Elizabeth I was queen of England for seventy years and died at the height of Shakespeare's literary career (Luminarium, 2008).

In a documentary shown on the CBC, Martin Seligman (2010) argues that positive emotions even protect us against colds ("How to be Happy," para. 2).

Electronic communications have proven to be helpful as a means of monitoring and assessing student progress as writers ("Writing and Discussion Groups," n.d.)

For an electronic source with no page numbers, use the paragraph number if it is available, preceded by the abbreviation *para.* and a space.

If neither paragraph nor page numbers are available, cite the heading and the number of the paragraph following it.

If no page numbers, paragraph numbers, or headings are provided, it may be necessary to omit a location reference.

As Myers (2011, para. 7) aptly phrased it, "positive emotions are both an end—better to live fulfilled, with joy [and other positive emotions]—and a means to a more caring and healthy society."

Panic disorder currently affects six million American adults (NIMH, 2010, "Panic Disorder," para. 3).

STRATEGIES

Some Basic Requirements in APA References

1. All references appear at the end of the paper, on a separate page, in alphabetical order by the first author's last name.
2. Each entry has a hanging indent, which means that all lines except the first are indented.
3. Use initials rather than complete names to avoid sexism.
4. When listing multiple references to the same author or authors, list in order of publication, starting with the earliest.
5. Use headline style for titles of journals; that is, capitalize all important words.
6. Use capitals only on the first word of titles of books, articles, or Web pages, as well as the first word of subtitles (unless, of course, the title includes proper nouns that must be capitalized).
7. Italicize titles of books and periodicals, but not of shorter works, which remain unadorned.

For every citation in the text of your paper, there must be a matching entry in a list of references at the end of the paper. Only sources used in the research and preparation of the paper are included in the reference list.

The following section presents guidelines for setting up a list of references and model entries for common types of sources. If the source you have used in your research paper is not described in this section, consult the *Publication Manual of the American Psychological Association*, 6th ed. (Washington: APA, 2010). Some tips and guidelines are also available on the APA website at www.apastyle.org.

TITLE AND PLACEMENT

Begin the list of references at the end of your paper on a separate page. Centre the title, *References*. Do not italicize (or underline) the title or put it within quotation marks; use boldface. Use an initial capital only, not all caps.

PAGINATION

Number the page or pages of your reference list sequentially with the rest of the research paper.

SPACING

Double space all entries in your reference list.

INDENTATION

Use a hanging indent format, with the first line of each reference flush left and subsequent lines indented 1.25 cm (0.5 in.).

References   17

Anandarajah, G. (2008). The 3 H and BMSEST models for spirituality in multicultural whole-person medicine. *Annals of Family Medicine, 6*(5), 448–458.

Baydala, A., Hampton, M., Kinunwa, L., Kinunwa, G., & Kinunwa, L., Sr. (2006). Death, dying, grieving, and end of life care: Understanding personal meanings of Aboriginal friends. *The Humanistic Psychologist, 34*(2), 159–176.

Blair, L. (1995). Update: Cultural variation in attitudes towards death. *Canadian Family Physician, 41*, 515–521.

See the reference list on pages 13–15 of the sample APA-style essay at the end of this chapter (pages 254–56).

Sale, K. (1991). *The conquests of paradise: Christopher Columbus and the Columbian legacy.* New York: Plume.

Alphabetize entries by the authors' surnames.

Riso, L. P., Klein, D. N., Anderson, R. L., & Ouimette, P. C. (2000). A family study of outpatients with borderline personality disorder and no history of mood disorder. *Journal of Personality Disorders, 14*, 208–217.

Robins, E., & Guze, S. B. (1970). Establishment of diagnostic validity in psychiatric illness: Its application to schizophrenia. *American Journal of Psychiatry 126*, 107–111.

Schulz, P. M., Soloff, P. H., Kelly, T., & Morgenstern, M. (1989). A family history study of borderline subtypes. *Journal of Personality Disorders, 3*, 217–229.

Rogers, C. R. (1953). Some directions and end points in therapy. In O. H. Mowrer (Ed.). *Psychotherapy: Theory and research* (pp. 44–68). Oxford: Ronald Press.

Rogers, C. R. (1957). The necessary and sufficient conditions of therapeutic personality change. *Psychotherapy: Theory, Research, Practice, Training, 44*(3), 240–248. doi: 10.1037/0033-3204.44.3.240

ARRANGEMENT OF ENTRIES

All sources used for your research paper and cited in the text must be listed alphabetically in your reference list.

TWO OR MORE WORKS BY THE SAME AUTHOR

Give the author name(s) each time and organize the works chronologically by their year of publication.

When the author is the sole author of one or more works and the leading co-author of others, put the entry or entries for the single-author works first.

For references with the same first author and different second or third authors, arrange entries alphabetically by the surname of the second author.

Arrange entries alphabetically by title, and add lowercase letters—*a, b, c,* and so on—immediately after the year within the parentheses.

Bradford, N. (2004a). Canada's urban agenda: A new deal for the cities? In J. Bickerton & A. G. Gagnon (Eds.), *Canadian politics* (4th ed., pp. 425–446). Peterborough, ON: Broadview Press.

Bradford, N. (2004b). Place matters and multilevel governance: Perspectives on a new urban policy paradigm. *Policy Options, 25*(2), 2–13.

If no author is given, alphabetize by the first significant word of the title. Do not consider initial articles—*A, An,* or *The*—when you alphabetize.

Algorithm. (n.d.) In *Merriam-Webster's online dictionary* (11th ed.). Retrieved from http://www.merriam-webster.com/dictionary/algorithm

If an organization published a work, list it by the full name of the organization alphabetically. Use full official names rather than abbreviations.

Canadian Pharmaceutical Association. (2008). *Compendium of pharmaceuticals and specialties (Canada)*. Ottawa: Author.

6-2B   ELEMENTS OF ENTRIES

AUTHOR
Invert all author names. Give the last name, followed by a comma, and then the initial(s)—do not use the full first name.

One Author

Field, J. (2003). *Social capital*. London and New York: Routledge.

Two or More Authors

Killackey, E., Jackson, H., & McGorry, P. (2008). Vocational intervention in first-episode psychosis: Individual placement and support versus treatment as usual. *British Journal of Psychiatry, 193*(2), 114–120.

When there are two or more authors, use the ampersand (&) rather than the word *and*. Separate author names with commas, including before an ampersand.

Edited Work

Csikszentmihalyi, M., & Csikszentmihalyi, I. S. (Eds.). (1992). *Optimal experience: Psychological studies of flow in consciousness*. New York: Cambridge University Press.

For an edited book, place the name of the editor or editors in the author position, followed by the abbreviation *Ed.* or *Eds.* in parentheses.

If the reference has no author, move the title to the author position.

Part of an Edited Work

Cacioppo, J. T., Hawkley, L. C., Kalil, A., Hughes, M. E., Waite, L., & Thisted, R. A. (2008). Happiness and the invisible threads of social connection: The Chicago health, aging, and social relations study. In M. Eid & R. J. Larsen (Eds.), *The science of subjective well-being*. New York: Guilford Press.

More than Eight Authors

Latimer, E., Lecomte, T., Becker, D. R., Drake, R. E., Duclos, I., Piat, M., ... Xie, H. (2006). Generalisability of the individual placement and support model of supported employment: Results of a Canadian randomised controlled trial. *British Journal of Psychiatry, 189*, 65–73.

For references with more than eight authors, insert an ellipsis mark after the name of the sixth author, followed by the last author's name.

The author element of the entry should end with a period; if it closes with a parenthesis—for example, with *(Ed.)*—add a period after the closing parenthesis. If an author's initial with a period ends the element, do not add an extra period.

PUBLICATION DATE

Place the publication date in parentheses after the last author's name or the closing parenthesis after *Ed.* or *Eds.*

For a published work, give the year the work was copyrighted; for an unpublished work, give the year it was produced.

For magazines, newsletters, or newspapers, give the year followed by the exact date of publication as it appears on the issue: the month or months, the season, or the month and day. Spell the names of months in full.

If no date is given, place *n.d.* in parentheses. For articles accepted for publication but not yet published, write *in press* in parentheses.

Finish the date element of the entry with a period after the closing parenthesis.

Laumakis, S. J. (2008). *An introduction to Buddhist philosophy*. Cambridge, UK: Cambridge University Press.

Kirby, J. (2011, July 25). The great white tax haven. *Maclean's*, *124*(28), 38–41.

Nielsen, M. E. (n.d.). Notable people in psychology of religion. Retrieved from http://www.psywww.com/psyrelig/psyrelpr.htm

Title of Article

> Umaña-Taylor, A. J., Bhanot, R., & Shin, N. (2006). Ethnic identity formation during adolescence: The critical role of families. *Journal of Family Issues, 27*, 390–414.

Title of Chapter

> Neimeyer, R. A., & Raskin, J. D. (2000). On practicing postmodern therapy in modern times. In R. A. Neimeyer and J. D. Raskin (Eds.), *Construction of disorder: Meaning-making frameworks for psychotherapy* (pp. 3–14). Washington, DC: American Psychological Association.

TITLE

Italicize book titles and subtitles. Capitalize only the first word of the title and of the subtitle as well as any proper nouns. End the title with a period, unless you will be adding additional information (see next item).

ADDITIONAL INFORMATION

Give edition, report number, or volume number, if applicable, in parentheses immediately after the title. Do not use a period between the title and the parenthetical information and do not italicize.

Following any parenthetical information, give a description of the form of the work, if necessary, enclosed in brackets—for example, *[Brochure]* or *[Videotape]*. End with a period.

PLACE OF PUBLICATION

Give the city where the work was published. If the city could be confused with another location, also give the state or province and, if necessary, the country. Use two-letter postal abbreviations for states and provinces. Use a colon to separate the place of publication from the publisher's name.

TITLE OF ARTICLE OR CHAPTER

Do not italicize or underline article or chapter titles or place them within quotation marks.

Capitalize only the first word of the title and of the subtitle and any proper nouns.

After the article title, other identifying information may be included in brackets, for example, *[Letter to the editor]* or *[Abstract]*.

Finish the element with a period.

TITLE OF WORK AND PUBLICATION INFORMATION
Non-periodicals

For a non-periodical such as a book, after the author name(s) and date give the following information: title of work; additional information such as edition; a description of the form of the work, if applicable; place of publication; publisher; and digital object identifier.

PUBLISHER

Give the publisher's name in brief, omitting words and abbreviations such as *Publishers, Co.,* and *Inc.,* but retaining the words *Books* and *Press*. End with a period.

PART OF A NON-PERIODICAL

When referencing part of a non-periodical, such as a book chapter, give the author, date, and chapter title as described above, and then add the following elements:

1. The word *In* followed by the editor's name, not inverted, followed by the abbreviation *Ed.* in parentheses (If there is no editor, simply include the word *In* followed by the title of the work.)
2. The title of the work in italics
3. Inclusive page numbers for the chapter, in parentheses and preceded by the abbreviation *pp.*
4. The publication information as outlined above

Periodicals

After the author(s), date, and title of article, additional information appears in the following order: periodical name, volume number (if applicable), issue number (if applicable), and inclusive page numbers.

PERIODICAL NAME

Give the complete name, in italics, followed by a comma. Capitalize the first letter of all significant words (see 14-3c).

VOLUME NUMBER

Give the volume number, if any, in italics. Do not use *Vol.* before the volume number. Place a comma after the volume number unless it is followed by an issue number. If there is no volume number, include the month or season with the year, for example, *(2006, September)*.

ISSUE NUMBER

If each issue of the periodical begins on page 1, give the issue number in parentheses immediately after the volume number, leaving no space, followed by a comma.

PAGE NUMBERS

Give inclusive page numbers after the volume (or issue) number. Use the abbreviations *p.* or *pp.* for newspaper articles but not for magazine or journal articles.

BOOKS

One Author

Rogers, C. R. (1961). *On becoming a person: A therapist's view of psychotherapy.* Boston: Houghton Mifflin.

Two or More Authors

Alper, S., Schloss, P. J., Etscheidt, S. K., & Macfarlane, C. A. (1995). *Inclusion: Are we abandoning or helping students?* Thousand Oaks, CA: Corwin Press.

Coon, D., & Mitterer, O. *Introduction to psychology: Gateway to mind and behavior.* Belmont, CA: Thomson Learning, 2007.

Edited Book

Reker, G. T., & Chamberlain, K. (Eds.) (2000). *Exploring existential meaning: Optimizing human development across the life span.* London: Sage.

Translation

Frankl, V. (1963). *Man's search for meaning: An introduction to logotherapy* (I. Lasch, Trans.). New York: Simon & Schuster.

Corporate Author

Canadian Psychological Association. (2000). *Canadian code of ethics for psychologists* (3rd ed.). Ottawa, ON: Author.

No Author or Editor

Geological field trips in southern British Columbia. (2003).
Vancouver, BC: Geological Association of Canada, Cordilleran
Section.

Subsequent Editions

Gifford, D. (1982). *Joyce annotated* (2nd ed.). Berkeley:
University of California Press.

Multi-volume Work

Rieber, R. W., & Carton, A. S. (1987). *The collected works of L. S.
Vygotsky* (Vols. 1–3). New York: Plenum Press.

Article in an Edited Book

Hill, R. D., Lund, D., & Packard, T. (1996). Bereavement. In J. I.
Sheikh & I. D. Yalom (Eds.). *Treating the elderly* (pp. 45–74).
San Francisco: Jossey-Bass.

Article in a Reference Book

Watkins, C. (1998). Indo-European and the Indo-Europeans. In
Canadian Dictionary of the English Language (pp. 1631–
1637). Toronto: ITP Nelson.

Article in a Journal Paginated by Volume

Dodd, D. (2001). Helen MacMurchy, MD: Gender and professional conflict in the medical inspection of Toronto schools, 1910–1911. *Ontario History, 93*, 127–149.

Article in a Journal Paginated by Issue

Martin, R. (2002). The virtue matrix: Calculating the return on corporate responsibility. *Harvard Business Review, 80*(3), 69–75.

Article in a Magazine

Chapin, A. (2010, October 18). A worldly workforce. *Maclean's, 123*(40), 55–56.

Article in a Newspaper

MacKinnon, M. (2010, October 10). Jailed dissident's award infuriates China. *The Globe and Mail*, p. A26.

Anonymous Article

Newsmakers. (2010, October 18). *Maclean's, 123*(40), 12, 14.

Letter to the Editor

Fournier, S. (2010, October 18). Questioning Quebec [Letter to the Editor]. *Maclean's, 123*(40), 6.

Review

> Grant, A. M. (2009). Review of *Positive psychology coaching: Putting the science of happiness to work for your clients* by R. Biswas-Diener & B. Dean. *The Journal of Positive Psychology 4*(5), 426–429.

6-2D ELECTRONIC SOURCES

One stable method of finding the source, if it is an online periodical, is the digital object identifier (DOI) if it is given. It is usually found on the first page of a scholarly article retrieved from a database. If there is no DOI listed, you should seek out the scholarly journal on the Internet and include its uniform resource locator (URL).

APA references are often scholarly articles, drawn from library databases. In an effort to standardize the process of locating online sources, APA requires a digital object identifier in any reference found this way, if it is available. If it is not, the URL of the journal from which the article comes should be included.

ARTICLE WITH A DOI
The retrieval statement containing a DOI for the journal in question supplements the publication information typically provided for print references.

> Ortiz, S. O. (2006). Multicultural issues in school psychology practice: A critical analysis. *Journal of Applied School Psychology, 22*(2), 151–167. doi: 10.1300/J370v22n02_08

Smith, T. B., Dean, B., Floyd, S., Silva, C., Momoko, Y., Durtschi, J., & Heaps, R. A. (2007). Pressing issues in college counseling: A survey of American College Counseling Association members. *Journal of College Counseling, 10*, 64–78. Retrieved from http://www.collegecounseling.org/resources/index.html

Strain, L. A. (2000). Seniors' centres: Who cares? *Canadian Journal of Aging, 20*, 471–491.

Leonard, A. (2010, October 8). America's mighty offshore wind … potential. *Salon.com*. Retrieved from http://www.salon.com/news/env/environment/index.html

Driscoll, D. L., & Brisee, A. (2010, June 16). *Quoting, paraphrasing, and summarizing*. Retrieved from http://owl.english.purdue.edu/owl/resource/563/1

ARTICLE WITH NO DOI (URL INSTEAD)

If there is no DOI, use the journal's URL instead. If a URL runs over a line, break it before most punctuation and make sure no hyphens are inadvertently added at line breaks. No final period appears after the end of the URL, and the URL is not placed in angle brackets.

ARTICLE BASED ON A PRINT SOURCE

Often articles retrieved from online publications are exact duplicates of print versions. In these cases, follow the format of the print form.

INTERNET-ONLY JOURNAL

Reference online-only journals as in the preceding example. However, if no volume or issue numbers are used, simply provide the name of the periodical and the URL.

NON-PERIODICAL WEB DOCUMENT

Give all the information you can find about a Web page, in the normal order. This may require some searching.

NEWSPAPER ARTICLE
Include the information you would use in print and the URL.

Markoff, J. (2010, October 9). Google cars drive themselves in traffic. *The New York Times*. Retrieved from http://www .nytimes.com/2010/10/10/science/10google.html?bl

ELECTRONIC BOOK
For books available in print and in digital form, make sure you give the date of publication after the name of the author. If you cannot access the book directly online or you must purchase it, use *Available from* rather than *Retrieved from*.

Larsson, S. (2009). *The girl who kicked the hornet's nest.* Available at http://www.ebooks.com/ebooks/book_display.asp?IID=456625

ONLINE LECTURE NOTES AND SLIDES
Provide the format of the digital information in brackets after the title, for example, *[PDF document]*, *[Word document]*.

Myers, M. *Overcoming test anxiety* [PowerPoint slides] Retrieved from http://www.slideworld.org/viewslides.aspx/ OVERCOMING-TEST-ANXIETY-ppt-2184279

ONLINE DISCUSSION SOURCES
Often newsgroups, forums, discussion groups, and electronic mailing lists are not referenced because they are not peer reviewed and posts are not retrievable. If the source is archived, cite the author's name or screen name and the exact date of online posting. Follow this with the subject line of the message and the address of the message group or forum

Nivalainen, M. (2002, December 17). The key and stupid web moments of 2002 [Online forum comment]. Message posted to Cybermind@listserv.aol.com

Barry, D. (2010, October 9). So much fun you'll want to kill yourself [Web log message]. Retrieved from http://blogs .herald.com/dave_barrys_blog/2010/10/index.html

Fernandez, R. (Interviewer). (2010, July 27). Drew Hayden Taylor on short stories [Audio podcast]. *CBC Book Club*. Retrieved from http://blip.tv/file/3930035

Emails are listed parenthetically in the text of your paper, though not in your reference list.

... negotiations had ended (P. Deane, personal communication, September 10, 2010).

beginning with *Message posted to*. Include the URL where the message is archived if it is available.

BLOG
Include the title of the message and the URL where you found it. Note that you do not italicize titles in online communities.

PODCAST
Provide any information you can find to identify the podcast and make it easy to retrieve, including perhaps the producer or director.

EMAIL
Since email messages are not retrievable by the reader, they should not be included in a reference list. They may be cited in the text as a personal communication.

MISCELLANEOUS SOURCES 6-2E

MUSIC RECORDING

Manuel, R. (1968). Lonesome Suzie. [Recorded by The Band]. On *Music from Big Pink* [CD]. Hollywood, CA: Capitol. (2003)

TELEVISION BROADCAST

Sheppard, M. C. (Executive Producer). (2010, October 8). *The national* [Television broadcast]. Toronto: Canadian Broadcasting Corporation.

SINGLE EPISODE FROM A TELEVISION SERIES

Ferrand, C. (Director). (2006, February 11). People of the ice. [Television series episode]. In M. Allder (Executive Producer), *The nature of things with David Suzuki.* Toronto: Canadian Broadcasting Corporation.

MOTION PICTURE

Anderson, W., Mendel, B., & Rudin, S. (Producers), & Anderson, W. (Director). (2001). *The royal Tenenbaums* [Motion picture]. United States: Touchstone Pictures.

DISSERTATION ABSTRACT

Karim, Y. (1999). Arab political dispute mediations (Doctoral dissertation, Wayne State University, 1999). *Dissertation Abstracts International, 61,* 350.

Solicitor General of Canada. (1995). *Annual report on the use of electronic surveillance.* Ottawa: Author.

Chorney, H. (1991). A regional approach to monetary and fiscal policy. In J. N. McCrorie & M. L. MacDonald (Eds.), *The constitutional future of the prairie and Atlantic regions of Canada* (pp. 107–121). Regina, SK: Canadian Plains Research Center Press.

Note that regularly published conference proceedings are treated as periodicals.

Nattika/Shutterstock.com

6-3A MATERIALS AND TYPEFACE

Use letter-size (22 × 28 cm, 8.5 × 11 in.), heavy (20-lb.) white bond paper. Type or print on only one side of the paper.

Use Times New Roman typeface, in 12-point size. Serif typeface is preferable since it enhances readability and reduces eyestrain. The type on the paper must be dark, clear, and easy to photocopy.

Sans Serif	Serif
Arial	Times New Roman
Calibri	Cambria

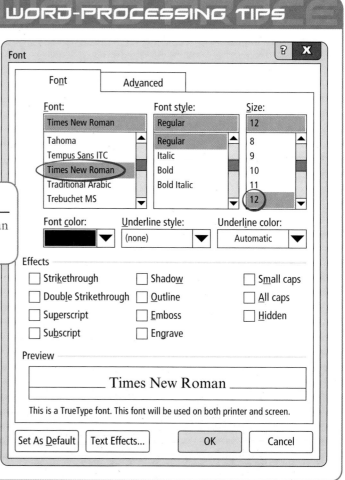

Infusing Cultural Differences:

Aboriginal Counselling Competency

Melissa Seaborg

GCAP 633-Section E-Fall 2009-Assignment 1

Athabasca University

April 15, 2010

Courtesy of Melissa Seaborg

Although APA style does not give specific guidelines for formatting a title page for college and university papers, the example to the left and the following guidelines are typical of the format most instructors require. Check with your instructor for the format you should use.

Note that APA wants you to put a running head (a shortened version of your title) as a heading on every page of your paper. You need also to identify this running head on page 1 as shown in the example.

In a manuscript intended for publication, APA suggests that, in the upper half of the title page, you type the title in uppercase and lowercase letters, centred between the left and right margins. If the title is more than two lines, double-space it.

About half-way down the page, provide your name.

Centred in the bottom third of the title page are the course name and section number, your instructor's name, and the date you submitted the paper. Double space throughout.

Leave margins of at least 2.5 cm (1 in.) at the top, bottom, left, and right sides of every page.

Double space the text throughout, including the title, headings, quotations, footnotes, and figure captions. Text should be ragged right rather than right justified. Do not divide words at the end of a line or use the hyphenation feature of your word-processing software.

Indent the first line of every paragraph 1.25 cm (0.5 in.). APA style specifies that quotations of 40 or more words should be further indented by 1.25 cm and double-spaced, without an opening paragraph indent and without quotation marks.

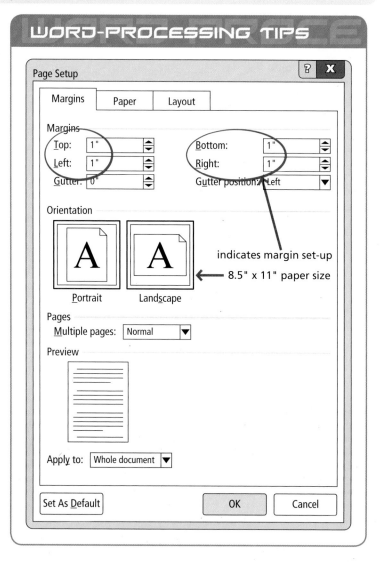

indicates margin set-up

8.5" x 11" paper size

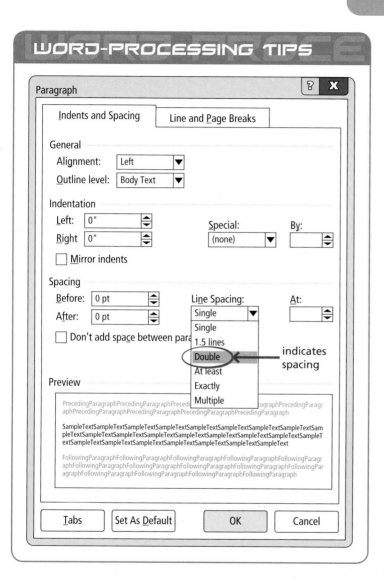

Paragraph ⟨?⟩ ⟨X⟩

| Indents and Spacing | Line and Page Breaks |

General

Alignment: [Left ▼]

Outline level: [Body Text ▼]

Indentation

Left: [0" ⬍]   Special: [(none) ▼]   By: [⬍]

Right: [0" ⬍]

☐ Mirror indents

Spacing

Before: [0 pt ⬍]   Line Spacing: [Single ▼]   At: [⬍]

After: [0 pt ⬍]

| Single |
| 1.5 lines |
| **Double** ← indicates spacing |
| At least |
| Exactly |
| Multiple |

☐ Don't add space between para

Preview

PrecedingParagraphPrecedingParagraphPreceding...agraphPrecedingParagraphPrecedingParagraphPrecedingParagraphPrecedingParagraphPrecedingParagraph

SampleText

FollowingParagraphFollowingParagraphFollowingParagraphFollowingParagraphFollowingParagraphFollowingParagraphFollowingParagraphFollowingParagraphFollowingParagraphFollowingParagraphFollowingParagraphFollowingParagraphFollowingParagraphFollowingParagraph

[Tabs]   [Set As Default]   [OK]   [Cancel]

HOW TO PLACE PAGE NUMBERS

First page is the title page

ABORIGINAL COUNSELLING COMPETENCY   (2)

Infusing Cultural Differences: Aboriginal Counselling Competency

While attending a conference, I ran into a long-time colleague of mine. Later that day, over tea, we began exchanging our present career paths. My colleague had just accepted an offer to work in Stony Plain, Alberta. She has been asked to begin a healthy-living counselling initiative within the high school. Stony Plain is a Cree

---

ABORIGINAL COUNSELLING COMPETENCY   2

Infusing Cultural Differences: Aboriginal Counselling Competency

While attending a conference, I ran into a long-time colleague of mine. Later that day, over tea, we began exchanging our present career paths. My colleague had just accepted an offer to work in Stony Plain, Alberta. She has been asked to begin a healthy-living counselling initiative within the high school. Stony Plain is a Cree Nation with a large population. I asked her how she was planning on integrating their cultural beliefs into this initiative. After thinking for a moment, she looked directly

Double space

Ragged Right

How to Insert an Em Dash

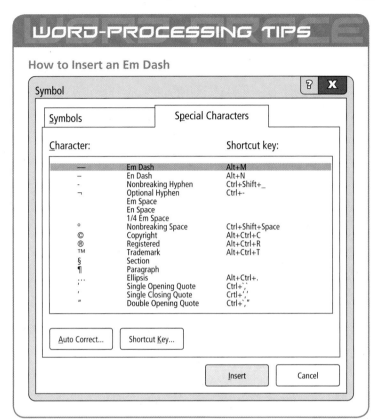

Symbol	?	X

S_ymbols	Sp_ecial Characters

_Character: Shortcut key:

—	Em Dash	Alt+M
–	En Dash	Alt+N
-	Nonbreaking Hyphen	Ctrl+Shift+_
¬	Optional Hyphen	Ctrl+-
	Em Space	
	En Space	
	1/4 Em Space	
°	Nonbreaking Space	Ctrl+Shift+Space
©	Copyright	Alt+Ctrl+C
®	Registered	Alt+Ctrl+R
™	Trademark	Alt+Ctrl+T
§	Section	
¶	Paragraph	
…	Ellipsis	Alt+Ctrl+.
'	Single Opening Quote	Ctrl+`,`
'	Single Closing Quote	Crtl+','`
"	Double Opening Quote	Ctrl+`,`"

A_uto Correct...   Shortcut K_ey...

Insert   Cancel

The dash is used to indicate a sudden break in the sentence, a startling interruption. Most often it is used like a colon, though it indicates less formality and more feeling than a colon.

I live for one thing—your love.

That is something I will never tell you—how I came to meet your father.

Sometimes a pair of dashes may be used instead of a parenthetical set of commas, if there is a need to indicate some sudden interruption.

I bought special gifts at the mall—dog treats and a flea collar—for Pepé, of course.

She heard a noise—a loud shriek—coming from the garage.

Avoid using dashes as a ready substitute for other punctuation. Their purpose is quite specific.

For more information on using dashes, see 11-6d.

6-3E ABSTRACT

Your instructor may ask you to include an abstract—a brief summary of your research paper. An abstract appears separately on page 2 and is one paragraph, double-spaced, and typed as a block without indentation. The length for an abstract ranges from 150 to 250 words. It is meant to provide a summary of your paper, including your thesis and the main points of your research. It should also suggest what your research implies and how it might be applied. Centre the heading *Abstract* over the paragraph.

PEDIATRIC BIPOLAR DISORDER   2

Abstract

This paper explores issues related to the phenomenology and diagnosis of pediatric bipolar disorder (PBD) that have led to an explosion in its incidence in America, though not elsewhere. It examines proponents, such as Biederman, Geller, and Kowatch, and their critics. The paper focuses on divergent interpretations of the DSM-IV-TR's criteria for diagnosis, and the relationship of the rise in incidence to comorbidity, particularly with Attention Deficit and Hyperactivity Disorder (ADHD). The paper suggests that PBD may now be over-diagnosed and that caution is necessary in the treatment of young children, given the side effects of current medications, the long-term treatment needed, and the relatively early stages of research on PBD and on the pharmacology and other treatments related to it.

6-3F HEADINGS

Headings are encouraged in APA style. They define the hierarchy of ideas and help the reader understand the structure and organization of the paper.

The APA guidelines for formatting headings are as follows:

Main Headings: centred, boldface, uppercase and lowercase (first letter of important words capitalized)

Second-Level Headings: flush left, boldface, uppercase and lowercase

Third-Level Headings: indented, boldface, lowercase paragraph heading (with initial capital) ending with a period

 See 14-3c for information on capitalizing titles.

Table 1

Favourite Harry Potter Movies among Male and Female Viewers

Movie Title	Males	Females
Harry Potter and the Sorcerer's Stone	25	25
Harry Potter and the Chamber of Secrets	35	20
Harry Potter and the Prisoner of Azkaban	35	15
Harry Potter and the Goblet of Fire	25	60
Harry Potter and the Order of the Phoenix	30	10
Harry Potter and the Half-Blood Prince	30	55
Harry Potter and the Deathly Hallows: Part 1	50	60
Harry Potter and the Deathly Hallows: Part 2	70	55

Note. 300 males and 300 females participated in this survey.

Figure 1. Maslow's hierarchy of needs. Maslow believed we progress toward higher psychological needs once basic survival needs have been met.

In APA style, any type of illustration other than a table is called a figure, including charts, graphs, drawings, and photographs. While tables are preferred for the presentation of quantitative data, figures are used to convey structural or pictorial concepts. Use the following guidelines to identify illustrations.

TABLES
Above the table, number consecutively with Arabic numerals. Give the title of the table in italics, double-spaced.

FIGURES
Below the figure, number consecutively with Arabic numerals, in italics, followed by a period and a caption (no italics). The caption acts as both the title and an explanation of the figure. If you include a visual, make sure that it is mentioned and discussed in the body of your paper so that the reader is alerted to its presence and its significance to your argument.

Tables and figures may appear in the body of a student paper rather than at the end. Ask your instructor for guidelines regarding the preferred placement.

Melissa Seaborg, a graduate student in Counselling, wrote the research paper to the right as part of her requirements for a course on multicultural counselling. Her assignment was to review recent, credible, and reliable sources on counselling First Nations people and write a defence of culturally infused counselling.

Seaborg used the APA guidelines for manuscript formatting and documentation of sources that are presented in this handbook. Her in-text citations follow APA style, as does her list of references. Seaborg's instructor required that students provide a title page with their papers but not an abstract since the paper was to be fairly short.

Running head: ABORIGINAL COUNSELLING COMPETENCY   1

Infusing Cultural Differences:

Aboriginal Counselling Competency

Melissa Seaborg

GCAP 633-Section E-Fall 2009-Assignment 1

Athabasca University

April 15, 2010

Infusing Cultural Differences: Aboriginal Counselling Competency

While attending a conference, I ran into a long-time colleague of mine. Later that day, over tea, we began exchanging our present career paths. My colleague had just accepted an offer to work in Stony Plain, Alberta. She has been asked to begin a healthy-living counselling initiative within the high school. Stony Plain is a Cree Nation with a large population. I asked her how she was planning on integrating their cultural beliefs into this initiative. After thinking for a moment, she looked directly at me and replied: "I understand that I have been offered this opportunity so that I can help them begin adapting in real life. I don't think that I will have to fully understand and integrate their culture in order to do this. They must have some knowledge of Canadian culture already, and if I can clarify their knowledge, then I will be well on my way."

It is apparent that my colleague believes that the integration of multicultural counselling is unnecessary. She has made a large assumption that all First Nations people must assimilate to Western society's values and beliefs. This paper will explore the importance of infusing cultural differences when counselling First Nation's people. The first section will include recent literature advocating for multicultural counselling. I will begin by outlining the key aspects of culture-infused counselling and carry on by integrating the importance that this infusion has on the client's expectations as well as the working alliance. In the next section, I will focus on critically analyzing why counsellors must be competent in multicultural counselling in an Aboriginal community, and how it may benefit this diverse group of clients, and discuss how

The running head is a shortened version of the paper's title that appears on every page.

The title of the paper is centred without embellishment.

Note that the font is 12-point Times New Roman.

my colleague and others may apply the material to an Aboriginal school counselling setting. Note that I use the terms First Nations, Cree, and Aboriginal peoples interchangeably throughout my paper.

Multicultural Counselling

Culture is an all-encompassing concept that involves not only one's ethnicity but must constitute all other aspects of one's life including beliefs, traditions, morals, values, society, sexual identity, and language, to name only a few (Arthur & Collins, 2010). Speaking from a Canadian perspective, Hadjistavropoulos (2009) stated that psychology has been touched by many different cultures as it continues to grow in population. In order to understand any diverse population, it is important to understand the origins of cultures present in various countries. In this case, Aboriginal people established settlements in Canada and are still part of the Canadian population throughout the provinces. In all countries, multiculturalism is prevalent, and for that reason multicultural counselling must be a key aspect of counselling and psychology (Arthur & Collins, 2010; Corenblum & Stephan, 2001). Understanding different cultures can benefit the connection that people can develop with each other. As previously mentioned, culture is all-encompassing, and thus it is difficult to create a working alliance when there is little understanding of another's culture (Corenblum & Stephan, 2001; Pedersen, 1990).

Literature Review of Multicultural Counselling

Counsellors provide support to clients; hence, they need to provide support

Main level headings are usually boldfaced, capitalized, and centred. Lesser headings are then boldfaced, capitalized, and flush left. More minor headings are then boldfaced, indented, lower-case paragraph headings. APA does allow for variations, but the headings must be consistently presented. For more information, see the APA manual.

Citations include author and date. Note the ampersand (&) with two authors in citations.

A level 2 heading should be flush left and bold.

to clients from various cultures. It is important therefore for counsellors to be educated in multiculturalism as well as competent in the process of infusing culture into their work (Smith, Constantine, Graham, & Dize, 2008; Sue, Bingham, Porche-Burke, & Vasquez, 1999). That said, Arthur and Collins (2010) noted that there are many graduate programs that have offered multicultural courses since the 1990s. In the current scenario, my colleague has implied that she believes that assimilation is an important aspect of counselling, especially when working with non-dominant cultures such as the Aboriginal population. Smith et al. (2008) noted that assimilation does not allow both parties to speak evenly; even if the push of assimilation is unintentional, the client will be more aware of the ramifications that it places on the working alliance. Clients from non-dominant populations do benefit from a multicultural stance insofar as there are no right or wrong beliefs, values, or thoughts. Multicultural counselling focuses on listening and learning from one another (Pedersen, 1990).

Infusing culture benefits the working alliance. Client expectations have great influence on how a counselling relationship can flourish (Bedi, Davis, & Williams, 2005; Shaw, McMahon, Chan, & Hannold, 2004). It is difficult if not impossible to create a successful working alliance when there is little understanding of another's culture (Corenblum & Stephan, 2001). Thus, these expectations can be applied to a client's value placed on culture. Day-Vines et al. (2007) solidify the idea that if a counsellor abstains from acknowledging cultural differences, he or she can harm the working alliance. Clients may distinguish this as an intentional concealment tool to deter personal biases (Day-Vines et al., 2007). Instead,

See APA manual for level of headings beyond what is used here.

Note that *et al.* Is used to indicate multiple authors after the first mention of them when there are three to five authors. Here, because there are more than five authors, *et al.* is acceptable on the first mention.

it is important for both parties to be comfortable enough to ignite cultural conversation. Through the acknowledgment of and openness for one another, the working alliance will thrive rather than wilt. Smith et al. (2008) suggested that therapists will be most effective if they make an effort to self-reflect and understand how cultural variations affect them personally.

   Diversity is accepted. Essentially, counselling should happen in an accepting environment. It is true that racism is prevalent all over the world, and this discrimination can be harmful to any relationship. Smith et al. (2008) explained that discrimination can be decreased through an individual's understanding that cultural beliefs are unique between all individuals. Both clients and counsellors arrive at the session coming from different backgrounds, neighbourhoods, lifestyles, and so on. These variables all relate back to their differing cultures. The point is that a person's culture is prevalent in all aspects of their lives and that counsellors are responsible for bridging cultural gaps by acknowledging the importance that culture plays in one's life. Sue et al. (1999) explained that diversity is essential in order to facilitate goals or personal change in a counselling setting because the therapist must be empathic to the client's unique experiences and influences. For instance, Arthur and Collins (2010) pointed out that Aboriginal clients often bear the discrimination that plagued their nation for over a century through residential schools. Clients who feel comfortable in sharing their cultural influences openly and honestly will benefit greatly in the long run. This openness promotes effective change as well as personal understanding both for the client and the counsellor. Sue et al. (1999) also noted that infusing culture into the counselling will result in improved competence and understanding on the part of the counsellor.

Critical Analysis of Aboriginal Counselling

Infusing Aboriginal Culture in a School Setting

While each person, situation, and counselling approach is unique, there are many areas that one must be aware of. Using recent literature pertaining to Aboriginal culture and counselling, I will outline eight areas that counsellors must be attentive to in an Aboriginal counselling setting.

Current problems stem from past traumas. Cote and Schissel (2002) identified the pain and suffering that tens of thousands of First Nations children and their families experienced for over a century in residential schools. These authors explained how the anguish of separation, abuse, and forced assimilation to Western-European culture affected First Nations people and how the repercussions of those events have continued to affect present Aboriginal generations. Cote and Schissel (2002) as well as Arthur and Collins (2010) have called this tragic Canadian era as a cultural genocide. For those Aboriginal people forced from their families and culture, the suffering continues into later life. Cote and Schissel (2002) explain that many residential school survivors turned to alcohol and/or drugs in an attempt to numb the pain they continued to carry with them. Cote and Schissel (2002) made a valid point in questioning whether a dominate society could ever fully grasp the great loss of their marginalized culture. While the history is tragic, it is important for

Note level 3 paragraph heading in boldface.

Note that the ampersand (&) is used in parentheses, but *and* is used when authors are referred to in the text.

my colleague and others to understand that this cannot be brushed off as insignificant. Life in residential schools will have affected some of her future clients in Stony Plain, Alberta. Regardless if it was a great-grandparent or parent, the consequences can remain present through addictions or present abuse (Cote & Schissel, 2002). To deny this as a current issue in a school setting would be to diminish cultural growth.

Past injustice potentially pushes for present cultural growth. This second point continues exploring historical traumas but with a greater focus on Aboriginal culture. It is only recently that many of the people who experienced residential schools are beginning to see a glimmer of justice. For example, Stephen Harper wrote a letter of apology on behalf of Canada (Arthur & Collins, 2010). Gone's (2009) study examined the therapeutic impact that healing lodges have on Aboriginal people who are dealing with historical suffering. Gone (2009) explains that in addition to the repeated torture that these children experienced, they were also forced to lose their Aboriginal cultural beliefs, including their language. In reaction to this cultural genocide (Arthur & Collins, 2010; Cote & Schissel, 2002), Gone (2009) notes that an Aboriginal Healing Foundation has been established in an attempt to restore Aboriginal cultural rights for current and future generations. By combining funding for therapeutic healing programs and developing ideal Aboriginal-focused projects, the foundation will be effective in advocating for those silenced for so many years (Gone, 2009). One healing technique found involved encouraging Aboriginal people affected by trauma to verbalize their personal pain (Gone, 2009). This is an important aspect for my colleague to infuse into her counselling initiative. She must

Note that multiple citations are divided by a semicolon.

be available to listen and acknowledge past hurts through understanding since, for some Aboriginals, this is an effective method in healing.

Counsellors must recognize the importance of healing. Gone (2009) pointed out that effective therapy for Aboriginal people is through healing rather than treatment. He noted that unlike the focus of treatments on well-being, healing encompasses reclaiming spiritual and cultural identification as well as sense of a purposeful existence. I believe that this variation of therapy is essential in any Aboriginal counselling setting, especially in a school. McCabe (2007) focused on the helpful factors of traditional Native healing. The study included Cree, Dakota, Ojibwa, and Métis people, so this study will be conducive for my colleague's work in a Cree population. These factors included personal readiness for healing, internalized self-actualization, lesson in daily life, challenge to personal change, empathy, acceptance and respect, leading as an example, genuineness, trust and safety, spiritual teachings, ceremonies and rituals, and most importantly the belief in the healing spirit.

Cree healers. Struthers (2000) researched the experiences of four Cree and Ojibwa healers, and while a healer's ability is a natural gift, multicultural counsellors can benefit greatly through understanding the traditional work. Struthers (2000) made note of the healers' ability to facilitate personal healing rather than produce healing effects on someone. While some of the themes are unique to a traditional Cree or Ojibwa healer, there a few themes that my colleague and other counsellors in an Aboriginal setting should take note of: placing faith in the ability to heal from suffering; having confidence and understanding of indigenous culture, values, and traditions;

being wholesome; recognizing that all things are interconnected; having balance within one's life; and embracing others (Struthers, 2000). The most important theme to embrace in a multicultural setting is understanding indigenous culture. Struthers (2000) found that through the infusion of cultural experience, healing is possible. On a personal note, my aunt is an Aboriginal medicine woman who through her internal connection with cultural traditions is able to explore and understand the earth as a healing agent. Essentially, for non-Aboriginal counsellors, it is the wholeness of healing rather than treatment that facilitates another's healing.

Stress can be experienced culturally. Kirmayer, Boothroyd, Tanner, Adelson, and Robinson (2000) found that psychological distress can be ignited by lack of a social network, pressures to conform, early loss, as well as little time spent in nature. These are aspects that are important to consider when addressing cultural stress. Adelson's (2000) article fits well with the discussion of Aboriginal cultural needs from a counselling standpoint. Social suffering is an apparent aspect of Aboriginal culture for the reasons mentioned previously. Adelson (2000) examined a Native gathering that takes place each summer in Quebec for the Cree population. The premise is that through cultural gatherings, Cree persons are able to focus on and grow in their cultural beliefs and values and as a community through this celebration of Aboriginal culture. In any Aboriginal community, the people would benefit greatly from an Aboriginal gathering, and this could be instituted into the high school in Stony Plains.

Acculturation is experienced uniquely. With regards to achieving personal healing, McCabe (2007) found that one of the greatest barriers

Aboriginal people face is conquering cultural disconnection. Arthur and Collins (2010) explained acculturation as the conjoining aspects of cultures that vary from one's own. Gone's (2008) article pointed out how cultural diversity in mental health can properly accommodate individuals. He explained that it is detrimental to only offer Western-European methods and traditions to Aboriginal people. That said, I agree that if there are choices available, people are more likely to advance in their acculturation rather than being pushed to assimilate. Thus, my colleague will be more helpful if she is able to integrate cultural options rather than pushing her own cultural values onto her student clients. Arthur and Collins (2010) explained that the client must be willing and ready to merge any culture beliefs they have as there will be various pressures from other people in their lives who are not experiencing acculturation at the same rate.

Aboriginals are often required to live in two worlds. Juntunen et al. (2001) studied the meaning of career development for First Nations people. These authors were interested in seeing how acculturation lends itself to this aspect of life. Being aware of career meanings is essential in a high school setting as my colleague will most likely work with students who are considering future goals and plans. Interestingly, Juntunen et al. (2001) found that success is rated on a more societal level rather than individual level. The authors explained that Aboriginal people are likely to feel successful when they are helping the greater community. An important aspect to point out to my colleague is that this study concluded that one of the greatest obstacles that First Nations people experience is the lack of support in exploring career options. Also,

Juntunen et al. (2001) found a common theme about Aboriginal culture and White culture being quite separate worlds. However, these findings varied between adults who found the two worlds to be completely separate, and a group of college students were able to utilize aspects from both worlds. My colleague can benefit from these findings as they determined that the younger generation is more open to acculturation. Through the encouragement of their own cultural identity, they will be more adaptable and confident in combining the two worlds rather than disregarding one or the other.

There is not one way to counsel all Aboriginal people. Sue et al. (1999) addressed the fact that multiculturalism is essential in social justice. Social justice is possible through equal opportunities for all people regardless of their culture. However, I must make note that this is not implying that there is a specific way to counsel any and all people, but rather, this is geared toward providing available resources while also maintaining that clients are having their individual needs met (Sue et al., 1999). As stated previously, culture includes multiple facets of one's life (Arthur & Collins, 2010). Within a school setting, there will be teenagers who are coping with many different cultural issues and/or situations in which they require assistance. Thus, an effective counsellor is one who can be readily available and flexible for the individual needs of any student. Being in an Aboriginal cultural setting requires some interest and knowledge of the cultural heritage in order to bring some empathy or understanding to the client (Smith et al., 2008). This is the most significant aspect of counselling in an Aboriginal setting. Counsellors should be aware of their use of culturally infused counselling for each individual's unique situation rather than getting caught up in providing uniform Aboriginal counselling.

Conclusion

Reconnecting the Facts

There are benefits to infusing culture into counselling. First Nations people were the first Canadians. As a counsellor myself, I realize that understanding different cultures can deepen any working alliance. Multicultural counselling focuses on listening and learning from one another, which is one of a counsellor's greatest strengths (Pedersen, 1990). We know that the client's expectations have great influence on the working alliance, and thus, if we are to ignore a key aspect of a person, such as their culture, it will be difficult to create an alliance (Corenblum & Stephan, 2001). As Smith et al.'s (2008) article shows, self-reflection about how cultural differences affect us will ensure a greater awareness for multiculturalism. Thus, infusing culture into the counselling will result in improved competence and understanding by the counsellor.

Aboriginal culture is alive and well. I will encourage my colleague to take a look at the variables that affect Aboriginal people: current problems stem from past traumas, past injustice demands present cultural growth, and healing has great importance. While stress can be experienced culturally, acculturation is experienced uniquely. Aboriginals are often required to live in two worlds, and consequently there is not one way to counsel all Aboriginal people.

> **References**

Adelson, N. (2000). Re-imaging aboriginality: An indigenous peoples' response to social suffering. *Transcultural Psychiatry, 37*(1), 11–34.

Arthur, N., & Collins, S. (2010). *Culture-infused counselling*. Calgary, AB: Counselling Concepts.

Bedi, R. P., Davis, M. D., & Williams, M. (2005). Critical incidents in the formation of the therapeutic alliance from the client's perspective. *Psychotherapy: Theory, Research, Practice, Training, 42*(3), 311–323. doi: 10.1037/0033-3204.42.3.311

Corenblum, B., & Stephan, W. G. (2001). White fears and native apprehensions: An integrated threat theory approach to intergroup attitudes. *Canadian Journal of Behavioural Science, 33*(4), 251–268. doi: 10.1037/h0087147

Cote, H., & Schissel, W. (2002). Damaged children and broken spirits: A residential school survivor's story. In B. Schissel & C. Brooks (Eds.), *Marginality and Condemnation: An Introduction to Critical Criminology* (pp. 175–192). Black Point, NS: Fernwood Publishing.

Day-Vines, N., Wood, S. M., Grothaus, T., Craigen, L., Holman, A., Dotson-Blake, K., & Douglass, M. J. (2007). Broaching the subjects of race, ethnicity, and culture during the counselling process. *Journal of Counseling and Development, 85*(4), 401–409.

Gone, J. P. (2008). "So I can be like a Whiteman": The cultural psychology of space and place in American Indian mental health. *Culture and Psychology, 13*(3), 369–399.

List all references included in the paper alphabetically. Start *References* on a new page. Double space.

Note that books and journal articles have capitals only to start and to signal a subtitle. Journal titles, on the other hand, are in headline style, with important words capitalized.

ABORIGINAL COUNSELLING COMPETENCY 14

Gone, J. P. (2009). A community-based treatment for Native American historical trauma: Prospects for evidence-based practice. *Journal of Consulting and Clinical Psychology, 77*(4), 751–762. doi: 10.1037/a0015390

Hadjistavropoulos, T. (2009). Canadian psychology in a global context. *Canadian Psychology, 50*(1), 1–7. doi: 10.1037/a0013398

Juntunen, C. L., Barraclough, D. J., Broneck, C. L., Seibel, G. A., Winrow, S. A., & Morin, P. M. (2001). American Indian perspectives on the career journey. *Journal of Counselling Psychology, 48*(3), 274–285.

Kirmayer, L. J., Boothroyd, L. J., Tanner, A., Adelson, N., & Robinson, E. (2000). Psychological distress among Cree of James Bay. *Transcultural Psychiatry, 37*(1), 35–56.

McCabe, G. H. (2007). The healing path: A culture and community-derived indigenous therapy model. *Psychotherapy: Theory, Research, Practice, Training, 44*(2), 148–160. doi: 10.1037/0033-3204.44.2.148

Pedersen, P. (1990). The constructs of complexity and balance in multicultural counselling theory and practice. *Journal of Counseling & Development, 68*(5), 550–554.

Shaw, L. R., McMahon, B. T., Chan, F., & Hannold, E. (2004). Enhancement of the working alliance: A training program to align counsellor and consumer expectations. *Journal of Vocational Rehabilitation, 20*, 107–125.

Use a digital object identifier (DOI) when you have located a source electronically.

Smith, L., Constantine, M. G., Graham, S. V., & Dize, C. B. (2008). The territory ahead for multicultural competence: The "spinning" of racism. *Professional Psychology: Research and Practice, 39*(3), 337–345. doi: 10.1037/0735-7028.39.3.337

Struthers, R. (2000). The lived experience of Ojibwa and Cree women healers. *Journal of Holistic Nursing, 18*, 261–279.

Sue, D. W., Bingham, R. P., Porche-Burke, L., & Vasquez, M. (1999). The diversification of psychology: A multicultural revolution. *American Psychologist, 54*(12), 1061–1069.

Italicize names of books and journals. Also italicize the volume number of journals.

Chicago Style of Documentation

7

Style comes only after long, hard practice and writing.

—William Styron

Chicago Style of Documentation

7

This chapter outlines the basic style guidelines published in *The Chicago Manual of Style*, 16th ed. (Chicago: University of Chicago Press, 2010) and concludes with sample pages that follow Chicago format and documentation style.

Chicago recommends two basic systems of documentation: (1) the author–date system and (2) the notes and bibliography system.

In Chicago style, the note will be formatted in one of two ways, depending on whether or not the paper includes a bibliography. Here is the key used to identify the type of example shown in the following sections:

SN = shortened note

FN = full note

B = bibliography entry

The *Chicago Manual of Style* website also provides information to subscribers on documentation style and format.

For examples of cited materials, follow the "Tools" link. The "Q & A" page allows you to submit questions, and the "Search the Manual" link allows you to find materials relevant to your questions.

(Lopez 2006, 60–61)

B   Lopez, Emilia C. 2006. "Targeting English Language Learners: Tasks and Treatments in Instructional Consultation." *Applied School Psychology* 22:59–79.

FN   1. D. Kern Holoman, *Writing about Music: A Style Sheet*, 2d ed. (Berkeley: University of California Press, 2008), 91–92.

FN   2. Bryan A. Garner, *The Elements of Legal Style*. 2d ed. (New York: Oxford University Press, 2002), 60.

AUTHOR–DATE SYSTEM

This system is recommended for writers in the physical, natural, and social sciences. Sources are given in brief in-text citations in parentheses, with full details supplied in a complete list of sources cited, usually called *References*. This system is recommended if all or most of the sources are easily convertible to author–date references. The author–date system follows the same principle as APA style with only minor differences. See Chapter 6 for detailed guidelines and examples.

NOTES AND BIBLIOGRAPHY SYSTEM

Also called "humanities style," this system is favoured by many writers in literature, history, and the arts. Notes (either endnotes or footnotes) are used instead of in-text citations. If the notes give full bibliographical information, the bibliography may be omitted.

With a Bibliography

All notes, including the first reference to a particular source, are shortened, giving the author's last name, a shortened version of the title, and the page number(s). Readers wanting additional information about the source will find it in the bibliography. Chicago recommends this practice since it minimizes duplication and is user-friendly and economical.

SN	1. Holoman. *Writing about Music,* 91–92.
SN	2. Garner, *The Elements of Legal Style,* 60.

Without a Bibliography

In a work without a full bibliography, the first citation of a particular source gives complete bibliographical information, and subsequent references to that source are shortened.

FN	3. Theodore M. Bernstein. *Miss Thistlebottom's Hobgoblins: The Careful Writer's Guide to the Taboos, Bugbears, and Outmoded Rules of English Usage.* (New York: Farrar, Straus and Giroux, 1971), 11–12.
FN	4. Bernstein, *Miss Thistlebottom,* 11–12.

It is preferable, however, to give complete details in the bibliography, in which case the notes may be shortened to avoid unnecessary duplication. Check with your instructor to determine which approach is preferred and whether to format notes as footnotes or endnotes.

Famine is an important anthropological issue: it is an expanding global crisis capable of being resolved through preventative measures.[1] More than 100 000 people have died in Africa in the last ten years alone due to famines. Famine has been present in the media for decades.[2]

---

[1] Stephen Devereux, "Why Does Famine Persist in Africa?" *Food Security* 1, no. 1 (2009): 25–35.

[2] Miriam S. Chaiken, J. Dixon, Colette Powers, and Erica Wetzler, "Asking the Right Questions: Community-Based Strategies to Combat Hunger." *National Association for the Practice of Anthropology Bulletin* 32, no. 1 (2009): 42–54.

Notes can appear either together at the end of your research paper, as **endnotes**, or at the foot of the page on which the citation appears, as **footnotes**. Use the footnote or endnote function of your word processor to create notes. Note numbers should be placed at the end of a sentence or at the end of a clause, indicating that the information in that sentence or clause is from another source. When readers wish to locate specific source information, they can do so by locating the note with the corresponding number.

IN A WORK WITH A BIBLIOGRAPHY 7-1A

B   Frow, John. *Marxism and Literary History.* Cambridge, MA: Harvard University Press, 1986.

SN   1. Frow, *Marxism*, 7.

Complete information about the source is given in the bibliography. (For guidelines on formatting bibliography entries, see 7-3.)

Note that citations (even the first citation of a work) are shortened to avoid duplication of information given in the bibliography entry. Shortened notes typically include the author's last name, a condensed version of the title, and the page number.

The first note gives complete bibliographical information.

Subsequent notes can be shortened.

If a work cited is identical in two successive notes, the abbreviation *ibid.* (from *ibidem*, "in the same place") may be used in place of the author/editor name, the title, and other identical information.

FN   1. John Frow, *Marxism and Literary History* (Cambridge, MA: Harvard University Press, 1986), 7.

SN   7. Frow, *Marxism*, 156.

9. Frow, *Marxism*, 112–13.

10. Ibid.

11. Ibid., 132.

QUICK TIP

For guidelines on formatting full notes, see 7-3.

7-2   BIBLIOGRAPHY

Although not always necessary provided that full bibliographic details are given in notes, an alphabetical bibliography is a convenience for the reader since it provides an overview of all sources and an easy reference to individual sources cited.

A bibliography is placed at the end of the paper and should list any sources you have cited in your notes. Some bibliographies also include entries for works consulted but not cited. Check with your instructor to determine if a bibliography is required and which sources should be included.

QUICK TIP

For guidelines on formatting a bibliography, see 7-3. A sample bibliography is also included in 7-5.

The following key identifies the elements of the example shown:

SN = shortened note

FN = full note

B = bibliographical entry

Entries in the following pages provide model notes and bibliographic entries for most of the types of resources you will use in your research.

BOOKS 7-3A

ONE AUTHOR

SN 1. Roberts, *Empire of the Soul*, 85.

FN 1. Paul William Roberts, *Empire of the Soul: Some Journeys in India* (Toronto: Stoddart, 1994), 85.

B Roberts, Paul William. *Empire of the Soul: Some Journeys in India.* Toronto: Stoddart, 1994.

TWO OR THREE AUTHORS
Note that in the bibliographic entry only the name of the first author is reversed and a comma precedes the *and*. Do not use an ampersand.

SN 2. Johnson and Blair, *Logical Self-Defence*, 17.

FN 2. Ralph H. Johnson and J. Anthony Blair, *Logical Self-Defence*, 2nd ed. (Toronto: McGraw-Hill Ryerson, 1983), 17.

B Johnson, Ralph H., and J. Anthony Blair. *Logical Self-Defence*, 2nd ed. Toronto: McGraw-Hill Ryerson, 1983.

FOUR OR MORE AUTHORS

This work has seven authors. Chicago recommends that all authors are listed in the bibliography.

SN   3. Newman et al., *Echoes from the Past*, 168.

FN   3. Garfield Newman et al., *Echoes from the Past: World History to the Sixteenth Century* (Toronto: McGraw-Hill Ryerson, 2001), 168.

B   Newman, Garfield, Elizabeth Graham, Osman Y. Mohamed, Gerry Schaus, Narinder Wagle, Rick Guisso, and David Pendergast. *Echoes from the Past: World History to the Sixteenth Century.* Toronto: McGraw-Hill Ryerson, 2001.

EDITED WORK WITHOUT AN AUTHOR

Note that the abbreviation *ed.* or *eds.* is omitted in shortened notes.

SN   5. Lamb and Arnold, *Reading*, 29.

FN   5. Pose Lamb and Richard Arnold, eds., *Reading: Foundations and Instructional Strategies* (Belmont, CA: Wadsworth, 1976), 29.

B   Lamb, Pose, and Richard Arnold, eds. *Reading: Foundations and Instructional Strategies.* Belmont, CA: Wadsworth, 1976.

EDITED WORK WITH AN AUTHOR

Note that *Edited by* is spelled out in a bibliography but abbreviated in notes.

SN   6. Mill, *On Liberty*, 45–46.

FN   6. John Stuart Mill, *On Liberty*, ed. Currin V. Shields (New York: Macmillan, 1956), 45–46.

B   Mill, John Stuart. *On Liberty*. Edited by Currin V. Shields. New York: Macmillan, 1956.

SN	7. Sartre, *Iron in the Soul*, 58.
FN	7. Jean-Paul Sartre, *Iron in the Soul*, trans. Gerard Hopkins (Harmondsworth, UK: Penguin Books, 1978), 58.
B	Sartre, Jean-Paul. *Iron in the Soul*. Translated by Gerard Hopkins. Harmondsworth, UK: Penguin Books, 1978.

TRANSLATED WORK

Note that *Translated by* is spelled out in a bibliography but abbreviated in notes.

SN	8. Abrams, *Norton Anthology*, 117–48.
FN	8. M. H. Abrams, ed., *The Norton Anthology of English Literature*, 5th ed. (New York: W. W. Norton, 1987), 117–48.
B	Abrams, M. H., ed. *The Norton Anthology of English Literature*. 5th ed. New York: W. W. Norton, 1987.

EDITIONS OTHER THAN THE FIRST

SN	10. Kallen, *The 1400s*, 50–55.
FN	10. Stuart A. Kallen, ed., *The 1400s*. (San Diego, CA: Greenhaven Press, 2001), 5:50–55.
B	Kallen, Stuart A., ed. *The 1400s*. Vol. 5, *Headlines in History*. San Diego, CA: Greenhaven Press, 2001.
FN	10. Stuart A. Kallen, ed., *The 1400s*, vol. 5, *Headlines in History* (San Diego, CA: Greenhaven Press, 2001), 50–55.

PARTICULAR VOLUME IN A MULTI-VOLUME WORK

The full note shown above indicates that all volumes of the Kallen work appeared in 2001. If only volume 5 had been published in 2001, the note would be formatted as shown here.

WORK IN AN ANTHOLOGY

SN   11. Morrison, "The Site of Memory," 185–206.

FN   11. Toni Morrison, "The Site of Memory," in *Inventing the Truth: The Art and Craft of Memoir*, ed. William Zinsser (Boston: Houghton Mifflin, 1998), 185–206.

B   Morrison, Toni. "The Site of Memory." In *Inventing the Truth: The Art and Craft of Memoir*, edited by William Zinsser, 185–206. Boston: Houghton Mifflin, 1998.

WORK IN A SERIES

SN   12. Lecker, David, and Quigley, *Bissoondath*, 29.

FN   12. Robert Lecker, Jack David, and Ellen Quigley, *Bissoondath, Clarke, Kogawa, Mistry, Skvorecky*: Canadian Writers and Their Works 11 (Toronto: ECW Press, 1996), 29.

B   Lecker, Robert, Jack David, and Ellen Quigley. *Bissoondath, Clarke, Kogawa, Mistry, Skvorecky*. Canadian Writers and Their Works, vol. 11. Toronto: ECW Press, 1996.

DICTIONARY OR ENCYCLOPEDIA

Well-known reference books are normally cited in notes rather than in bibliographies, with the facts of publication often omitted, but with the edition specified. Certain reference works, however, may be listed with publication details, as shown here. For an alphabetically arranged work, cite the item preceded by *s.v.* (for the

SN   13. *Nelson Canadian Dictionary*, s.v. "saltire."

FN   13. *Nelson Canadian Dictionary of the English Language* (Toronto: ITP Nelson, 1999), s.v. "saltire."

B   *Nelson Canadian Dictionary of the English Language*. Toronto: ITP Nelson, 1998.

FN   14. *Wikipedia*, s.v. "Michael J. Fox," accessed July 13, 2011, http://en.wikipedia.org/wiki/Michael_J._Fox

Note that encyclopedias and dictionaries do not normally appear in bibliographies.

Latin *sub verbo*, which means "under the word"). Note that online dictionaries or encylopedias contain the same elements. If there is no posting date, give the date of your access. Use a shortened, more stable version of the URL if it is offered, unless there is a DOI (digital object identifier) given for a particular article. Note that dictionaries and encyclopedias, if well known, do not typically appear in bibliographies, only in notes.

PERIODICALS   7-3B

Most journal citations include both volume and issue numbers, although the issue number may be omitted if pagination is continuous throughout a volume or when a month or season precedes the year.

In these entries, note that, while specific page references are given in the notes, inclusive pages for the article are given in the bibliographic entries.

ARTICLE IN A JOURNAL

SN   15. Beattie, "Real Place," 11.

FN   15. Ann Beattie, "Real Place, Imagined Life," *Literary Imagination: The Review of the Association of Literary Scholars and Critics* 4, no. 1 (2002): 11.

B   Beattie, Ann. "Real Place, Imagined Life." *Literary Imagination: The Review of the Association of Literary Scholars and Critics* 4, no. 1 (2002): 10–16.

ARTICLE IN A MAGAZINE

SN	16. Lazare, "False Testament," 40.
FN	16. Daniel Lazare, "False Testament: Archeology Refutes the Bible Claim to History," *Harper's*, March 2002, 40.
B	Lazare, Daniel. "False Testament: Archeology Refutes the Bible Claim to History." *Harper's*, March 2002, 39–47.

ARTICLE IN A NEWSPAPER

SN	17. Reynolds, "UN to Add 'Nazi' Stamp," A2.
FN	17. Matt Reynolds, "UN to Add 'Nazi' Stamp to Auschwitz Camp Site," *Toronto Star*, July 13, 2006, A2.
B	Reynolds, Matt. "UN to Add 'Nazi' Stamp to Auschwitz Camp Site." *Toronto Star*, July 13, 2006, A2.

An initial *The* is omitted from a newspaper name. Except for well-known national papers, if the city is not part of the name, it should be added in italics, along with the abbreviated form for the province in parentheses if necessary. For example, *National Post* needs no clarification, but *Daily Gleaner* becomes *Fredericton (NB) Daily Gleaner.*

For unsigned articles, the name of the newspaper stands in place of the author.

7-3C ELECTRONIC SOURCES

ONLINE BOOK

Many of the rules for citing print sources apply to electronic sources, so it is important to indicate the medium from which the source was retrieved. A URL is added to the citation to indicate that a source was

SN	18. Jameson, The History of Historical Writing.
FN	18. John Franklin Jameson, *The History of Historical Writing in America* (Boston: Houghton Mifflin, 1891; Electronic Library of Historiography, 1996), accessed July 17, 2010, http://www.eliohs.unifi.it/testi/800/ jameson/jameson.html.

> **B** Jameson, John Franklin. *The History of Historical Writing in America*. Boston: Houghton Mifflin, 1891; Electronic Library of Historiography, 1996. Accessed July 17, 2010. http://www.eliohs.unifi.it/testi/800/jameson/jameson.html.

Wherever possible, include the original facts of publication when citing electronic editions of older works, as in the preceding example. Note that the date of access is included before the URL or DOI. Note that you should cite only the version you used if the text appears in both print and online formats. A date of access is not required unless your instructor asks for one.

retrieved from the Internet. If the material is time-sensitive or if the discipline demands it, the retrieval date should immediately precede the URL or DOI.

If a URL has to be broken at the end of a line, do not add a hyphen to denote a line break and do not break a line after a hyphen that is part of the URL. The line break should occur *after* a slash or double slash or *after* a period, comma, hyphen, tilde (~), or underscore.

ONLINE JOURNAL

> **SN** 19. Robson and Turner, "Teaching Is a Co-learning Experience," 41.
>
> **FN** 19. Sue Robson and YvonneTurner, "Teaching Is a Co-learning Experience: Academics Reflecting on Learning and Teaching in an Internationalized Faculty," *Teaching in Higher Education* 12, no. 1 (2010): 50, doi: 10.1080/13562510601102115.
>
> **B** Robson, Sue, and Yvonne Turner. "Teaching Is a Co-learning Experience: Academics Reflecting on Learning and Teaching in an Internationalized Faculty." *Teaching in Higher Education* 12, no. 1 (2010): 41–54, doi: 10.1080/13562510601102115.

Use the DOI if it is available. If not, use the URL. You may also wish to include the date of access in that case, if your instructor requires it.

SN	20. Green, "Poisoned Ears," para. 23.
FN	20. Reina Green. "Poisoned Ears and Parental Advice in *Hamlet*," *Early Modern Literary Studies* 11, no. 3 (2006), para. 23, accessed July 17, 2006, http://www.shu.ac.uk/emls/11-3/greeham2.htm.
B	Green, Reina. "Poisoned Ears and Parental Advice in *Hamlet*." *Early Modern Literary Studies* 11, no. 3 (2006). Accessed May 19, 2010. http://www.shu.ac.uk/emls/11-3/greeham2.htm.

Note the descriptive locator, *para. 23,* in the shortened and full notes above, directing readers to a specific location in the article. If the page range were available, it would be included in the bibliography.

WEBSITE

SN	21. Giblin, "Introduction: Diffusion and Other Problems."
FN	21. James Giblin, "Introduction: Diffusion and Other Problems in the History of African States," *Arts and Life in Africa Online*, accessed March 15, 2006, http://www.uiowa.edu/~africart/toc/history/giblistat.html. (site discontinued)
B	Giblin, James. "Introduction: Diffusion and Other Problems in the History of African States." *Arts and Life in Africa Online.* Accessed March 15, 2006. http://www.uiowa.edu/~africart/toc/history/giblistat.html.

If a site ceases to exist, as in the above example, state this information in the text or in a note.

In Text

In an email on July 17, 2011, Damian Collom indicated his displeasure with the new strategic plan.

In a Note

N   22. Damian Collom, email message to author, July 17, 2011.

Personal communications are rarely listed in a bibliography. Be aware, too, that a personal email address may be cited only with the permission of its owner.

N   23. Molly Millar to The Design Café mailing list, July 17, 2011, http://lists.graphic-design.net/mailman/listinfo/cafe.

SN   24. Lagapa, "Something from Nothing," 54.

FN   24. Jason Lagapa, "Something from Nothing: Disontological Poetics of Leslie Scalapino," *Contemporary Literature* 47, no. 1 (Spring 2006): 54, accessed July 18, 2010, http://muse.jhu.edu.ezproxy.library.yorku .ca/journals/.

B   Lagapa, Jason. "Something from Nothing: Disontological Poetics of Leslie Scalapino." *Contemporary Literature* 47, no. 1 (Spring 2006): 30–61. Accessed July 18, 2010. http://muse.jhu.edu.ezproxy.library.yorku.ca/journals/.

EMAIL MESSAGE

References to personal communications such as email messages, letters, and conversations are usually run into the text or given in a brief note.

ELECTRONIC MAILING LIST

Citations to mailing lists are generally limited to text and notes.

DATABASE

GOVERNMENT DOCUMENT

Follow these general guidelines for the order of citation elements when citing government documents:

1. division of government issuing the document
2. legislative body, department, court, committee, and so forth
3. subsidiary divisions, regional offices, and so forth
4. document title
5. author or editor (if given)
6. report number or other identifying information
7. publisher, if different from the issuing body
8. date
9. page (if relevant)

The order of these items may vary to suit the subject matter. If the government body issuing the document is not obvious from the context, begin the citation with *Canada*, followed by the provincial or territorial legislature.

SN   25. Treasury Board of Canada, *Canada's Performance*, 8.

FN   25. Treasury Board of Canada, *Canada's Performance: The Government of Canada's Contribution*, 2005, 8.

B   Treasury Board of Canada. *Canada's Performance: The Government of Canada's Contribution*. 2005.

Zhong Chen/Shutterstock.com

SN	26. Warbey, "The Acquisition of Modal Notions," 90.
FN	26. Margaretta Warbey, "The Acquisition of Modal Notions by Advanced-Level Adult English as a Second Language Learners" (PhD diss., University of Victoria, 1986), 90.
B	Warbey, Margaretta. "The Acquisition of Modal Notions by Advanced-Level Adult English as a Second Language Learners." PhD diss., University of Victoria, 1986.

UNPUBLISHED DISSERTATION

PERSONAL COMMUNICATION
See "Email Message" under "Electronic Sources."

INTERVIEW

SN	27. Diski, interview.
FN	27. Jenny Diski, interview by Eleanor Wachtel, *Writers & Company*, CBC Radio, July 23, 2006.
B	Diski, Jenny. Interview by Eleanor Wachtel. *Writers & Company*. CBC Radio. July 23, 2006.

SOUND RECORDING

SN	28. Gould, *The Goldberg Variations*.
LN	28. Glenn Gould, *The Goldberg Variations*, by Johann Sebastian Bach, Sony Music SMK 52594, compact disc.
B	Gould, Glenn. *The Goldberg Variations*, by Johann Sebastian Bach. Sony Music SMK 53594, compact disc.

DVD

SN   29. Young, "When God Made Me."

LN   29. Neil Young, "When God Made Me," *Neil Young: Heart of Gold*, directed by Jonathan Demme (Hollywood, CA: Paramount, 2005), DVD.

B   Young, Neil. "When God Made Me." *Neil Young: Heart of Gold*. Directed by Jonathan Demme. Hollywood, CA: Paramount, 2005, DVD.

7-4) MANUSCRIPT FORMAT AND TYPEFACE

Use letter-size (22 × 28 cm, 8.5 × 11 in.), good-quality white paper. Type or print on only one side of the paper.

Use the same typeface throughout and avoid sans serif fonts, since these do not clearly distinguish between 1, *l*, and *I* (Arabic numeral one, lowercase letter *L*, and Roman numeral one/capital *I*).

SANS SERIF   SERIF

CREATING A BIBLIOGRAPHY PAGE IN CHICAGO STYLE

PLACEMENT

The bibliography is placed at the end of the paper.

INDENTATION

Use a hanging indent, with the first line of the entry flush left and subsequent lines indented.

AUTHOR NAME

Invert names to put the surname first. For multiple authors, only the first name is inverted.

ARRANGEMENT OF ENTRIES

All sources are arranged alphabetically by the last name of the author or editor.

If a source has no author or editor, alphabetize by the first main word of the title. Do not consider articles—*A, An,* or *The*—when alphabetizing.

A single-author entry precedes a multi-author entry beginning with the same name.

For successive entries by the same author, a 3-em dash (———) followed by a period replaces the name after the first appearance.

PUBLICATION INFORMATION

Do not place publication information within parentheses.

PAGE NUMBERS

Give inclusive page numbers for an article or specific chapter. Otherwise, do not provide page numbers in the bibliography.

QUICK TIP

For an example of a correctly formatted bibliography, see page 288 in 7-5.

In this sample, you will find these model elements of a Chicago-style research paper:

- title page
- text pages
- notes page
- bibliography page

A page number is not placed on the title page. However, this page is counted as the first page of the paper.

The title page should include the full title of the paper, your name, the course name, the instructor's name, and the date the paper was submitted.

Note that title pages of student papers are not specifically addressed in *The Chicago Manual of Style*. Follow the requirements established by your instructor.

The Digital Revolution and the Decentralized World

Dustin Manley

Communication Studies 1A03

Professor Faiza Hirji

March 23, 2010

© Dustin Manley

The majority of the world is in the midst of a digital revolution. Communities are becoming more and more personally detached on a micro scale while the world is continuing to grow much more interconnected and smaller on a macro level. The technology created to build culture within a society is now being used to dominate through cultural imperialism, a problem Canada faces with the United States. A contemporary exception to this, however, can be found in the North, where micro communities are growing closer and more centralized due to the digital revolution. It can be argued that the world has been on this path since the domination of vernacular forms of communication by more complex systems of writing.

The Industrial/capitalist Revolution of the 18th and 19th centuries aided in the facilitation and refinement of complex communication systems within society. Machines, as Marshall McLuhan contends, were being created as extensions of human limbs to increase ease and efficiency of labour/capitalism. Radio, telegraph, television, and eventually the computer can be seen as refined extensions of vernacular communication, allowing extraordinary ease in keeping people and societies in contact with one another, albeit in an isolated manner.

In "Minerva's Owl" Harold Innis surveys the deterministic role of technology in history from the discovery of writing by the Sumerians and Egyptians to the printing press and the Industrial Revolution. Innis describes vernacular traditions as being bound to "primitive," or rather less-developed cultures, implying some xenophobia toward those vernacular societies that keep within themselves rather than spread across territories as literate societies do. Aboriginal societies in the North, however, who continue to maintain

The page number appears in the upper right-hand corner. You may include your last name there, as well, as part of the header.

Use margins of at least 2.5 cm (1 in.) on all four sides of the page. Double space the entire text, including notes and bibliography. Leave one space after periods and colons. Text should be flush left and ragged right. Do not use full justification. Indent the first line of a paragraph. Indent block quotations (100 words or 8 lines or more) and leave extra space above and below them.

vernacular traditions in the 20th and 21st centuries, are not necessarily "primitive" and "xenophobic" cultures as Innis describes.[1] The harsh geographical conditions of the North make it difficult for technological and physical communication with the rest of Canada. In fact there are no stoplights and only one paved road in the whole territory of Nunavut, which occupies one-fifth of Canada's total landmass.[2] Recently technology has made its way to the North through the Internet, broadcasting, and machinery, which the Aboriginal societies combine with their vernacular and cultural traditions. For example, "many Inuit hunters still travel along the ancient dog sled routes while out hunting on their skidoos, an interesting combination of old traditions and new technology,"[3] adopted from the more developed provinces of Canada.

One of Innis' primary points is that the systems of knowledge that any civilization develop are not created out of a vacuum: they are built upon those that precede them. There always has to be a pre-existing medium or technology that is built upon to create new technology. Both Innis and McLuhan contend that there is a dialectical relationship between society and technology in that they have mutual influence. Similarly, the tools of "clay, the stylus and cuneiform script from the beginnings of civilization"[4] were appropriated and refined upon by other cultures throughout time until these mediums of communication became the printing press, radio and television and "thereafter.... shape us."[5] Marshall McLuhan gives an interesting aphorism for the detachment that visual and literary media give to society: "People don't actually read newspapers—they get into them every morning like a hot bath."[6]

Following Innis' deterministic view of technology, as well as McLuhan's view of the "Global Village," the telegraph, a prototype of telecommunications,

---

Note numbers indicate an acknowledgement of a source. The number corresponds to the entries in the Notes section of the paper. Notes may also be placed at the bottom of each page.

represents a key advance in people's ability, as Karl Marx describes, to "shrink space through time" with technology.[7] The telegraph eventually led to the creation of the telephone and radio, which today we view as the primary tools for personal communication, but should be seen first and foremost as business tools. The Canadian government saw radio as an opportunity for nation building, and sought to connect the nation via radio, just as the Canadian Pacific Railway physically connected the nation in 1887.[8] The Canadian Radio Broadcasting Commission (CRBC) was established as Canada's first national broadcaster in 1932, succeeded by the Canadian Broadcasting Corporation (CBC) in 1936.[9]

The Prime Minister at the time, Richard Bennett, stressed the importance of the publicly owned and operated CRBC: "This country must be assured of complete Canadian control of broadcasting from Canadian sources. Without such control, broadcasting can never be the agency by which national consciousness may be fostered and sustained and national unity still further strengthened."[10]

Though the CRBC, later the crown-owned CBC, brought Canadians together nationwide, the United States also had its own selection of radio programs that Canadians were able to listen to. Due to economies of scale it was, and remains, cheaper and more profitable for Canadian distributors of media markets to sell "American books, magazines, TV shows, and films than those made specifically for the Canadian market"[11] and radio programming is no different. American content began to dominate Canadian airwaves, threatening Canadian culture with cultural imperialism. The legislature of the 1932 Broadcasting Act stressed the importance of the preservation and growth

> The *Chicago Manual of Style* does not give guidelines specifically for student papers. Check with your instructor to determine the preferred page numbering system.

of Canadian culture and was responsible for regulating and controlling the amount of content broadcast in Canada within privately owned radio broadcast stations. Currently the Canadian content quota dictated by the CRTC's Music, Artist, Performance and Lyric (MAPL) points system for radio is 35% (raised from 30% in 1998) for English-language popular music stations and 55% (raised from 50% in 1998) for French-language popular music stations.[12] Radio stations are, however, able to exploit loopholes by relegating Canadian content to low-audience hours.

Television, like radio, was and is also used by the Canadian government to promote and build national community. Marshall McLuhan contended that television, a multi-modal binding of sensory and auditory process, was a more effective community builder than radio. Television as a "cool" medium puts an individual "into in-depth involvement with the screen and acting out a constant creative dialog with the iconoscope"[13] unlike the more passive "hot" medium of radio where a detached voice speaks to you from a box. Like radio, Canadian television programming is threatened, particularly by American cultural imperialism as well as by the increase of narrowcasting to niche audiences. Canada's own broadcasting channel via the CBC was established in 1951 and the Canadian Radio-television and Telecommunications Commission was created in 1968 in order to regulate the amount of American television that floods the nation.[14]

The unifying effect of Canada's broadcast systems became more and more fragmented by the amount of choice the audience had with American and foreign content, and narrowcasting to specific audiences. In the early stages of broadcast there was little selection, and families and communities would gather together and listen to weekly radio broadcasts or watch a television broadcast in the living room. Television began to broadcast to narrower and more specific audiences over the years: In 1962 Toronto was the trial site for closed-circuit pay-TV; in 1982 the CRTC licenced Canada's first pay-TV services; and in 1999 Web-TV service began.[15] Radio followed suit with the ability of Canadians to receive from the United States with satellite/subscription radio. The media began catering to the choice of individuals, and the once communal activities of watching television with the family or listening to radio broadcasts increasingly became solo activities.

The digital revolution of the Internet has turned virtually every form of media that was intended to be used for nation and community building into an individual activity, accessible at an individual's fingertips from the majority of the developed world. All media have been refined and conflated by the computer. This continual repackaging and refinement of media is Horkheimer and Adorno's term of cultural industry[16] in practice.

Music has gone from being appreciated only by attending a live performance, to being captured on a record, to being broadcast on the radio, to being in an individual's pocket along with 10,000 other songs on an iPod, allowing an individual to turn any public space private with a pair of headphones. Films went from being available to be viewed only in nickelodeons and cinemas, to being broadcast on television, to being purchased via VHS or DVD, to being downloaded free within minutes and viewed upon personal computing devices whenever desired. The printing press has gone from physical newspapers to online publications able to be read anywhere at any time worldwide. Media of encounter like telephones are enabling people to encounter each other even less: personal cellular phones have replaced household landlines, thus allowing people to send pictures, videos, and text messages instead of communicating verbally.

Computers are massive media of both encounter and administration. Emails and instant messaging are replacing physical mail, and since 2007, the use of Skype makes voice messaging available for no charge beyond Internet access.[17] Apple iPhones allow people to listen to music, surf the Internet, check mail, and watch television from virtually anywhere at any time. In the post-Fordist economy, businesses are able to administer their companies much more quickly, efficiently, and interpersonally via email and video monitoring, holding video conferences rather than having to travel. The 8-hour workday is a concept of the past now that people are able to continue their work at home by being constantly connected to their jobs through Blackberries and email.

Though the digital revolution gives us access to the media that allow us to interact with people from all over the world at any time, in a substantivist view, it seems that in this era we are more isolated and detached than ever before. As Gary Farmer wrote: "Seventy-five years ago, we were all we had except for Saturday night radio. A hundred and fifty years ago, we were all we had. We must have been a hell of a lot more fascinating. We had to have been great storytellers. We certainly had a lot of time for each other.... No TV to keep us amused, or e-mail love to find a relationship."[18]

Harold Innis and Marshal McLuhan both believe that the transition from traditional oral societies to the literary led to the information-based, capitalist society we live in today. In an oral cultural "the primary medium of communication was speech, and thus no man knew appreciably more or less than any other—which meant that there was little individualism and specialization, the hallmarks of "civilized" Western man."[19] Innis and McLuhan both contend that the phonetic alphabet served to numb the freshness, elasticity, and spontaneity of culture. Literacy focuses upon the visual sense, and it is this sense alone that detaches us, and leaves us spectators of the world we live in; "all other senses involve us but the detachment bred by literacy disinvolves and detribalizes man."[20] The oral tribal culture endured until the invention of the printing press in the 16th century that "hit ... like a 100-megaton H-bomb,"[21] with print ensuring the primacy of visual bias and vastly extending phonetic literacy across the developed, developing, and colonized world.

The Inuit communities in Canada's northern regions, predominately in Yukon, Nunavut, and Northwest Territories, are an oral tribal culture whose community has been brought closer together by the digital revolution: "Inuit are nomads—There is nothing that frustrates Inuit more than being made to remain in one spot.... It is no wonder that Inuit treasure the Internet, for if they cannot bodily leave their communities, at least their minds can wander at will.... [They] rejoice in the ability to compare opinions abroad, as they did when travelling at will. For the hamlet is the new igloo, and the Internet is the new land."[22]

Canadian actor and author Gary Farmer, a member of the Cayuga nation and Wolf Clan, warns the Aboriginal communities about the detachment that the Internet and technology bring as the Inuit in Northern and remote communities embrace the peer-to-peer system of the Internet and telecommunications, stating, "The road to Nunavut is along the information highway."[23] The Television Northern Canada (TVNC)—a $10 million, federally funded satellite transponder service—became the primary First Nations broadcasting distribution service in the North on June 18, 1991.[24] The TVNC brought together over ninety-four Aboriginal communities, from the Alaska–Yukon border to the Labrador coast "broadcasting cultural, social, political and educational programming to Canada's Native people."[25]

The "small-town" qualities of Northern Canada continue into the digital age, and in many ways, the "Internet and satellite technology have picked up where town meetings left off. In some cases, they have *become* the town meetings." [26] The Internet and other forms of telecommunication enable people to convene when weather, distances, and budgets would prohibit travel and help bring Aboriginal people to each other and the rest of Canada. The new telecommunication systems help to "mainstream" marginalized media ... a chance for Aboriginal people to 'send the information the other way.'"[27] The risks of losing Inuit culture and sense of heritage because of the predominantly English Internet is acknowledged, and the Northwest Territories Community Access Program (CAP) was established in order to aid Aboriginal communities in developing their own websites for preservation and presentation of their culture, and to teach uses of the Internet to the people in the North.[28] For the Inuit, technology is used instrumentally—it is neither inherently good nor bad, but depends upon how it is used.

Technology and the media have changed the world; however, as technological determinists Harold Innis and Marshall McLuhan argue, society has been on this path since the discovery of the phonetic alphabet and the adoption of the literary over vernacular forms of communication. The entire world is currently greatly interconnected, yet at the same time its inhabitants are growing more and more detached. A pocket-sized device allows someone to communicate with almost anyone from anywhere in the world, to read any global news article, to listen to any form of music, or to use it in a myriad of other ways—so why go to a friend's house when you can text him, or why meet with your colleagues at the office to work on a project when it can be done online? For communities like the Inuit in Canada's North, technology is used instrumentally as a tool to better their difficult way of life. One wonders how long it will be before they become as reliant upon technology as the rest of Canada and the developed world, and if they will lose their unique sense of tribal culture in the process.

Notes

1. Harold A. Innis, "Minerva's Owl," in *Introduction to Communication*, 2nd ed., edited by Alexandre Sévigny (Dubuque, IA: Kendall-Hunt Publishing, 2010), 1.

2. Minister of Indian Affairs and Northern Development, "Travel in the Northwest Territories and Nunavut," *Affaires Indiennes et Du Nord Canada/Indian and Northern Affairs Canada*, accessed March 3, 2010, http://www.ainc-inac.gc.ca/ach/lr/ks/cr/pubs/trav-eng.asp.

3. Ibid.

4. Innis, "Minerva's Owl," 1.

5. Rowland Lorimer, Mike Gasher, and David Skinner, *Mass Communication in Canada* (Don Mills, ON: Oxford University Press), 2008.

6. Eric McLuhan and Frank Zingrone, eds., "Playboy Interview with Marshall McLuhan," in *Introduction to Communication,* edited by Alexandre Sévigny (Dubuque, IA: Kendall-Hunt Publishing, 2010), 17.

7. Karl Marx, *The Grundrisse* (New York: Harper & Row, 1972).

8. Lorimer, Gasher, and Skinner, *Mass Communication in Canada*, 69.

9. Ibid., 67.

10. Ibid.

11. Ibid., 68.

12. Ibid., 175–176.

13. McLuhan and Zingrone, "Playboy Interview with Marshall McLuhan," 25.

14. Lorimer, Gasher, and Skinner, *Mass Communication in Canada*, 156.

15. Ibid., 159.

16. Andrew Edgar, *Cultural Theory: The Key Concepts* (London: Routledge, 2006), 103.

17. Lorimer, Gasher, and Skinner, *Mass Communication in Canada*, 6.

18. Valerie Alia, *Uncovering the North* (Vancouver: UBC Press, 1999), accessed February 11, 2010. http://site.ebrary.com.libaccess.lib.mcmaster.ca/lib/oculmcmaster/docDetail.action?docID=10210495, 133.

19. McLuhan and Zingrone, "Playboy Interview with Marshall McLuhan," 22.

20. Ibid., 22.

21. Ibid., 23.

22. Alia, *Uncovering the North,* 142.

23. Ibid., 133.

24. Ibid., 136

25. Ibid.

26. Ibid., 142.

27. Ibid., 142–144.

28. Ibid., 144.

Centre the title
Bibliography and
place it 2.5 cm
(1 in.) from the top
of the page.

The first line of an
entry in the bibliog-
raphy is flush with
the left margin.
Indent subsequent
lines 1.25 cm
(0.5 in.).

Bibliography

Alia, Valerie. *Uncovering the North*. Vancouver: UBC Press, 1999. Accessed
     February 11, 2011. http://site.ebrary.com.libaccess.lib.mcmaster.ca/lib/
     oculmcmaster/docDetail.action?docID=10210495.

Edgar, Andrew. *Cultural Theory: The Key Concepts*. London: Routledge, 2006.

Innis, Harold A. "Minerva's Owl." In *Introduction to Communication*. 2nd ed.
     Edited by Alexandre Sévigny, 1–16. Dubuque, IA: Kendall-Hunt Publishing,
     2010.

Jackson, John D., and Paul Millen. "English-Language Radio Drama: A Com-
     parison of Central and Regional Production Units." *Canadian Journal
     of Communication*, 15, no. 1. (1990): 1–18. Accessed February 4, 2010.
     http://www.cjconline.ca/index.php/journal/issue/view/55/showToc.

Lorimer, Rowland, Mike Gasher, and David Skinner. *Mass Communication in
     Canada*. Don Mills, ON: Oxford University Press, 2008.

Marx, Karl. *The Grundrisse*. New York: Harper & Row, 1972.

McLuhan, Eric, and Frank Zingrone, eds. "Playboy Interview with Marshall
     McLuhan." In *Introduction to Communication*. Edited by Alexandre
     Sévigny, 17–41. Dubuque, IA: Kendall-Hunt Publishing, 2010.

Minister of Indian Affairs and Northern Development. "Travel in the North-
     west Territories and Nunavut." *Affaires Indiennes et Du Nord Canada/
     Indian and Northern Affairs Canada*. Accessed March 3, 2011. http://www.
     ainc-inac.gc.ca/ach/lr/ks/cr/pubs/trav-eng.asp.

PUBLICATION IS THE
AUCTION OF THE
MIND
OF MAN.
–EMILY DICKINSON

Online Style

CSE Style and Columbia Online Style

The Council of Science Editors (CSE) is the recognized authority on documentation style in all areas of science and related fields. Documentation guidelines presented in *Scientific Style and Format: The CSE Manual for Authors, Editors, and Publishers* (7th ed., 2006) are outlined in 8-1.

Columbia Online Style (COS) has variations for humanities and scientific disciplines and can be useful for citing electronic sources no matter which specific style of documentation you are required to use. Documentation guidelines presented in *The Columbia Guide to Online Style* (2nd ed., 2006) are outlined in 8-2.

8-1A DOCUMENTATION STYLES

The CSE Manual outlines three styles of documentation: name–year, citation–sequence, and citation–name.

NAME–YEAR

This system is very similar to APA style (see Chapter 6). Sources are identified in the text in parenthetical name–year references with complete bibliographical information given at the end of the paper in a reference list organized alphabetically by author surname. As the following examples illustrate, CSE style emphasizes simplicity, avoiding effects such as italics and reducing punctuation to a minimum.

In CSE style, names are given for up to ten authors in the reference list, with *et al.* used only after the tenth. Notice that journal names are abbreviated and use of spaces and punctuation is minimal.

In-Text Reference

Dietary soy intake in man is proposed to provide cardiovascular protection, but it is not established whether this property is attributable to the soy protein per se or to associated dietary isoflavones (Douglas et al. 2006).

End Reference

Douglas G, Armitage JA, Taylor PD, Lawson JR, Mann GE, Poston L. 2006. Cardiovascular consequences of life-long exposure to dietary isoflavones in the rat. J Physiol. 571(2):477–487.

… the incidence of T cells was seen[2,9,17–23] to decrease …

In-Text Reference

Savage-Rumbaugh and Lewin's[1] work on Kanzi describes a chimpanzee who understands a good deal of spoken English, and the text expands our notions of what constitutes animal intelligence. McCarthy and Masson[2] wrote a book that not only touched on a subject not much examined before—animals' emotions—but became a popular nonfiction work as well.

End Reference

1. Savage-Rumbaugh ES, Lewin R. The ape at the brink of the human mind. New York: Wiley; 1994. 299 p.

2. McCarthy S, Masson JM. When elephants weep: the emotional lives of animals. New York: Delacorte; 1995. 291 p.

Note that the last element of these entries indicates the total number of pages in a book. This is an optional component of a book reference, but it can be useful for the reader.

CITATION–SEQUENCE

In this system, superscript numbers in the text correspond to numbered references in a list at the end of the document. References are numbered in the order in which they appear within the text, with the number placed immediately after the reference in the text and before any punctuation. If the sentence uses the authority's name, the number is inserted after the name. If a single reference points to more than one source, numbers are given in a series, with commas and no spaces separating discontinuous numbers and a hyphen inserted to show more than two inclusive source numbers.

Once a source has been assigned a number, it is referred to by that number throughout.

In the reference list, entries are ordered in the sequence in which they first appear in the text, with numbers placed on the line followed by a period and a space. For example, if the first reference in the text is to a work by Zeleny, number 1 in the reference list at the end of the paper will be Zeleny.

CITATION–NAME

In this system, the list of end references is compiled alphabetically by author surname. The references are then numbered in that sequence, with Aaba number 1, Backnell number 2, and so on. These numbers are used for in-text references regardless of the sequence in which they appear in the text. If Mobbitt is number 38 in the reference list, the in-text reference is number 38, and the same number is used for subsequent in-text references.

When several in-text references occur at the same point, place their corresponding reference numbers in numeric order. In-text reference numbers not in a continuous sequence are separated by commas with no spaces. For more than two numbers in a continuous sequence, connect the first and last by a hyphen.

Formats for end references are similar to those used in the citation–sequence style, as shown above and in 8-1b.

In-Text Reference

For example, Jaini and colleagues[5] targeted the breast-cancer antigen alpha-lactalbumin with a vaccine containing the recombinant protein mixed with complete Freund's adjuvant, which provided signifcant protection against development of autochthonous tumors in transgenic mouse models of breast cancer.

End Reference

5. Jaini R, Kesaraju P, Johnson JM, Altuntas CZ, Jane-Wit D, Tuohy VK. An autoimmune-mediated strategy for prophylactic breast cancer vaccination. Nat Med. 2010;16:799–803.

… in several research projects[2,7-11,16,25] that had shown …

PAGE LAYOUT

Begin your reference list on a separate page with the centred title *References* or *Cited References* at the top. Double space throughout. Use a flush-left style for entries (no hanging indent).

SEQUENCE OF REFERENCES

Give the reference number in regular type followed by a period and a space. For the name–year system, place references in alphabetical order by author. For citation–sequence, list and number references in the order in which they are cited in the text. For citation–name, place references in alphabetical order by author and then number the in-text references in the same sequence.

AUTHOR NAME(S)

Names are inverted, with surnames followed by initials with no punctuation and no space between initials. Names of multiple authors are separated with a comma, with no *and* before the last author's name and a period following.

SAMPLE BIBLIOGRAPHY IN CSE STYLE

References

1. Qaddoumi I, Sultan I, Gajjar A. Outcome and prognostic features in pediatric gliomas: a review of 6212 cases from the Surveillance, Epidemiology, and End Results database. Cancer 2009;115:5761–70.
2. Rickert CH, Paulus W. Epidemiology of central nervous system tumors in childhood and adolescence based on the new WHO classification. Childs Nerv Syst. 2001;17:503–11.
3. Louis DN, Ohgaki H, Wiestler OD, Cavenee WK, Burger PC, Jouvet A, Scheithauer BW, Kleihues P. The 2007 WHO classification of tumours of the central nervous system. Acta Neuropathol. 2007;114:97–109.

TITLE

In both citation–sequence and citation–name styles, the title follows the author name. In the name–year system, the title follows the year of publication. If no author is given, the title always begins the reference. Titles of books should not be italicized and titles of articles should not be placed in quotation marks. Only the first word and proper nouns are capitalized. Subtitles are preceded by a colon and space; note that the first word in a subtitle is not capitalized. End the title with a period.

PUBLICATION INFORMATION
Books

Reference in CSE Style with No Author

> 4. Protocol for sterile procedures. Toronto (ON): Association for Microbiological Standards: 2004. 35 p.

Reference in CSE Style with Multiple Authors

> 5. Stroup DF, Berlin JA, Morton SC, et al. Meta-analysis of observational studies in epidemiology: a proposal for reporting. JAMA 2000;283:2008–2012.

City of publication
If clarification is needed, include the abbreviation for the state/province and/or country in parentheses. Use postal abbreviations—for example, UK, US, or ON—with no periods or spaces. Place a colon and a space after the place of publication.

Publisher's name
Omit an initial *The*. Well-known publisher names may be abbreviated, so that, for example, *J. B. Lippincott Company* becomes *Lippincott*, although such abbreviations should be used with caution to avoid confusion. If no publisher can be determined, put *publisher unknown* in square brackets. When using the citation–name and citation–sequence systems, use a semicolon and a space after the publisher's name; with the name–year system, use a period.

Year of publication
If no year of publication can be determined, use the year of copyright preceded by *c*; if neither a year of publication nor the copyright date can be found, use the words *date unknown* in square brackets. The exception to this is with electronic references, in which case the dates of update/revision or citation (or both) are used instead.

Journal or newspaper name

Put the name in title case, using standard abbreviations for journal names unless the name is only one word; end with a period. Newspaper names are never abbreviated, although an initial *The* may be dropped. If it is not part of the title, add the city either within or after the title. If the city is not well known, give the two-letter postal abbreviation for the U.S. state or Canadian province; for other countries, give the country name. All location information is in parentheses. End with a period.

Date

The year of publication is required for all journal references. In the name–year system, the year follows the author name; in the citation–sequence and citation–name systems, it follows the journal title. Give the month and day only for a journal that has no volume or issue number, abbreviating the month to the first three letters with no period—for example, 2011 Aug 20. In the citation–sequence and citation–name systems, the date is followed by a semicolon; in the name–year system, it is followed by a period.

Volume and issue information

The volume number must be included, followed by the issue number, if there is one, in parentheses. No other punctuation is used. For citation–sequence and citation–name systems, include this information immediately after the semicolon following the date, with no space. Conclude with a colon.

Page numbers

Location within a work—for example, a journal article or a chapter of a book—is a required part of an end reference. For a chapter or other part of a book, give inclusive pages preceded by the abbreviation *p.* (note the period). For a journal article, list inclusive page numbers but do not precede them with *p.* and do not leave any space between the preceding colon and the first digit.

The extent of a work—for example, the length of an entire book—is an optional part of a reference. Extent is expressed as the total number of pages followed by a space, as in *672 p.*

EXAMPLES OF CSE STYLE

The following examples illustrate the correct formatting for end references as they would occur in either the citation–sequence or citation–name system. For the name–year system, the date is moved up to follow the author name. Refer to Chapter 6 for detailed information about the name–year system, which follows much the same format as APA style.

Book with One Author

1. Hawking SW. The universe in a nutshell. New York: Bantam; 2001. 216 p.

Book with More than One Author

2. McCarthy S, Masson JM. When elephants weep: the emotional lives of animals. New York: Delacorte; 1995. 291 p.

Edited Book

3. Bowling AT, Ruvinsky A, editors. The genetics of the horse. New York: Oxford University Press; 2000. 527 p.

Chapter from an Edited Book

4. Polanyi JC. The transition state. In: Zewail AH, editor. The chemical bond: structure and dynamics. Boston: Academic Press; 1992. p. 201–227.

Edition Other than the First

5. Lyon MF, Searle AG, editors. Genetic variants and strains of the laboratory mouse. 3rd ed. New York: Oxford University Press; 1989. 896 p.

Journal Article with Volume and Issue Numbers

6. Reimann N, Barnitzeke S, Nolte I, Bullerdick J. Working with canine chromosomes: current recommendations for karyotype description. J Hered. 1999;90(1):31–34.

Journal Article with Discontinuous Pagination

7. Crews D, Gartska WR. The ecological physiology of the garter snake. Sci Am. 1981;245:158–164,166–168.

Newspaper Article

8. Vincent D. 1st West Nile case reported. Toronto Star. 2006 Aug 20;Sect. A3 (col. 5).

Website

9. Canadian Science Writers' Association [Internet]. Toronto (ON): Canadian Science Writers' Association; c2006 [updated 2006 Aug 15; cited 2006 Aug 22]. Available from: http://www.sciencewriters.ca/index.html

Online Book

10. Farabee MJ. The online biology book [Internet]. Avondale (AZ): Estrella Mountain Community College; c1992–2002 [updated 2001 Sep 17; cited 2006 Aug 22]. Available from: http://www.emc.maricopa.edu/faculty/farabee/BIOBK/BioBookTOC.html

Online Article

11. Brown VW. Neurofeedback and Lyme's disease: a clinical application of the five phase model of CNS functional transformation and integration. JNT [Internet]. 1995 Fall [cited 2006 Aug 22]; 1(2):[about 32 screens]. Available from: http://www.snr-jnt.org/journalnt/jnt(1–2)6.html

Online Database

12. Alcohol and Alcohol Problems Science Database (ETOH) [Internet]. Bethesda (MD): National Institute on Alcohol Abuse and Alcoholism. 1972–2003 [cited 2006 Aug 22]. Available from: http://etoh.niaaa.nih.gov/Archive.htm

The following material is based on Janice R. Walker and Todd Taylor's *The Columbia Online Style*, 2nd ed. (New York: Columbia UP, 2006).

Citing information from online sources can be difficult. For one thing, sites often move or disappear; for another, websites often fail to supply the detailed information necessary to cite them properly. To date, no single standard exists for documenting online sources.

Columbia Online Style offers practical guidelines for citing electronic sources in both the humanities and the sciences. In both cases, COS advocates a citation style that includes as much information as necessary stated as briefly as possible.

8-2A) HUMANITIES STYLE

COS uses a humanities style based on MLA criteria but modified for online sources. As with other styles, citations include a note in the text and a matching entry in a list of works cited that gives complete bibliographic information.

Citation

North American audiences responded negatively (Cohen).

Bibliography

Cohen, Mark. Abstract. "Just Judgment: Censorship of and in Canadian Literature." Diss. McGill University, 1999. ProQuest Dissertations and Theses. ProQuest. AAT NQ50133 (8 Nov. 2006).

QUICK TIP

Page numbers are not usually needed for Internet documents.

Cohen states that North American audiences responded negatively.

In the 2006 census, it was found that both divorce and marriage were on the rise (Statistics Canada).

In the CBC radio program "Sunday Edition," experts challenged current thinking about the Western diet ("Worldwide Obesity").

(18165.html)

IN-TEXT REFERENCES

Although page numbers are usually given in the case of print documents, they rarely appear within an electronic document or file.

In-text references, therefore, usually include only the author's last name, either in the body of the text or in parentheses next to quoted or paraphrased material.

Placement of Author's Last Name

Corporation Name

If no author is named, cite the name of the corporation or organization.

No Author Given

When no author or organization is listed, use the document title or a shortened version of the title.

No Author or Title Given

For citations with no author or title, use the file name.

Multiple Works by Same Author

For multiple works by the same author, include the author's last name followed by a comma and a shortened version of the title. This information can be given either in a parenthetical note or in the text.

BIBLIOGRAPHIC ENTRIES

The list of works cited should begin on a separate page and should be double-spaced throughout. When citing electronic sources, attempt to include in bibliographic citations as many of the following key information elements as you can:

1. Author's last name, followed by a comma and the first name and initial(s) (if known). Sometimes, the only designation of authorship is an email address, login name, or alias. Use a comma after the last name and end with a period.
2. Title of document, usually a Web page or article, in quotation marks with the first word and all major words capitalized. For untitled files, give a designation

It is a truism that the author's work gets darker through the years: readers begin with lighthearted caricature (Dickens, *Pickwick*) and move on to works shrouded in mystery and peopled with despairing characters (Dickens, *Dorrit*).

Article in Online Magazine

Macklem, Katherine. "A 'Devastated' Leonard Cohen." Macleans.ca 17 Aug. 2005. Macleans.ca. http://www.macleans.ca/topstories/finance/article.jsp?content=20050822_110877_110877 (8 Nov. 2006).

Website

National Association of Photoshop Professionals (NAPP). Home page. 2006. http://www.photoshopuser.com/ (6 Nov. 2006).

Full-Text Article from Library Database

Goldie, Terry. "The Canadian Homosexual." *Journal of Canadian Studies* 33.4 (Winter 1998/1999): 132–143. *Research Library*. ProQuest. ISSN 00219495 (8 Nov. 2006).

Abstract from Library Database

Cohen, Mark. Abstract. "Just Judgment: Censorship of and in Canadian Literature." Diss. McGill University, 1999. *ProQuest Dissertations and Theses*. ProQuest. AAT NQ50133 (8 Nov. 2006).

Online Reference Work

"Philistine." *Merriam-Webster Online Dictionary*. Merriam-Webster OnLine. 2006. http://www.m-w.com/dictionary/Philistine (6 Nov. 2006).

Mailing List

Long, Tom. "Re: Certification." 6 Nov. 2006. *Editors' Association of Canada Members' Discussion List*. eac-acr-l@list.web.net (6 Nov. 2006).

SAMPLE BIBLIOGRAPHY IN CGOS STYLE (HUMANITIES)

Works Cited

Brook, George Leslie. *An Introduction to Old English*. Manchester: Manchester University Press, 1962. http://books.google.com/books?id= LpSxAAAAIAAJ&source=gbs_book_other_versions_r&cad=3 1. (7 Nov. 2010).

Echard, Sian. "Old English Poetry." *University of British Columbia*. (no date). http://faculty.arts.ubc.ca/sechard/492oe.htm (7 Nov. 2010).

Everett, Glenn. "Gerard Manley Hopkins: A Brief Biography." *The Victorian Web*. 1988. http://www.victorianweb.org/authors/hopkins/hopkins12.html (7 Nov. 2010).

(for example, *Home Page*), with no quotation marks or italics. End with a period.

3. Title of complete work, such as a website or online book or journal, in italics. Capitalize the first word and all major words. End with a period.

4. Version or edition, if applicable, followed by a period.

5. Date of publication or last revision, if available, in international date format (day, month, year), followed by a period.

6. Protocol and address, or name of database (in italics) and publisher.

7. Access path, directories, key words, or file numbers, if applicable, in parentheses.

8. Date of access, in parentheses, in day-month-year format, followed by a period.

For scientific sources, COS style is designed to complement APA guidelines for citing print sources while providing more complete suggestions for citing electronic sources. As with other styles, citations include a note in the text and a matching entry in the list of references, which gives complete bibliographic information.

IN-TEXT REFERENCES
Subsequent references may omit the date, giving only the author's name.

Since most electronic sources are not paginated, in-text references include only the author's last name followed by a comma and the year of publication.

First Reference

> The glycerol produced during transesterification contains a very high percentage of excess methanol (Kemp, 2006).

No Publication Date
If there is no publication date, use the date of access (day-month-year).

> There is no concrete evidence to suggest that the drug is effective in controlling performance anxiety (Millar, 8 Nov. 2006).

Placement of Date
If the author's name is given in the text, include the date in parentheses immediately after the author's name.

> Fenton (2006) claims that many events are either silent or clinically unrecognized.

Two or More References in the Same Note
Two or more references in the same note are separated with a semicolon.

> (Peters & Collom, 2005; Stendall, 2006)

No Author Given
If no author is given, use the document or Web page title and the date.

> ("Quirks & Quarks," 2006)

Web Page

> Nobel Foundation. (2006). The Nobel Prize in Chemistry. Nobel-prize.org. http://nobelprize.org/nobel_prizes/chemistry/ (8 Nov. 2006).

Website

> National Biodiesel Board. (2006). Home page. http://www.biodiesel.org/ (8 Nov. 2006).

Full-Text Article from Library Database

> Maviglia, M.A. (2006). Alcohol and drug abuse intervention in the emergency department. *Psychiatric Times*, 23(1), 40. ProQuest Nursing & Allied Health. ProQuest. (ISSN 08932905). (8 Nov. 2006).

Abstract from Library Database

> Kuhlen, M. (2006). Adventures in numerical cosmology [Abstract]. *ProQuest Dissertations and Theses*. ProQuest. (9780542705502). (8 Nov. 2006).

Online Reference Work

> Maquiladora. (2006). In *Encyclopaedia Britannica* online. http://www.britannica.com/eb/article-9050713/maquiladora (8 Nov. 2006).

BIBLIOGRAPHIC ENTRIES

The list of works cited should begin on a separate page and should be double-spaced throughout. When citing electronic sources, attempt to include in bibliographic citations as many of the following key information elements as you can:

1. Author's last name and initial(s), or the author's email, login name, or alias. Use a comma after the last name and end with a period.
2. Date of document, in parentheses, followed by a period.
3. Title of document, capitalizing only the first word, any proper nouns, and the first word following a colon, if applicable. End with a period.
4. Title of complete work, in italics, capitalizing only the first word and any proper nouns. End with a period.
5. Edition or revision, if applicable, enclosed in parentheses and followed by a period.

6. Protocol and address, or name of database (in italics) and database publisher.
7. Access path, or directories or document or file number, in parentheses.
8. Date of access, in parentheses, followed by a period.

Note that hanging indents should not be used if the material for an essay is to be published online. Instead they should be flush left.

Mailing List

Fennel, R. (2006, November 8). Re: Editing science texts. Editors' Association of Canada members' discussion list. eac-acr-l@list.web.net (8 Nov. 2006).

SAMPLE BIBLIOGRAPHY IN COS SCIENTIFIC STYLE

References

d'Errico, F. et al. (1998). Neanderthal acculturation in Western Europe? A critical review of the evidence and its interpretation. *Current Anthropology*, *39*. http://www.journals.uchicago.edu/doi/pdf/10.1086/204689 (29 July 2011).

Ravilious, K. (2008). Neanderthals grew fast but sexual maturity came late. *National Geographic News*. http://news.nationalgeographic.com/news/2008/09/080908-neanderthal-brain.html (28 July 2011).

Sample, Ian. (2006). Neanderthal DNA reveals human divergence. *Guardian News & Media*. http://www.guardian.co.uk/science/2006/nov/16/fossils.research (6 July 2011).

Grammar

9

IT IS WELL
TO
REMEMBER
THAT
GRAMMAR
IS COMMON
SPEECH
FORMULATED.

—W. SOMERSET
MAUGHAM

Grammar

9

Nouns name people, places, things, or concepts.

> **Luxury** is the **wolf** at the **door** and its **fangs** are the **vanities** and **conceits** germinated by **success**.
>
> —Tennessee Williams

Articles are words that accompany and quantify nouns.

> **The** good writing of any age has always been **the** product of someone's neurosis, and we'd have **a** mighty dull literature if all **the** writers that came along were **a** bunch of happy chunkleheads.
>
> —William Styron

Pronouns are used in the place of nouns.

> **I** never desire to converse with a man **who** has written more books than **he** has read.
>
> —Samuel Johnson

Adjectives modify nouns or pronouns.

> If you would be **thrilled** by watching the **galloping** advance of a **major** glacier, you'd be **ecstatic** watching changes in publishing.
>
> —John D. MacDonald

This section will teach you the basic concepts of grammar you will need in order to understand how your sentences are put together. This knowledge can be used to explain or to justify what you have written and why. When in doubt about a grammatical issue, whether in your first or subsequent drafts, consult this section.

Knowing how grammar works in your sentences will improve your ability to write and revise.

Adverbs modify verbs, adjectives, other adverbs, or larger units of the sentence.

> I never reread what I've written. I'm **far too** afraid to feel ashamed of what I've done.
>
> —Jorge Luis Borges

Prepositions describe the position of nouns and pronouns in relation to other words.

> When I stepped **from** hard manual work **to** writing, I just stepped **from** one kind **of** hard work **to** another.
>
> —Sean O'Casey

Conjunctions join words and phrases.

> The critic should describe, **and** not prescribe.
>
> —Eugene Ionesco

Interjections are words expressing emotion that are not part of the grammatical pattern of the sentence.

> **Darn!** I can't find a quotation with an interjection in it!

Adjectives with Plural Nouns:
In many languages, adjectives agree in number with the nouns they modify; however, in English, adjectives do not change number this way. For example,

His puppies are adorable (not *adorables*).

Adjective Sequence:
Be careful how you place adjectives in a sentence. For example, you should write *"these beautiful blue marble tiles"* instead of *"these blue beautiful marble tiles."*

Nouns can be classified by type:

A **noun** names a person, place, or thing. Whenever an **article** (*a, an, the*) could precede a word without destroying the logic of a sentence, that word is a noun.

Table 9.1   Types of Nouns

Noun Type	These Nouns Name	Examples	See also
proper	specific people, places, and things (always with an initial capital)	*Buckminster Fuller, Moose Jaw, Honda*	14-3A
common	general people, places, or things	*architect, town, car*	14-3A
concrete	things you experience through your senses	*gravel, ice cream, storm*	13-2B
abstract	things you do not experience through your senses	*knowledge, liberation, fear*	13-2B
collective	groups	*jury, police*	10-3E, 10-3A
non-count	things that cannot be counted	*snow, porridge*	15-1A, 15-1B, 15-1D
count	things that can be counted	*books, cornflakes*	15-1D
possessive	things that are owned by someone	*Nathan's, Maria's, Daddy's*	11-4A

NOUN

My **attempts** to dance are sometimes met with ridicule.

STRATEGIES

Checklist for Identifying Nouns
A word may be a noun if
- you can make it singular or plural
- you can make it possessive; that is, it can indicate ownership
- you can put an *a, an,* or *the* in front of it
- you find a suffix like *-tion, -ance, -ence, -ment, -ty,* or *-ness*

Count and Non-count Nouns

Most nouns change from singular (one) to plural (more than one) when you add the suffix *-s* or *-es* or another suffix: *duck, ducks; touch, touches; die, dice; datum, data*. Some count nouns have irregular plural forms: *woman, women; child, children; deer, deer.*

Non-count nouns cannot be made plural because they name things that cannot be easily counted: *dust, water, hockey, weather, poetry, mathematics, Chinese, Spanish.*

9-1B   ARTICLES

Articles, or determiners, come before nouns. The **indefinite** articles are *a* and *an*, and the **definite** article is *the*.

Articles are actually related to adjectives since they are used to identify and quantify nouns.

A Chihuahua, **the** Boston terrier, **an** Afghan
What is **the** point?

9-1C   PRONOUNS

A **pronoun** can replace a noun. The word (or words) replaced by a pronoun is called the **antecedent.**

ANTECEDENT
Homer lives in Springfield.

PRONOUNS
He is married to Marge.

His children—Bart, Lisa, and Maggie—also live with **him**.

PERSONAL PRONOUNS
Subjective
We asked Hermione, but **she** wouldn't tell.

Who do **you** think **you** are?

Objective
Don't look at **me**; look at **him**.

The audience hated **us** and loved **her**.

POSSESSIVE PRONOUNS
Every dog has **its** day.

My ambitions are high, but **my** motivation is not.

ABSOLUTE POSSESSIVE PRONOUNS
The bank account is **mine**, the property is **yours**, and the debt is **ours**.

RELATIVE PRONOUNS
People **who** live in glass houses shouldn't throw stones.

That is the reason **that** I will not be attending graduation.

Her wedding dress, **which** she bought on sale, was beautiful.

TYPES OF PRONOUNS
Personal
Personal pronouns refer to people, places, or things. When **subjective** (*I, you he, she, it, we, they*), personal pronouns refer to people or things who are performing actions or that are the subject being described.

Objective personal pronouns (*me, you, him, her, it, us, them*) refer to people or things that are acted on. They often follow a preposition.

Possessive
Possessive pronouns (*my, your, his, her, its, our, their*) indicate ownership, or possession. They function like adjectives in front of a noun.

Absolute possessive pronouns (*mine, yours, his, hers, its, ours, theirs*) also indicate ownership. They stand in for both the owner and the thing owned.

Relative
Relative pronouns (*who, which, that*) introduce subordinate clauses (see 9-3e) that operate as adjectives, describing the noun or pronoun in the main clause.

Demonstrative

Demonstrative pronouns (*this, these, that, those*) point to nouns. They may function as adjectives modifying a noun, or they may replace the noun entirely.

Interrogative

Interrogative pronouns (*who, whose, what, which,* and others) begin questions.

Reflexive and Intensive

Reflexive pronouns (*myself, yourself, himself, herself, itself, ourselves, yourselves, themselves*) name the receiver of an action who is identical to the performer of an action.

    Intensive pronouns look like reflexive pronouns but are used to emphasize a noun or pronoun.

Reciprocal

Reciprocal pronouns (*each other, one another*) refer to the separate parts of a plural antecedent.

Indefinite

Indefinite pronouns (*all, anybody, anyone, anything, each, either, everybody, everyone, everything, neither, no one,*

DEMONSTRATIVE PRONOUNS

Those who ignore history are condemned to repeat it.

Those shoes hurt my feet.

Those hurt my feet.

INTERROGATIVE PRONOUNS

Who wants to be a millionaire?

Whatever do you mean by that?

Whose life is it anyway?

REFLEXIVE PRONOUNS

Cats keep **themselves** very clean.

Sleeping Beauty looked at **herself** in the mirror with dire consequences.

INTENSIVE PRONOUNS

You **yourself** scorn a daily bath.

What matters is the work **itself**.

RECIPROCAL PRONOUNS

Kathleen and Aitken despise **each other**.

The kittens licked **one another** lazily.

INDEFINITE PRONOUNS

Everyone should have **someone** to love.

Table 9.2 Indefinite Pronouns

all	each	more	one
another	either	most	several
any	everybody	neither	some
anybody	everyone	nobody	somebody
anyone	everything	no one	someone
anything	few	none	something
both	many	nothing	

nobody, none, nothing, one, some, somebody, someone, something) refer to general (not specific) people or things. Many are always singular, some are always plural, and some may be either singular or plural.

VERB

When she **attempts** to dance, she **is** often embarrassed by her lack of grace.

STRATEGIES

Checklist for Identifying Verbs
A word may be a verb if
- you can change its tense, often by adding the ending -*ed.*
- you can change its form in the present tense with *he, she,* or *it.* Almost all verbs in English add -*s* or -*es* in that situation.

Remember that infinitives (base forms beginning with *to*) and gerunds (-*ing* forms) cannot act as verbs unless they are connected to other verbs.

Smoking is bad even for innocent by-standers. (Here *smoking* is not a verb, but a gerund.)

Marge's sister was smoking a cigarette. (Here *smoking* is a verb, but it has an auxiliary verb, *is*, connected to it.)

Verbs may be passive or active:

I am bringing takeout food from the café. (active)

Takeout food was brought from the café. (passive)

The **verb** in a sentence usually expresses an action (*work, climb*), an occurrence (*became*) or a state of being (*is, seemed*). It may be one verb or a phrase made up of a main verb and an auxiliary verb. In English, the verb frequently appears as the second element of a sentence.

Verbs may be **regular** or **irregular**.

- **Regular** verbs have this conjugation:

   Singular:
   I love
   you love
   he/she/it loves

   Plural:
   we love
   you love
   they love

- **Irregular** verbs have irregular conjunctions:

  Singular:
  I am
  you are
  he/she/it is

  Plural:
  we are
  you are
  they are

KINDS OF VERBS

Transitive and Intransitive

Transitive verbs always take an object.

The verb *hates* is transitive because it is followed by the object *math*.

Intransitive verbs do not take an object.

The verb *giggled* is intransitive because it does not take an object.

Linking and Action

Linking verbs (e.g., forms of *to be, to feel, to seem,* etc.) join the subject to the complement.

The linking verb, *feel,* joins the subject, *I,* to the complement, the adjective *pretty.*

Action verbs are verbs that involve some activity, movement, or action, rather than expressing a state of being.

VERB EXPRESSING ACTION
Cupid **shot** his arrow.

VERB EXPRESSING OCCURRENCE
It **happened** one night.

VERB EXPRESSING STATE OF BEING
Blondie and Dagwood **have been married** for decades.

TRANSITIVE VERBS
Ken **hates** math.

INTRANSITIVE VERBS
Barbie **giggled**.

LINKING VERBS
I **feel** pretty.

Procrastination **is** the thief of time.

ACTION VERBS
The bomb **exploded**.

Sheila **hit** her brother with a pillow.

VERB FORMS: MAIN AND AUXILIARY

Byron **mocked** Keats.

He *had* **scorned** other poets for years.

MODAL VERBS

You *might* **have called** before barging in.

"*May* I **suggest** the duck confit salad?" asked the waiter.

Betting on the stock market *could* **be** dangerous.

CHANGES IN VERB FORMS

Tense (present, past, future): I bring, I brought, I will bring

Person: I bring, he brings

Number: they bring, she brings

Mood: Bring my supper! (imperative)
I am bringing a sandwich. (indicative)

Voice: I am bringing takeout food from the café. (active)
Takeout food will be brought from the café. (passive)

VERB FORMS

Main and Auxiliary

A **main** verb describes a simple action or state of being.

Auxiliary verbs are helping verbs. *Be, do,* and *have* operate as auxiliary verbs in English.

Modal

Modal verbs (like *can, could, may, might, should, would, must,* and *ought to,* or the most common modals, *do, have,* and *be*) are used with the present tense form of the verb to express doubt or certainty, necessity or obligation, probability or possibility. They are also often used to make polite requests.

CHANGES IN VERB FORMS

Verb forms vary according to

- tense
- person
- number
- mood
- voice

Tense

The **tense** of a verb refers to when an action occurs, in the **past**, in the **present**, or in the **future**. Tense expresses the time of an action. To show changes in time, verbs change form and combine with auxiliary verbs.

The **simple** tenses describe a one-time or regular occurrence; the **progressive** form refers to an ongoing event. The **perfect** tenses express completed actions. (See 10-4f.)

Table 9.3 Simple Tenses

Type	Example	Progressive Form
Present	I laugh	I am laughing
Past	I laughed	I was laughing
Future	I will laugh	I will be laughing

Table 9.4 Perfect Tenses

Type	Example	Progressive Form
Present Perfect	I have laughed	I have been laughing
Past Perfect	I had laughed	I had been laughing
Future Perfect	I will have laughed	I will have been laughing

Person and Number

Depending on the **person** the verb is attached to, its form may change. Look at the conjugation of a regular verb in English; note that, in the present tense, regular verbs take an *s* in the third person singular (with *he, she,* or *it*).

The **number** of a verb tells you whether the verb refers to a singular subject or a plural subject. *She works* is singular, but *they work* is plural, and the form of the verb changes to reflect the change in number of the subject.

First Person Singular: I work

Second Person Singular: you work

Third Person Singular: he/she/it works

First Person Plural: we work

Second Person Plural: you work

Third Person Plural: they work

For more information on the person and number of verbs, see 10-3.

MOOD

Indicative Mood
He who **laughs** last **laughs** best.

Imperative Mood
Don't **laugh** at me.

Subjunctive Mood
If I **were** you, I would learn to laugh at myself.

It is necessary that you **be** in attendance.

VOICE

Active Voice
Customers **found** the wait staff to be inattentive, careless, and rude.

Passive Voice
The wait staff **was found** to be inattentive, careless, and rude.

Passive voice can be wordy:
A trick **was played** on me by my brother.

Passive voice can also be appropriate:
My new house **will be completed** in 2013.

Mood
The **mood** of a verb refers to whether it is indicative, imperative, or subjunctive.

The **indicative** mood is used for events that are real or that commonly recur.

The **imperative** mood is used for commands. The subject in these cases is left out, but is understood to be *you*.

The **subjunctive** mood is used to express hypothetical situations, things contrary to fact, wishes, requirements, and speculations.

Voice
The **voice** of a verb refers to whether the subject *performs* the action or whether it *receives* the action.

Because the active voice emphasizes the performer of an action, it is more direct and less wordy than the passive voice. On the other hand, because the passive voice stresses the receiver of an action, it is especially useful when the performer of an action is unknown or unimportant.

For more information on active and passive voice, see 10-4h.

9-1E ADJECTIVES

Adjectives modify or describe nouns or pronouns. They give information about *which one, what kind,* or *how many.*

ADJECTIVE FORMS
Common Adjective
Life is **beautiful**.

Proper Adjective
The play was set in **Edwardian** times.

COMPARATIVE ADJECTIVE
I prefer you in **redder** lipstick.

SUPERLATIVE ADJECTIVE
The **reddest** lipstick is my favourite.

Words with the suffixes *-ful, -ish, -less,* and *-like* are usually adjectives.

9-1F ADVERBS

An **adverb** can modify a verb, an adjective, another adverb, or a complete sentence. Adverbs give information about *when, where, how,* and *how much.*

Many adverbs, though not all adverbs, end in *-ly;* however, it is important to realize that many adjectives do as well (e.g., *jolly, silly,* and *smelly*).

Note that adjectives and adverbs may also be **comparative** or **superlative**.

ADVERB MODIFYING VERB
Buffy screamed **loudly**.

ADVERB MODIFYING ADJECTIVE
Computers are a **very** significant cause of a sedentary lifestyle.

ADVERB MODIFYING ADVERB
I cannot swim now because I have eaten **too** recently.

ADVERB MODIFYING SENTENCE
Mercifully, the lost children were reunited with their frightened parents.

COMPARATIVE ADVERB
The younger child came **more willingly**.

SUPERLATIVE ADVERB
I will share my sandwich with you **most willingly**.

After the party, they had lots of bottles to throw out.

In summer, they eat **on** the patio.

Between you and me, this place is a mess.

Note that prepositions are always followed by nouns or pronouns in the object form, which is why it is always "between you and me" and not "between you and I."

Prepositions are words that often express position. They form phrases with nouns and pronouns, which often provide information about time and space.

The use of prepositions in English is complex. For more discussion of prepositions, see 15-3g.

Table 9.5   Common Prepositions

about	between	next	through
above	beyond	of	throughout
across	by	off	till
after	concerning	on	to
against	considering	onto	toward
along	despite	opposite	under
among	down	out	underneath
around	during	outside	unlike
as	except	over	until
at	for	past	unto
before	from	plus	up
behind	in	regarding	upon
below	inside	respecting	with
beneath	into	round	within
beside	like	since	without
besides	near	than	

Conjunctions are words that connect.

When one of these seven words joins two complete sentences, it is working as a **coordinating** conjunction. Coordinating conjunctions join two coordinate or balanced structures.

SUBORDINATE CONJUNCTIONS

Subordinate conjunctions connect main clauses with subordinate clauses. (See 9-3e.)

Note that subordinate clauses that appear in front of main clauses are followed by a comma. When the subordinate clause follows the main clause, however, there is no comma.

CORRELATIVE CONJUNCTIONS

Correlative conjunctions work in pairs to balance sentence structure. (See 9-4a.)

COORDINATING CONJUNCTIONS

and	or	nor
but	yet	so

for (meaning *because*)

On holidays, we go to theatres, **and** we eat in expensive restaurants.

Table 9.6 Common Subordinate Conjunctions

after	if	though
although	if only	till
as	in order that	unless
as if	now that	until
as long as	once	when
as though	rather than	whenever
because	since	where
before	so that	wherever
even if	than	whereas
even though	that	while

Because he had gained fifty pounds, the doctor put him on a diet.

I did not attend university **until** I had spent some time in the work force.

CORRELATIVE CONJUNCTIONS

Either that wallpaper goes, **or** I do.

—Oscar Wilde, on his deathbed

Table 9.7 Correlative Conjunctions

both … and	not only … but also
either … or	whether … or
neither … nor	and not … so much as

CONJUNCTIVE ADVERBS

I have a headache; **therefore**, I'm going to bed.

Jason wanted the job; **however**, he needed to finish his degree first.

Some words that may be used as conjunctive adverbs are the following:
- *to compare*: conversely, however, likewise, nevertheless, similarly
- *to add information*: additionally, furthermore
- *to show cause and effect*: consequently, hence, therefore, thus
- *to show time sequence*: finally, next, subsequently, then

CONJUNCTIVE ADVERBS

Conjunctive adverbs are used to indicate a connection between main clauses. (See 10-2b and 11-2b.)

Many adverbs can function as conjunctive adverbs. Learning to distinguish between conjunctive adverbs and coordinating conjunctions is essential to avoid comma splice errors and to punctuate correctly. (See 10-2, 11-1a, and 11-2b.)

INTERJECTIONS 9-1I

Ouch! I hate going to the dentist.

Hey, what you are up to?

An **interjection** is a word that expresses strong feeling. Interjections also are sometimes used to address someone. These words are seldom used in formal writing.

Voronin76/Shutterstock.com

English sentences are usually composed of (a) subjects and (b) verbs, often completed with (c) objects or complements.

A sentence is composed of a subject and a predicate. The latter is the name for the verb, its modifiers, and the object or complement in the sentence.

STRATEGIES

Checklist for Identifying Basic Sentence Patterns

1. Subject and verb
   S   V
   Dogs bark.

2. Subject and verb and complement
   S   V   C
   Dogs are good companions.

3. Subject and verb and direct object.
   S   V   DO
   Dogs chew everything.

4. Subject and verb with indirect object and direct object.
   S   V   IO   DO
   Dogs give people their loyalty.

5. Subject and verb with direct object and object complement.
   S   V   OC   DO
   Dogs keep people safe.

9-2A   SUBJECTS

The subject (S) of a sentence is what the sentence is about. To find the **complete** subject, ask *who* or *what* of the verb.

COMPLETE SUBJECTS

S

My professor writes grammar textbooks.

Finding Subject: Who writes grammar textbooks? *My professor.*

S

Grammar books that are genuinely useful are hard to come by.

Finding Subject: What are hard to come by? *Grammar books that are genuinely useful.*

SIMPLE SUBJECTS

    SS

My <u>professor</u> writes grammar textbooks.

      SS

Grammar <u>books</u> that are genuinely useful are hard to come by.

COMPOUND SUBJECTS

 S   *S*

<u>Time</u> and <u>tide</u> wait for no man.

SUBJECT IN A COMMAND

  S

[<u>You</u>] Use it or lose it.

SUBJECT AFTER THE VERB

     S

There *is* <u>an owl</u> sitting on that branch.

SUBJECT AT THE END OF THE SENTENCE

         S

In the doorway *stood* <u>her father</u>.

SUBJECT BETWEEN PARTS OF VERB

 S

Do <u>you</u> *know* the answer?

The **simple** subject (SS) is the one-word subject that is left after all modifiers, phrases, and clauses are stripped away. A simple subject is always either a noun or a pronoun.

Remember, though, that some subjects can be **compound** if they are joined by a coordinating conjunction such as *and* or *or*.

In commands (or **imperatives**), *you* is understood to be the subject.

Sometimes subjects do not appear before the verb in English sentences. If a sentence begins with an **expletive,** such as *there is* or *there are* (or *there was* or *there were*), then the subject follows the verb. Expletives function as placeholders to begin the sentence.

Subjects sometimes appear at the end of sentences for dramatic effect.

In questions, the subject often appears between parts of the verb.

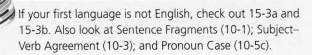

ELL Note

If your first language is not English, check out 15-3a and 15-3b. Also look at Sentence Fragments (10-1); Subject–Verb Agreement (10-3); and Pronoun Case (10-5c).

Checklist for Identifying Subjects
- First find the verb. It is usually in the middle of the sentence and constitutes the action of the sentence, if there is any. If there is no action, it describes a state of being.
- After finding the verb, ask who or what is performing the action of the verb.

Every cloud has a silver lining. (Active voice)
What has a silver lining?
A **cloud** (the subject)

A good time was had by all. (Passive voice)
What was had by all?
A good **time** (the subject)

9-2B VERBS, OBJECTS, AND COMPLEMENTS

As you saw in 9-1d, verbs may be categorized as linking, if followed by a complement; transitive, if followed by an object; or intransitive, if the verb cannot take an object.

LINKING VERBS AND COMPLEMENTS

A linking verb (LV) must take a complement, or **subjective completion** (SC), which is a word (or words) that completes the meaning of the subject (S) by renaming or describing that subject.

Verb with a complement: He is obsessive about his work.

Transitive verb (followed by a direct object): He writes romance novels.

Intransitive verb: He frets constantly about his workload.

LINKING VERBS AND COMPLEMENTS

  S   *LV*   *SC*
<u>Recess</u> *is* <u>the part of school we enjoy most</u>.

  S *LV*   *SC*
<u>Life</u> *is* <u>what you make it</u>.

   S   *LV* *SC*
<u>The lake</u> *was* <u>calm</u>.

When a subjective completion, or complement, renames the subject, it is a noun or pronoun, or a phrase beginning with a noun or pronoun, such as *the part of school we enjoy most* or *what you make it*. When it describes the subject, it is an adjective, such as *calm*.

Table 9.8 Common Linking Verbs

appear	grow	smell
be	look	sound
become	prove	stay
feel	remain	taste
get	seem	turn

TRANSITIVE VERBS (VERBS TAKING OBJECTS)

S   TV   DO
You *will pay* the price.

S   TV   DO
[You] Answer me.

*   S   TV   DO*
Active Voice: The Stratford Festival *presented* the play.

*   S   TV   phrase*
Passive Voice: The play *was presented* by the Stratford Festival.

*   S   TV*
Passive Voice: The play *was presented*.

The direct object (*the play*) becomes the subject when the sentence is made passive; the original subject moves to the end of the sentence, in a prepositional phrase beginning with *by*. Sometimes these *by* phrases are left out in passive constructions, leaving the performer of the action unstated.

Linking verbs are often forms of the verb *to be: be, am, is, are, was, were, being, been*. Verbs that have no action are also linking verbs when they are followed by a word or word group that names or describes the subject of the sentence.

TRANSITIVE VERBS THAT TAKE DIRECT OBJECTS

Remember, transitive verbs (TV) always take an object. They may take a **direct object** (DO). Direct objects name the receiver of an action. A simple direct object must be a noun or pronoun.

Transitive verbs are often in the active voice, with the subject (or performer of the action) at the beginning of the sentence and the direct object (the receiver of the action) following the verb. Only transitive verbs may appear in the passive voice, where the receiver of the action becomes the subject and the performer of the action is moved to the end of the sentence.

TRANSITIVE VERBS WITH BOTH INDIRECT AND DIRECT OBJECTS

Sometimes transitive verbs take both direct and **indirect objects** (IO). In this case, the indirect object comes first.

TRANSITIVE VERBS, DIRECT OBJECTS, AND OBJECT COMPLEMENTS

A transitive verb and a direct object are sometimes followed by an **object complement** (OC), a word or group of words that completes the direct object's meaning by describing it or renaming it. If the object complement is used to rename the direct object, it is a noun (or noun phrase) or a pronoun. If the object complement describes the direct object, it is an adjective or adjective phrase.

INTRANSITIVE VERBS

An intransitive verb (IV) cannot take either an object or a complement.

Intransitive verbs may, however, be followed by adverbs or **adverbial phrases** that modify them. An adverbial phrase is a group of words that

TRANSITIVE VERBS WITH INDIRECT AND DIRECT OBJECTS

  S   TV   IO DO   S   TV   IO DO

You *catch* [for] me a fish, and I *will cook* [for] you dinner.

     S   TV   DO   OC

Some people *find* stamp collecting a dull hobby.

The object complement renames the direct object, *stamp collecting, a dull hobby.*

     S   TV   DO   OC

The passage of time *makes* antiques more valuable.

The object complement describes the direct object, *antiques,* as *more valuable.*

INTRANSITIVE VERBS

    S   IV

The soccer team *succeeds.*

There is no receiver for the action in this sentence because *succeed* is an intransitive verb.

S IV
Tarzan and Jane *exercise* every day.

The intransitive verb *exercise* takes no object, but it is followed by an adverbial phrase that modifies it: *every day*.

TRANSITIVE AND INTRANSITIVE VERBS

S TV DO
Transitive: The coach *swam* the Australian crawl.

S IV
Intransitive: The coach *swam* every morning.

In the first sentence, the verb *swam* takes a direct object (*the Australian crawl* answers the question *swam what?*). In the next sentence, *swam* takes no object and is followed by an adverbial phrase (*every morning* answers the question *swam when?*).

modifies a verb, an adverb, or an adjective; for example, *slowly but surely* is an adverbial phrase in the sentence *He walked, slowly but surely, to the closet door.*

Check a dictionary to determine whether a verb is transitive or intransitive. Sometimes a verb can be both, depending on its context.

PHRASES AND CLAUSES (9-3

PHRASES

A phrase is a group of words that lacks a subject and verb and thus does not form a sentence. Phrases work in sentences like nouns, verbs, adjectives, or adverbs.

Participial Phrase: eating chocolate

Noun Phrase: the director Atom Egoyan

Verb Phrase: has been found

CLAUSE

A clause is a group of words with both a subject and verb.

I chose freedom. (independent clause or sentence)
If I chose freedom (subordinate clause)

Each sentence, no matter how complex, has a **main** clause—the clause containing the main idea, subject, and verb of the sentence.

A main clause, also known as an **independent** clause, can always stand alone as a sentence.

Phrases are word groups lacking a subject or verb—or both—and they cannot stand alone (although exceptions to this rule are often allowed in works of fiction). They are used within sentences, usually as adjectives, adverbs, or nouns.

9-3A PREPOSITIONAL PHRASES

Prepositional phrases are groups of words that begin with a preposition, such as *at, across, by, beside, for, from, in, into, off, on, over, to,* or *without.* (See 9-1g.) Prepositional phrases always include a noun or a pronoun, which serves as the object of the preposition.

A bird **in the hand** is worth two **in the bush**.

Here, the prepositional phrases are used as adjectives and hence follow the noun they modify.

We ate **with gusto** the picnic she had brought for us.

Here, the prepositional phrase is used as an adverb and follows the verb, though it might also have appeared at the beginning of the sentence.

You can't judge a book **by its cover**.

Prepositions can be difficult because their use is often idiomatic. For advice on "*on, at, in*" and their usage, see 15-3g.

9-3B VERBAL PHRASES

Verbal phrases are formed from parts of the verb, but they function as nouns, adjectives, or adverbs. There are three kinds of verbal phrases: those formed with infinitives, those formed with present participles, and those formed with past participles.

INFINITIVE PHRASES
The **infinitive** is *to* + the base form of the verb: for example, *to be, to do, to love.* The infinitive often functions as a noun in a sentence, but it can also be an adjective or an adverb.

INFINITIVE PHRASES
S
To be or not to be is the question. [infinitive phrase as subject]

Donating food **to help those in need** feels good. [infinitive phrase as adjective]

He swims laps **to relieve stress**. [infinitive phrase as adverb]

PARTICIPIAL PHRASES

Standing there among the gardenias, the gardener could see what the problem was.

The baby, **crying in the dark**, had been abandoned.

Exhausted, Geoffrey finished the application at midnight.

The envelope, **sent by express courier**, arrived just in time.

Gerunds and infinitives, when used as objects, sometimes pose problems for ESL students. See 15-2g for a discussion of gerunds and infinitives.

PARTICIPIAL PHRASES

Participial phrases can use either present participles or past participles. **Present participles** are formed with *-ing* and act like adjectives.

　　Past participles are formed with *-ed,* or the equivalent forms of irregular verbs. They, too, operate like adjectives in a sentence.

APPOSITIVE PHRASES　9-3C

Sanitary engineers, **otherwise known as garbage collectors**, are going on strike.

Appositives and **appositive phrases** are used to rename nouns or pronouns. They function like nouns.

ABSOLUTE PHRASES　9-3D

Her head spinning with confusion, Ethel left the exam room.

An **absolute** phrase modifies a clause or a sentence. It usually is made up of a noun followed by a participial phrase.

Subordinate clauses (SC), like main clauses, contain a subject and a verb, but they cannot stand alone as complete sentences, and instead function in sentences as adjectives, adverbs, or nouns. Subordinate clauses are usually indicated by the presence of a subordinate conjunction or a word beginning with *wh-*, such as *as, because, since, that, when, where, whereas, wherever,* or *whether.*

SUBORDINATE CLAUSES OR DEPENDENT CLAUSES

All that I need to know I learned in kindergarten. (noun clause)

Rear Window, **which is one of Hitchcock's most successful films,** is mostly seen from the perspective of one window. (adjective clause)

Just as you predicted, I found the conference dull. (adverb clause)

ADJECTIVAL CLAUSES

An adjectival subordinate clause modifies a noun or a pronoun. Adjectival clauses often start with a relative pronoun (*who, whom, whose, which,* or *that*) or with a word like *when* or *where.*

ADJECTIVAL CLAUSES

SC
The boat <u>that I am rowing</u> has sprung a leak.

SC
The man <u>whom I marry</u> will have to be taller than I am.

ADVERBIAL CLAUSES

Subordinate clauses can act as adverbs by modifying adjectives, adverbs, or verbs. They usually answer at least one of the questions *when? where? why? how? under what conditions?* or *to what degree?* These clauses usually begin with a subordinate conjunction.

ADVERBIAL CLAUSES

SC
<u>If I had a hammer</u>, I'd hammer in the morning.

SC
<u>Whether you like it or not</u>, it's your turn.

NOUN CLAUSES

SC

<u>Whatever frog she kisses</u> will become a prince.

Here, the subordinate noun clause is a subject.

SC

I want to understand <u>why you feel that way</u>.

Here, the subordinate noun clause is an object.

SC

I will be <u>whoever you want me to be</u>.

Here, the subordinate noun clause is a complement.

NOUN CLAUSES

Subordinate noun clauses are used as subjects, objects, or complements. They usually begin with one of these words: *how, that, which, who, whoever, whom, whomever, what, whatever, when, where, whether, whose, why.*

SENTENCE TYPES 9-4

There are two approaches to the classification of sentences.

Sentences may be categorized according to their structure or their function.

SENTENCE STRUCTURE 9-4A

SENTENCE VARIETIES

Sentences can be

- simple
- compound
- complex
- compound-complex

Sentences can be simple, compound, complex, or compound-complex, depending on the number and types of clauses they contain. In order to be a sentence, there must be at least one independent (or main) clause (IC). A subordinate clause, like the main clause, has a subject and a verb, but it cannot stand alone as a sentence.

Simple sentences have one independent clause with no subordinate clauses. A simple sentence has just one subject and verb.

Compound sentences have two or more independent (or main) clauses, with no subordinate clauses. The main clauses may be joined by a comma and a coordinating conjunction (*and, or, nor, for, but, yet,* or *so*) or with a semicolon.

Complex sentences are made up of one independent clause and at least one subordinate clause.

Compound-complex sentences are made up of at least two independent clauses and at least one subordinate clause.

This sentence has two main clauses, and each main clause contains a subordinate clause.

SIMPLE SENTENCE

IC

Yesterday, <u>the dog was sick</u>.

COMPOUND SENTENCE

IC   *IC*

<u>Potatoes are healthy</u>, but <u>potato chips are not</u>.

IC   *IC*

<u>Life is not fair</u>; <u>it is just fairer than death</u>.

COMPLEX SENTENCE

SC   *IC*

<u>If you go into the woods today</u>, <u>you're in for a big surprise</u>.

COMPOUND-COMPLEX SENTENCE

IC   *IC*

SC   *SC*

Give me whatever money you can spare, and I will see to it that you get a tax receipt.

SC

IC

Here are examples of each sentence function:

DECLARATIVE
To err is human.

IMPERATIVE
To yourself be true.

INTERROGATIVE
What vision do I see before me?

EXCLAMATORY
You must listen to me!

Sentences can also be classified by function. Sentences can function in any of the following ways:

- as statements (declarative)
- as requests or commands (imperative)
- as questions (interrogative)
- as exclamations (exclamatory)

Alexey Lysenko/Shutterstock.com

Common Sentence Errors

> Blot out,
> correct, insert, refine,
>
> Enlarge, diminish, interline,
>
> Be mindful, when
> invention fails,
>
> To scratch your head,
> and bite your nails.
>
> —Jonathan Swift

Common Sentence Errors

LEARN TO IDENTIFY COMMON ERRORS IN ENGLISH

Sentence fragment

Fused sentence

Comma splice

Subject–verb agreement errors

Verb errors (form, tense, mood, voice)

Pronoun agreement errors

Pronoun reference errors

Pronoun case errors

Adjective and adverb errors

Modifier errors

STRATEGIES

Ways to Improve Your Grammar
1. Keep a list of "favourite" errors and edit with them especially in mind.
2. Use grammar checkers judicially.
3. Use a "buddy system." Ask a friend to read and make suggestions with an eye to clarifying your meaning.

The following sections catalogue a number of common errors made by writers in English. Use these sections to revise your work and to respond to questions and suggestions about your use of language. If you discover that you have a tendency to make any one of these errors with some frequency, review the relevant section carefully to internalize the information you find. Current grammar-checkers are mainly quite reliable, but it is still up to you to accept or reject the changes suggested, and to understand them. The grammar in this chapter reflects formal usage in academic documents, but usage is key: email and instant messaging have created increasingly informal usage. Be aware of the level of formality you need in a given document.

A sentence is, at the very least, one complete independent clause that contains a subject and verb. A **sentence fragment**, on the other hand, is part of a sentence that is set off as if it were a whole sentence by a beginning capital letter and a final period or other end punctuation. However, the fragment lacks the essential requirements of a grammatically complete and correct sentence.

LEARN TO IDENTIFY SENTENCE FRAGMENTS

The fragment may lack a main verb:

> Just Phil and I.

A sentence fragment can lack a subject:

> Pacing the hallway.

Note that even a phrase such as *Just Phil and I, pacing the hallway* does not have a main verb. Don't confuse the participle *pacing* with a main verb. Here, the participle operates as an adjective and modifies *Phil and I*; it doesn't provide a main action for the sentence.

A sentence fragment could also be a subordinate clause commencing with a subordinating word:

> When I fly a kite.

Sentence fragments give readers a fragment of a thought as opposed to a complete thought, and they interfere with writing clarity. In any type of academic writing, sentence fragments are considered a serious writing error, and they must be eliminated.

Everett Collection/CP Images

It has been twenty years since the release of *Rain Man* and now information about autism has certainly become much more widespread in our culture. I was curious to see how stereotypes regarding autism might have changed over the years, so I asked several of my friends and colleagues what characteristics stood out to them most about Hoffman's character in *Rain Man*. I found it interesting that most of them mentioned only his strange walk, odd behaviour and major social impairment. All of the traits that remained salient in their minds were negative. ~~Although what I found most distinct was his incredible gift with numbers and his innocent, child-like nature.~~ *Fix fragment*

TESTING FOR SENTENCE
FRAGMENTS
Fragments can be spotted
easily when they appear in iso-
lation, but they are more difficult to identify when they are
near complete sentences.

GET ORGANIZED

How to Identify Sentence Fragments

1. Does the word group have a verb?
   - ❏ YES. Consider the next question.
   - ❏ NO. The word group is a fragment and must be revised to include a verb.

2. Does the word group have a subject?
   - ❏ YES. Consider the next question.
   - ❏ NO. The word group is a fragment and must be revised to include a subject.

3. Does the word group start with a subordinating word, making it a subordinate clause?
   - ❏ YES. The word group is a sentence fragment and must be revised to create a complete sentence that is an independent clause.
   - ❏ NO. If you answered yes to the two previous questions and no to this one, the word group is a complete sentence and does not require revision for sentence completeness.

Make sure to consider all three questions when reviewing your sentence, since a fragment could be missing more than one essential sentence element. If your evaluation indicates that you have a sentence fragment, use the following strategies to transform it into a complete sentence.

ELIMINATING SENTENCE FRAGMENTS

ELIMINATE SENTENCE FRAGMENTS

To fix a sentence fragment and make it a complete sentence, do one of the following:

1. Attach the sentence fragments to an independent clause or a clause that contains the essential element lacking in the fragment (e.g., a subject or a verb), or add the missing element to the fragment.

   Just Phil and I **were** pacing the hallway.

2. Compose an independent clause from the fragment.

   At the emergency ward, **the parents were** pacing the hallway.

3. Drop the subordinating word.

   ~~When~~ I fly a kite.

 ELL Note

Subjects may not be omitted in English, except in the case of imperative sentences. Verbs may not be omitted either. If English is not your first language, consult 15-2i and 15-3a for further information.

10-1A SUBORDINATE CLAUSES

A subordinate clause contains a subject and a predicate, or verb, but the clause begins with a subordinating word or phrase (e.g., *after, although, if, until*) or a relative pronoun (*that, which, what, who*). Therefore, the clause is not independent.

CORRECT FRAGMENTS THAT INVOLVE SUBORDINATE CLAUSES

You can make a subordinate clause into an independent clause in one of two ways:

1. Merge the subordinate clause with a nearby sentence.

   Many of Elmore Leonard's novels have been made into movies.
   because
   ~~Because~~ he is an amazingly popular crime writer.

2. Delete the subordinating element of the clause.

   Many of Elmore Leonard's novels have been made into
   He
   movies. ~~Because he~~ is an amazingly popular crime writer.

CORRECT FRAGMENTS THAT INVOLVE PHRASES

Look at these examples of phrases:

to go kayaking

for the umpteenth time

with great trepidation

To make these examples into complete sentences, you must add a subject and verb.

To go kayaking, **you need stamina**.

For the umpteenth time, **pay attention**! (Here, the subject *you* is understood.)

The stray cat approached me with great trepidation.

Our community library has an amazing array of
. which is there for
resources. ~~For~~ every local citizen to use.

The phrase *for every local citizen to use* has been added to the sentence in a subordinate clause.

. a
He took part in the smudging. ~~A~~ ceremony that uses smoke to purify the psychic energy field, or aura, around a person.

The writer has used the phrase beginning *A ceremony that uses smoke* as an appositive to rename *smudging*.

Smokejumpers land with heavy gear, including two parachutes, puncture-proof Kelvar suits, freeze-dried food, fire shelters, and personal effects.
Next. cardboard   containing
^ ~~Cardboard~~ boxes ^ ~~heaved out of the airplane~~ chain
are heaved out of the airplane
saws, shovels, and axes^.

Cardboard boxes has become the subject, and the verb has been changed to *are heaved*.

A phrase is a group of words that does not have either a subject or a verb and, therefore, cannot stand alone as an independent clause or sentence.

Major types of phrases include noun phrases, adjective phrases, adverb phrases, and prepositional phrases. (For more information about phrases, see 9-3.)

FIXING PHRASE FRAGMENTS

You can address phrase fragment problems in two ways:

1. Incorporate the phrase into a nearby sentence.
2. Turn the phrase into a complete sentence by adding a subject, predicate (verb), or both.

Other commonly fragmented word groups include

- compound predicates
- examples introduced by *for example*, *such as*, and *for instance*
- lists

CORRECTING OTHER FRAGMENT PROBLEMS

DEFINITION:

Subject: Who or what is performing the action or being described

Predicate: What the subject is doing or experiencing, or what can be said about the subject.

Examples

   S   P

Kyle hit a home run. (The subject is *Kyle*; the predicate is *hit a home run*.)

   S   P

Kyle is a great baseball player. (The subject is *Kyle*; the predicate is *is a great baseball player*.)

COMPOUND PREDICATES

A **compound predicate** contains two or more predicates with the same subject.

FRAGMENTS WITH A COMPOUND PREDICATE

but

Joel wanted to buy a new computer and printer. ~~But~~ could only afford to purchase a used laptop.

The fragment starting *But could only* has been made part of the compound predicate. Note that no comma is required between compound elements of this predicate.

EXAMPLES INTRODUCED BY *FOR EXAMPLE, SUCH AS,* AND *FOR INSTANCE*

Often you will need to introduce examples, illustrations, and explanations to support arguments and ideas in your academic writing. Here are some common words and phrases used to introduce examples, illustrations, and explanations.

also	besides	as an illustration
and	such as	for example
but	namely	in particular
like	especially	furthermore
or	including	specifically
mainly	for instance	to illustrate
that is	in addition	equally important

Example

Any treatment of early-seventeenth-century English literature must include a discussion of the period's leading figures.~~—~~
such
~~Such~~ as John Donne, Ben Jonson, and John Milton.

Sometimes a fragment introduced by *such as* or *for example* or *for instance* can be attached to the sentence before it to create a complete sentence.

Example

Jan Morris's travel pieces cover many interesting cities.
　　　　she explores　　*visits*
For instance, ~~exploring~~ Beirut, ~~visiting~~ Chicago, and
　discovers
~~discovering~~ "The Navel City" of Cuzco.

However, in some instances you may find it necessary to change the fragment containing the examples into a new sentence.

Example

FRAGMENTS IN LISTS
Occasionally, list elements are fragmented. This type of writing problem can usually be corrected through the use of a colon or dash.

During my rare vacations, I work on my three R's.~~—~~
: reading
~~Reading,~~ rest, and running.

ACCEPTABLE FRAGMENTS　10-1D

USE ACCEPTABLE FRAGMENTS
CREATING EMPHASIS

> A strange place it was, that place where the world began. A place of incredible happenings, splendours and revelations, despairs like multitudinous pits of isolated hells. A place of shadow-spookiness, inhabited by the unknowable dead. A place of jubilation and of mourning, horrible and beautiful.

—Margaret Laurence, "Where the World Began," in *Heart of a Stranger*
(Toronto: McClelland & Stewart, 1976).

Professional writers may use sentence fragments intentionally for emphasis or effect.

Many instructors do not accept sentence fragments, even intentional ones, in formal writing. Fragments may be acceptable in less formal writing contexts, such as an informal personal essay or an article for a campus newspaper.

Even in contexts where they are permitted, do not overuse sentence fragments.

MAKING TRANSITIONS
Now for the con side.

RESPONDING STRONGLY
Not bloody likely!

ANSWERING QUESTIONS
And should we go along with this position? Under no circumstances.

ADVERTISING
Proven effective.

10-2) COMMA SPLICES AND FUSED SENTENCES

Incorrectly joining two or more independent clauses within a sentence is a common writing error. An independent (or main) clause contains at least a subject and a verb, and the clause can stand on its own as a separate grammatical unit. When two independent clauses appear in a single sentence, they must be joined in one of two ways:

1. Using a comma and one of the seven coordinating conjunctions (*and, but, for, nor, or, so, yet*)
2. With a semicolon or other acceptable punctuation mark such as a dash or a colon

LEARN TO IDENTIFY COMMA SPLICES

I gave up watching television, I started surfing the Internet.

You say "tomato," I say "tomato."

USE A COMMA WITH *AND, OR, NOR, FOR, BUT, YET, SO* TO JOIN TWO INDEPENDENT CLAUSES.
I gave up watching television, but I started surfing the Internet.

USE A SEMICOLON TO INDICATE A CLOSE CONNECTION BETWEEN INDEPENDENT CLAUSES.
You say "tomato"; I say "tomato."

IDENTIFY FUSED SENTENCES

> IC
> Canada's most famous racing ship is the *Bluenose* it
> IC
> was primarily designed to fish the Atlantic coast.

The first independent clause in this fused sentence is *Canada's most famous racing ship is the* Bluenose. The second independent clause is *it was primarily designed to fish the Atlantic coast.*

IDENTIFY COMMA SPLICES

A comma is too weak to join two main clauses by itself.

- ⊕ Canada's most famous racing ship is the *Bluenose*, it was primarily designed to fish the Atlantic coast.

COMMA SPLICE INVOLVING CONJUNCTIVE ADVERB

- ⊕ Canada's most famous racing ship is the *Bluenose*, however, it was primarily designed to fish the Atlantic coast.

- ⊕ Algernon hated winter, therefore, he decided to become a snowbird.

Fused sentences (also known as run-on sentences) or **comma splices** occur when two independent clauses are incorrectly joined within the same sentence.

FUSED SENTENCES

In a fused sentence, no punctuation or coordinating conjunction appears between the two independent clauses (IC).

FIXING COMMA SPLICES

In a sentence that contains a comma splice, the independent clauses are joined (or spliced) with a comma but no coordinating conjunction.

Often, writers use conjunctive adverbs in place of coordinating conjunctions and, in doing so, create comma splice errors. A coordinating conjunction is one of these seven words: *and, but, or, nor, for, so,* and *yet.*

A **conjunctive adverb** is a word such as *furthermore*, *however*, or *moreover*. Merely placing commas and one of these words between the two independent clauses does not correct a comma splice error.

Table 10.1 Common Conjunctive Adverbs

accordingly	however	now
also	incidentally	otherwise
anyway	indeed	similarly
besides	instead	specifically
certainly	likewise	still
consequently	meanwhile	subsequently
conversely	moreover	then
finally	namely	thereafter
further	nevertheless	therefore
furthermore	next	thus
hence	nonetheless	undoubtedly

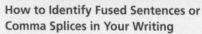

GET ORGANIZED

How to Identify Fused Sentences or Comma Splices in Your Writing

Use the following checklist to determine if a sentence is fused or is a comma splice.

- The sentence contains two independent clauses.
  - ❏ NO. Neither of the errors applies.
  - ❏ YES. Proceed to the next question.
- The independent clauses are joined by a comma and a coordinating conjunction.
  - ❏ YES. The clauses are correctly joined.
  - ❏ NO. Proceed to the next question.
- The independent clauses are joined by a semicolon or other acceptable punctuation, such as a colon or a dash.
  - ❏ YES. The clauses are correctly joined.
  - ❏ NO. Use one of the revision strategies provided in the next section to correct the fused sentence or comma splice.

In Canadian academic contexts, many readers will find a series of short sentences choppy and distracting. To connect two independent clauses into one sentence, join them with a comma followed by a coordinating conjunction or with a semicolon. Conversely, you should also try to avoid writing a series of very long sentences in a row. Balance your writing with appropriate numbers of long and short sentences.

CORRECT FUSED SENTENCES AND COMMA SPLICES

CORRECT A COMMA SPLICE WITH A COORDINATING CONJUNCTION

Canada's most famous racing ship is the *Bluenose*, **yet** it was primarily designed to fish the Atlantic coast.

CORRECT A COMMA SPLICE WITH A SEMICOLON

Canada's most famous racing ship is the *Bluenose*; it was primarily designed to fish the Atlantic coast.

OR

Canada's most famous racing ship is the *Bluenose*; **however,** it was primarily designed to fish the Atlantic coast.

CORRECT A COMMA SPLICE BY CREATING A SUBORDINATE CLAUSE IN PLACE OF ONE OF THE CLAUSES

Even though Canada's most famous racing ship is the *Bluenose,* it was primarily designed to fish the Atlantic coast.

CORRECT A COMMA SPLICE BY DIVIDING THE CONSTRUCTION INTO TWO COMPLETE SENTENCES

Canada's most famous racing ship is the *Bluenose*. **It** was primarily designed to fish the Atlantic coast.

STRATEGIES FOR CORRECTING FUSED SENTENCES OR COMMA SPLICES

You have four main options for correcting fused sentences or comma splices.

1. Add a comma and a coordinating conjunction (*and, but, for, nor, or, so, yet*).
2. Add a semicolon or other appropriate punctuation, such as a colon or a dash.
3. Revise the sentence to subordinate one of the clauses.
4. Turn each independent clause into a separate complete sentence.

10-2A REVISION WITH COORDINATING CONJUNCTION

A comma must precede the coordinating conjunction (*and*, *but*, *for*, *nor*, *or*, *so*, *yet*).

USE A COMMA BEFORE A COORDINATING CONJUNCTION JOINING TWO MAIN CLAUSES

It was minus 30 degrees with the wind-chill factor^ *,but* I still had to walk my dogs.

Mordecai Richler was a fine novelist,^ *and* he was also an amusing essayist.

10-2B REVISION WITH SEMICOLON OR COLON

Use a semicolon without a conjunction if the relationship between the two independent clauses is very clear.

USE A SEMICOLON TO JOIN TWO LOGICALLY RELATED MAIN CLAUSES

The results of the chemistry experiment were disappointing; our attempt to turn salad dressing into fine cognac had failed miserably.

USE A SEMICOLON AND A COMMA WITH INDEPENDENT CLAUSES THAT ARE JOINED WITH A CONJUNCTIVE ADVERB OR TRANSITIONAL PHRASE, SUCH AS THOSE IN THE FOLLOWING LIST:

also	as a result	besides
consequently	conversely	for example
for instance	furthermore	in addition
in fact	meanwhile	moreover
nonetheless	next	on the other hand
otherwise	similarly	subsequently
then	therefore	thus

Margaret Atwood is Canada's foremost living novelist; **furthermore,** she is among our leading poets.

USE A COLON IF THE FIRST INDEPENDENT CLAUSE INTRODUCES THE SECOND

The requests are thorough and varied: a chicken or rabbit will be skinned, boned, quartered, shredded, turned into patties, prepared for stew, the liver used for this, the kidney for that.

CORRECT A FUSED SENTENCE BY ADDING A SUBORDINATE CONJUNCTION

When the
~~The~~ ^family visited Niagara Falls^ we enjoyed visiting the wax museum, playing mini-golf, and taking pictures of the falls.

The rules of hockey developed in the 1870s~~, they~~
that
stipulated^ there be nine players on a team instead of six as there are today.

Since there
~~There~~ is a smog alert in south-central Ontario, people with breathing difficulties are not supposed to go outside.

This option for correcting fused sentences and comma splices is usually the most effective since it provides the most revision choices. You will first need to decide which of the independent clauses you would like to emphasize.

CORRECT A FUSED SENTENCE BY FORMING TWO COMPLETE SENTENCES

. The
Those who run for office are required to speak~~, the~~ speeches must be no longer than five minutes in length.

There is one council member from each region
. The
~~the~~ chairperson is elected by the council members.

Since the clauses in fused sentences and comma splices are independent, they can stand on their own as separate grammatical units.

Every sentence has a subject (stated or implied) and a verb. **Subject–verb agreement** refers to the relationship between the subject and the verb.

In the present tense, verbs must agree with subjects in two ways:

1. In **number**. Number means the subject can be singular (e.g., *I*) or plural (e.g., *we*).
2. In **person**. Person can be first person (*I*, *we*), second person (*you*), or third person (*she, he, it,* or *they*).

Often, if you have been speaking or writing English for a long time or know it well, problems with subject–verb agreement will be obvious to your ear or eye.

However, some subject–verb agreement problems are more difficult to spot. A number of English sentence constructions make the subject difficult to identify—often the subject is located far from the verb—and, as a result, it is easy to make subject–verb-agreement mistakes.

LEARN TO IDENTIFY SUBJECT–VERB AGREEMENT ERRORS

Being able to find subjects and verbs expertly will improve your grammatical accuracy.

Watch for third-person singular agreement in the present tense.

If the verb is a regular verb and the subject is in the third-person singular, use the -*s* (or -*es*) form of the verb.

Amir **works** for his godfather.

His godfather **stresses** the importance of being on time.

Table 10.2 Present-Tense Forms of *Work*

	Singular	Plural
First Person	I work	we work
Second Person	you work	you work
Third person	she/he/it works	they work

Notice how the following irregular verbs achieve subject–verb agreement.

Table 10.3 Present-Tense Forms of Common Irregular Verbs

Present-Tense Forms of *Do*

I do	we do
you do	you do
she/he/it does	they do

Present-Tense Forms of *Have*

I have	we have
you have	you have
she/he/it has	they have

The verb *to be* has different forms for the present and past tense.

Table 10.4 Forms of *To Be*

Present-Tense Forms of *Be*

I am	we are
you are	you are
she/he/it is	they are

Past-Tense Forms of *Be*

I was	we were
you were	you were
she/he/it was	they were

James look good in his new tuxedo.
James looks good in his new tuxedo.

WATCH FOR SUBJECT–VERB AGREEMENT WHEN WORDS COME BETWEEN THE SUBJECT AND VERB

You might consider drawing an arrow to connect the subject with the verb, as has been done in the example below.

The **first ten minutes** of a blind date **are** the most frightening.

practise

The women in my residence ~~practises~~ kung fu for hours every day.

The *subject* of the sentence above is *women*, not *residence*. The sentence verb is *practise*. Since the subject is in the third-person plural, the correct verb form is *practise,* not *practises*.

is

The **objective** in both cases ~~are~~ to give the students hands-on experience dealing with real-life situations.

The subject of the sentence is *objective*, not *cases*. The sentence verb is a form of the verb *to be*. The subject, *objective*, is in the third-person singular. To be correct, the verb form should be *is*, not *are*.

The **prime minister**, along with the cabinet, was photographed in the glamour shot.

The *prime minister* is the main subject of the sentence. If the writer had wanted to emphasize both the prime minister and the cabinet, he or she might have structured the sentence as follows: *The prime minister and the cabinet were photographed in the glamour shot.*

Occasionally, the modifying words between the sentence subject and verb include a noun, which might be mistaken for the subject. As a result, some writers use a verb that does not agree with the actual subject.

When evaluating any sentence for subject–verb agreement, in your mind, delete any modifying elements, such as prepositional phrases, so that only the sentence subject and verb remain. Then, assess whether or not the subject and verb agree.

Phrases beginning with *along with, as well as, in addition to,* and *together with* do not change the number of the subject because they are not really part of the subject. They are prepositional phrases used to modify the subject only.

10-3B SUBJECTS WITH *AND*

A compound subject contains two or more independent subjects joined by *and*. The compound subject requires a plural verb.

However, when the parts of the subject refer to a single person or idea, they require a singular verb.

The pronoun *each* is singular and requires a singular verb, even if the subjects it precedes are joined by *and*.

WATCH FOR SUBJECT–VERB AGREEMENT WITH COMPOUND SUBJECTS JOINED BY *AND*

Tina and Mauri were inseparable.

The American bulldog's unforgettable face and amazing

have

athletic ability ~~has~~ helped to make Harley a star of advertising media.

Rice and tomato is a San Francisco treat.

Spaghetti and clam sauce has been a favourite in our house for years.

Each woman and man is allowed one vote.

10-3C SUBJECTS WITH *OR* OR *NOR*

When a compound subject is joined by *or* or *nor*, make the verb agree with the part of the subject nearer to the verb.

WATCH FOR SUBJECT–VERB AGREEMENT WITH SUBJECTS JOINED BY *OR* OR *NOR*

Neither the tour guide nor his passengers know if the CN Tower is the world's tallest building.

Either the Beatles or Elvis Presley has had the most gold albums.

are

If my aunt or my cousins ~~is~~ available, they will come to the quilting bee.

is

Neither the cabinet members nor the prime minister ~~are~~ going to wave to the crowd.

WATCH FOR SUBJECT–VERB AGREEMENT WITH INDEFINITE PRONOUNS

The following are indefinite pronouns:

all	either	everybody	some
anybody	neither	everyone	somebody
anyone	nothing	everything	someone
anything	nobody	one	something
each	no one	none	

Everybody from our class **was** at the nudist colony.

smells
Something in the garage ~~smell~~ fishy.

pays
Everyone in our house ~~pay~~ bills on time.

Neither **is** correct.

Of the guests who were sent RSVP invitations, none **has** deigned to respond.

Neither of those flattering adjectives **applies** to my parents.

None of these programs **offers** bonus air miles.

An **indefinite pronoun** refers to an unspecified person or thing.

Even though many indefinite pronouns seem to refer to more than one person or thing, most require a singular verb. Note especially that *each*, *either*, and words ending in *-body* and *-one* are singular.

NEITHER AND *NONE*

When used alone, the indefinite pronouns *neither* and *none* require singular verbs.

When prepositional phrases with plurals follow the indefinite pronouns *neither* and *none*, in some cases a plural or singular verb may be used. However, it is best to treat neither and none consistently as singular.

INDEFINITE PRONOUNS THAT CAN BE SINGULAR OR PLURAL

A few indefinite pronouns, such as *all, any, more, most,* and *some,* can be singular or plural, depending on the noun or pronoun to which they refer.

Singular: All of the money **is** in a Swiss bank account.

Plural: All of his accounts **are** frozen because of the terrorist connection.

In the first example, *money* is a singular noun, so a singular verb is required. In the second example, *accounts* is a plural noun, so a plural verb is required.

10-3E   COLLECTIVE NOUNS

A collective noun names a class or a group of people or things. Some examples of collective nouns include *band, committee, family, group, jury,* and *team.*

Use a singular verb with the collective noun when you want to communicate that the group is acting as a unit.

Use a plural verb when you want to communicate that members of the group are acting independently.

WATCH FOR SUBJECT–VERB AGREEMENT WITH COLLECTIVE NOUNS

The band **agrees** that it needs a new drummer.

The first-year law class ~~have~~ *has* a test on Monday.

The *class* is considered a single unit, and individual action is not important to the sentence meaning. Therefore, a singular verb is required.

The original band **have** gone on to pursue solo careers and spend time in rehabilitation centres.

The first-year law class ~~has~~ *have* their fingerprints on file.

Each member of the class has his or her fingerprints on file.

Sometimes it is possible to better capture the idea of individual action by recasting the sentence with a plural noun.

The original band members **have gone** on to pursue solo careers and spend time in rehabilitation centres.

WATCH FOR SUBJECT–VERB AGREEMENT WITH THE WORD *NUMBER*

The number of ways to cheat death **is** increasing.

If *number* is preceded by *a*, treat it as a plural.

A number of Scrabble players **have** gotten a triple word score.

WATCH FOR SUBJECT–VERB AGREEMENT WITH UNITS OF MEASUREMENT

One-half of the fat in those French fries **is** unsaturated.

Only one-half of your promises **are** likely to be kept.

DECIDING WHETHER TO TREAT *NUMBER* AS SINGULAR OR PLURAL

If the collective noun *number* is preceded by *the*, treat it as a singular noun.

UNITS OF MEASUREMENT

Use a singular verb when the unit of measurement is used collectively—that is, when the thing described by the noun cannot be counted.

Use a plural verb when the unit of measurement refers to individual persons or things that can be counted.

SUBJECT AFTER VERB   10-3F

WATCH FOR SUBJECT–VERB AGREEMENT WHEN THE SUBJECT DOES NOT PRECEDE THE VERB

As goes the weather, so **goes** the oil stocks.

As goes the weather, so **go** the oil stocks.

There **are** significant differences among the pop stars of the '60s.

Most often the verb follows the subject in sentences. However, in certain cases, the verb may come before the subject, making it difficult to evaluate subject–verb agreement.

EXPLETIVE CONSTRUCTIONS

Expletive constructions include phrases such as *there is, there are, it is,* and *it was.* When these phrases appear at the beginning of a sentence, the verb often precedes the subject.

INVERTING SENTENCE ORDER

To achieve sentence variety, you may from time to time wish to invert traditional subject–verb order. Ensure that when you do this, you check that the subject and the verb agree.

are
Nestled on the couch ~~is~~ <u>a beautiful black malamute and a spectacular red setter</u>.

The compound subject, _a beautiful black malamute and a spectacular red setter_, requires a plural verb.

10-3G SUBJECT COMPLEMENT

A **subject complement** is a noun or adjective that follows a linking verb and renames or describes the sentence subject, as in _Elvis Presley is a cult figure_. (See 9-2b.) Because of its relationship to the subject, the complement can often be mistaken for the subject and result in subject–verb agreement errors.

MAKE SURE THE VERB AGREES WITH THE SUBJECT (BEFORE THE VERB) AND NOT THE COMPLEMENT (AFTER THE VERB)

_is_
The socialite's central <u>concern</u> ~~are~~ facial lines.

The subject of the sentence is _concern_, which is singular. If the subject is singular, the sentence requires a singular verb. The plural _lines_ is the complement.

are
<u>The advice column and the comics</u> ~~is~~ all I read in the newspaper.

The subject of the sentence is _the advice column and the comics_. Since it is plural, it requires a plural verb.

10-3H SUBJECT WITH RELATIVE PRONOUN

WHO, WHICH, AND _THAT_

A relative pronoun such as _who, which,_ or _that_ usually introduces an adjective clause that modifies the subject. The relative pronoun must agree with its antecedent. The antecedent is the noun or pronoun to which the relative pronoun refers. Thus, the verb in the adjective clause must agree with the antecedent.

WATCH FOR SUBJECT–VERB AGREEMENT IN SENTENCES WITH RELATIVE PRONOUNS

The wealthy industrialist <u>who</u> **donates** money to the food bank expects a tax deduction.

The singular noun _industrialist_ is the antecedent of _who_. The verb _donates_ must then be singular.

WATCH SUBJECT–VERB AGREEMENT IN SENTENCES USING *ONE OF THE* AND *THE ONLY ONE OF THE*

The stiletto heel is one of the styles of footwear <u>that</u>

cause
~~causes~~ a lot of medical problems.

The antecedent of *that* is *styles*, not *heel* or *footwear*. Since the antecedent is plural, to agree, the verb *cause* must also be plural.

is
The roller coaster is the only one of the rides <u>that</u> ~~are~~ worth the price.

The antecedent of *that* is *one*, not *rides*. Since the antecedent is singular, to agree, the verb must also be singular: *is*.

CONSTRUCTIONS USING *ONE OF THE* AND *THE ONLY ONE OF THE*

Subject–verb agreement mistakes are often made with relative pronouns when the sentence contains *one of the* or *the only one of the*.

Generally, use a plural verb with constructions containing *one of the*, and use a singular verb with constructions containing *the only one of the*.

PLURAL FORM, SINGULAR MEANING   10-3I

WATCH SUBJECT–VERB AGREEMENT WITH WORDS THAT LOOK PLURAL BUT ARE ACTUALLY SINGULAR

was
The news ~~were~~ encouraging.

When nouns such as *mathematics*, *physics*, and *statistics* refer to a particular item of knowledge, as opposed to the collective body of knowledge, they are treated as plural.

Environment Canada <u>statistics</u> **reveal** that the area experienced record amounts of smog.

Some words ending in *-ics* or *-s* are singular in meaning, even though they may seem plural in appearance. These words include *athletics, economics, ethics, physics, politics, statistics, mathematics, measles, mumps,* and *news*. Nouns such as these generally require a singular verb.

TITLES AND WORDS AS WORDS   10-3J

deals
<u>Dog Days</u> ~~deal~~ with the hilarious consequences of Peter's disenchantment with his job.

refers
In this report, <u>*illegal aliens*</u> ~~refer~~ to people who enter the country without following prescribed immigration procedures.

A work referred to by its title is treated as a singular entity, even if the title includes a plural word.

The verb communicates vital information in any sentence, often by indicating what is occurring, what has occurred, or what will occur. For writers, there are several major potential trouble spots relating to verbs. You'll know from the previous section that one common problem is making sure that a sentence's subject and verb agree. Unfortunately, there are other areas where writers frequently experience problems with verb usage.

ELL Note

If your first language is not English, you may also wish to consult 15-2, which offers advice on working with verbs in English.

Some potential trouble spots in using verbs include
- irregular verb forms (such as *drink, drank, drunk*)
- *lie* and *lay*
- *-s* (or *-es*) endings with verbs
- *-ed* endings
- omitted verbs
- verb tenses
- the subjunctive mood
- the active versus the passive voice

10-4A) IRREGULAR VERBS

With the exception of the verb *to be*, English verbs have five forms. These forms are shown here in brief sample sentences using the regular verb *talk* and the irregular verb *ring*.

With regular verbs, such as *talk*, the past tense and past participle verb forms are created by adding *-ed* or *-d* to the **base**, or simple, form of the verb. As you can see, this pattern is not followed for the irregular verb *ring*. In fact, many writers mix up the past tense and past participle of irregular verb forms, creating non-standard English sentences.

USE THE CORRECT FORM OF VERBS

Base (Simple) Form: Today I (talk, ring).
Past Tense: Yesterday I (talked, rang).
Perfect: I (have talked, have rung) many times in the past.
Progressive: I (am talking, am ringing) at this moment.
-s Form: She/he/it (talks, rings).

Non-standard: Many **have rang** the old church bell.
Standard: Many have rung the old church bell.

DEFINITIONS

Non-standard English is language other than edited English. You may encounter and use it in very informal speaking contexts, and also in much modern literature, but it is not acceptable in formal, academic writing and speaking contexts. Standard English should be used in all formal writing and speaking situations.

USE STANDARD VERB FORMS

❌ I ain't never going to graduate.

✓ I am never going to graduate.

PAST TENSE

Yesterday I **laughed** at Donna's joke.

Last May I **paid** the first installment on our big-screen television set.

PAST PARTICIPLE

Since that time I **have paid** two more installments.

My parents **have** never **understood** why I do not want to get married.

Yesterday there was snow, but today **it has gone** away.

Before we met, I **had never enjoyed** playing tennis.

shaken
Yesterday we were ~~shook~~ by a violent tremor.

sang
At the pep rally, I ~~sung~~ victory songs.

According to the insurance agent, the windshield was
broken
~~broke~~ before the accident.

swam
On the weekend, my grandfather ~~swum~~ one length of the pool.

Past Tense Form

Past tense verbs are used to communicate action that happened completely in the past. These verbs do not require helping verbs forms such as *was* or *were*.

Past Participle Form

The past participle always requires a helping verb. For the perfect tenses, these helping verbs could be *has*, *have*, or *had*. For the passive voice, the helping verbs are *be*, *am*, *is*, *are*, *was*, *were*, *being*, or *been*. (For a complete list of helping verbs, see 10-4e.)

How Do I Choose?

When you want to choose the standard English verb form for formal writing, first check to see if the verb is irregular. See if it is listed on the chart of common irregular verbs on pages 356 to 359. If the verb in your sentence does not require a helping verb, select the appropriate past tense verb. If the verb does require a helping verb, use the past participle form listed in the chart. Of course, regular verbs will follow the pattern outlined above for the regular verb *talk*.

COMMON IRREGULAR VERBS

This three-column chart lists many of the more common irregular verbs in the base (simple), past-tense, and past-participle forms. When composing a sentence or editing your work, find the relevant verb in the first column, then determine if you have used the correct past-tense or past-participle form. If you cannot find the verb in the chart, check in a good Canadian dictionary that lists irregular verb forms.

Table 10.5 Common Irregular Verbs

Base (Simple) Form	Past Tense	Past Participle
arise	arose	arisen
awake	awoke, awaked	awaked, awoken
be	was, were	been
bear (carry)	bore	borne
bear (give birth)	bore	born
beat	beat	beaten, beat
become	became	become
begin	began	begun
bend	bent	bent
bet	bet	bet
bid	bid	bid
bind	bound	bound
bite	bit	bitten, bit
blow	blew	blown
break	broke	broken
bring	brought	brought
build	built	built
burst	burst	burst
buy	bought	bought
catch	caught	caught
choose	chose	chosen
cling	clung	clung
come	came	come
cost	cost	cost
creep	crept	crept
cut	cut	cut
deal	dealt	dealt
dig	dug	dug
dive	dived, dove	dived
do	did	done
drag	dragged	dragged
draw	drew	drawn

Base (Simple) Form	Past Tense	Past Participle
dream	dreamed, dreamt	dreamed, dreamt
drink	drank	drunk
drive	drove	driven
eat	ate	eaten
fall	fell	fallen
feed	fed	fed
feel	felt	felt
fight	fought	fought
find	found	found
flee	fled	fled
fling	flung	flung
fly	flew	flown
forbid	forbade, forbad	forbidden
forget	forgot	forgotten, forgot
freeze	froze	frozen
give	gave	given
go	went	gone
grow	grew	grown
hang (execute)	hanged	hanged
hang (suspend)	hung	hung
have	had	had
hear	heard	heard
hide	hid	hidden
hit	hit	hit
hold	held	held
hurt	hurt	hurt
keep	kept	kept
know	knew	known
lay (put)	laid	laid
lead	led	led
leave	left	left
lend	lent	lent
let (allow)	let	let

(continued)

Base (Simple) Form	Past Tense	Past Participle
lie (recline)	lay	lain
light	lighted, lit	lighted, lit
lose	lost	lost
make	made	made
mean	meant	meant
pay	paid	paid
prove	proved	proved, proven
put	put	put
quit	quit	quit
read	read	read
ride	rode	ridden
ring	rang	rung
rise (get up)	rose	risen
run	ran	run
say	said	said
see	saw	seen
seek	sought	sought
send	sent	sent
set (place)	set	set
shake	shook	shaken
shine	shone, shined	shone, shined
shoot	shot	shot
show	showed	shown, showed
shrink	shrank	shrunk, shrunken
sing	sang	sung
sink	sank	sunk
sit (be seated)	sat	sat
slay	slew	slain
sleep	slept	slept
slide	slid	slid
sling	slung	slung
sneak	sneaked	sneaked
speak	spoke	spoken

Base (Simple) Form	Past Tense	Past Participle
spend	spent	spent
spin	spun	spun
spring	sprang	sprung
stand	stood	stood
steal	stole	stolen
sting	stung	stung
stink	stank, stunk	stunk
strike	struck	struck, stricken
strive	strove	striven
swear	swore	sworn
swim	swam	swum
swing	swung	swung
take	took	taken
teach	taught	taught
tear	tore	torn
tell	told	told
think	thought	thought
throw	threw	thrown
understand	understood	understood
wake	woke, waked	waked, woken
wear	wore	worn
win	won	won
wring	wrung	wrung
write	wrote	written

**DECIDING BETWEEN
LIE AND *LAY***

The forms of the verbs *lie* and *lay* are frequently confused.

1. *Lie*, meaning "to recline," is an intransitive verb, which means it cannot be followed by a direct object.
2. *Lay*, meaning "to set down," is a transitive verb, which means it must be followed by a direct object.

USE THE CORRECT VERB: *LIE* OR *LAY*

I am going to **lie** on the beach this afternoon.

Jack **lay** his weary head on the table.

Table 10.6 *Lie* and *Lay*

Base (Simple) Form	Past Tense	Present Participle
lie	lay, lain	lying
lay	laid, laid	laying

Yesterday I ~~laid~~ *lay* in the hammock for a few hours.

Since the meaning is "to recline," the verb should be a form of *to lie*. The correct past-tense form of *lie* is *lay*.

The workers were ~~lying~~ *laying* the new tile floor in my bathroom.

Here the meaning is "to set down," so the correct verb is *lay*. The present participle of *lay* is *laying*.

The book has ~~laid~~ *lain* on my desk, unopened, for two days.

An additional meaning of *lie* is "to rest on a surface," so a form of the verb *to lie* is appropriate here. The past participle of *lie* is *lain*.

USE THE -S IN THE THIRD-PERSON SINGULAR PRESENT TENSE

I tell, you tell, we tell, you tell, they tell, visitors tell

BUT

THIRD-PERSON SINGULAR

she tells, he tells, it tells, Jane tells, the parrot tells, everybody tells

As you can see, the third-person singular includes nouns such as *Jane* and *parrot*; the pronouns *she*, *he*, and *it*; and the indefinite pronoun *everybody*.

involves
Pre-production ~~involve~~ all the planning up to the day the camera

takes
operator ~~take~~ out the camera.

The sentence subject *pre-production* is third-person singular, so the verb must end in -s. In the subordinate clause, the subject is *camera operator*, which is also third-person singular and thus requires the -s ending, as in *takes*.

DO NOT USE -S EXCEPT WITH THIRD-PERSON SINGULAR IN THE PRESENT TENSE

draft
First, I ~~drafts~~ a script for the video.

serve
We often ~~serves~~ cheese and crackers instead of a dessert course.

buzz
The bees ~~buzzes~~ around my head whenever I go near their hive.

In the first sentence the subject is *I*, which is first-person singular; thus, the -s ending is not required. In the second sentence, the subject is *we* (second-person plural), and in the third sentence, the subject is the *bees* (third-person plural). Neither requires the -s verb ending.

Use the -s (or -es) form of a verb in the present when the subject is third-person singular. Often, people who speak English dialects or who are just learning English omit verb endings such as -s (or -es). Although the -s verb ending may be omitted in some non-standard English speech, it should *never* be omitted in standard English speaking and writing situations. (See 10-3.)

WHEN NOT TO ADD AN -S (-ES) VERB ENDING
If the subject is not third-person singular, do not add an -s (-es) verb ending.

has
That expressway usually ~~have~~ heavy traffic jams in the morning.
Does
~~Do~~ anybody know what time it is?
doesn't
The stage manager ~~don't~~ think it is necessary to alter the backdrop.

10-4D *-ED* ENDINGS

For regular verbs, the past tense and past participle are formed by adding *-ed* or *-d* to the base verb, as in *talked* and *have talked,* or *used* and *have used.*

Make sure to add the *-ed* or *-d* ending to the base (simple) verb for all regular past-tense or past-participle verbs.

Some speakers omit *-ed* endings from past-tense and past-participle regular verbs and also omit the endings from these words in their writing. Often, it can be difficult to remember the *-ed* ending because in some verbs it is not very distinctly pronounced (for example, *asked, learned, licensed, passed, practised, supposed to*).

PAST TENSE

The past tense indicates an action that has happened at a particular time in the past. To form the past tense of a regular verb, add *-ed* or *-d* to the base (simple) verb form.

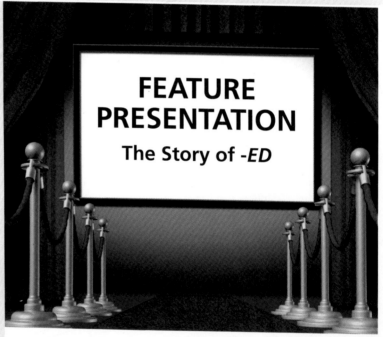

Lightspring/Shutterstock.com

ADD *-ED* TO THE ENDING OF PAST-TENSE REGULAR VERBS

watched
Last January we ~~watch~~ an opera by Verdi at the Four Seasons Centre.
licensed
Amazingly, the province ~~license~~ his great uncle to drive.

USE PAST PARTICIPLES CORRECTLY

1. **to form one of the perfect tenses**
   In this case, the past participle follows *have*, *has*, or *had*.

   developed
   The scientist had ~~develop~~ a new technique for destroying cancer cells.

   Had developed is the past perfect tense (*had* followed by a past participle; here *developed*).

   For more information on the perfect tenses, see page 366 in 10-4f.

2. **to form the passive voice**
   In this case, the past participle follows *be*, *am*, *is*, *are*, *was*, *were*, *being*, or *been*.

   created
   The decorations were ~~create~~ by the social club.

   Were created is in the passive voice. The subject, *the decorations*, is the receiver of the action. In the passive voice, a form of *be* (here *were*) is followed by the past participle (here *created*).

3. **as an adjective modifying nouns or pronouns**
   weakened
   The medics carried the ~~weaken~~ soldier to the field hospital.

   Here, the past participle *weakened* modifies the noun *soldier*.

PAST PARTICIPLES
Past participles may be used in three ways.

For more information on the passive voice, see 10-4h.

For more information on using participles as adjectives, see 9-3b.

OMITTED VERBS   10-4E

DO NOT OMIT LINKING OR AUXILIARY VERBS

After tracing the call, the police discovered that the caller
was
^ a fellow employee.

LINKING VERBS

I *am* overcome by shock.

He *was* short, dark, and handsome.

The dodo *has been* extinct for many years.

LINKING VERBS
A linking verb is a main verb that links a subject with a subject complement (a word or words that renames or describes the subject). Linking verbs indicate a condition or state of being. They are often forms of the verb *to be*, such as *am*, *was*, or *been*.

Some linking verbs appear in contractions, such as in *I'm* for *I am* or *it's* for *it is*. Especially in formal writing, do not leave out linking verbs.

For more information on linking verbs, see 9-2b.

HELPING, OR AUXILIARY, VERBS

A helping verb, also known as an auxiliary verb, is a form of *to be, do, can, have, may, will, shall, could, would, might,* or *must* that combines with a main verb to express tone, and voice.

Like linking verbs, helping verbs can be contracted as in *she's going* or *they've been warned*. Especially in formal writing, do not leave out helping verbs.

For more information on helping verbs, see 9-1d.

HELPING VERBS

A tutor *can* help you improve your study skills.

I *will* never desert my husband.

We *must* have left the door unlocked.

have
Housing prices ^ escalated in recent months.

 If English is not your first language, you might consult the section on omitted verbs, 15-2i.

Avoid contractions in formal writing.

 Atwood and Munro are among the most popular Canadian writers. They've written many works that have become bestsellers here and in other countries.

10-4F TENSE

Tense indicates the time or duration of an action. The following section outlines some common writing problems associated with verb tenses and suggests strategies for avoiding these problems and ways of correcting them. One major problem connected with verb tense—shifts from one verb tense to another—is covered

LEARN TO IDENTIFY VERB TENSES

QUICK TIP

Overview of Verb Tenses
There are three basic verb tenses.
1. Present
2. Past
3. Future

Each tense has three forms, also known as aspects.
1. Simple
2. Perfect
3. Progressive

The *simple present tense* indicates something that happens regularly or in the present.

I **wipe** the counters.

The *simple past tense* indicates a completed action that happened at a particular time in the past.

She **skated** at the recreation centre yesterday.

The *simple future tense* indicates an action that will happen sometime in the future.

We **will ask** the neighbours to our housewarming party.

The table below provides the simple forms for the regular verb *to cook*, the irregular verb *to take*, and the irregular verb *to be*.

in detail in 12-1b. Before exploring tense problems in detail, it is important to understand English verb tenses.

SIMPLE FORMS
The three simple tenses divide time into present, past, and future.

Table 10.7 Simple Forms for All Tenses

Simple Present

Singular		Plural	
I	cook, take, am	we	cook, take, are
you	cook, take, are	you	cook, take, are
she/he/it	cooks, takes, is	they	cook, take, are

Simple Past

Singular		Plural	
I	cooked, took, was	we	cooked, took, were
you	cooked, took, were	you	cooked, took, were
she/he/it	cooked, took, was	they	cooked, took, were

Simple Future

I, you, she/he/it, we, they	will cook, will take, will be

PERFECT FORMS

There are perfect forms for present, past, and future tenses.

The *present perfect tense* indicates action that has happened in the past.

We **have shovelled** the driveway twice this morning.

The *past perfect tense* indicates an action that has been completed at some time in the past before another past action.

We **had shovelled** the driveway before the snowplow circled our street.

The *future perfect tense* indicates an action that will take place before some time in the future.

I **will have finished carving** the pumpkin before the little goblins arrive.

Table 10.8   Perfect Forms for All Tenses

Present Perfect	
I, you, we, they	have cooked, have taken, have been
she/he/it	has cooked, has taken, has been
Past Perfect	
I, you, she/he/it, we, they	had cooked, had taken, had been
Future Perfect	
I, you, she/he/it, we, they	will have cooked, will have taken, will have been

Table 10.9 Progressive Forms for All Tenses

Present Progressive	
I	*am cooking, am taking, am going*
she/he/it	*is cooking, is taking, is going*
Past Progressive	
I, she/he/it	*was cooking, was taking, was going*
you, we, they	*were cooking, were taking, were going*
Future Progressive	
I, you, she/he/it, we, they	*will be cooking, will be taking, will be going*
Present Perfect Progressive	
I, you, we, they	*have been cooking, have been taking, have been going*
she/he/it	*has been cooking, has been taking, has been going*
Past Perfect Progressive	
I, you, she/he/it, we, they	*had been cooking, had been taking, had been going*
Future Perfect Progressive	
I, you, she/he/it, we, they	*will have been cooking, will have been taking, will have been going*

ELL Note

Verbs that involve mental activity, such as *think, know,* and *imagine,* usually do not use progressive forms. (See 15-2b.)

PROGRESSIVE FORMS

The progressive forms indicate that an action, occurrence, or state of being is ongoing, or progressive. This ongoing action can take place in the present, past, or future, and can be either completed or not yet completed (i.e., still going on). Progressive verb forms are created by combining the present participle and forms of the verb *to be* as a helping, or auxiliary, verb.

OBSERVING SPECIAL USES OF THE PRESENT TENSE

As well as being used to indicate that something happens or can happen in the present, the present tense has several special uses in formal academic writing.

QUICK TIP

The present tense is used in literature and in general truths and scientific principles to indicate things that are universally true and present.

DISCUSSING CONTENT IN LITERARY WORKS

The **literary present tense** refers to the use of the present tense to discuss events that have happened in the past. Using the present tense to describe fictional events in novels, short stories, or films makes these events feel more immediate.

USE THE PRESENT TENSE TO DISCUSS LITERATURE AND FILM

In Todd Field's *In the Bedroom,* the mother's grief
seethes   *reaches*
~~seethed~~ until it ~~reached~~ a boiling point.

In Martin Scorsese's film about George Harrison, *Living in the Material*
                    witnesses
World, the viewer ~~witnessed~~ interviews with fellow Beatles and with George Harrison himself from the days of Beatlemania until near the end of his life.

GENERAL TRUTHS AND SCIENTIFIC PRINCIPLES

General truths and scientific principles should appear in the present tense.

However, if a scientific principle has been disproved, the verb can be presented in the past tense.

USE THE PRESENT TENSE TO EXPRESS THINGS THAT ARE UNIVERSALLY TRUE

                              reduces
According to mechanical advantage, a machine ~~reduced~~ the force necessary to move a load.

According to the early Greeks, the brain **pumped** blood through the body.

USE THE PRESENT TENSE TO SUMMARIZE OR PARAPHRASE IDEAS

contends

John Stuart Mill ~~contended~~ that "genius can only breathe freely in an atmosphere of freedom."

Note that John Stuart Mill (1806–73) is no longer alive. The present tense is used to introduce an author's view, even if the author is dead.

G. Temple (1995) **described** the patient's way of transforming words and numbers into images.

USE THE PAST PERFECT TENSE TO INDICATE AN ACTION PERFORMED BEFORE ANOTHER ACTION IN THE PAST

I **had completed** a draft of the essay before we learned about Britain's post-colonial involvement.

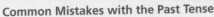

STRATEGIES

Common Mistakes with the Past Tense

1. Using the simple past tense when the sentence's meaning and grammar require the past perfect tense.
2. Overusing the past perfect tense. Do not use the past perfect tense if two past actions in the sentence happened at the same time.

---

had left

By the time I arrived at the station, the bus ~~left~~.

Both actions took place in the past, but one took place before the other. The past perfect is used to indicate that one action was completed (*the bus had left*) before the other happened (*I arrived*).

SUMMARIZING, PARAPHRASING, AND QUOTING

Often, to introduce ideas or support your own, you will need to present the views of another author. When summarizing, paraphrasing, or directly quoting an author's views as expressed in a non-literary work, use the present tense.

Exception: If you are following the American Psychological Association style for in-text citation, use the past tense when the date and author's name are provided.

USING THE PAST PERFECT TENSE CORRECTLY

The past perfect tense (i.e., the perfect form of the past tense) indicates an action that has been completed at some time in the past, before another action. The past perfect is formed by using the helping verb *had* before the past participle of a verb.

Do not use past perfect when two actions happened at the same time in the past.

had

By the time the hikers came, we ^ cleared the trail.

The action of clearing the trail had been completed before the hikers arrived, so the past perfect tense is required.

As the train approached the Zurich station, the conductor ~~had~~ arrived to check our tickets.

USING CORRECT TENSES WITH INFINITIVES AND PARTICIPLES

Infinitives

An infinitive is a verb form consisting of the simple verb form and, usually, *to*.

Present Tense Infinitive:

Use the present tense infinitive (*to exercise, to fly*) to indicate action that takes place at the same time as, or later than, the action of the sentence's main verb.

Present Perfect Infinitive:

The perfect form of the infinitive is created by placing the helping verb *to have* in front of the past participle (*to have exercised, to have flown*). Use the present perfect infinitive to indicate action that takes place before the action of the main sentence verb.

BE CAREFUL WITH VERB TENSES USED WITH INFINITIVES AND PARTICIPLES

"I'm not afraid of death; I just don't want to be there when it happens."

—Woody Allen

lose

Bert had tried to ~~have lost~~ weight before his vacation.

The action of the infinitive (*to lose*) took place at the same time or later than the action of the sentence verb (*had tried*).

have finished

I would like to ~~finish~~ the paper on time.

The time of the main verb, *would like*, is the present. Since the paper should have been finished before the present, the present perfect infinitive is used.

PRESENT PARTICIPLE

Flying over British Columbia, Danielle spotted her hometown through the clouds.

The present participle is required since Danielle spotted her hometown at the same time as she was flying over British Columbia.

PAST PARTICIPLE

Made of cedar, the canoe floated well.

The making of the canoe took place before the canoe floated.

PRESENT PERFECT PARTICIPLE

Having invested all his money in a dot-com, Yuri lost it all when profits in the high-technology sector dramatically declined.

Yuri's investment took place before his unfortunate financial loss.

Participles

The tense of the participle is determined by the tense of the main sentence verb.

Present Participle: Use the present participle (*risking, making*) when the action occurs at the same time as that of the main sentence verb.

Past Participle or Present Perfect Participle: Use the past participle (*risked, made*) or the present perfect participle (*having risked, having made*) to indicate action that occurred before that of the main sentence verb.

MOOD   10-4G

LEARN TO IDENTIFY THE MOOD OF THE VERB

INDICATIVE MOOD

The indicative mood states a fact or opinion or asks a question.

The library **needs** our assistance.

IMPERATIVE MOOD

The imperative mood gives an order or a direction.

Be at the library by eight.

SUBJUNCTIVE MOOD

The subjunctive mood expresses demands, recommendations, requests, and conditions that are either contrary to fact or desired.

If I **were** you, I would try to avoid the boss today.

The mood of a verb indicates the manner of action. There are three moods of a verb: the **indicative**, the **imperative**, and the **subjunctive**. By using one of three verb moods, a writer can show how he or she views a thought or action. For instance, through his or her choice of mood, a writer can indicate if he or she is expressing an opinion or a wish.

The subjunctive mood is used to express demands, recommendations, and requests

Other Problems with Verbs **10-4**

in clauses using *that*. It is also used to express conditions that are contrary to fact or are wished for. Finally, it is seen in idiomatic expressions such as *be that as it may*. Note that the subjunctive mood appears more commonly in North American than in British usage. Many writers frequently use the subjunctive mood incorrectly.

FORMING THE SUBJUNCTIVE

To create the subjunctive mood with *that* clauses, use the base (simple) form of the verb (e.g., *come, decide, produce*). Do not change the verb to indicate whether the subject is singular or plural.

It is crucial that I **be** [not **am**] at the interview on time.

The judge requested that he **produce** [not **produces**] more evidence.

If you are employing the subjunctive to express a contrary-to-fact clause starting with *if* or to express a wish, use *were*, the past subjunctive mood tense form of *to be*. Do not use *was*.

I wish that I **were** [not **was**] seventeen again.

It is necessary that you **be** in class every morning.

I wish I **were** in Dixie.

If only I **were** able to be with you!

I recommend that he **answer** the question.

Be that as it may, we have no choice but to detain you.

APPROPRIATE USES OF THE SUBJUNCTIVE

The subjunctive mood is used in the following writing situations:

- contrary-to-fact clauses beginning (usually) with *if* or *as if*
- contrary-to-fact clauses expressing a wish
- *that* clauses after verbs such as *ask, insist, recommend, request, require, suggest,* and *urge*
- idiomatic expressions such as *suffice it to say* or *be that as it may*

were
If she ~~was~~ our class president, she would fight for the cause.

were
Denise acts as if Roger ~~was~~ her slave.

Not Contrary to Fact: If he **gets** a flight, he will cancel his bus ticket.

Contrary-to-Fact Clauses Beginning with *If* or *As If*
In the subjunctive, use *were* to express a contrary-to-fact clause starting with *if* or *as if*.

The *if* clauses express conditions that do not exist—they are contrary to fact; therefore, they require the subjunctive.

The subjunctive is not used when the *if* clause expresses a condition that does exist or may exist.

Formal (Writing): I wish that the reading material in Dr. Vavougis's medical office **were** better.

Note: In informal speech, people often use the indicative mood in place of the subjunctive.

Informal (Speech): I wish that the reading material in Dr. Vavougis's medical office **was** better.

In a formal writing context, when you need to express a wish, always use the subjunctive.

Contrary-to-Fact Clauses Expressing a Wish
In the subjunctive, use *were* to express a wish.

be
The memorandum requires that all employees ~~are~~ there.

present
It is suggested that the examination candidate ~~presents~~ himself or herself at 9:30 a.m.

These sentences are expressed in the subjunctive because they involve suggestions, requirements, or requests.

That* Clauses after Verbs Such as *Ask*, *Insist*, *Recommend*, *Request*, *Require*, *Suggest*, and *Urge
The following verbs can indicate a requirement or a request: *ask, insist, recommend, request, require, suggest,* and *urge*. These verbs often come before a clause starting with *that*. These sentences require the subjunctive.

The subjunctive mood is used in idioms and expressions (e.g., *as it were, be that as it may, come rain or shine, far be it from me, God be praised, suffice it to say*).

Suffice it to say, they concur.

10-4H VOICE

Voice refers to whether the sentence subject is the actor performing the action communicated by the sentence verb or the receiver of that action. In the active voice the subject (S) performs the action, while in the passive voice the subject is acted upon. Only transitive verbs (TV)—those verbs requiring a direct object (DO)—can be active or passive.

The passive voice consists of a helping, or auxiliary, verb (some form of *to be*) plus the past participle, as in *was taken*.

LEARN TO DISTINGUISH BETWEEN ACTIVE AND PASSIVE VOICE

ACTIVE VOICE

$$S \quad TV \quad DO$$

The <u>guard</u> **took** the <u>prisoner</u> to his cell.

PASSIVE VOICE

$$S \qquad TV$$

The <u>prisoner</u> **was taken** to his cell by the guard.

For more information on the active and passive voice, see 9-2b.

CHANGING A SENTENCE FROM THE PASSIVE TO THE ACTIVE VOICE

In most cases, use the active voice in your academic writing. The active voice tends to be clearer and more concise,

Every spring, ~~gardens are planted by~~ millions of North
   plant gardens
American homeowners^.

In this sentence, the main sentence verb is *plant*. Who plants? *Millions of homeowners*. Therefore, to make the sentence active, make the homeowners the subject and the gardens the direct object.

Remember, most grammar-checkers will point out passive voice very quickly, and you can then decide whether to make a change in wording.

> I was interrupted by a salesman who came to my door. He wanted to sell me magazines.

direct, powerful, and dramatic. Passives, by contrast, tend to be wordier, more awkward, and less direct.

To change a sentence from the passive to the active voice, identify the sentence actor (who or what performs the main sentence action) and make that actor the sentence subject.

WHEN THE PASSIVE VOICE IS APPROPRIATE

Although the active voice is often preferable, the passive voice does have important functions. It is appropriate when the actor is unknown or unimportant, or when responsibility for an action should not or cannot be assigned.

The passive voice is often used in technical and scientific writing in which a process, as opposed to a person, is important.

When writing about historical events, you may wish to use the passive voice to avoid assigning blame for an action or to emphasize that a certain group was acted upon.

USE THE PASSIVE VOICE WHEN THE SUBJECT IS UNIMPORTANT OR UNKNOWN

The bank **was robbed** late last night.

A tornado **was spotted** heading this way.

The solution **is pumped** through a special filter where harmful impurities **are extracted**.

During the 1950s in British Columbia's Kootenay region, Doukhobor parents **were compelled** to send their very young children to a residential school.

ELL Note

Do not always avoid the passive voice. It is, in many cases, appropriate. For information on how to transform the active voice to the passive, consult 15-2c.

Other Problems with Verbs **10-4**

A pronoun is a word that replaces a noun or another pronoun. Three major types of pronoun problems occur frequently in writing:

1. Antecedent agreement problems: The pronoun does not agree with the noun or pronoun to which it refers.
2. Reference problems: It is not clear to which noun or pronoun the pronoun refers.
3. Case problems: The case of a pronoun is its form in a particular sentence context—whether the pronoun functions as a subject, object, or a possessive. Writers sometimes confuse pronoun case.

STRATEGIES

Identifying Pronoun Errors
There are three kinds of errors to watch for:
1. Pronoun agreement
2. Pronoun reference
3. Pronoun case

COMMON PRONOUN ERRORS

PRONOUN ANTECEDENT AGREEMENT
Someone has left their silver slipper behind.

PRONOUN REFERENCE
When the fire alarm rang in the classroom, they all trooped out.

PRONOUN CASE
I would like to thank everyone who helped Kate and I on this trip.

10-5A PRONOUN–ANTECEDENT AGREEMENT

The antecedent is the word the pronoun replaces. (*Ante* in Latin means *before*.) A pronoun must agree with its antecedent.

LEARN TO IDENTIFY ERRORS IN PRONOUN AGREEMENT

If the antecedent is singular, the pronoun that refers to it must also be singular.

The microbiologist adjusted **his** microscope.

Similarly, if the antecedent is plural, the pronoun must be plural.

The choir members opened **their** song books.

Pronouns like *he, she, his, her,* and *its* agree in gender with their antecedents, not with the words they modify: <u>Lorna</u> travelled with <u>her</u> [not *his*] chauffeur to Saskatoon.

Indefinite pronouns do not refer to any specific person, thing, or idea:

another	everybody	no one
anybody	everyone	nothing
anyone	everything	one
anything	neither	somebody
each	nobody	someone
either	none	something

<u>Anyone</u> who knows the answer should enter it using ~~their~~ *his or her* keyboard.

CORRECT ERRORS IN AGREEMENT WITH INDEFINITE PRONOUNS

1. Change the plural pronoun to a singular, such as *he* or *she*.

   When the airplane hit severe turbulence, everyone feared for ~~their~~ *his or her* safety.

2. Make the pronoun's antecedent plural.

   When the airplane hit severe turbulence, ~~everyone~~ *the passengers* feared for their safety.

3. Recast the sentence to eliminate the pronoun agreement problem.

When the airplane hit severe turbulence, ~~everyone feared for their safety.~~ *safety was a common fear among all those on board.*

Since the use of *his* or *her* can be awkward and wordy, especially if used repeatedly, you might consider correction strategies 2 and 3 as preferable alternatives. Do, however, be careful to use inclusive language when gender is involved.

GENERIC NOUNS

A **generic noun** names a typical member of a group, such as a typical *classroom teacher*, or a typical *dentist*. Generic nouns might appear to be plural; however, they are singular.

If a plural pronoun incorrectly refers to a generic noun, there are three major ways to remedy the error. As you will notice, they are the same as those outlined above for correcting indefinite pronoun–agreement problems.

COLLECTIVE NOUNS

A collective noun names a group of people or things. Examples of collective nouns include *audience, army, choir, class, committee, couple, crowd, faculty, family, group, jury, majority, number, pack,* and *team*.

CORRECT ERRORS IN PRONOUN AGREEMENT WITH GENERIC NOUNS

Each Olympic <u>athlete</u> must sacrifice if **he or she plans** [not **they plan**] to win a gold medal.

1. Although the average Canadian complains about
   he or she feels
   overwork, ~~they feel~~ powerless to cut back.
   Canadians complain
2. Although ~~the average Canadian complains~~ about overwork, they feel powerless to cut back.
   The
3. ~~While the~~ average Canadian complains about overwork,
   but feels
   ~~they feel~~ powerless to cut back.

CORRECT PRONOUN AGREEMENT WITH COLLECTIVE NOUNS
If the Collective Noun Refers to a Unit
Use the singular pronoun.

The <u>audience</u> stood and applauded to show **its** approval.

If Parts of the Collective Noun Act Individually
Use a plural pronoun.

The <u>audience</u> folded up **their** lawn chairs and left the park.

Often it is a good idea to emphasize that the antecedent is plural by adding a word, such as *members*, describing individuals within the group.

The audience <u>members</u> folded up **their** lawn chairs and left the park.

Maintain Singular or Plural Consistency

The faculty ~~have~~ *has* completed **its** review of courses for the upcoming term.

Its is a singular pronoun but *have* is a plural verb form. To be consistent, the verb should be changed to *has*. The sentence could also be revised to read: *The faculty have completed their review of courses for the upcoming term*, but in that case it might be preferable to add the word *members* after *faculty*.

Whether you treat the collective noun as singular or plural, ensure that you consistently treat references within the sentence as singular or plural, respectively.

WATCH FOR PRONOUN AGREEMENT WITH COMPOUND ANTECEDENTS

Dave and Michaela were hungry after **their** [not **his and her**] day of skiing in Whistler.

COMPOUND ANTECEDENTS
Two or More Antecedents Joined by *And*
Antecedents joined by *and* form a **compound antecedent** and require a plural pronoun whether the antecedents are plural or singular.

Two or More Antecedents Connected by *Or, Nor, Either … Or, Neither … Nor*

Make the Pronoun Agree with the Nearest Antecedent

Either Melodie or the Chans will have **their** way.

   Note: With a compound antecedent such as the one above, place the plural noun last to prevent the sentence from sounding awkward.

Neither the captain nor the other players could explain **their** lopsided defeat.

   In a sentence with a compound antecedent in which one antecedent is masculine and the other is feminine, rewrite the sentence to avoid any gender problem.

Original: Either Michelle or Yuri will be selected to have **his** documentary previewed at the campus film festival.

Rewrite: The judges will select Michelle's or Yuri's documentary for a preview at the campus film festival.

A pronoun is a word that replaces a noun or another pronoun. Using pronouns allows you to avoid repeating nouns in speech and writing.

However, when the relationship between the antecedent and the pronoun is ambiguous, implied, vague, or indefinite, the intended meaning can become unclear or completely lost to the reader.

AVOIDING AMBIGUITY ABOUT PRONOUN REFERENCE

When it is possible for a pronoun to refer to either one of two antecedents, the sentence is ambiguous.

LEARN TO IDENTIFY PRONOUN REFERENCE ERRORS

Once <u>Jarod</u> made the <u>sandwich</u>, **he** packed **it** in a brown bag.

The noun or pronoun that the pronoun replaces is its antecedent. Here the pronoun *he* clearly relates to the antecedent *Jarod*, and the pronoun *it* clearly relates to the antecedent *sandwich*.

CORRECT AMBIGUOUS PRONOUN REFERENCES

Ambiguous: <u>Franz</u> told **his**

?

<u>father</u> that **his** car needed a new transmission.

In this sentence the second possessive pronoun *his* could refer to *Franz* or *his father*: is Franz talking about his father's car or his own car?

To eliminate the ambiguity, either repeat the clarifying antecedent or rewrite the sentence.

Option 1: Franz told his father that his father's car needed a new transmission.

Option 2: Franz said, "Dad, your car needs a new transmission."

Before the raging fire spread too close to nearby farms,
the residents
~~they~~ were ordered to leave their homes.

Although in the original sentence it is implied that the occupants of the farms were the ones ordered to leave, it is not explicitly stated. The pronoun *they* has no clear antecedent.

Make sure that antecedents refer to nouns present in, or near, the sentence.

Naomi Wolf

In ~~Naomi Wolf's~~ *The Beauty Myth*, ~~she~~ explores the relationship between gender and work.

In the original sentence, it is not clear who is doing the exploring. The wording allows the possibility that it is not *Naomi Wolf*, but a contributor to her book.

CORRECT BROAD PRONOUN REFERENCES SO THAT THEY REFER TO A SPECIFIC NOUN

The international figure skating organization agreed to a
the change
major overhaul of the judging process; however, ~~it~~ took time.

A spot forecast may state that a temperature range for a specific canyon in the forest will be between 25 and 30 degrees; the humidity between 12 and 14 percent, and the winds 15 kilometres an hour.
All of these details interest
~~This interests~~ firefighters.

AVOIDING IMPLIED ANTECEDENTS

The reader should be able to clearly understand the noun antecedent of any pronoun you use. This antecedent must be stated and not implied or merely suggested.

AVOIDING VAGUENESS WHEN USING PRONOUNS

Pronouns such as *this*, *that*, *which*, and *it* should refer clearly to a specific noun antecedent and not large groups of words expressing ideas or situations.

AVOIDING INDEFINITE USE OF *IT, THEY,* OR *YOU*

The pronouns *it, they,* and *you* must have clear, definite antecedents.

CORRECT PRONOUN REFERENCES THAT LACK CLEAR ANTECEDENTS

Using It

Do not use the pronoun *it* indefinitely (e.g., *In this book it says* …).

~~In~~ Chapter 23 of the textbook ~~it~~ states that one of the most important factors in transforming Canadian culture was the change in immigration patterns.

Using They

Never use *they* without a definite antecedent.

the director, screenwriter(s), and actors

In a typical Hollywood movie, ~~they~~ manipulate the audience's emotions.

Using You

In formal writing, the use of *you* is acceptable when you are addressing the reader directly—for example, when you are writing instructions.

If **you** do not want the beeper on, select OFF, and if **you** want it loud, select HIGH.

In formal writing, do not use *you* as an indefinite pronoun.

one

In ancient Greece, ~~you~~ dropped a mussel shell into a certain jar to indicate that a defendant was guilty.

10-5C   PRONOUN CASE

Case refers to the form a pronoun takes according to the function of that pronoun in a sentence. In English there are three cases.

1. The **subjective case** indicates that the pronoun functions as a subject or a subject complement.

LEARN TO DISTINGUISH AMONG PRONOUN CASES

Table 10.10   Pronoun Cases

Subjective	Objective	Possessive
I	me	my, mine
we	us	our, ours
you	you	your, yours
she/he/it	her/him/it	her/his/its, hers
they	them	their, theirs

Two common pronoun case difficulties are

1. when to use *I* instead of *me*, *he* instead of *him*, *they* instead of *them*, and so on (that is, the subjective and objective cases of personal pronouns)
2. when to use *who* instead of *whom*

Subjective Case: when the pronoun is the performer of the action or is being described

She is brilliant.

Objective Case: when the pronoun is the receiver of the action

Give *her* an A+.

Possessive Case: when the pronoun owns something

That is *her* book.

CORRECT PRONOUN CASE TO MAKE IT FUNCTION CORRECTLY IN THE SENTENCE

As a Subject

I

Tony and ~~me~~ split the cost of the video.

As a Subject Complement

she

The students who did the most work are Ivan and ~~her~~.

In all formal writing, ensure that you use the subjective pronoun case when the pronoun is part of the subjective complement.

The <u>woman</u> Anatole married is **she**.

The subject complement of the subject *woman* is the pronoun *she*.

If the construction sounds too unnatural, you may wish to recast the sentence.

She is the <u>woman</u> Anatole married.

2. The **objective case** indicates that the pronoun functions as the object of a preposition or a verb.
3. The **possessive case** indicates that the pronoun shows ownership.

The remainder of this section will help you to clearly distinguish between the subjective and the objective case; it also explains how to avoid common pronoun case errors. The final part of the section explains common uses of pronouns in the possessive case.

SUBJECTIVE CASE

The subjective case (*I, we, you, she/he/it, they*) must be used when the pronoun functions as a subject or as a subject complement.

A subject complement is a noun or adjective that follows a linking verb and renames or describes the sentence subject. Since the way pronouns are used in the subjective case often sounds quite different than the way you might use pronouns in informal speech, subjective case pronouns as subject complements frequently cause writing difficulties.

OBJECTIVE CASE

An objective case pronoun (*me, us, you, her/him/it, them*) is used when the pronoun functions as an object.

Compound Subjects and Objects

A **compound subject** or a **compound object** includes more than one pronoun or noun.

The fact that the subject or object is compound does not affect the case of the pronoun. However, compound structures often cause writers to confuse pronoun case.

To determine if you have selected the correct pronoun case, try mentally blocking out the compound structure and focusing on the pronoun in question. Then, decide if the pronoun case you have selected is correct.

As a Direct Object
The instructor asked **her** to read the poem.

As an Indirect Object
The invigilator gave pencils to Sam, Duncan, and **me**.

As the Object of a Preposition
Just between you and **me**, the Russian's routine was superior.

Since *between* is a preposition, it requires the objective form of the pronoun: *me*.

WATCH FOR PRONOUN CASE ERRORS WITH COMPOUND SUBJECTS AND OBJECTS

In a Compound Subject
She and I went to the multiplex to see a movie.

In a Compound Object
The park proposal surprised **her** and **me**.

~~My two roommates and~~ me ⟶ did the driving.
~~My two roommates and I~~

You would say *I did the driving,* so the correct choice for the compound is *My two roommates and I did the driving.*

I
In spite of our difficulties, my uncle and ~~me~~ had a wonderful vacation in Mexico.

You wouldn't say *me had a wonderful vacation*, so the correct choice is *my uncle and I*. The pronoun is part of the subject of the sentence, so the subjective case is required.

$\overset{me}{}$

After the class, the librarian gave detentions to Rachel and ~~I~~.

You wouldn't say *gave detentions to I*, so the correct choice is *to Rachel and me*. The pronoun is the indirect object, so the objective case is required.

Resist the impulse to use a reflexive pronoun such as *myself* or *himself* when you are uncertain about the pronoun case.

$\overset{me}{}$

The contest organizers sent the entry forms to Del and ~~myself~~.

In this sentence, *Del* and *me* are the indirect objects of the verb *sent*, so the objective case (*me*) is correct.

As an Appositive

$\overset{I}{}$

Three members of the debating team—Clara, Michael, and ~~me~~—were mentioned in the article.

Clara, Michael, and I is an appositive for the sentence subject *three members*. As a result, the subjective case of the pronoun is required.

$\overset{me}{}$

Let's you and ~~I~~ take the weekend off and go to the St. Jacob's market.

You and me is an appositive to *us* (*let's* is a contraction of *let us*). *Us* is the objective of the verb *let*; therefore, the objective case of the pronoun is required.

Appositives

An appositive is a noun or noun phrase that renames a noun, noun phrase, or pronoun. When a pronoun functions as an appositive, it has the same function, and hence the same case, as the noun or pronoun it renames.

WE OR US BEFORE A NOUN

Sometimes you may need to decide whether *we* or *us* should come before a noun or noun phrase. Mentally block out the noun so that only the pronoun remains. Then, decide which pronoun case is correct.

Before a Noun

We ~~piano players~~ ⟶

Us ~~piano players~~ ⟶ play scales every day.

We is correct since the subjective case of the pronoun is required.

Follow the same procedure when considering pronouns that function as sentence objects.

> *us*
The teacher yells at ~~we~~ banjo players during every practice.

You wouldn't say *The teacher yells at we*. The word *us* functions here as an object of the preposition *at*, so the objective case is required.

COMPARISONS USING THAN OR AS

When making comparisons using *than* or *as*, writers frequently leave out words because these words are clearly understood by readers.

The case of the pronoun is determined by its function in the implied part of the sentence, which has been omitted. To determine the correct pronoun case in a sentence that uses *than* or *as* to make a comparison, supply the implied or missing part of the sentence. Then, decide if the pronoun case is correct.

In Comparisons

Last year Bill Gates made more money *than* I ~~made~~.

> *she*
The groom is a full metre taller than ~~her~~.

When the omitted words are supplied, the sentence reads: *The groom is a full metre taller than she [is]. She* is the subject of the verb *is*; therefore, the subjective case of the pronoun is required.

> *me*
My late grandmother left my cousin as many family heirlooms as ~~I~~.

When the omitted words are supplied, the sentence reads: *My late grandmother left my cousin as many family heirlooms as [she left] me. Me* is the indirect object of *left*.

INFINITIVES

The infinitive is the base (simple) form of a verb, usually following *to*, as in *to jump*.

As the Subject of an Infinitive

The minister asked **her** [not **she**] to sing at the wedding.

As the Object of an Infinitive

Club members decided to elect **him**.

As a Modifier to a Gerund

his
The physical trainer disapproved of ~~him~~ eating bacon before workouts.

Nouns as well as pronouns can modify gerunds; as with pronouns, you must use the possessive case of the noun. The possessive is formed by adding an apostrophe and -*s* to the end of the noun.

Wayne's <u>smoking</u> is the cause of his bad breath.

Wayne's
The physical trainer disapproved of ~~Wayne~~ eating bacon before workouts.

For more information on possessives, see 11-4a.

Both the subject and the object of an infinitive are in the objective case.

MODIFYING A GERUND

A **gerund** is a form of a verb that ends in -*ing* and is used as a noun; for example, *Fencing is my favourite sport*. Use a pronoun in the possessive case (*my, our, your, her/his/its, their*) to modify a gerund or gerund phrases.

WATCH FOR PRONOUN CASE ERRORS WHEN USING *WHO* AND *WHOM*

⊘ I know who you saw last night.

⊘ He is a specialist whom, people say, will find a cure for cancer.

◗ The woman whom we saw yesterday at city hall is running for mayor.

◗ She is a candidate who, I believe, will do an excellent job of serving her constituency.

Who and *whom* are pronouns. *Who* is the subjective case; it must be used only for subjects and subject complements. *Whom* is the objective case; it must be used only for objects.

Who and *whom* are used as interrogative pronouns to open questions. They are also used as relative pronouns, to introduce subordinate clauses.

AS INTERROGATIVE PRONOUNS OPENING QUESTIONS

To decide whether to use *who* or *whom*, you must first determine the pronoun's function within the question. Does the interrogative pronoun function as a subject or subject complement, or is it an object? Determine whether the subjective or objective case is required by recasting the question as a statement—that is, giving a possible answer to the question. Temporarily substitute a subjective case pronoun, such as *he*, or an objective case pronoun, such as *him*.

AS RELATIVE PRONOUNS INTRODUCING SUBORDINATE CLAUSES

Use *who* and *whoever* as relative pronouns for subjects, and use *whom* and *whomever* for objects. When deciding which pronoun to use, you must determine whether the relative pronoun functions as a subject or object within the subordinate clause. A good technique to employ when making this decision is to mentally block off the subordinate clause you are considering.

AS INTERROGATIVE PRONOUNS

Who

~~Whom~~ commanded the coalition forces during the war in Afghanistan?

A possible answer would be *He commanded the coalition forces. Him commanded* would not work. *He* is the subject of the verb *commanded*. Therefore, the subjective case is required, and *who* is the correct interrogative pronoun.

Whom

~~Who~~ did the human resources manager interview?

A possible answer to the question would be *The human resources manager interviewed her. Interviewed she* would not work. *Her* would be the direct object of the verb *did interview*. Therefore, the objective case is required, and *whom* is the correct interrogative pronoun.

AS RELATIVE PRONOUNS

whoever

The Nobel Prize for Literature is presented to [~~whomever~~ has made the most significant contribution to literature over the course of a writing career.]

When determining the correct relative pronoun, consider only the subordinate clause. Hence, the main clause (*The Nobel Prize for Literature is presented to*) is mentally set aside. The relative pronoun of the subordinate clause is the subject of the verb *has made*. The subjective pronoun case is required; thus, the relative pronoun *whoever* is the correct choice. Notice, however, that the entire subordinate clause functions as the object of the preposition *to*.

whom

We don't know [~~who~~ the university president nominated to chair the committee.]

Mentally set aside *We don't know* to enable you to focus exclusively on the subordinate clause. The relative pronoun is the object of the verb *nominated*. Thus, the objective case is required, and the correct pronoun is *whom*.

Do not be misled by interrupting expressions such as *I know*, *they think*, or *she believes*, which often come after *who* or *whom* in a subordinate clause.

The car dealer intends to invite only the customers

who

[~~whom~~ *he thinks* will want to attend.]

Mentally set aside *The car dealer intends to invite only the customers* and *he thinks*. The relative pronoun of the remaining subordinate clause is the subject of the verb *will want*. Therefore, the subjective case is required, and the correct relative pronoun is *who*.

ADVERBS AND ADJECTIVES (10-6

STRATEGIES

Identifying Problems with Adverbs and Adjectives

Adverbs can modify
- verbs
  He left the examination **early**.
- adjectives
  Her cheeks were **slightly** red.
- other adverbs
  They ate dinner **very** late.

Adjectives can modify
- nouns
  The **blue** ball is in the corner.
- pronouns
  He is **tired**.

Adjectives and adverbs are modifiers. Adjectives modify nouns and pronouns. Adverbs modify verbs, adjectives, and other adverbs.

Many adverbs end in *-ly* (*quickly, oddly*); however, some do not (*often, very*). As well, a number of adjectives end in *-ly* (*lovely*).

Problems can occur when adjectives are incorrectly used as adverbs or vice versa. The best way to decide whether a modifier should be an adjective or an adverb is to determine its function in the sentence. If you are in doubt about whether a word is an adjective or an adverb, you might also consult a good Canadian dictionary.

ELL Note

Adjectives in English do not have to agree in number or gender with the words they modify. *The white [not whites] tree ornaments were purchased during my last holiday.*

10-6A ADVERBS

In modifying a verb, another adverb, or an adjective, an adverb answers questions such as *why? when? where? how?*

USE ADVERBS TO ANSWER *HOW, WHEN, WHERE, WHY*

The following are some common misuses of adjectives in situations where adverbs are required:

1. Using adjectives to modify verbs

          loudly   *clearly*
   The choir <u>sang</u> ~~loud~~ and ~~clear~~ at the concert.

2. Using the adjective *good* when the adverb *well* is required

   The minister of education indicated to the media that he wants

                 well
   students within the province to be able to <u>write</u> ~~good~~.

For more detail on the correct uses of *good* and *well*, see page 570 in the usage glossary.

3. Using adjectives to modify adjectives or adverbs

                really
   The museum in Niagara Falls has a ~~real~~ <u>unusual</u> collection of artifacts.

ELL Note

For help with placement of adjectives and adverbs in English, see 15-3e.

WATCH THE PLACEMENT OF ADJECTIVES IN A SENTENCE
BEFORE NOUN OR PRONOUN
She watched the **red** <u>dawn</u>.

AFTER LINKING VERB
<u>Silence</u> *is* **golden**.

Linking verbs communicate states of being as opposed to actions.

The <u>milk</u> at the back of the refrigerator *tasted* ~~sourly~~. *[sour]*

<u>She</u> *seems* ~~happily~~. *[happy]*

When my headache returned, I *felt* ~~badly~~. *[bad]*

In these examples, the verbs *taste*, *seem*, and *feel* communicate states of being that modify the subject, so adjectives are required.

MODIFYING THE SUBJECT
The girl looked **curious**.

Curious modifies the subject, *girl*. Here, *looked* is a linking verb and the modifier is an adjective. The adjective *curious* describes the girl's state of being.

MODIFYING THE VERB
The girl looked **curiously** at the man dressed in a bunny suit.

Here, *curiously* modifies the verb, *looked*. The adverb *curiously* describes how the act of looking was done.

Usually, adjectives come before the nouns or pronouns they modify.

However, adjectives can also function as subject complements that follow a linking verb. The subject complement renames or describes the sentence subject.

LINKING VERBS
Some verbs—such as *look, feel, smell,* and *taste*—may or may not be linking verbs. When the word after the verb modifies the subject, the verb is a linking verb, and this modifying word should be an adjective. However, when the word modifies the verb, it should be an adverb.

Adjectives and adverbs can take three forms:

1. The positive
2. The comparative
3. The superlative

WHEN TO USE THE COMPARATIVE FORM AND WHEN TO USE THE SUPERLATIVE FORM

When comparing two entities, use the comparative form.

When comparing three or more entities, use the superlative.

DO NOT USE DOUBLE COMPARATIVES OR SUPERLATIVES

DO NOT USE COMPARATIVES OR SUPERLATIVES WITH ABSOLUTE CONCEPTS

Absolute concepts by their very nature cannot be compared. If two diamonds are perfect, one cannot be more perfect than the other.

USE THE CORRECT FORM OF THE ADJECTIVE OR ADVERB

IN COMPARISONS OF TWO

lesser
Which is the ~~least~~ of the two evils?

faster
The jaguar moves ~~fastest~~ than the lion.

IN COMPARISONS OF THREE OR MORE

Of all the playwrights, I feel that William Shakespeare is the **greatest**.

most
She is the ~~more~~ selfish of the three sisters.

Of the two playwrights, I feel that William Shakespeare is the ~~more~~ greater.

beautiful
The painting is probably one of the most ~~beautifulest~~ in the museum.

The cat looks **more pregnant** than she did last week.
The cat's pregnancy is more obvious than it was last week.

That painting by Leonardo da Vinci is ~~very~~ unique.

unusual
The bizarre comedy was the most ~~unique~~ I have ever seen.

Some examples of absolute concepts are: *favourite, unique, perfect, pregnant, impossible, infinite,* or *priceless.*

Table 10.11 Forming Comparatives and Superlatives

ADJECTIVES		
Positive	**Comparative**	**Superlative**
One- and most two-syllable adjectives		
red	redder	reddest
crazy	crazier	craziest
Longer adjectives		
intoxicating	more intoxicating	most intoxicating
selfish	less selfish	least selfish
Irregular		
good	better	best
bad	worse	worst
No comparative or superlative form		
unique	—	—
pregnant	—	—

ADVERBS		
Positive	**Comparative**	**Superlative**
Ending in -*ly*		
selfishly	more selfishly	most selfishly
gracefully	less gracefully	least gracefully
Not ending in -*ly*		
fast	faster	fastest
Irregular		
well	better	best
badly	worse	worst
No comparative or superlative form		
really	—	—
solely	—	—

10-6D DOUBLE NEGATIVES

A *double negative* is a non-standard English construction in which negative modifiers such as *no, not, neither, none, nothing*, and *never* are paired to cancel each other. Double negatives should be avoided in any formal writing.

Two negatives are only acceptable in a sentence if they create a positive meaning.

In standard English, the modifiers *barely, hardly*, and *scarcely* are considered negative modifiers. These words should not be paired with words such as *no, not*, or *never*.

DO NOT USE DOUBLE NEGATIVES

The government ~~never~~ does <u>nothing</u> to solve the problems affecting the poor.

Canadians will <u>never</u> vote for ~~no~~ new taxes.

anything
Barry did not feel ~~nothing~~ during his hernia operation.

They could ~~not~~ <u>barely</u> hear the tiny girl speak.

10-7 PROBLEMS WITH MODIFIERS

A modifier is a word, phrase, or clause that describes or limits another word, phrase, or clause within a sentence. Modifiers must be placed carefully and correctly or else they will cloud—or, in some instances, destroy—sentence meaning.

LEARN TO IDENTIFY MODIFIER ERRORS

Not all modifier errors are funny, though some are:

I shot an elephant in my pyjamas.

Lincoln wrote the Gettysburg address while travelling there on the back of an envelope.

QUICK TIP

Generally, modifying words should be kept close to the words they modify.

WATCH FOR MODIFIER ERRORS WITH LIMITING MODIFIERS LIKE *ONLY* AND *EVEN*

She **nearly** <u>missed</u> the swim team's practice.

Place limiting words such as *just, even, only, almost, hardly, nearly,* and *merely* directly before the verb they modify.

If a limiting word modifies another word in the sentence, place the modifier in front of that word.

Incorrect: In the first quarter, Steve Nash did not **even** score <u>one point</u>.
Correct: In the first quarter, Steve Nash did not score **even** <u>one point</u>.

In this example, *even* must modify *one point* instead of *score*, so the modifier should be placed in front of *one point*.

Incorrect: Louis Cyr **only** weighed <u>250 pounds</u>.
Correct: Louis Cyr weighed **only** <u>250 pounds.</u>

Here, *only* must modify *250 pounds* instead of *weighed*, so the modifier should be placed in front of *250 pounds*.

The modifier *not* is often misplaced, a situation that can create confusing or unintended meanings.

Unintended Meaning: All snake bites are **not** lethal.
Intended Meaning: Not all snake bites are lethal.

In the first version, one possible meaning is that no snake bite is lethal, which could be a dangerous assumption in certain parts of the world. The correction makes the meaning clear: one does not have to worry that all snake bites are lethal.

A **misplaced modifier** is a describing word, phrase, or clause that is incorrectly positioned within a sentence so that the modifier's meaning is illogical or unclear. The misplaced modifier relates to, or modifies, the wrong word or words in the sentence. When a modifier is misplaced, unusual misreadings can result.

WATCH FOR PHRASES OR CLAUSES THAT ARE NOT CLOSE ENOUGH TO WHAT THEY MODIFY

🔸 Jennifer sat waiting for her boyfriend to park the car **in a slinky red dress with a plunging neckline**.

✅ **In a slinky red dress with a plunging neckline**, Jennifer sat waiting for her boyfriend to park the car.

When the modifier is placed so far from what it modifies, the reader could easily conclude that it is Jennifer's boyfriend who is wearing the slinky dress.

🔸 The counter clerk at the soda fountain brought the sundae to the eager young boy **covered in chocolate sauce**.

✅ The counter clerk at the soda fountain brought the sundae **covered in chocolate sauce** to the eager young boy.

The first sentence can be misinterpreted two ways: either the clerk or the boy was covered in chocolate sauce. The second sentence makes it clear that the sundae was covered in chocolate sauce.

🔸 A beautiful painting attracts the viewer's eye **on the wall of the National Gallery**.

✅ A beautiful painting **on the wall of the National Gallery** attracts the viewer's eye.

The painting, not the viewer's eye, is on the wall.

Sometimes, modifier placement can lead to ambiguity so that two or more revisions are possible. The correction chosen will depend on the writer's intended meaning.

Ambiguous: The fellow we interviewed at the station **yesterday** turned up in London.
Clear: The fellow we interviewed yesterday at the station turned up in London.
Clear: The fellow we interviewed at the station turned up in London yesterday.

In the first sentence, it is unclear whether the fellow was interviewed yesterday or turned up in London yesterday. The first correction makes it clear the interview was yesterday, while the second makes it clear he turned up yesterday.

AWKWARDLY PLACED MODIFIERS   10-7C

Awkward: The dog, **after chasing the mail carrier**, wagged its tail and pranced triumphantly to the front porch.
Clear: **After chasing the mail carrier**, the dog wagged its tail and pranced triumphantly to the front porch.

There is no reason to separate the subject *dog* from the verb *wagged* with a fairly long modifying clause.

As well, keep auxiliary verbs near to the main verbs.

Awkward: I <u>have</u> **as long as I can remember** <u>had</u> a scar on my elbow.
Clear: I <u>have had</u> a scar on my elbow **as long as I can remember**.

The complete verb is *have had*, so the main and auxiliary verb should be placed together.

Sentences should generally flow in a pattern from subject to verb to object. Keep the subject as close to the main verb as possible and, where possible, don't separate the subject from the main verb of the sentence with a modifying adverb clause.

An infinitive consists of *to* and the verb, as in *to love*, *to leave*, and *to forget*. In a **split infinitive**, a modifier is placed between *to* and the verb. Frequently, including a split infinitive in a sentence will make the sentence awkward, and the sentence will need to be revised. One famous example of a split infinitive is in the opening to *Star Trek*, "To boldly go where no man has gone before"; it is parodied by Douglas Adams in *The Hitchhiker's Guide to the Galaxy*: "Men boldly split infinitives that no man had split before." Split infinitives are not considered grammatical errors in modern writing and are often very effective usage, but they are easy to spot, so use them at your peril.

WATCH FOR SPLIT INFINITIVES

While many people do not consider the split infinitive incorrect, it is easy to adjust for the sake of clarity.

Awkward: Financial analysts expected the stock prices **to**, after a period of sharp decline, dramatically **rise**.
Clear: Financial analysts expected the stock prices **to rise** dramatically after a period of sharp decline.

Here, the phrasing is awkward because of a long intervening phrase that splits the infinitive. A similar case is illustrated below:

Awkward: Try **to**, if you can get it, **see** her latest DVD.
Clear: Try **to see** her latest DVD if you can get it.

However, in some instances, split infinitives are preferable to alternative wordings. It might be argued that the following split infinitive is essential because of a slight nuance in meaning:

The audience failed **to** <u>completely</u> **understand** the argument.

This may mean that that the audience's understanding was incomplete, but not that their failure was complete, as it would in this example where the infinitive is not split:

The audience failed <u>completely</u> **to understand** the argument.

Generally, avoid split infinitives in formal writing. They are often pointed out as errors, even though they are quite common in informal writing. They are not errors, but it may be better to play it safe since many regard them as such.

WATCH FOR DANGLING MODIFIERS THAT DO NOT CONNECT TO A WORD OR PHRASE IN YOUR SENTENCE

A dangling modifier can be any of the following:

- a participial phrase
  <u>Believed to be dangerous</u>, an old lady was accosted on the street.

- a gerund phrase
  <u>After eating dinner</u>, the turkey was left sitting on the table.

- an infinitive phrase
  <u>To win first place on a reality-TV show</u>, a strong stomach is needed.

To repair dangling modifier problems, use one of the following revision strategies:

ADD A NEW SUBJECT

- Believed to be dangerous, an old lady was accosted on the street.
- Believed to be dangerous, **an escaped convict** accosted an old lady on the street.

EXPLICITLY STATE THE IMPLIED SUBJECT OF A GERUND PHRASE

- After eating dinner, the turkey was left sitting on the table.
- After eating dinner, **we** left the turkey sitting on the table.

EXPLICITLY STATE THE IMPLIED SUBJECT OF AN INFINITIVE PHRASE

- To win first place on a reality-TV show, a strong stomach is needed.
- To win first place on a reality-TV show, **a contestant** needs a strong stomach.

> A **dangling modifier** is a word, phrase, or clause that does not relate to any word within the sentence and, as a result, confuses the reader. Dangling modifiers usually appear at the start of the sentence, and the person who performs the action is not mentioned.

Also watch out for elliptical phrases. The subject of the participle must be explicitly stated in order to avoid dangling modifiers.

⊘ Keep stirring the meat until browned.

As it stands, this sentence implies that the person stirring the meat is being browned, not the meat.

✓ Keep stirring the meat until **it is** browned.

In an **elliptical clause**, a word or phrase required by the rules of grammar is omitted because the clause is thought to be understood without it. Above, the elliptical clause has an implied subject and verb; *it is* means "the meat is," a connection that is implied but not stated in the unclear elliptical clause.

Punctuation

11

A strict and
succinct style
is that where
you can take
away nothing
without loss, and that
loss to be manifest.

—Ben Jonson

(image) ideeone/iStockphoto.com

Punctuation

This section on punctuation follows the one on grammar because so many issues of punctuation depend on a knowledge of grammar. For this reason, grammar-checkers cannot easily catch routine comma errors, so don't rely on them to do so. Refer to this section for advice on problem areas you encounter as you compose and revise.

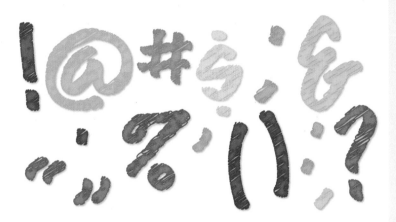

THE COMMA 11-1

⊕ While emailing Mary Beth spoke on the telephone with her stockbroker.

⊕ When eating the baby spilled her porridge frequently.

Commas help readers understand how writers have grouped or separated words. Frequently, a comma is essential to ensure that readers clearly understand your intended meaning. Omitting or misplacing a comma can easily lead to misreadings.

11-1A COMMAS BETWEEN INDEPENDENT CLAUSES WITH A COORDINATING CONJUNCTION

Some writers may leave out the comma before the coordinating conjunction in less formal contexts or in very brief sentences. Also, the comma alone may be used if the clauses show sharp contrast or are direct speech. However, formal academic writing demands a period or a semicolon to separate clauses.

Never use a comma to separate independent clauses in formal writing. To do so is to make a comma splice error.

CONNECT INDEPENDENT CLAUSES WITH A COMMA AND *AND, OR, NOR, FOR, BUT, YET, SO*

I enjoy watching television, **but** I draw the line at World Wrestling Entertainment.

Blessed are the meek, **for** they shall inherit the earth.

Leave out the comma when independent clauses are brief or informal.

We ate supper and then we went to bed. (brief)

Phone the doctor and make an appointment. (informal)

LEAVE OUT THE CONJUNCTION WHEN INDEPENDENT CLAUSES SHOW SHARP CONTRAST OR ARE IN DIRECT OR REPORTED SPEECH

Dogs have masters, cats have staff. (contrast)

Young girls often pluck the petals from daisies and repeat, "He loves me, he loves me not." (reported speech)

11-1B COMPOUND ELEMENTS

Compound elements in a sentence do not require commas. Do not break up two subjects or two verbs or two subordinate clauses. Use a comma before a conjunction to separate independent clauses only.

NEVER USE A COMMA TO SEPARATE COMPOUND ELEMENTS OF A SENTENCE THAT ARE NOT COMPLETE INDEPENDENT CLAUSES

A good commercial pitches its wares to viewers with smooth language and is loud enough to reach those who have left the room during the break. (two predicates)

Margaret picked up dog food and bought a full tank of gas. (two verbs)

He will not quit smoking until he takes responsibility for his own health and until he shows responsibility for his immediate family. (two subordinate clauses)

Use a semicolon between independent clauses to correct a comma splice.

Abnormal psychology has benefited a great deal from the modern developments of neuroscience; *however*, it still owes much to pioneers like Freud and Adler.

The harmonized sales tax is controversial; *however*, its implementation may benefit the provincial deficit.

Note: Some words, such as *however, therefore, hence,* and *thus* may act as conjunctive adverbs between two independent clauses, but unlike coordinating conjunctions, they need to be introduced by a semicolon (see 11-2b).

COMMAS WITH INTRODUCTORY ELEMENTS 11-1C

USE A COMMA AFTER A PHRASE OR CLAUSE THAT APPEARS BEFORE THE MAIN SUBJECT AND VERB OF THE SENTENCE

Whenever I feel in need of cheering up, I indulge in online shopping. (introductory adverbial phrase)

After appetizers and an extended family dinner, my uncle fell asleep in his chair. (introductory prepositional phrase)

Elated about the court ruling, Renée phoned her probation officer. (introductory participial phrase)

By studying the stock market, Rafe found a way to add excitement to his life. (introductory gerund phrase)

To be considered by a casting director, an actor must demonstrate versatility as well as talent. (introductory infinitive phrase)

All things considered, it was an ideal first date. (absolute phrase modifying the whole sentence)

A comma is often used to separate introductory words, phrases, or clauses from the main clause or sentence.

In less formal writing, you may omit the comma if the introductory word, phrase, or clause is adverbial, short, and not likely to be misconstrued. If a phrase or clause indicates *where, when, why, how,* or *under what conditions,* it is adverbial.

Delete or omit commas in less formal situations.

In a flash͵it was over.

11-1D COMMAS BETWEEN ITEMS IN A SERIES

A series in a sentence is made up of three or more words, phrases, or clauses that have the same grammatical form and are of equal importance.

Place commas between the items in the series (e.g., *knife, fork, and spoon*). The comma before the last item, commonly called the "serial comma," is optional, though preferred in academic writing because it is useful in preventing ambiguity. If you decide to use the serial comma, use it consistently throughout your writing.

USE COMMAS BETWEEN ITEMS IN A SERIES OF THREE OR MORE ITEMS

The Barenaked Ladies have four members now: Jim Creeggan,ˆKevin Hearn,ˆEd Robertson,ˆand Tyler Stewart.

I enjoy eating turkey,ˆdrinking eggnog,ˆand sleeping heavily over the holidays.

Wet,ˆscrawny,ˆand angry,ˆthe cat attempted to dry itself off after the bath. (The comma after *angry* sets off the introductory phrase; do not put a comma after the last item in a list.)

The funniest Canadians I know are Mary Walsh,ˆCathy Jones,ˆand Russell Peters,ˆall of whom are well known on television in this country. (The last comma is necessary to introduce the non-restrictive clause that follows; do not put a comma after the last item in a list.)

QUICK TIP

Do NOT place a comma before the first or after the last item in a series unless another comma rule makes a comma there necessary.

USE COMMAS BETWEEN COORDINATE ADJECTIVES

The <u>cold</u>, <u>smelly</u>, <u>wet</u> basement was off-limits to the children as a play area. (coordinate adjectives)

Pumpkin was a <u>fluffy</u>, <u>playful</u>, <u>tiny</u> kitten. (coordinate adjectives)

Vic disliked his <u>boring</u>, <u>low-paying</u>, <u>menial</u> job. (coordinate adjectives)

She wants to date a <u>tall</u>, <u>dark</u>, <u>handsome</u> man. (coordinate adjectives)

The book talk featured <u>three</u> <u>well-known</u> <u>English</u> authors. (cumulative adjectives)

His résumé included <u>various</u> <u>short-term</u> <u>landscaping</u> jobs. (cumulative adjectives)

An exhibit of <u>authentic</u> <u>early</u> <u>Incan</u> art was on display at the Royal Ontario Museum. (cumulative adjectives)

The music festival featured <u>many</u> <u>Canadian</u> <u>folk</u> acts. (cumulative adjectives)

QUICK TIP

Some adjectives are cumulative. They do not make sense if you change their order. For example,

She bought a little white dog.

Do not separate cumulative adjectives with commas.

Coordinate adjectives are two or more adjectives that separately and equally modify a noun or pronoun. If you change the order of these adjectives, the meaning of the sentences does not change. Coordinate adjectives can be joined by *and*.

11-1F COMMAS WITH NON-RESTRICTIVE ELEMENTS

A non-restrictive element adds non-essential, or parenthetical, information about an idea or term that is already limited, defined, or identified; hence, a non-restrictive element is set off with a comma or commas.

If you remove items that are non-restrictive, the meaning of the sentence does not change, and the sentence still makes sense. *Note:* When a non-restrictive element occurs in the middle of a sentence, use commas around it to set it off from the rest of the sentence.

By contrast, a restrictive element limits, defines, or identifies what it modifies. The information in a restrictive element is essential to a sentence's meaning. Do not set off a restrictive element with commas.

QUICK TIP

Non-restrictive elements can be removed from a sentence without changing its meaning. They should be set off with commas. Restrictive elements are essential to meaning and cannot be set off with commas.

USE COMMAS TO INDICATE NON-RESTRICTIVE ELEMENTS

The man who is the chief robbery subject has a scar, which is above his left eyebrow. (non-restrictive)

The man who has the scar above his left eyebrow is the chief robbery suspect. (restrictive)

Tofino, which is well over 200 kilometres from Victoria, attracts many tourists during November for storm-watching. (non-restrictive adjective clause)

People who drink excessively should be banned from driving. (restrictive adjective clause)

The poodle that won the trophy for Best in Show was stylishly groomed. (*Note:* Restrictive clauses often use *that* rather than *which*)

RESTRICTIVE AND NON-RESTRICTIVE ELEMENTS HAVE DIFFERENT GRAMMATICAL FUNCTIONS:

Canadian tourists, especially when travelling in foreign countries, often wear a Canadian flag. (non-restrictive adjective phrase)

Shoppers using debit cards to make small purchases are becoming more common than those using cash. (restrictive adjective phrase)

Emmy Lou, who runs the daycare centre, is a retired karate teacher. (non-restrictive appositive)

Leonard Cohen's song "Hallelujah" has become his most admired musical work. (restrictive appositive)

He missed the turn for the expressway, even though signs for the on-ramp were well posted. (non-restrictive concluding adverb clause)

Water boils at sea level when it reaches a temperature of 100 degrees Celsius. (restrictive concluding adverb clause)

USE COMMAS TO INDICATE ELEMENTS THAT ARE PARENTHETICAL OR TRANSITIONAL

Frankly, I am not worried about you. (parenthetical word)

George is, to be honest, not the son-in-law I would have chosen. (parenthetical phrase)

Jeffrey is embarrassed easily; therefore, I decided not to mention the rip in his pants. (transitional word)

I was upset by the speeding ticket; as a result, I burst into tears. (transitional phrase)

A word or phrase is parenthetical if it offers information not necessary to the meaning of the sentence. You may choose to enclose such elements in parentheses when you want to de-emphasize their role in a sentence. By contrast, you may choose commas when the information is more central to the sentence.

Transitional elements allow the reader to progress from one idea to the next and to see how ideas are connected.

When you use a transitional or parenthetical element in the middle of a sentence, use commas around it.

USE COMMAS FOR EMPHASIS OR TO INDICATE A CONTRASTING ELEMENT SET OFF FROM THE MAIN PART OF THE SENTENCE

We must inoculate against the virus, not wait until an epidemic strikes. (contrast)

By George, I think you've got it. (interjection)

Use a comma when you find that information given later in a sentence contrasts with that found earlier. The comma emphasizes the contrast.

Such contrasts may occur with interjections—words that add emotion or surprise and do not fit neatly into the sentence structure.

Use commas after a word or phrase that indicates direct address, that is, when you speak directly to someone.

Listen, I'm warning you! (direct address)

Henriette, have you seen my keys? (direct address)

Use commas with tag questions or sentences at the end of a sentence since they, too, add emphasis.

You know the truth, don't you? (tag question)

He answered the summons without delay, I assure you. (tag sentence)

11-1I COMMAS WITH QUOTATIONS

Use commas with speech tags, that is, short clauses like *he said*.

Note: You should punctuate quotations as if the quoted words were yours. That is, the standard rules of punctuation still apply. For that reason, you will introduce quotations after a complete sentence with a colon rather than a comma. Similarly, if the quotation fits into your sentence smoothly, you do not need a comma.

USE COMMAS WITH SPEECH TAGS SUCH AS *SHE WROTE* OR *HE SAID* TO SET OFF DIRECT QUOTATIONS

Woody Allen writes, "It is impossible to experience one's death objectively and still carry a tune."

"I am so excited about Canadians ruling the world," opined John Diefenbaker.

When Prime Minister Harper says, "As a religion, bilingualism is the god that failed," he means that Canada's attempts to become bilingual did not come to fruition.

"Answer the door," Darlene yelled, "and tell that pesky salesman to go away."

11-1J COMMAS WITH DATES, ADDRESSES, TITLES, AND NUMBERS

Use commas between date and year, and between day and date. When the date appears in a full sentence, also put a comma after the year. There is no need for commas with only

USE COMMAS IN DATES WITH THESE FORMATS

December 29, 2011 (date, year)

Wednesday, November 25, 1953 (day, date, year)

The Romantic poet John Keats was born on October 31, 1795, in England. (date, year, in a full sentence)

Compare with these dates:
December 2011
Winter 2011
25 November 1953

USE COMMAS IN ADDRESSES BETWEEN CITY AND PROVINCE AND BETWEEN CITY AND COUNTRY

We visited London, England.

Stephen Leacock died in Toronto, Ontario, in 1944.

I would appreciate it if you would courier the book to Ella James at 126 Mayburn Drive, Oakville, Ontario L6P 1K8. (no comma before the postal code)

Use a comma between the city and province or city and country. When a sentence continues on after the city and province or city and country, also use a comma after the province or country.

USE COMMAS BEFORE TITLES, BUT NOT BEFORE FAMILY DESIGNATIONS

Patrick Deane, Ph.D.

Desmond Pouyat, M.S.W.

Queen Elizabeth II

Martin Luther King Jr.

Philip Bacho, Ph.D., taught the course on writing scripts.

Use a comma before a title, such as a degree, but not before a designation such as Jr., Sr., III, or IV. When an abbreviated title follows a name in a sentence, place a comma after the name and a second comma after the title.

DO NOT USE COMMAS IN NUMBERS IN THE INTERNATIONAL METRIC SYSTEM

4673

233 971

62 299 381

QUICK TIP

Note that readings of American origin will use the comma in numbers of four digits or more. Canada's system of metric measurement uses spaces rather than commas to separate sets of three digits.

Canada follows the international system of metric measurement (SI), which does not use commas in numbers. Instead, spaces are used to separate sets of three digits. Four-digit numbers may be grouped together. Be aware that many U.S. style guides use the imperial system instead and, hence, do not conform to the international system of metric measurement.

The month and year, or only the season and year, or when the date appears in inverted form.

In your reading, you may encounter commas used for numbers that are four digits or more. This system was used before Canada adopted the international metric system.

Never use commas to separate sets of digits in years, telephone numbers, street numbers, or postal codes.

❌ 17, Brandon Avenue

❌ John A. MacDonald was born in 1,815.

11-1K   PREVENTING CONFUSION

In many writing situations, commas are required to prevent reader confusion. Commas may be used to indicate omitted words, to clarify intention, or to separate echoing words.

USE COMMAS TO PREVENT CONFUSION

Tasha adored jazz; Bert, gospel. (omitted words)

Dedicated runners who can, run every chance they get. (clarified intention)

Undeterred by the possibility of plane hijackings, Barry believes that whatever happens, happens. (echoing words)

11-1L   INCORRECT USES OF THE COMMA

Don't use commas injudiciously or believe the old saying that commas should be inserted wherever you pause for breath.

Don't use a comma

- to separate two main clauses, except in a series of clauses
- to separate a subject from a verb
- to separate a verb from an object

DON'T USE COMMAS IN SENTENCES LIKE THESE

I am sure you will pay me on time, I know where you live. (comma splice)

Tom Patterson, originated the idea for the Stratford Festival in 1952.

The superior boxer mercilessly punched, his staggering opponent.

"Watch out for the logging truck!," he bellowed.

Neither he, nor I had ever been to a tanning booth before.

It was a gruesome, thankless, investigation.

The party was victorious in the hotly, contested riding.

April likes to play the guitar, apply moisturizer, and eat cookies before she goes to bed.

Many Canadian recording artists will be in attendance, such as Jann Arden, Sarah McLachlan, and Joni Mitchell.

The journalist has been to some of the most dangerous trouble spots in the world, and she has lived to tell about them.

People who live in glass houses shouldn't throw stones.

We all started to sing that "We stand on guard for thee."

Did you know that "mondegreen" means a "misheard word or phrase that is said or sung"?

On the other hand, there are some Catalans (usually women who've never worked outside the home) who haven't spoken Spanish since their school days.

GET ORGANIZED

How to Determine When to Use Commas

❏ Check for introductory elements in each sentence and follow them with commas.

❏ Check for coordinating conjunctions (*and, or, nor, for, but, yet, so*) that separate independent clauses, and use a comma before them.

❏ Check for non-restrictive phrases or clauses in the sentence, and set them off with commas.

- with an exclamation mark or a question mark
- to separate two nouns, verbs, predicates, or objects
- to separate an adjective from a noun
- to separate an adverb from what it modifies
- before or after a series of items
- after *like* or *such as*
- after a coordinating conjunction (*and, or, nor, for, but, yet, so*)
- with restrictive modifiers
- with quotations that flow directly into your sentence
- with quotation marks that indicate titles or set off words as words
- before a parenthesis

A semicolon (;) is used to separate major elements of a sentence that are of equal grammatical rank or closely connected in thought. A semicolon is also used to separate phrases or clauses when a comma would be unclear or too weak.

It is not important whether you win or lose; it is how you play the game.

I would be happy to write a letter of recommendation for you; however, it must remain confidential.

11-2A SEMICOLONS BETWEEN INDEPENDENT CLAUSES WITH NO COORDINATING CONJUNCTION

An independent clause expresses a complete thought and can stand on its own as a sentence. When related independent clauses appear in a sentence, they are usually linked by a comma and a coordinating conjunction (*and, but, for, nor, or, so,* or *yet*). The conjunction indicates the relationship between the clauses.

When the relationship between independent clauses is clear without the conjunction, you may instead link the two clauses with a semicolon.

The semicolon is often used stylistically to emphasize contrast.

USE SEMICOLONS TO CONNECT TWO OR MORE MAIN CLAUSES

A teacher affects eternity; no one can tell where his influence stops.

—Henry Adams

I like broccoli; Ethel cannot stand it.

I must leave immediately; I am not well.

There are three options: you can make an appointment with an academic advisor; you can attend a workshop; you can deal with the problem on your own.

His position was terminated; he was escorted summarily to the door.

USE SEMICOLONS WITH CONJUNCTIVE ADVERBS AND TRANSITIONAL PHRASES TO JOIN MAIN CLAUSES

She is an authority on the H1N1 virus; **furthermore**, we need someone with her expertise. (conjunctive adverb)

For teachers, education never ends; **for example**, we attend professional development workshops at least once each semester. (transitional phrase)

Sometimes, you may use a conjunctive adverb such as *therefore*, *however*, or *hence* or a transitional phrase such as *for instance*, *as a consequence*, or *that is* to clarify how two main clauses are connected logically.

In this situation, you should use a semicolon between the main clauses and a comma after the conjunctive adverb or transitional phrases.

QUICK TIP

Note that transitional words may change their function. In a single sentence, only commas are needed:

The weather, however, did not improve.

Joining two main clauses, you need a semicolon:

The long weekend was approaching; however, the weather did not improve.

SEMICOLONS IN A SERIES WITH INTERNAL PUNCTUATION **11-2C**

USE SEMICOLONS TO SEPARATE ELEMENTS IN A SERIES WHEN THEY ALREADY CONTAIN COMMAS

Here is the list of remaining speakers and topics: Gurdeep, the rewards of working at a student newspaper; Miles, the elements of hip-hop; and Mustapha, the wonders of wireless technology.

Usually, commas separate items in a series. However, when series items contain commas, a semicolon is placed between items to make the sentence easier to read.

Semicolons should be used to join only sentence elements of equal rank. In other words, do not use a semicolon to separate a subordinate clause from a main clause or an introductory phrase from the clause that follows. Semicolons are like soft periods, so using one incorrectly inadvertently creates a sentence fragment.

Semicolons, unlike colons, do not typically introduce material. Therefore, do not use a semicolon to introduce a list or a quotation. Quotations are usually introduced by a comma; however, when a quotation is introduced by a complete sentence, a colon is used.

Don't use semicolons

- between independent clauses joined by *and*, *but*, *for*, *nor*, *or*, *so*, or *yet*
- between a subordinate clause and the remainder of the sentence
- between an appositive and the word to which it refers
- to introduce a list
- to introduce a quotation

DON'T USE SEMICOLONS IN SENTENCES LIKE THESE

The painter was very prolific during his lifetime, yet he only achieved the fame he deserved after death.

After she had made the lemon curd, Leona whipped the cream she needed to ice the cake.

Raj's favourite television program is *Mad Men*, a great ensemble dramatic series set in the early '60s.

A number of great novels are covered in the course: *Bleak House*, *Pride and Prejudice*, and *Gulliver's Travels*.

Oscar Wilde made this clever observation: "Some people cause happiness wherever they go; others whenever they go."

GET ORGANIZED

How to Determine When to Use Semicolons

❏ Use semicolons between closely connected thoughts where you could use a period.

❏ Use semicolons to separate items in a list when simple commas would be unclear.

❏ Don't use semicolons between independent clauses joined by *and*, *but*, *for*, *nor*, *or*, *so*, or *yet*.

❏ Don't use a semicolon between a subordinate clause and the remainder of the sentence.

❏ Don't use a semicolon between an appositive and the word, phrase, or clause to which it refers.

❏ Don't use semicolons to introduce lists or quotations.

The Cherokees offer the following advice on how you should live: When you were born, you cried and the world rejoiced. Live your life so that when you die, the world cries and you rejoice.

Ebenezer Scrooge lived for one thing: money.

The colon is most often used as a formal and emphatic method to introduce a word, phrase, or clause that follows. It operates like a pointing finger and is commonly used in typography. Note, however, that colons have this introductory function only after a complete main clause. Remember not to use a colon directly after a verb or after any incomplete main clause. If you can't use a period at the end, you can't use a colon either.

COLONS BEFORE LISTS, QUOTATIONS, OR APPOSITIVES 11-3A

USE A COLON AFTER A MAIN CLAUSE TO INTRODUCE A LIST

"A boy can learn a lot from a dog: obedience, loyalty, and the importance of turning around three times before lying down."

—Robert Benchley

For this experiment, you will need the following materials: three small cups, a transparent sheet, a waterproof marker, an eye dropper, and three paper towels.

USE A COLON AFTER A MAIN CLAUSE TO INTRODUCE A QUOTATION

Erikson describes the concreteness of ego integrity in his final book: "Integrity has the function of promoting contact with the world, with things and above all, with people."

Mackenzie King summed up his position with this epigrammatic line: "Not necessarily conscription, but conscription if necessary."

LISTS
After a main clause, you should use a colon to introduce a list. Often, the preceding clause contains words such as *the following* or *as follows*.

QUOTATIONS
A colon is used at the end of a main clause if a long quotation, typically one sentence or more, follows. If you use something shorter than a complete sentence to introduce a quotation, use a comma before it, or if the

quotation flows directly into your sentence structure, omit punctuation altogether.

APPOSITIVES

A colon is often used in formal writing to introduce a word or phrase that functions as an appositive—that is, a part of the sentence that renames something or offers more explanation. In informal writing, a colon may be replaced by a dash in these instances.

USE A COLON AFTER A MAIN CLAUSE TO INTRODUCE AN APPOSITIVE

Rock stars stereotypically have three preoccupations: wine, women, and song.

While held hostage, the journalist had one all-consuming thought: survival.

11-3B   COLONS TO ILLUSTRATE MEANING BETWEEN MAIN CLAUSES

A colon is often used instead of a period when one sentence introduces a concept illustrated or elaborated on in the next sentence. You may use a capital letter on the first word of the second sentence or not, as long as you are consistent throughout your document. Typically, however, the second sentence does not require a capital letter unless it is a question.

USE A COLON TO INTRODUCE A SECOND SENTENCE THAT AMPLIFIES THE FIRST

I'll never forget you, mother: you gave away my dog.

In North America, there are two classes of travel: there is first-class travel, and then there is travel with children.

Kim lived for one thing: she loved going to the movies.

I would like an answer to my question: Do you think that tuition fees are too high?

USE COLONS IN CERTAIN CONVENTIONAL SITUATIONS

Dear Mr. Trump: (formal letter)

To: Mr. Weston
From: Mr. Harper
Date: July 18, 2012
Subject: Rising food costs
(headings in a memo)

7:45 p.m. (expression of time)

In 1926, John C. Miles, a Canadian, won the Boston Marathon, with a time of 2:25:40. (expression of time)

Checkmate: A Writing Reference for Canadians

15:20 means "15 to 20." (ratio)

Colons are conventionally used in formal correspondence after the salutation in an email or letter. In memos, colons are used after each part of the heading (*To:, From:, Date:, Subject:*).

Colons are used to separate hours, minutes, and seconds in expressions of time.

Colons are used to indicate a separation between a book's main title and its subtitle.
Colons are used to indicate a ratio.

DON'T USE COLONS IN SENTENCES LIKE THESE

The main ingredients in a good mushroom omelette are: eggs, mushrooms, and butter.

The open-area portion of the dome house consisted of: a kitchen, living room, and master bedroom.

The content of the botanist's lecture included: boreal forests, a Carolinian forest, and an Amazonian rainforest.

Don't use colons

- between verbs and their subjects or objects
- between prepositions and their objects
- after *for example, for instance, such as, including,* or *included*

An apostrophe (') can be used to form the possessive case or to indicate contractions—that is, places where letters have been omitted. Apostrophes are also often used in the plural form of letters, numbers, symbols, and words as words.

Polly's maternity leave (possessive case)

ne'er-do-well (contraction)

catch some z's (plural letter)

11-4A   POSSESSIVE NOUNS

An apostrophe (') appears as part of a noun to indicate that the word is possessive.

USE APOSTROPHES TO MAKE NOUNS POSSESSIVE

Mishka's hockey stick
The instructor's briefcase

QUICK TIP

To test if a noun is possessive, see if you can state it as an "of" phrase. According to this test, both nouns below, "journey's" and "river's," are possessive.

The journey's end = the end of the journey
The river's tributaries = the tributaries of the river

A SINGULAR OR PLURAL NOUN THAT DOES NOT END IN S

man's, men's, woman's, women's, child's, children's, person's, people's

The <u>women's</u> shelter needs volunteers. (plural noun not ending in *s*)

It was the <u>team's</u> wish that the donation be made in his name. (collective singular noun)

The <u>commodore's</u> cabin cruiser ran aground. (singular noun)

A SINGULAR NOUN THAT ENDS IN S

dress's, walrus's, glass's, Elvis's

<u>Gus's</u> father owns a single-engine plane.

A PLURAL NOUN THAT ENDS IN S

<u>Workers'</u> rights were neglected by the military regime.

The <u>boys'</u> tent was flattened in the storm.

The party was at the Mark <u>Jones'</u> house.

A NAME THAT ENDS IN A Z SOUND

Moses'

A SINGULAR NOUN ENDING WITH AN "EEZ" SOUND

Sophocles'

<u>Euripides'</u> tragedy *Medea* is his best-known work.

POSSESSIVES FORMED BY ADDING AN APOSTROPHE AND AN S

The apostrophe and the letter *s* form the possessive in most cases.

POSSESSIVES FORMED BY ADDING AN APOSTROPHE ONLY

An apostrophe by itself may indicate possession when the noun is plural and ends in -*s*.

Names that end in a *z* sound or singular nouns that end in an "eez" sound may take an apostrophe only. You may see this usage with other nouns ending in *s* as well; however, the preferred style is to add an apostrophe and *s* except in these specific cases.

11-4B POSSESSIVE INDEFINITE PRONOUNS

An indefinite pronoun refers to a general or non-specific person or thing.

Add *'s* to the end of the indefinite pronoun to make it possessive.

USE APOSTROPHES TO MAKE INDEFINITE PRONOUNS POSSESSIVE

Examples of indefinite pronouns are *somebody, anything,* and *anyone.*

It is not <u>anybody</u>**'s** business what I do in my free time.

<u>Someone</u>**'s** laptop was stolen from the reference library.

11-4C POSSESSIVE WITH COMPOUNDS

COMPOUND SUBJECTS

To show joint possession with compound subjects, use *'s* (or *s'*) with the last noun only.

To show individual possession with compound subjects, make all nouns in the compound subject possessive.

COMPOUND NOUNS

Use *'s* (or *s'*) with the last element in a compound noun to show possession.

USE APOSTROPHES APPROPRIATELY TO SHOW INDIVIDUAL OR JOINT POSSESSION WITH COMPOUND SUBJECTS

You should see <u>Doug and Dino</u>**'s** modified stock car. (joint ownership)

<u>Manuela and Jesus</u>**'** new house overlooks the valley. (joint ownership)

<u>Todd</u>**'s** and <u>Charles</u>**'s** ideas on how to decorate the home were diametrically opposed. (individual ownership)

USE APOSTROPHES TO MAKE COMPOUND NOUNS POSSESSIVE

My in-<u>laws</u>**'** parties are always worth attending. (compound noun)

My sister-in-<u>law</u>**'s** film won a Genie. (compound noun)

11-4D CONTRACTIONS

The apostrophe takes the place of missing letters in contractions. Occasionally, in informal situations, the apostrophe can also indicate that the first two digits of years have been left out.

USE APOSTROPHES TO INDICATE CONTRACTIONS

It <u>doesn't</u> matter <u>who's</u> going to do it. (missing letters)

There will be a reunion for the class of <u>'88</u>. (missing numbers)

Contractions are usually used in informal writing, such as personal letters or emails or reported speech. Contractions are often discouraged in academic writing, though depending on the context, they may be acceptable.

PLURALS OF NUMBERS, LETTERS, ETC. | 11-4E

USE APOSTROPHES TO FORM PLURALS OF LETTERS, SYMBOLS, ABBREVIATIONS, AND WORDS AS WORDS

Tiny *X*'s and *O*'s were embroidered on the scarf.

I don't want to have to deal with any more *what if*'s.

The Calgary-area *M.P.*'s met to discuss the issue.

He has trouble writing 6s. [MLA style]

I bought some new DVDs. [MLA style]

In some common writing situations, an apostrophe plus *s* is used to form the plural of numbers, letters, abbreviations, symbols, and words as words, but this is not always the case. These elements may take an apostrophe and an *s* or simply an *s* alone.

Sometimes, the decision will depend on the style guide that you are using—for example, MLA style—and sometimes it will depend on your consistent preference throughout a document. The letter, word as word, or symbol should appear in italics, and the ' and *s* should follow in regular type. It is not necessary for abbreviations to be italicized.

11-4F INCORRECT USES OF THE APOSTROPHE

Don't use apostrophes with

- nouns that aren't possessive
- possessive pronouns (*his, hers, its, ours, theirs, whose*)
- present-tense verbs in third-person singular

DON'T USE APOSTROPHES IN SENTENCES LIKE THESE

Employee's must wear security badges at all times.

The clients' had expected us to pick up the tab for dinner.

The dog must wear it's collar when outdoors.

The opposition party typically disagree's with the prime minister.

GET ORGANIZED

How to Determine When to Use Apostrophes
- ❏ Use apostrophes when possession or ownership is involved.
- ❏ Use caution when choosing between *its* and *it's*. The first, without an apostrophe, is possessive, like *his* or *her*. The second is a contraction meaning *it is*.

11-5 QUOTATION MARKS

Quotation marks are used mainly to indicate direct speech or words that have been copied exactly from another source. They are also used around titles of short works (poems, short stories, essays).

11-5A DIRECT QUOTATIONS

Direct quotations are the exact words copied from a print source or transcribed from what a person says. Direct quotations must be enclosed within quotation marks.

"The international community didn't give one damn for Rwandans because Rwanda was a country of no strategic importance."

—Romeo Dallaire (direct quotation)

"I don't know," Mark said. (direct quotation)

John Dowd in *Kayaking: A Manual for Long-Distance Touring* professes that, usually, the open ocean is a safe place to sea kayak. (indirect quotation)

QUICK TIP

Indirect quotations, which paraphrase or summarize what appears in a print source or what someone has said, are not placed in quotation marks.

USE QUOTATION MARKS TO INDICATE DIALOGUE

Harper emphasized the importance of recognizing the former prime minister's contributions: "Meighen's love of the language went beyond political speeches. He could quote Shakespeare and other poets at length. He also had success as a lawyer and a businessman, but it was public service which he loved the most.

"Arthur Meighen's portrait has hung in these hallways for decades. But today, he finally receives the belated tributes that have for too long been his due."

> "I said me, not you."
> "Oh. You got a car outside?"
> "I can walk."
> "That's five miles back to where the van is."
> "People have walked five miles."

—Alice Munro, "Friend of My Youth,"
from *Friend of My Youth* (Toronto: McClelland & Stewart, 1990).

USE QUOTATION MARKS AROUND SHORT QUOTATIONS IN ACADEMIC PAPERS

Atwood records Toby's thoughts about the new day in *The Year of the Flood*: "What breaks in daybreak? Is it the night? Is it the sun, cracked in two by the horizon like an egg, spilling out light?" (17).

—Margaret Atwood,
The Year of the Flood. (chapter 3)

QUOTING LONGER PASSAGES BY A SINGLE SPEAKER

If you are directly quoting passages by a single speaker, start each new paragraph with quotation marks, but do not use closing quotation marks until the end of the quoted material.

MARKING A CHANGE IN SPEAKER WITHIN DIALOGUE

Start a new paragraph to signal a change in the speaker. Each speaker's speech should have its own set of quotation marks.

QUOTATION MARKS WITH SHORT QUOTATIONS IN ACADEMIC PAPERS

There are differences in formatting of short quotations depending on what style you use. In MLA style, for instance, a short quotation is shorter than four lines of prose text or three lines of poetry.

In APA, by contrast, a quotation is considered short if it is fewer than forty words.

In either style, short quotations should be set off with quotation marks.

As Flora and Bobby put it, "Just as a child with a hammer discovers new things that 'need' to be hammered, when psychiatry finds new drugs it discovers new people who 'need' to be treated with them" (p. 42).

—Flora, S. R., & Bobby, S. E.
(2008). The bipolar bamboozle. *Skeptical Inquirer 32*(5), 41–45.

11-5B   QUOTATION MARKS WITH LONG QUOTATIONS

PROSE IN MLA STYLE

In MLA style, a long quotation of prose is any passage that is more than four typed or handwritten lines. Start the quotation 2.5 cm (1 in.) from the left margin. You do not need to enclose the longer quotation within quotation marks because the indented format establishes for the reader that the quotation is taken exactly from a source. Usually, longer quotations are introduced by a sentence ending with a colon.

Placing the page number reference within parentheses follows the citation style prescribed by the Modern Language Association.

DON'T USE QUOTATION MARKS AROUND LONG QUOTATIONS IN ACADEMIC PAPERS

LONGER PROSE QUOTATIONS IN MLA STYLE

Alamian and Paradis discuss the risk factors that lead to smoking among Canadian adolescents and conclude that several of these would benefit from early intervention:

> The present study contributes new knowledge about correlates of multiple chronic disease behavioral risk factors among children and adolescents. In particular, the findings point to a range of individual and social variables which could be used as potential targets in lifestyle intervention strategies aimed at changing multiple behavioral risk factors among youth. Though more research is needed to determine the effectiveness of multiple behavioral interventions in primary prevention settings, this study provides evidence that older youth, those with low self-esteem, those living in a lone-parent family or a family with low education, those whose parents/friends smoke cigarettes, and those whose friends drink alcohol may be the most at risk and might require special attention. (1287)

LONGER POETRY QUOTATIONS IN MLA STYLE

P. K. Page is more personal in "After Rain" than in "The Stenographers."
In "After Rain," she defines her own poetic sensibility through the poem-within-a-poem of stanza three:

> the clothes-reel gauche
> as the rangy skeleton of some
> gaunt delicate spidery mute
> is pitched as if
> listening;
> while hung from one thin rib
> a silver web—
> its infant, skeletal, diminutive,
> now sagged with sequins, pulled ellipsoid,
> glistening. (122)

Reprinted from *The Hidden Room* (in two volumes) by P.K. Page
by permission of the Porcupine's Quill. Copyright © P. K. Page, 1997.

LONGER PROSE QUOTATIONS IN APA STYLE

Selective optimization with compensation (SOC) theory, developed by
Freund and Baltes (2002), examines three processes—selection, optimization, and compensation—used by older adults that Moraitou et al. (2006) explain as follows:

> Older adults become more selective in their personal goals, mainly because of age-related changes in their resources. They use the resources to optimize their functioning in these selected goal areas and compensate for the losses they experience. Compensation involves the use of resources to change goals in response to loss of past goal-relevant means. (p. 73)

POETRY IN MLA STYLE

A long quotation of poetry is more than three lines of the poem. Start the quotation 2.5 cm (1 in.) from the left margin. You do not need to enclose the longer quotation within quotation marks because the indented format establishes for the reader that the quotation is taken exactly from the poem. Only use quotation marks within the quotation if they are part of the poem.

PROSE IN APA STYLE

In APA style, a long, or block, quotation is more than forty words. It has no quotation marks around it and is indented one-half inch from the left margin throughout.

11-5C QUOTATIONS WITHIN QUOTATIONS

Single quotation marks are used only to enclose quotations within quotations. Some confusion arises because this is a North American convention.

USE SINGLE QUOTATION MARKS TO INDICATE A QUOTATION INSIDE A QUOTATION

According to Newman et al., Charles de Gaulle "spoke the words that jolted a nation: 'Vive le Québec libre!'"

QUICK TIP

British usage is the reverse (i.e., single quotation marks are the norm, and double quotation marks are only used inside single quotation marks).

11-5D QUOTATION MARKS TO INDICATE TITLES OF SHORT WORKS

Use quotation marks around titles of works that are included within other works, such as poems, short stories, songs, published essays, newspaper and magazine articles, radio programs, television episodes, photographs, unpublished speeches, pages on a website, and chapters and other subdivisions of books.

USE QUOTATION MARKS AROUND TITLES OF SHORT WORKS IN YOUR ACADEMIC WORK

His talk focused on point of view in Edgar Allan Poe's short story "The Tell-Tale Heart." (title of short story)

Joni Mitchell's song "A Case of You" is a classic. (title of song)

The first chapter of *David Copperfield* is "I Am Born," which emphasizes the apparent autobiographical stance of the novel. (title of chapter)

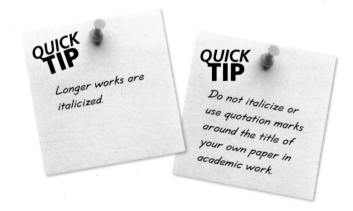

QUICK TIP

Longer works are italicized.

QUICK TIP

Do not italicize or use quotation marks around the title of your own paper in academic work.

USE ITALICS OR QUOTATION MARKS TO SET OFF WORDS AS WORDS

I remember once displaying my ignorance by using the word *irregardless* when I should have used *regardless*.

I remember once displaying my ignorance by using the word "irregardless" when I should have used "regardless."

Italics are preferred for setting off words used as words. However, it is also acceptable to use quotation marks for this purpose.

The following section provides rules for using punctuation with quotation marks.

PLACE COMMAS AND PERIODS INSIDE QUOTATION MARKS

"I'm not finished yet," she said. "The books I looked at were of no help."

John Stuart Mill's masterpiece, "On Liberty," is essential reading for philosophers. (title of work)

The entry I just looked up, "Internet," is a recent addition to the dictionary. (word used as a word)

"I'm studying for my history exam," said Siddia. "I expect to be up all night."

For more information on single quotation marks, see 11-5c.

PLACE PUNCTUATION AFTER PARENTHESES IN IN-TEXT CITATIONS

Clarkson and McCall contend "Davis was apprehensive that Trudeau's pugnacity might scupper the possibility" (368).

COMMAS AND PERIODS
Place commas and periods inside quotation marks. (Note that this is a North American convention; British usage generally places commas and periods outside quotation marks.)

Also follow the above punctuation rule in the following cases:

- with single quotation marks
- for titles of works
- for words used as words

Exception: For parenthetical in-text citations, the period follows the final parenthesis. In this case, the period is therefore outside the quotation marks.

SEMICOLONS AND COLONS

Place semicolons and colons outside quotation marks.

PLACE SEMICOLONS AND COLONS OUTSIDE QUOTATION MARKS

He explained his term "in the moment": the individual focuses himself or herself on the elusive present.

As the bank's head economist, she asserts that the economy will soon "take off"; several of her colleagues at other banks strongly disagree.

QUESTION MARKS AND EXCLAMATION MARKS

If the question mark or exclamation mark is part of the quoted material, place it *inside* the quotation marks.

If the question mark or exclamation mark applies to the entire sentence, place it *outside* the quotation marks.

PLACE EXCLAMATION MARKS AND QUESTION MARKS INSIDE QUOTATION MARKS WHEN THEY ARE PART OF THE QUOTED MATERIAL

When Parminder heard what Susan had done, he shouted, "She made the shot from centre court!"

PLACE QUESTION MARKS OR EXCLAMATION MARKS OUTSIDE QUOTATION MARKS WHEN THEY APPLY TO THE ENTIRE SENTENCE

What do you think of Napoleon's view that "history is a set of lies agreed upon"?

Oliver Sacks ponders, "If this was the case in Virgil, what might happen if visual function was suddenly made possible, demanded?" (291).

QUICK TIP

In in-text citations, the question mark or exclamation mark is placed before the final closing quotation mark; a sentence period is then placed after the final parenthesis in the parenthetical citation.

11-5G   INTRODUCING QUOTED MATERIAL

You have three major punctuation options when using a group of words to introduce a quotation:

1. a colon
2. a comma
3. no punctuation

1. Forrest Gump had it right: "Stupid is as stupid does."
2. My mother always says, "You can't take it with you."
3. The batter yelled "Heads up!" as the foul ball sailed toward the crowd of spectators.

USE A COLON TO INTRODUCE A QUOTATION FORMALLY

In *The Globe and Mail*, John Stackhouse presents the following insight about political change in Africa: "The economic revolution that has swept through Africa, from the highlands of eastern Kenya to the rain forests of Ivory Coast, has affected almost every African—and altered few governments."

USE A COMMA TO INTRODUCE A QUOTATION AFTER AN EXPRESSION LIKE *HE SAID*

With a wry smile, the firefighter remarked, "Where there's smoke, there's fire."

"I'm a Canadian," I protested.

According to Pierre Elliott Trudeau, "Power only tires those who don't exercise it."

USE NO PUNCTUATION WHEN A QUOTATION BLENDS GRAMMATICALLY INTO THE SENTENCE

In summertime, all expeditions were planned tentatively; sentences ended with the phrase "if it doesn't rain."

USE A COMMA AFTER A QUOTATION THAT BEGINS A SENTENCE

"I'll be back in a moment," I told my students, and half out of my mind with anxiety, I went down in the lift, dashed across the street, and burst into Jai Lu's house.

USE NO PUNCTUATION IF THE INTRODUCTORY QUOTATION ENDS IN A QUESTION OR AN EXCLAMATION

"What are you doing?" I demanded.

USE COMMAS TO SET OFF WORDS THAT INTERRUPT A QUOTATION

"No," he called back, "I can see it breathing!"

WHEN TO USE THE COLON
Use the colon if the quotation has been formally introduced. A formal introduction is a complete independent clause.

WHEN TO USE THE COMMA
Use a comma if a quotation is introduced with or followed by an expression such as *she said* or *he uttered*, or when the introduction is not a complete sentence.

WHEN TO USE NO PUNCTUATION
Don't use any punctuation before a quotation that blends into the sentence smoothly and grammatically.

WHEN A QUOTATION BEGINS A SENTENCE
Use a comma to set off a quotation at the beginning of a sentence.

However, a comma is not needed if the opening quotation ends with a question mark or an exclamation mark.

WHEN A QUOTED SENTENCE IS INTERRUPTED BY EXPLANATORY WORDS
Use commas to set off the explanatory words.

Use a comma within the quotation marks of the first quotation. End the explanatory words with a period.

PUNCTUATE INTERRUPTED QUOTATIONS BY USING A COMMA BEFORE EXPLANATORY WORDS AND A PERIOD AFTER

"We are simply not well prepared for the rapid development that we have been experiencing," <u>Dr. Muangman said</u>. "Politicians and decision-makers think that if we make a lot of money, that is enough."

11-5H   INCORRECT USES OF QUOTATION MARKS

Do not use quotation marks around indirect quotations.

Do not use quotation marks to call attention to a word or expression. Never use quotation marks to distance yourself from an expression or to call attention to slang. Quotation marks used in this way are often called *scare quotes*. They are best avoided because they send an ambiguous message. Trust your words to speak for you, without the addition of quotation marks. Relying on such artificial devices is like explaining a joke; it reduces the effect, rather than increasing it.

Finally, do not use quotation marks to set off the title of your document.

DON'T USE QUOTATION MARKS FOR INDIRECT QUOTATIONS

My mother always said longingly that she'd "like to visit Greece."

I wondered "if you wanted to come to lunch with me."

DON'T USE QUOTATION MARKS TO DRAW ATTENTION TO WORDS

Some might say the mechanic went on a "busman's holiday."

Many academics find the language of "political correctness" objectionable.

DON'T USE QUOTATION MARKS AROUND TITLES OF UNPUBLISHED MATERIALS

I handed in my essay "A Critique of John Donne's *Holy Sonnets*" to my professor.

Periods are commonly used to indicate the end of a sentence. They are also used in abbreviations.

USE PERIODS TO END SENTENCES

Rock climbing on the Bruce Trail can be dangerous.

ENDING SENTENCES
Use the period after statements, indirect questions, and mild commands.

USE A PERIOD AFTER A STATEMENT

I went to bed early last night.

Statement
Use a period after a statement.

USE A PERIOD AFTER AN INDIRECT QUESTION

The hike leader inquired if they wanted to walk the Gun Point Loop section of the trail.

Indirect Question
After a **direct question**, use a question mark. (See 11-6b.)

However, if the question is **indirect**, use a period to end the sentence.

Commands
After a strong command, use the exclamation mark. (See 11-6c.)

However, after a **mild command**—an imperative or declarative sentence that is not an exclamation—use a period.

USE A PERIOD AFTER MILD COMMANDS

Please pick up the groceries.

ABBREVIATIONS

Use periods in abbreviations such as those in the top table.

Do not use periods with Canada Post abbreviations, such as *SK*, *ON*, and *NB*.

Widely recognized abbreviations for organizations, companies, and countries do not require periods, such as the examples in the second table.

If you are in doubt about whether or not an abbreviation requires a period, check in a good Canadian dictionary or encyclopedia. To check the abbreviation of a name of a company, you might consult that company's website.

Do not add a second period if the sentence ends with an abbreviation's period.

USE A PERIOD IN ABBREVIATIONS

Abbreviations

a.m.	p.	B.A.	Dr.	Inc.
p.m.	etc.	M.A.	Ms.	Ltd.
B.C. (or B.C.E.)	e.g.	M.B.A.	Mrs.	Dec.
A.D. (or C.E.)	i.e.	Ph.D.	Mr.	St.

CBC	CSIS	NFB	UK	USA
IBM	UN	NBA	CFL	

At 6 a.m., the neighbour's dog woke us.

He always wanted to complete his M.A.

11-6B   QUESTION MARK

Use a question mark after any direct questions.

Also use a question mark after a polite request.

Use a period after an indirect question. (See 11-6a.)

QUESTIONS IN A SERIES

Use a question mark to end each question in a series, even if series questions are not complete sentences.

USE A QUESTION MARK AFTER A DIRECT QUESTION

Are you coming or going?

USE A QUESTION MARK AFTER A POLITE REQUEST

Would you please forward me a copy of the article for my files?

USE A QUESTION MARK TO END EACH QUESTION IN A SERIES

We are curious to hear what Justin's career goal will be this week. Maybe a brain surgeon? A stockbroker? Or perhaps a travel agent?

USE AN EXCLAMATION MARK FOR EMPHASIS, BUT DO NOT OVERUSE IT

The plane will hit the mountain!

Get out of the way, quickly!

⊘ We climbed the mountain on Hornby and had an incredible view! On one side was the snowcapped Coastal Range! On the other side, we could see majestic Mt. Washington!

⊘ We climbed the mountain on Hornby and had an incredible view. On one side was the snowcapped Coastal Range. On the other side, we could see majestic Mt. Washington.

Use the exclamation mark with an emphatic declaration or a strong command.

Do not overuse the exclamation mark.

If every sentence ends with an exclamation mark, the mark loses its effectiveness in communicating emphasis. Communicate strong impressions through the powerful use of words, not through overuse of the exclamation mark.

USE DASHES TO INDICATE AN INTERRUPTION IN THOUGHT

Our civilization is decadent and our language—so the argument runs—must inevitably share in the general collapse.

—George Orwell, "On Politics and Government," in *Shooting an Elephant and Other Essays* (London: Secker and Warburg, 1950).

USE DASHES TO SET OFF APPOSITIVES

Teachers—those educators, parents, entertainers, babysitters, and counsellors—are undervalued and underpaid by society.

USE DASHES TO INDICATE AN ABRUPT SHIFT IN THOUGHT

At the NBA All-Star Game, Michael Jordan took the pass, eluded the defender, hit full stride, soared—and missed an uncontested dunk.

USE DASHES TO AMPLIFY

Although they are close together—living only a few kilometres apart—they may as well be on different sides of the planet.

The dash marks a strong break in the continuity of a sentence. It can be used to add information, to emphasize part of a sentence, or to set part of the sentence off for clarity.

Dashes are used for the following purposes:

- to enclose a sentence element that interrupts the flow of thought, or to set off parenthetical material that deserves emphasis
- to set off appositives that contain commas (for more information on appositives, see 11-1f)

- to show a dramatic shift in tone or thought
- to restate
- to amplify
- to introduce a list

USE DASHES TO INTRODUCE A LIST

Peanut butter was everywhere—in their hair, on their clothes, smudged on their glasses.

In the storage room are all the paint supplies—paints, paint thinner, drop cloths, brushes, rollers, and paint trays.

QUICK TIP

To make a dash using your computer, you can enter two unspaced hyphens (--). Do not leave a space before the first hyphen or after the second hyphen. Many computer programs automatically format dashes when you enter two consecutive hyphens.

This kind of dash (—) is called an em dash. You can also select it in Word by going to the Insert menu, choosing Symbol, and then selecting Em Dash from the Special Characters option.

For more information on inserting em dashes in Word, see page 239.

Do not overuse dashes. If overused, dashes can lose their effectiveness and make writing disjointed. The Modern Language Association manual suggests limiting the number of dashes in a sentence to two paired dashes or one unpaired dash.

DO NOT OVERUSE DASHES

- Three students—Anwar, Sanjah, and Pete—won prizes—scholarships, books, and medallions. This is quite an achievement—especially for Pete, since he studies only minimally—if at all.

- Three students—Anwar, Sanjah, and Pete—won prizes, which included scholarships, books, and medallions. This is quite an achievement, especially for Pete, since he studies only minimally, if at all.

Parentheses are used to set off helpful, non-essential, additional information. While dashes usually call attention to the information they enclose, parentheses often de-emphasize the information they enclose.

Parentheses can be used for the following purposes:

- to enclose supplemental information, such as a definition, an example, a digression, an aside, or a contrast
- to enclose letters or numbers that label items in a series

USE PARENTHESES TO ENCLOSE SUPPLEMENTAL INFORMATION

Calgary is second among cities in Canada for number of head offices located within its city limits (92 in 1995).

Kenner taught at Assumption College (now University of Windsor) from 1946 to 1948.

USE PARENTHESES TO NUMBER ITEMS IN A LIST

Follow these directions to make a puppet: (1) put your hand inside a white sock, (2) form the puppet's mouth with your thumb and fingers, and (3) draw a face on the sock with a felt-tipped marker.

DO NOT OVERUSE PARENTHESES

The second phase of railway building in Canada ~~(starting 1867)~~
came with Confederation *in 1867*.

QUICK TIP

Do not overuse parentheses. Including too much parenthetical information can make your writing seem choppy and awkward. Often, you can integrate information from parentheses into your sentences so they flow more smoothly.

11-6F   BRACKETS

Brackets (also called square brackets—not to be confused with parentheses) are used to enclose any words you have inserted into quoted material.

TO ADD OR SUBSTITUTE CLARIFYING INFORMATION IN A QUOTATION

TO INDICATE ERRORS IN ORIGINAL MATERIAL

The Latin word *sic* means "so" or "thus." The word *sic* is placed in square brackets immediately after a word in a quotation that appears erroneous or odd. *Sic* indicates that the word is quoted exactly as it stands in the original. The term is always in italics to indicate that it is a foreign word.

USE BRACKETS TO ADD CLARIFYING INFORMATION

This short passage is from *Bury My Heart at Wounded Knee* and offers oral accounts from a Native perspective of fighting between Native Americans and soldiers. Within the context of the book, the information in square brackets clarifies which white soldiers were doing the fighting.

"I rode swiftly toward Sitting Bull's camp. Then I saw the white soldiers [Reno's men] fighting in line."

USE BRACKETS TO INDICATE ERRORS IN ORIGINAL MATERIAL

"Growing up on the small island [*sic*] of Nanaimo, British Columbia, Diana Krall has made a name for herself as a jazz singer."

[*Sic*] indicates to the reader that the writer who is quoting the sentence realizes the author of the original article is wrong in calling Nanaimo an island, when in fact it is a city.

11-6G   ELLIPSIS MARK

An ellipsis mark consists of three spaced periods (…). The ellipsis is used to indicate that you have omitted material from the original writer's quoted words.

In their introduction to the *ITP Nelson Canadian Dictionary of the English Language*, the authors write, "We have … sought to show how the development of … Canadian English … mirrors our development as a nation."

USE ELLIPSES TO DELETE MATERIAL FROM A QUOTATION

Gagnon states that "as much as 65% to 70% of semen volume originates from the seminal vesicles ... and about 5% from the minor sexual glands."

Alliteration in "Pied Beauty" contributes to imagery; however, unlike "God's Grandeur" the images convey God's power through his creations. The second to the fifth line of the poem all encompass images that are strengthened by Hopkins' choice of words that create alliteration. The use of "fresh-firecoal chestnut falls" compares the falling chestnut to a fresh firecoal, allowing the reader to better imagine the colour and texture of this chestnut and better appreciate the complexity of its creation (Hopkins 4). Also, the poet mentions how the landscape was "plotted, pieced [... and] plough[ed]" (5). In the same line, he interposes "fold, fallow" to further create alliteration (5). The repetition of the "p" and "f" sounds is used to provide a greater emphasis on the phrase itself, resulting in an increased sensitivity to the image it invokes.

For clarity, the square brackets here enclose the ellipsis.

USE FOUR ELLIPSIS POINTS TO INDICATE THE DELETION OF A COMPLETE SENTENCE

Priestly's ideas on nationalism are not flattering. He says, "If we deduct from nationalism all that is borrowed or stolen from regionalism, what remains is mostly rubbish.... Almost all nationalist movements are led by ambitious, frustrated men determined to hold office."

WHEN DELETING MATERIAL FROM A QUOTATION

The Modern Language Association used to recommend placing brackets around an ellipsis inserted by the quoting writer. The brackets indicated to the reader that the ellipsis did not appear in the original material. Though the MLA no longer recommends using brackets in this way, many instructors like the idea. You may wish to check with yours to clarify which style he or she would like you to follow.

An ellipsis is not required at the beginning of a quotation. Do not place an ellipsis at the end of the quotation, unless you have omitted content from the final quoted sentence.

WHEN DELETING A FULL SENTENCE FROM THE MIDDLE OF A QUOTED PASSAGE

Use a period before the three ellipsis points if you need to delete a full sentence or more from the middle of a quoted passage.

WHEN QUOTING POETRY

Use a full line of spaced dots the length of the line above to indicate that you have omitted a line or more from the quotation of a poem.

USE ELLIPSES TO INDICATE A DELETED LINE IN POETRY

Death, be not proud, though some have called thee
Mighty and dreadful, for thou art not so;

. . . .

From rest and sleep, which but thy pictures be,
Much pleasure; then from thee much more must flow,

—John Donne

WHEN INDICATING INTERRUPTION OR HESITATION IN SPEECH OR THOUGHT

Often, in story dialogue or narration, an ellipsis is used to indicate hesitation or interruption in speech or thought.

USE ELLIPSES TO INDICATE INTERRUPTED OR HESITANT SPEECH OR THOUGHT

"Well ... I couldn't make it. I didn't get to the exam."

11-6H   SLASH

USING THE SLASH TO INDICATE LINES OF POETRY

The slash is used most often in academic writing to mark off lines of poetry when these have been incorporated into the text. According to MLA style, up three lines from a poem can be quoted in the text.

Leave one space before and one space after the slash. For quoted passages of poetry that are four or more lines in length, start each line of the poem on its own line, indented in the style of block quotations.

USE A SLASH TO INDICATE THE END OF A LINE OF POETRY

Atwood's "Death of a Young Son by Drowning" opens with the haunting lines, "He, who navigated with success / the dangerous river of his own birth / once more set forth."

"Death of a Young Son by Drowning" by Margaret Atwood

In "Low Tide on Grand Pre," Bliss Carman describes the aging process: "I deemed / That time was ripe, and years had done / Their wheeling underneath the sun."

USE A SLASH TO INDICATE OPTIONS

Since the orchestra was short of funds, he served as artistic director/conductor.

AVOID INFORMAL AND AWKWARD USE OF THE SLASH IN YOUR WRITING

- We need to determine if he/she is a suitable subject for our study.
- An applicant must give his/her social insurance number before the bank will release information.
- The author contends that use of pesticides is dangerous and/or inappropriate in food production.

USING THE SLASH TO INDICATE OPTIONS OR PAIRED ITEMS

Sometimes the slash is used between options or paired items. Examples include *actor/producer, life/death, pass/fail.* In these cases, do not leave a space before and after the slash.

Avoid the use of *he/she, his/her,* and *and/or,* as they are informal and awkward in writing.

Sentence Structure and Style

A change of
style is a change
of subject.

—Wallace Stevens

Sentence Structure and Style

12

Revising for Clarity

To make your writing active and direct, follow these instructions:

1. Let your writing sit for a period of time, and then revise according to these principles.
2. Make sure that your ideas are easy to follow. Do this by reducing shifts in point of view, tense, mood, or voice.
3. Improve logical connections by following conventional sentence patterns.
4. Use structures, such as parallelism and clear comparisons, to enhance clarity.
5. Reduce wordiness and your use of the passive voice.
6. Use precise language, checking to make sure that the words mean what you think they mean.
7. Keep your audience, its expectations, and its level of expertise in mind.

Chapter 10, "Common Sentence Errors," is designed to deal with the nuts and bolts of putting a sentence together. At a later stage in revision, you may give more thought to why you structured a sentence in a particular way. This section provides you with information on how to make your sentences work better for you in your efforts to persuade the reader of the point you are making.

12-1) SHIFTS

A **shift** is a sudden and unnecessary change in point of view, verb tense, mood, or voice, or a change from indirect to direct questions or quotations. Shifts can occur within and between sentences. They often blur meaning and confuse readers.

⊘ I am curious to know how do you install an operating system?

⊘ I am curious to know how to install an operating system.

Moving from an indirect question to a question is a shift.

12-1A) POINT OF VIEW

In writing, **point of view** is the perspective from which the work is written. Often this is indicated by the pronouns the writer uses.

- The first-person point of view emphasizes the writer. It often appears in more informal types of writing, such as journals, diaries, and personal letters.
- The second-person point of view emphasizes the reader and is often found in directions or instructional types of writing, such as this handbook.
- The third-person point of view emphasizes the subject. It is used in informative writing, including the writing you do in many academic and professional contexts.

1. First person: *I, we*
2. Second person: *you*
3. Third person: *he/she/it/one* or *they*

FIRST-PERSON POINT OF VIEW
I believe that individuals should all do their part to clean up the environment by participating in local initiatives that improve its beauty and safety.

SECOND-PERSON POINT OF VIEW
If you want to help, remember that you must reduce, reuse, and recycle.

THIRD-PERSON POINT OF VIEW
A priority of environmental protection in Canada is chemical management that obliges industries to show how they use and manage chemicals identified as dangerous to individuals and the environment.

KEEP POINT OF VIEW CONSISTENT

One must keep one's cool when faced with big crowds in orientation week. You need to appreciate the opportunities of your widening environment. (shift in point of view from third person, *one*, to second person, *you*)

Some hikers have their dogs carry the food pack on longer

their

trips. As ~~our~~ journey progresses and stops are periodically made for meals, the dog's pack becomes lighter. (shift from third person, *some hikers*, to first person, *our*)

Your fax machine supports both tone and pulse dialling. The

you do

default setting is TONE, so ~~one does~~ not need to change the

you use

setting if ~~he or she uses~~ that kind of line. If you are using a pulse dial line, change the setting to PULSE by following these steps. (shift from second person, *you*, to third person, *one* and *he or she*, and back to second person)

MAINTAIN SINGULAR OR PLURAL STATUS OF NOUNS

they prefer

Since malamutes have very heavy fur coats, ~~it prefers~~ to sleep outside even in extremely cold temperatures. (shift from third-person plural, *malamutes*, to third-person singular, *it*; note that the verb needed to be changed, too)

SHIFTS IN POINT OF VIEW

Shifts in point of view occur when a writer begins his or her piece of writing in one point of view, then shifts carelessly back and forth to other points of view. To prevent needless shifts, think about the most appropriate point of view for your writing situation, establish the point of view in your writing, and keep to that point of view.

SHIFTS FROM SINGULAR TO PLURAL

A common problem among student writers is shifting from the third-person singular to the third-person plural or vice versa.

12-1B   VERB TENSE

The verb tense tells the reader when the action in the piece of writing is taking place. Shifting from one verb tense to another without a sound reason only confuses the reader.

The convention in essays about literature is to describe fictional events consistently in the present tense. Sometimes, of course, shifts in tense are necessary if you are discussing literature in its historical context.

KEEP VERB TENSES CONSISTENT AND LOGICAL

TENSE SHIFT

He is so vain that he always sits at a restaurant table facing

the sunlight, since he ~~thought~~ *thinks* the rays might add to his precious tan. (shift from present tense to past tense)

You told me yesterday that you thought my new dress ~~looks~~ *looked* appropriate for the wedding. (shift from past to present tense)

SHIFT FROM LITERARY PRESENT

As an egocentric, Gabriel has "restless eyes" early in "The Dead." However, when he displays empathy near the end of the story, he ~~possessed~~ *possesses* "curious eyes." (shift from literary present tense to past tense)

Throughout *Lady Chatterley's Lover*, D.H. Lawrence uses sexually explicit language and curse words. This use of profane language **was** a departure from the conventions of the novel in the early twentieth century. (exception to rule; tense shift is necessary to relate the literary work to its context)

12-1C   VERB MOOD AND VOICE

MOOD

Shifts can also occur in the mood of verbs. The mood of the verb indicates the manner of action.

There are three moods in English.

USE THE APPROPRIATE MOOD OF THE VERB

⊘ I wish my son was here with me. (indicative mood is incorrect since the subjunctive mood expresses a wish)

INDICATIVE MOOD

He wrote a short story.

Did he win a prize for the story?

IMPERATIVE MOOD

Don't do that!

Rewind the videotape before returning it.

SUBJUNCTIVE MOOD

If I were lucky, I might have won the lottery.

If wishes were horses, beggars would ride.

AVOID SHIFTS IN THE MOOD OF VERBS

Include more foreground by focusing in front of your main subject

To include more background, do the reverse.

while keeping the subject within the depth of field.^ ~~The reverse is also true.~~ (shift from imperative mood, *Include*, to indicative mood, *is*)

ACTIVE VOICE

Shelley baked the pie.

PASSIVE VOICE

The pie was baked by Shelley.

1. The indicative mood is used to state facts or opinions, or to ask questions.
2. The imperative mood is used to give a command or advice, or to make a request.
3. The subjunctive mood is used to express doubt, wishes, or possibility. It also expresses conditions contrary to fact.

Shifts in Mood

The writer's purpose is to give advice on photography. He or she appropriately begins in the imperative mood, but erroneously shifts into the indicative mood.

VOICE

Voice refers to whether a verb is active or passive. A verb is active when the subject of the sentence is the performer of the action. A verb is passive when the performer of the action is an object in the sentence or is not present.

Active voice is easier to read because it puts the agent of the action first.

Shifts in Voice

If the writer suddenly shifts between voices, it can be jarring and confusing to the reader. The subordinate clause is in the passive voice, while the main clause is in the active voice.

USE THE ACTIVE VOICE WHEN YOU NEED TO IMPROVE CLARITY

I could immediately comprehend the devastation of the avalanche

as soon as ^*I reached* the peak overlooking the valley ~~was reached~~.

12-1D   DIRECT AND INDIRECT QUESTIONS OR QUOTATIONS

DIRECT AND INDIRECT QUOTATIONS

In a direct quotation, the writer repeats a speaker's words exactly, placing those words within quotation marks. In an indirect quotation, the writer summarizes or paraphrases what the speaker has said.

SHIFT FROM INDIRECT TO DIRECT QUOTATIONS

If you start by paraphrasing a quotation, continue to do so throughout the sentence. Likewise, if you start with a direct quotation, keep quoting directly. Note, however, that you may use both direct and indirect quotations in an academic paper; just don't do so in the same sentence.

USE DIRECT AND INDIRECT QUOTATIONS AND QUESTIONS APPROPRIATELY

Direct: U.S. General William C. Westmoreland said, "We'll blow them back into the Stone Age."

Indirect: U.S. General William C. Westmoreland said his forces would bomb the enemy so relentlessly that they would be blown back into the Stone Age.

KEEP YOUR USE OF QUOTATIONS CONSISTENT

The dog trainer told me to keep Pepé by my side and *not* ~~don't~~ give the dog more than a foot of slack on his lead. (consistently indirect quotation)

Alternative revision: The dog trainer said, "Keep Pepé by your side and don't give the dog more than a foot of slack on his lead." (consistently direct quotation)

DIRECT QUESTION

Which road do you take to get to Lions Head?

Do you know how to use a GPS?

INDIRECT QUESTION

I asked which road to take to get to Lions Head. I'm wondering if you know how to use a GPS.

DO NOT COMBINE INDIRECT AND DIRECT QUESTIONS

I'm asking you if you'd like to hike the Bruce Trail, and if so,
whether you'd like
~~would you like~~ to start at Tobermory or St. Catharines.

Alternate revision: Would you like to hike the Bruce Trail, and if so, would you like to start at Tobermory or St. Catharines? (direct question)

Note the difference in punctuation.

DIRECT AND INDIRECT QUESTIONS

A direct question stands alone as a question. It is not introduced by or included in any statement.

An indirect question reports that a question was asked or could be asked but does not actually ask the question.

Shifting from indirect to direct questions can make writing awkward and confusing.

SHIFTS FROM INDIRECT TO DIRECT QUESTIONS

An alternate revision would be to pose both questions directly.

MIXED CONSTRUCTIONS (12-2

⊕ By working overtime and watching my pennies should make it possible to save enough money for a new car.

☺ Working overtime and watching my pennies should make it possible to save enough money for a new car.

A sentence with a **mixed construction** incorrectly changes from one grammatical construction to another, thereby confusing the sentence's meaning.

When you draft a sentence, your options for structuring that sentence are limited by the grammatical patterns of English. (See 9-2 and 9-3.) You must consistently follow the pattern you choose within the sentence. You cannot start the sentence using one grammatical pattern and then abruptly change to another. *Don't switch horses* [grammatical structures] *in the middle of a stream* [sentence] is an idiom that can help you remember this key grammatical guideline.

KEEP SENTENCE PATTERNS IN MIND AND MAKE SURE MODIFIERS ARE CLOSE TO WHAT THEY MODIFY

Mixed: By multiplying the number of specialty stations available to viewers via digital television **increases** the chance that cultural communities within Canada's diverse cultural mosaic will be better served.

Revised: Multiplying the number of specialty stations available to viewers via digital television **increases** the chance that cultural communities within Canada's diverse cultural mosaic will be better served.

OR

Revised: By multiplying the number of specialty stations available to viewers via digital television, **satellite and cable companies increase** the chance that cultural communities within Canada's diverse cultural mosaic will be better served.

Mixed: Although satellite dishes have become popular in many northern Canadian communities, **but** many viewers still prefer local stations.

Revised: Satellite dishes have become popular in many northern Canadian communities, **but** many viewers still prefer local stations.

OR

Revised: Although satellite dishes have become popular in many northern Canadian communities, many viewers still prefer local stations.

Mixed: In communicative language teaching, students' errors are corrected only when they interfere with comprehension **rather than by the direct method in which** students' errors are corrected immediately to avoid habit formation.

Revised: In communicative language teaching, students' errors are corrected only when they interfere with comprehension; **in the direct method**, students' errors are corrected immediately to avoid habit formation.

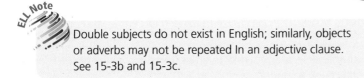

Double subjects do not exist in English; similarly, objects or adverbs may not be repeated In an adjective clause. See 15-3b and 15-3c.

The museum you want to visit ~~it~~ is not open on Sunday.

Upset at the news, she ran to the school that her son was attending ~~it~~.

Another mixed construction is incorrectly combined clauses.

It is often wise to rethink what you want to say, and then completely recast the sentence so it is clear, straightforward, and logical.

Often, trying to pack too much information into a sentence causes confusion.

ILLOGICAL CONNECTIONS   12-2B

CHECK TO SEE THAT YOUR SUBJECT AND VERB MAKE SENSE WHEN USED TOGETHER

Originally,
~~The original function of~~ the Internet was created to exchange academic and military information.

Was the function created or the Internet?

The decisions on who would make Canada's 2002 Olympic
were made
hockey team ~~was chosen~~ by a management committee headed by Wayne Gretzky.

Were the decisions chosen or made?

A number of sentence faults can occur when elements of the sentence do not logically fit together. **Faulty predication** is one example of such a problem. In faulty predication, the subject and predicate do not make sense together. To remedy this problem, either the subject or the predicate must be revised.

An appositive is a noun or noun phrase that renames or explains a noun or noun phrase immediately before it. The appositive must logically relate to the noun or noun phrase that precedes it; otherwise **faulty apposition** occurs.

MAKE SURE APPOSITIVES RELATE TO THEIR ANTECEDENTS

Stock ~~speculators~~ *speculation*, a very risky business, demands nerves of steel and a healthy bank account.

Stock speculation, not stock speculators, is a very risky business.

12-2C AVOIDING *IS WHEN, IS WHERE,* AND *THE REASON … IS BECAUSE*

These constructions are not grammatical and often add unnecessary words to a sentence. If you find such constructions in your drafts, revise the sentences that contain them.

DEFINE TERMS WITHOUT USING *IS WHEN* OR *IS WHERE*

In computer dating,
~~Computer dating is when~~ the computer is used to match potential romantic partners according to their compatibility, interests, and desirability.

AVOID THE REDUNDANT EXPRESSION *THE REASON IS BECAUSE*

~~The reason~~ I watch horror movies ~~is~~ because I need a release from the tensions of life.

12-3 COORDINATION AND SUBORDINATION

Coordination and **subordination** allow you to communicate the relationships between ideas in sentences. Use coordination to give equal emphasis to ideas; use subordination to emphasize one idea over another.

COORDINATION
Coordination balances two or more ideas in a sentence, giving equal emphasis to each.

CHECK YOUR USE OF COORDINATORS WHEN YOU REVISE

You can coordinate ideas at the level of words, phrases, or clauses by using the coordinating conjunctions *and, but, for, nor, or, so,* and *yet.*

COORDINATING WORDS

John is friendly **but** awkward.

I want candy **and** popcorn.

COORDINATING PHRASES

Suze likes long, hot bubble baths **and** big, cold bowls of ice cream.

It's not what you say **but** how you say it.

COORDINATING CLAUSES

Nelson Mandela spent twenty-eight years in a South African jail, **but** the great dignity with which he endured imprisonment made him a symbol of the struggle against apartheid.

In some cases, the semicolon is followed by a conjunctive adverb, such as *however, therefore, moreover, hence,* and *indeed.*

Nelson Mandela spent twenty-eight years in a South African jail; **moreover**, the great dignity with which he endured imprisonment made him a symbol of the struggle against apartheid.

CHECK YOUR USE OF SUBORDINATORS WHEN YOU REVISE

Usually, subordinate clauses begin with one of the following subordinating conjunctions:

after	since	when	while
although	than	whenever	who
as	that	where	whom
because	though	wherever	whose
before	unless	whether	
if	until	which	

When coordinating words or phrases, you need only use the coordinating conjunction. When coordinating independent clauses (remember that a clause is a group of words that can stand on its own as a sentence), join the clauses with a comma and a coordinating conjunction, a semicolon and a subordinating conjunction, or a semicolon alone.

SUBORDINATION

Subordination allows you to communicate the relative importance of ideas within sentences. You can emphasize important ideas by making them independent clauses or give ideas less emphasis by making them subordinate clauses, which cannot stand on their own as sentences.

When drafting a sentence, you must decide which idea you would like to emphasize. Subordinating a clause can give a sentence a very different meaning. If you aren't sure which sentence structure to use, try writing the sentence a few different ways, and then pick the one that best conveys your meaning.

The subordinating conjunction you choose, as well as the clause you subordinate, can alter the meaning of your sentence. Consider the differences between the following:

Although Nelson Mandela spent twenty-eight years in a South African jail, the great dignity with which he endured imprisonment made him a symbol of the struggle against apartheid. (suggests that the time spent in prison might have been worth it to become a symbol against apartheid)

While Nelson Mandela spent twenty-eight years in a South African jail, the great dignity with which he endured imprisonment made him a symbol of the struggle against apartheid. (emphasizes the role and effect of Mandela's dignity during imprisonment)

After Nelson Mandela spent twenty-eight years in a South African jail, he became a symbol of the struggle against apartheid because of the great dignity with which he endured imprisonment. (offers a temporal perspective and shows cause and effect)

None of these sentences is incorrect, but one is likely closer than the others to the writer's intended meaning.

12-3A   CHOPPY SENTENCES

Too many consecutive short sentences in a passage can make your writing seem mechanically repetitive and choppy. As well, probably not all of the ideas in the string of short sentences are equally important. Some sentence ideas you might wish to emphasize, some you might want to de-emphasize, and some ideas in pairs of sentences you might consider balancing.

These four very short sentences have become one by using the subordinator *which*

CONSIDER THE LENGTH OF SENTENCES AND REPETITIVENESS OF WORDING WHEN YOU REVISE; JOIN SENTENCES TO AVOID REDUNDANCY

QUICK TIP

Subordination and coordination allow you to combine sentences and thus eliminate the problem of choppy writing.

Choppy: Tennyson called lightning a "flying flame." Lightning travels at between 100 000 and 300 000 kilometres per second. Lightning reaches temperatures of 24 000 to 28 000 degrees Celsius. It kills 20 people each day.

Revised: Lightning, **which** Tennyson called a "flying flame," travels at between 100 000 and 300 000 kilometres per second **and** reaches temperatures of 24 000 to 28 000 degrees Celsius, **killing** 20 people each day.

Choppy: The basketball team huddled on the sidelines. The players were drenched in sweat. They looked dejected.
Revised: The basketball team, **drenched in sweat and looking dejected**, huddled on the sidelines.

Choppy: I received a call from the doctor about my dad's serious illness. I immediately booked the first possible flight to Victoria.
Revised: After I received a call from the doctor about my dad's serious **illness, I** immediately booked the first possible flight to Victoria.

Choppy: Harjeet was my adult literacy student. Harjeet was fighting a valiant battle against multiple sclerosis.
Revised: Harjeet, my adult literacy **student,** was fighting a valiant battle against multiple sclerosis.

Choppy: The marathon swimmer was coated with grease, and she listed as she made her way to the shore. She seemed a symbol of determination.
Revised: Coated with grease and listing as she made her way to the shore, the marathon swimmer seemed a symbol of determination.

Choppy: Miners in Nanaimo-area coal mines had to worry about shafts under the harbour collapsing. They had to be concerned about deadly gases. The miners also had to be worried about fires or explosions.
Revised: Miners in Nanaimo-area coal mines had to worry about **shafts under the harbour collapsing, deadly gases, and fires or explosions**.

ELL Note

Do not repeat the subject when you combine sentences. Also, do not repeat an adverb when it occurs in an adjective clause. See 15-3b and 15-3c.

The work that he completed ~~it~~ was sloppy.
The spot where the accident occurred ~~there~~ is dangerous.

and the coordinator *and.* Also note the use of the modifier *killing* to replace *it kills.*

Here, the two final sentences have been subordinated into an adjective clause modifying the basketball team.

The subordinating word *after* has been used to turn the first sentence into an adverbial clause.

A less important idea has been turned into an appositive describing Harjeet.

Less significant details about how the swimmer looked are placed in the participial phrase beginning *Coated.*

The three sentences have been combined into one sentence containing ideas of equal importance.
While these sentences serve as examples, you can also use them as models for strategies to improve your own writing. For example, you might consider combining sentences by turning a shorter sentence into an appositive or an adjectival phrase.

Coordination is effective when you want to point out to the reader that two ideas are of equal importance.

U.S. president Theodore Roosevelt quoted this adage in a speech in 1901. The balance of the sentence is central to Roosevelt's meaning. He thought American foreign policy should employ diplomacy (*speak softly*) but at the same time be backed up by military might (*a big stick*). Coordination is extremely effective here.

In the coordinated version of the next sentence, the two ideas could be unrelated. By adding the subordinating word *Since* and turning the opening independent clause into a subordinate one, the cause–effect relationship between the ideas is foregrounded.

The key idea that the doctor concluded there might be a crisis is given prominence in the sentence. The less significant idea is given less prominence as a participial phrase modifying the subject, the doctor.

The original sentence about P. K. Page contained too many coordinated independent clauses. In the revision, the

USE COORDINATION TO JOIN ONLY RELATED AND EQUAL IDEAS

Effective Coordination: <u>Speak softly</u> and <u>carry a big stick</u>.

Since cell
~~Cell~~ phones became very popular in the 1990s, ~~and~~ many users have experienced car accidents.

. observing
The doctor^ ~~observed~~ that there were an abnormal number of patients from the Walkerton area with gastrointestinal

disorders^ ~~and~~ alerted authorities that they could have a major health crisis on their hands.

Coordinated Unequal Ideas: Poet P. K. Page studied art in New York and Brazil, and then in the 1940s she was a filing clerk and historical researcher, but it was during the '40s that she became a founding member of the literary periodical *Preview*.

Revised: After studying art in New York and Brazil, poet P.K. Page worked as a filing clerk and historical researcher in the 1940s, but it was **also during this time** that she became a founding member of the literary periodical *Preview*.

opening clause has become dependent, which is appropriate since that clause contains less important information.

INEFFECTIVE SUBORDINATION 12-3C

GIVE IMPORTANT IDEAS PRIORITY IN YOUR SENTENCE STRUCTURE

Most important idea subordinated: Rajinder was riding the bus along West Hastings Street listening on his iPod to the Steve Miller song "Take the Money and Run," when he saw two bank robbers fleeing a TD Canada Trust branch on foot.

Revised: While Rajinder was riding the bus along West Hastings Street listening on his iPod to the Steve Miller song "Take the Money and Run," he saw two bank robbers fleeing a TD Canada Trust branch on foot. (explanation)

Main sentence ideas should be given emphasis within the sentence; do not relegate them to subordinate status. Structure your sentences so that important ideas appear in independent clauses, while less important ideas or information appears in subordinate dependent clauses.

EXCESSIVE SUBORDINATION 12-3D

WATCH SENTENCE LENGTH AND REDUCE EXCESSIVE SUBORDINATION WHEN IT INTERFERES WITH CLARITY

Unclear: While jogging is good aerobic exercise, as you get older, since running adversely affects deteriorating knees, it is advisable to do it in moderation.

Revised: Jogging is good aerobic exercise. However, as you get older, since running adversely affects deteriorating knees, it is advisable to do it in moderation.

Sometimes subordination can be overused. If you have more than two dependent clauses in a sentence, determine whether or not excessive subordination has made the sentence unclear or otherwise ineffective.

QUICK TIP

Usually there are two ways to address the excessive subordination problem:
1. Recast the sentence.
2. Divide the sentence in two.

12-4) PARALLELISM

Parallelism in writing means that equal grammatical structures are used to express equal ideas. Errors in parallelism, known as **faulty parallelism,** occur when *unequal* structures are used to express equal ideas. Words, phrases, and clauses should all be parallel when they express a similar idea and perform a similar function in a sentence. When using parallelism for effect, balance single words with single words, phrases with phrases, and clauses with clauses.

USE PARALLEL CONSTRUCTION, WHERE POSSIBLE, TO MAKE SENTENCES CLEAR AND MEMORABLE

The following three quotations from Winston Churchill all demonstrate parallel, balanced elements:

Words: I have nothing to offer but blood, toil, tears and sweat.

Phrases: Victory at all costs, victory in spite of all terror, victory however long and hard the road may be; for without victory there is no survival.

Clauses: You do your worst, and we will do our best.

12-4A   WITH ITEMS IN A SERIES

When the reader encounters items in a series, he or she expects them to be parallel in structure. When one or more items do not follow the parallel grammatical pattern, the sentence seems jarring and awkward to the reader.

MAKE SURE ITEMS IN A SERIES ARE PARALLEL

❌ Anatole liked the lawn, the hedge, and to garden.
✅ Anatole liked **the lawn**, **the hedge**, and **the garden**.

❌ Ace may not be the cutest or the largest dog in existence, but he's very smart.
✅ Ace may not be the **cutest** or the **largest** dog in existence, but he may be one of the **smartest**.

❌ Being outdoors, feeling the winds off the ocean, and to smell the Douglas fir are what I like about hiking British Columbia's West Coast Trail.
✅ **Being** outdoors, **feeling** the winds off the ocean, and **smelling** the Douglas fir are what I like about hiking British Columbia's West Coast Trail.

MAKE SURE PAIRED ITEMS ARE PARALLEL

HOW TO IDENTIFY THE NEED FOR PARALLEL STRUCTURES

Parallel ideas are often connected in one of three ways:

1. With a coordinating conjunction, such as *or*, *and*, or *but*
2. With a pair of correlative conjunctions, such as *not only ... but also* or *either ... or*
3. With comparative constructions using *than* or *as*

USE PARALLEL STRUCTURE WITH COORDINATING CONJUNCTIONS

- Alfred, you may go by train, boat, car, bus, or a jet will take you there.
- Alfred, you may go by **train**, **boat**, **car**, **bus**, or **jet**.

- Our debating team read Jordan's ideas, were discussing her arguments, and have decided they are not relevant to our debate position.
- Our debating team **read** Jordan's ideas, **discussed** her arguments, and **decided** they were not relevant to our debate position.

USE PARALLEL CONSTRUCTION WITH CORRELATIVE CONJUNCTIONS

not only ... but also

either ... or

both ... and

- When the staff met the sales target, the manager not only ordered new chairs, but also new desks, potted plants, and a microwave for the lunchroom.
- When the staff met the sales target, the manager ordered <u>not only</u> **new chairs**, <u>but also</u> **new desks**, potted plants, and a microwave for the lunchroom.

OR

- When the staff met the sales target, the manager <u>not only</u> **ordered** new chairs, <u>but also</u> **provided** new desks, potted plants, and a microwave for the lunchroom.

Whenever you relate ideas using coordination, correlation, or comparison, always emphasize the connection between or among ideas by expressing them in parallel grammatical form.

USING PARALLEL FORMS WITH COORDINATING CONJUNCTIONS

Coordinating conjunctions (*and, but, or, nor, for, yet,* and *so*) are words that connect ideas of equal importance. Avoid faulty parallelism by ensuring that all elements joined by coordinating conjunctions are parallel in grammatical form.

USING PARALLEL FORMS WITH CORRELATIVE CONJUNCTIONS

Avoid faulty parallelism by ensuring that each element linked by correlative conjunctions is parallel to the other.

Correlative conjunctions are pairs of words that join equal grammatical structures. Examples include *not only ... but also, either ... or,* and *both ... and.*

- ⊕ Viewers either criticized the television station for its inflammatory views, or it was criticized for its political stance.
- ✓ Viewers <u>either</u> **criticized** the television station for its inflammatory views <u>or</u> **criticized** it for its political stance.

OR

- ✓ Viewers criticized the television station <u>either</u> **for its inflammatory views** <u>or</u> **for its political stance**.

(Note that while the first revision is technically correct, the second is more economical, and the connection between the ideas is clearer.)

COMPARISONS LINKED WITH *THAN* OR *AS*

Often you will use *than* or *as* to make comparisons. To avoid faulty parallelism, make sure the elements being compared are expressed using parallel grammatical structure.

Use the matching -*ing* form on both sides of the comparison.

MAKE SURE COMPARISONS ARE PARALLEL

- ⊕ Having great wealth is not as satisfying as the completion of charitable works.
- ✓ **Having** great wealth is not as satisfying as **completing** charitable works.

Use the matching form—in this case, the infinitive form of the verb (with *to*)—on both sides of the comparison.

Note: For either of the examples shown, there are equally acceptable alternatives. In some instances, faulty parallelism corrections that occur to you may be improvements over what appears in the handbook.

- ⊕ It is better to give than do the receiving.
- ✓ It is better **to give** than **to receive**.

MAKE SURE TO INCLUDE NECESSARY WORDS

Other languages have different rules about which words can be omitted. Watch especially for missing articles, verbs, subjects, or expletive pronouns. See 15-1, 15-2i, and 15-3a.

In your efforts to write concisely by deleting words, be careful not to cut essential words.

Provide all words needed to make such sentences grammatically and logically complete.

QUICK
TIP

Check for clarity when balancing structures in your writing, especially
- *when using compound-structures*
- *when that is required to prevent misreading*
- *when using comparisons*

USE PARALLEL STRUCTURE IN COMPOUND SENTENCES

In the Big Sur event, some competitors will run in the marathon and some [will run] in the 10 km race. (*will run* can be omitted in the second instance)

- A funeral lasts for hours; some wakes for days.
- A funeral lasts for hours; some wakes **last** for days. (the verb form is different, so the verb must be repeated)

In compound constructions, two or more elements (e.g., words, phrases, clauses) have equal importance and function as a unit.

It is acceptable to omit words that are common to both parts of the compound structure.

However, when the parts in a compound structure differ in any way, all words must be included in each part of the compound construction.

🟢 I have and will continue to support your right to remain silent.
🔵 I have **supported** and will continue to support your right to remain silent. (the verb form is different, so the verb must be repeated)

🟢 Many little tots believe and leave milk and cookies for Santa Claus.
🔵 Many little tots believe **in** and leave milk and cookies for Santa Claus. (tots don't believe *for* Santa Claus, so the correct preposition must be included)

12-5B *THAT*

When the word *that* introduces a subordinate clause, it may sometimes be omitted, but only if the omission does not present a danger of misreading the sentence.

INCLUDE THE WORD *THAT* IF IT IMPROVES CLARITY

The movie [that] I saw most often when I was young was *The Mummy*. (meaning is clear without *that*, so it can be omitted)
BUT

🟢 Edgar noticed his brand new television, which he had purchased on credit, didn't match his new carpet. (may indicate that Edgar noticed the TV)
🔵 Edgar noticed **that** his brand new television, which he had purchased on credit, didn't match his new carpet. (makes it clear that Edgar noticed the mismatch, not the TV itself)

12-5C IN COMPARISONS

Make comparisons only between like items. Comparisons between unlike items are illogical and jarring to the reader.

MAKE SURE COMPARISONS ARE LOGICAL AND COMPLETE

🟢 I compared my short stories to Ernest Hemingway.
🔵 I compared my short stories to Ernest Hemingway**'s**.
OR
🔵 I compared my short stories to **those of** Ernest Hemingway.

The incorrect version compares short stories with Ernest Hemingway—two distinctly different items. The sentence requires that short stories be compared with short stories.

❌ In terms of special effects, James Cameron's version of the *Titanic* is more stunning than any other director.

✓ In terms of special effects, James Cameron's version of the *Titanic* story is more stunning than any other director**'s**.

In the incorrect sentence, version and director—two very different items—are compared. By adding the possessive *director's*, which implies version, you are comparing two like items: versions of the *Titanic* story.

other

Toronto has a larger population than any ^ city in Ontario.

Without *other*, the sentence suggests that Toronto has a larger population than itself.

Toronto has a larger population than any ~~other~~ city in Quebec.

With *other*, this sentence suggests that Toronto is in Quebec, which is untrue.

as

Canada's best authors are as renowned^, and probably more renowned than, those of any other small country.

The construction *as renowned … than* is grammatically incomplete.

❌ Sudsaway is a better dishwashing detergent.
✓ Sudsaway is a better dishwashing detergent **than Dentoxanol**.

❌ I gave him more soup than you.
✓ I gave him more soup than **I gave to** you.
OR
✓ I gave him more soup than you **gave him**.

USING *ANY* AND *ANY OTHER*

Comparisons using *any* and *any other* can be confusing. Writers sometimes omit *other*, making comparisons illogical.

Follow these guidelines:

1. Use *any other* when comparing an item with other items in the same group.
2. Use *any* when comparing an item with other items in a different group.

USING *AS* TO MAKE GRAMMATICALLY CORRECT COMPARISONS

Insert *as* when it is needed to make a comparison grammatically correct.

Comparisons must be complete so that it is clear to the reader just what is being compared.

Leave no chance for ambiguity in the comparisons you make.

12-6) SENTENCE VARIETY

When you carefully review the draft, you may find that many sentences are very similar in structure and length. By revising and crafting your work to create sentences of varied structures and lengths, you can make your writing livelier. However, when striving for sentence variety, be sure that you do not detract from your intended meaning or sentence clarity.

QUICK TIP

To check for sentence variety, count the number of sentences in a 100-word sample of your writing. Divide 100 by that number to find the number of words per sentence. Many more than 12–15 words per sentence may signify a lack of clarity; many fewer may signify a lack of coherence. Some rare exceptions, of course, may add interest to your writing.

12-6A   SIMPLE, COMPOUND, AND COMPLEX SENTENCES

Too many of any one type of sentence structure can make your writing repetitive and monotonous. Recall that sentences come in three basic structures—simple, compound, and complex—and that sentence structures can be combined to create, for example, compound-complex sentences. Guard against overuse of one sentence type: too many simple sentences can make your ideas sound simplistic, and too many complex sentences can make your writing seem tedious or pretentious.

CONSIDER SENTENCE VARIETY AS YOU REVISE

Bear in mind that about half of your sentences in academic prose are likely to be complex because you are making logical connections.

Simple: I like swimming.

Compound: I like swimming, and I even like diving.

Complex: I like swimming although it is inconvenient in the winter.

Compound-complex: I like swimming although it is inconvenient in the winter, but in that season, I often go skiing instead.

For a discussion on sentence types, see 9-4.

WHEN CLARITY IS AN ISSUE, BEGIN WITH THE SUBJECT AND FOLLOW DIRECTLY WITH THE VERB; WHEN CLARITY IS NOT LIKELY TO BE A PROBLEM, CONSIDER SOME VARIETY

When your writing seems monotonous, vary openings of sentences and vary their length to change the rhythm.

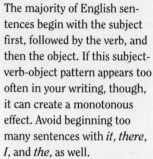

- The biggest problem yesterday was that too few students showed up to the orientation.

- Unfortunately, at the orientation yesterday, very few students showed up.

Soon the ferrets
~~The ferrets soon~~ returned from their sanctuary at the wildlife habitat.

For seven days, the
~~The~~ students stayed in their rooms ~~for seven days~~, where they were deprived of sleep, overwhelmed by assignments, and driven to distraction with worry.

ʙ   *the boxer*
~~The boxer,~~ broken and battered, ^ relinquished his heavyweight crown.

Expecting to be terminated, t
^ ~~The~~ provincial government employees~~, expecting to be terminated,~~ dusted off their résumés.

- Born prematurely, her father assumed she would be a delicate child.

Although we may understand what is meant, this sentence suggests that her father was born prematurely, rather than she.

For information on repairing dangling modifiers, see 10-7e.

The majority of English sentences begin with the subject first, followed by the verb, and then the object. If this subject-verb-object pattern appears too often in your writing, though, it can create a monotonous effect. Avoid beginning too many sentences with *it*, *there*, *I*, and *the*, as well.

To add variety and interest to your writing, consider beginning some sentences differently.

ADVERBIAL MODIFIERS
You can easily place an adverbial modifier in front of the sentence subject. These modifiers can be single words, phrases, or clauses.

ADJECTIVAL AND PARTICIPIAL PHRASES
Often, adjectival phrases and participial phrases can be moved to the start of the sentence without affecting meaning.

When using adjectival or participial phrases, ensure that the subject is clearly identified, or you may be creating a dangling modifier.

Changing the common subject-verb-object sentence pattern may not only create sentence variety but also—in some instances—add emphasis.

In an inverted sentence, the subject appears at the end of the sentence.

Use inverted sentences in moderation. They often sound awkward and artificial.

IF IT WON'T AFFECT CLARITY, CONSIDER INVERTING SENTENCE ORDER

Subject-Verb-Object: The world-famous painting rested against the far wall.
Inverted Order: Against the far wall rested the world-famous painting.

Subject-Verb-Object: The movie star sauntered into the suite for the press conference.
Inverted Order: Into the suite sauntered the movie star for the press conference.

12-7) WORDINESS

Effective writing is concise, clear, and direct. Concise writing does not necessarily mean fewer words or shorter sentences. It means words that function clearly and sentences that express their point without empty words.

When revising, review each sentence you write with an eye to eliminating any phrase or word that is not absolutely necessary to your intended meaning.

LEAVE OUT WORDS THAT ARE EMPTY OF MEANING OR REPETITIVE

❌ Notwithstanding the fact that the manager is late, the meeting will still take place.

✅ Although the manager is late, the meeting will still take place.

BE DIRECT

REMOVE WORDS THAT REPEAT AN IDEA

It is 6:30 <u>a.m.</u> <u>in the morning</u>.

~~The reason~~ Nebuchadnezzar stopped his conquest ~~was~~ because he heard of his father's death and his own succession to the throne.

The board members did not want to repeat the debate ~~again~~, so they had a frank ~~and honest~~ discussion during which they identified some basic ~~essential~~ ideas.

When people are in ~~situations of~~ conflict at a meeting, they should

achieve

circle ~~around~~ the speaker and try to attempt to ~~form~~ a consensus ~~of opinion~~.

The bridge ~~that people cross to get~~ to Burlington is ~~sort of~~ rectangular ~~in shape~~, and it is made of strong materials such as reinforced steel, and concrete, ~~etc.~~

Redundancy is the use of unnecessary words in a sentence. Often the same idea is expressed twice or more.

Common redundancies include *final completion*, *important essentials*, *close proximity*, *consensus of opinion*, and *actual fact*.

ELIMINATE REPETITION

The quarterback passed the football, but the lineman raised

it

his meaty, ~~heavy~~ hand and batted ~~the football~~ away.

The houses ~~where the people live~~ are not far from ~~the city of~~ Moncton.

DON'T USE TWO WORDS IF ONE WILL DO

As basketball fans, we journeyed to Almonte, Ontario, ~~which is~~ the birthplace of ~~Canadian~~ John Naismith.

The powerful

~~Loaded with power, the~~ car was considered unbeatable.

Sometimes you may wish to repeat words or phrases to create an effect or for emphasis, as in parallel constructions. However, when words are repeated for no apparent reason, they make writing seem sloppy and awkward.

As you revise, eliminate unnecessary repeated words.

Occasionally, to make your writing sound more important, you may be tempted to include certain phrases you've heard others use. When you examine your sentences carefully, you'll find these padded phrases only increase your word count and contain little or no meaning.

Effective writers state what they mean as simply and directly as possible. As you revise your work, trim sentences of any wordy, empty, or inflated phrases. These can often be easily spotted when you edit for conciseness. You don't need words like *I think* or *I feel* or *in my opinion*, for example, because your ownership as an author is established without them. Expressions like *in today's society* are also meaningless and should be avoided.

You can eliminate empty words or phrases without affecting your meaning.

REMOVE WORDS THAT HAVE LITTLE OR NO MEANING

Because currently
~~By virtue of the fact that at the current time~~ we do not have sufficient funding, the skateboard park will not be built.

Table 12.1   Eliminating Wordy or Inflated Phrases

Wordy/Inflated	Concise
along the lines of	like
as a matter of fact	in fact
at all times	always
at the present time	now, currently, presently
at this point in time	now, currently, presently
because of the fact	because
being that	because
by means of	by
by virtue of the fact that	because
due to the fact that	because
for the purpose of	for
for the simple reason that	because
have a tendency to	tend
have the ability to	be able to
in the nature of	like
in order to	to
in spite of the fact that	although, even though
in the event that	if
in the final analysis	finally
in the neighbourhood of	about
in the world of today	today
it is necessary that	must
on the occasion of	when
prior to	before
until such a time as	until
with regard to	about

MAKE VERBS STRONGER

make a recommendation: recommend

have a discussion: discuss

exhibit a tendency: tend

give a suggestion: suggest

accumulated

During the strike, the ~~accumulation of~~ garbage^ ~~carried on~~ for fifteen days.

REPLACE *BE* AND *HAVE* WHENEVER POSSIBLE

recommends

The budget proposal before the legislature ~~is to do with~~ tax cuts and massive reductions in public-sector spending.

AVOID BEGINNING SENTENCES WITH *HERE*, *THERE*, AND *IT*

A

~~There is a~~ picture of Pierre Trudeau playing baseball ~~that~~ shows the energy he brought to the prime minister's office.

Most importantly,

~~It is important that~~ you should remain calm if your kayak capsizes in rough water.

The following word-trimming strategies will help you make your sentences simple, clear, and direct.

STRENGTHEN THE VERB

Often nouns derived from verbs can be turned back into verbs to make the sentence more direct and active.

The noun phrase *the accumulation of garbage* has been turned into the subject *garbage* and active verb *accumulated*.

AVOID COLOURLESS VERBS

The verb forms *is/are, was/were,* and *has/have/had* are weak and often create wordy sentence constructions.

The weak verb *is* has been replaced with the more active verb *recommends*.

REVISE EXPLETIVE CONSTRUCTIONS

An expletive construction uses *there* or *it* and a form of the verb *to be* in front of the sentence subject. Often, these constructions create excess words. You might remove the expletive and revise the sentence to make it more concise and direct.

USE THE ACTIVE VOICE WHERE POSSIBLE

The active voice is generally more concise and direct than the passive voice. Use the active voice when you want to be direct and to focus on the action of a sentence.

Note: A grammar-checker can easily find instances of the passive voice, but it is up to you to decide whether or not to make the suggested changes, based on your knowledge and the context of the document you are working on.

USE THE ACTIVE VOICE TO PUT THE ACTION AND THE PEOPLE WHO PERFORM THE ACTION INTO THE SPOTLIGHT

Passive: The research was conducted by senior students who plan to enter graduate school.

Active: Senior students who plan to enter graduate school conducted the research.

For more information on active and passive voice, see 10-4h.

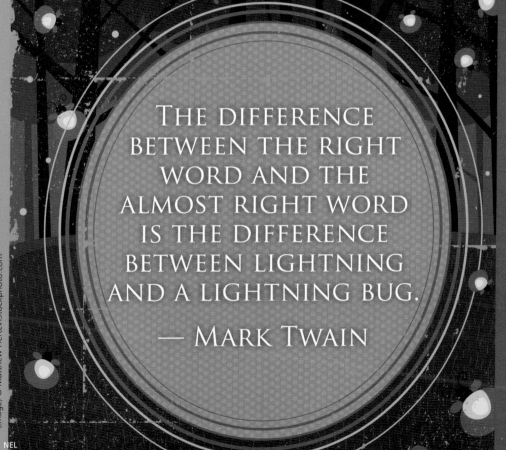

THE DIFFERENCE
BETWEEN THE RIGHT
WORD AND THE
ALMOST RIGHT WORD
IS THE DIFFERENCE
BETWEEN LIGHTNING
AND A LIGHTNING BUG.

— MARK TWAIN

Usage

13

WRITING IN CONTEXT

Consider how what you want to say fits with the reader's expectations, and with the occasion of your writing.

Figure 13. 1 Rhetorical Context

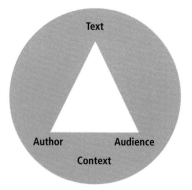

The effectiveness of your writing will in large measure depend on the appropriateness of the language you decide to use for your audience. Choose the wording that best suits the context and the audience of your writing. Consider these elements as you choose your words:

- subject
- audience (their needs, expectations, and feelings)
- purpose
- voice (as reflected in your unique writing style)

The following section provides guidance and information that will help you to select appropriate language for your writing assignments.

Jargon is the specialized language of a particular group or occupation. In some instances, you may need to use jargon—for example, if your audience is the particular group or occupation that uses the jargon or you can reasonably assume your audience will understand this specialized language. Generally, though, avoid jargon and use plain English in its place.

In addition to very specialized language, jargon often includes language that is intended to impress readers rather than to communicate information and ideas effectively. Jargon-filled language is often found in business, government, education, and military documents.

Sentences containing jargon are difficult to read and extremely unclear.

If you encounter inflated words or phrases in your writing draft, consider alternative words that are simple, clear, and precise in meaning.

CONSIDER YOUR AUDIENCE'S EXPERTISE BEFORE USING JARGON

Jargon: Positive input into the infrastructure impacts systematically on the functional base of the organization in that it stimulates meaningful objectives from a strategic standpoint.

Clear: Positive feedback to the organization helps it formulate concrete, strategic objectives.

Jargon: The Director of Instruction implemented the optimal plan to ameliorate poor test scores among reading-at-risk students.

Clear: The Director of Instruction carried out the best plan to improve poor test scores among students having trouble reading.

Jargon: We will endeavour to facilitate a viable trash recovery initiative for all residences in the neighbourhood.

Clear: We will try to create a workable garbage pickup plan for all neighbourhood homes.

Table 13.1 Eliminating Jargon

Words Designed to Impress	Simple Alternative(s)
ameliorate	fix, improve
commence	begin, start
components	parts
endeavour	attempt, try
exit	go, leave
facilitate	help
factor	cause, consideration
finalize	complete, finish
impact on	effect
implement	carry out
indicator	sign
initiate	start, begin
optimal	best
parameters	boundaries, limits
prior to	before
prioritize	order, rank
utilize	use
viable	workable

AIM FOR CLARITY IN LANGUAGE

Pretentious: It is **de rigueur** to expound on reification in Timothy Findley's fictional tome *The Wars.*

Plain Language: It is **necessary** to discuss the treatment of people as objects in Timothy Findley's novel *The Wars.*

Pretentious: Pursuant to our discussion yesterday, it is time to **operationalize** our business plan.

Plain language: As we discussed yesterday, it is time to act on our business plan.

Pretentious: For **optimal** results, we must **establish parameters** for clients and service providers.

Plain language: For best results, we must set boundaries for clients and service providers.

AVOID LANGUAGE THAT IS DELIBERATELY UNCLEAR, SUCH AS EUPHEMISMS

Table 13.2   Avoiding Euphemisms

Euphemism	Plain English
chemical dependency	drug addiction
correctional facility	jail
declared redundant	fired, laid off
developing nations	poor countries
downsizing	laying off or firing employees
economically deprived	poor
incendiary device	bomb
laid to rest	buried
leather-like	vinyl
military solution	war
misleading phrase	lie
pre-owned automobile	used car
starter home	small house
strategic withdrawal	defeat or retreat

AVOID PRETENTIOUS LANGUAGE

When writing for academic audiences and purposes, it is tempting to opt for elevated language. However, using uncommon or unnecessarily long words can highlight rather than obscure deficiencies in content—and make the writing seem pretentious. Academic writing does not require that you use longer, difficult words for their own sake. State your ideas in words that you understand.

AVOID EUPHEMISMS

A **euphemism** is a word or expression intended to lessen the impact of harsh or unacceptable words or phrases. An example of a euphemism in a military context is *collateral damage,* a term sometimes used to describe civilian casualties. In a few writing situations, using euphemisms is acceptable. For instance, when expressing condolences to a friend, you might use the euphemism *passed away* as a substitute for *died.* Generally, however, avoid euphemisms; they are highly indirect and blur meaning.

SLANG

Slang is the informal, colourful vocabulary that is often unique to and coined by subgroups such as teenagers, college students, musicians, skate-boarders, computer program-mers, street gangs, rap artists, and soldiers. Slang is often used to communicate the unique common experiences of these subgroups, and it is frequently not understood by all segments of society. Most often, slang attempts to be current and trendy, but such language is soon overused and quickly becomes dated.

Slang can often make story dialogue sound lively and authentic. However, it is inappropriate in formal writing such as academic essays and business letters.

AVOID SLANG; IT MAY BE INAPPROPRIATE FOR THE CONTEXT OR UNCLEAR IN MEANING

>   *failed*   *examination*
> Jeff ~~flunked~~ his final history ~~exam~~, and now his
>   *has been completely wasted*
> semester ~~is a total write-off~~.

Slang: Mel and her gang are coming over, and we're going to watch the tube and pig out.

Formal: Melanie and her friends are coming over. We are going to watch television and eat snacks.

DATED SLANG
the cat's pyjamas
groovy

STILL UNDERSTANDABLE?
a cool dude
bad
wicked
bummer
grunt
rip-off
wired
preppie

REGIONAL EXPRESSIONS

A regional expression is an expression that is common to a particular area of the country.

Regional expressions, like slang, can add colour and authenticity; however, they

AVOID REGIONAL EXPRESSIONS; THEY MAY NOT BE UNDERSTOOD BY YOUR AUDIENCE

Murray could see the skiff beyond the <u>barachois</u>.

In Atlantic Canada, a *barachois* is "a tidal pond partly obstructed by a bar" (*Nelson Canadian Dictionary*, p. 108).

After he caught the winning salmon, they threw the

ocean

fisherman in the ~~salt chuck~~.

Salt chuck is a regional expression used in British Columbia and the U.S. Pacific Northwest. It might not be known to all Canadians.

USE STANDARD ENGLISH IN FORMAL WRITING

Non-standard: The **guy** was **nowheres** in sight. He **could of** left town, but she didn't care **anyways**.

Standard: The **man** was **nowhere** in sight. He **could have** left town, but she didn't care **anyway**.

Some common examples of non-standard English include

anyways
bursted
nowheres
theirselves

If you speak a non-standard dialect, you may consult these sections of the handbook for advice on using standard English in your writing:

- *10-4a*: Misuse of verb forms
- *10-3* and *10-4c*: Omission of *-s* endings on verbs
- *10-4d*: Omission of *-ed* endings on verbs
- *10-4e*: Omission of necessary verbs
- *10-6d*: Double negatives

may not be familiar to a general audience and should be avoided in formal academic writing.

Many Canadian dictionaries have labels indicating if a word or expression is regional.

NON-STANDARD ENGLISH

Non-standard English is acceptable in informal social and regional contexts, but it should be avoided in any formal writing.

Standard English, on the other hand, is the written English commonly expected and used in educational institutions, businesses, government, and other contexts in which people must formally communicate with one another. Use standard English in all of your academic writing. If you are in doubt about whether a word or phrase is standard or non-standard English, check in the Glossary of Usage in this handbook or in a good Canadian dictionary.

QUICK TIP

Email conventions differ depending on cultural context and audience. In Canadian colleges and universities, use a formal tone for email and follow formal conventions of address, word choice, and spelling. Remember that there are multiple readers of email, and postings are typically archived. Decide—before you press the SEND button—whether your words are appropriate for email.

Informal writing is casual in language and tone, and it is appropriate for communication in such forms as notes, friendly letters, emails, journal entries, and brief memoranda to people you know very well.

Formal writing is professional in tone and language, and it is appropriate for academic and business writing such as essays, research reports, job application letters, and business letters and reports.

When deciding which level of formality to employ in a piece of writing, you should consider three key factors:

1. Subject
2. Audience
3. Context

USE THE LEVEL OF FORMALITY APPROPRIATE TO THE CONTEXT

Consider these factors:

Subject: How serious or lighthearted is the subject?

Audience: Who will be receiving this? Who might see it? How familiar am I with the audience?

Context: What do I want the message to accomplish? How will the message make me look to the reader?

QUICK TIP

Avoid the abbreviations of instant messaging in academic writing.

hfng/Shutterstock.com

SAMPLE BUSINESS LETTER 1: BLOCK STYLE WITH MIXED PUNCTUATION

12 Princess Dr.
Marktown, ON M2P 1L0

> Your address (You might also include your name and your email address here.)

January 15, 2011

> Date

Mr. Hal Cheng, Executive Director
Alliance of Part-time Undergraduate Students
202 Wells St., Room 4207
Toronto, ON M8P 1U7

> Address of the recipient

Dear Mr. Cheng:

> Salutation (Typically, you use an honorific like *Mr.* and a last name.)

SUBJECT: CHARITY COMMUNITY WEBSITE

> An optional Subject line

I would like to apply for the position of researcher in charge of educational opportunities for part-time students that you advertised in the *Globe and Mail* on January 10, 2011. I believe I would be an outstanding candidate for the position.

Over the past three years, I have worked as a researcher for various instructors at the University of Waterloo. A significant part of my work involved assisting professors in their research to determine which teaching strategies and materials are used within the educational community. I was responsible for helping to administer research surveys and questionnaires by mail, telephone, and email. As well, I proofread final analysis reports. My work often required contacting educational decision-makers at schools, school-board offices, colleges, universities, and departments of education.

Mr. Hal Cheng, January 15, 2011, page 2

I have also helped conduct market analysis research projects in the private sector. A recent project I worked on involved surveying telecommunications decision-makers to assess customer needs.

While a summer intern with the British Columbia Ministry of Education, I helped file in the Assessment Branch and gained organizational skills useful to researchers. I am sensitive to issues affecting part-time university students, having completed my second year on a part-time basis while working.

My writing skills are of a high standard. This past academic year, I won a prize for the best undergraduate essay, and I have published two short stories in the campus newspaper.

I would welcome the opportunity to meet with you to elaborate on my qualifications and discuss the advertised position.

Sincerely,

Naomi Bahadur

Naomi Bahadur

Enc.

cc Professor Theodore Resnick

Note that in block style (the most common), paragraphs are not indented, nor is anything else.

Complimentary close (You might use *Yours truly* or *Yours sincerely* in a formal letter also).

Enc. indicates an enclosure.

cc indicates other recipients of the letter

As you draft and revise your work, ask the following questions about the level of formality you select.

SUIT THE WORDS TO THE SUBJECT

1. Consider your purpose in writing.
2. Consider how serious the issue is.

SUIT WORDS AND STRUCTURES TO THE AUDIENCE

1. What does my audience expect?
2. How well do I know my audience?
3. What conventions do I need to respect?

Use specific, respectful language.

🔴 I'm just dropping you a few lines to put my name in for that fisheries biologist's assistant job I saw somewhere in the *Free Press* a few weeks back.

⚫ I am writing to apply for the fisheries biologist's assistant position advertised in the June 16 edition of the *Free Press.*

Too Formal: When the illustrious Maple Leafs exited from the frozen playing surface trailing their less renowned opponents, the Wild, by the modest score of 1–0, the assembled spectators vigorously voiced their disapproval. The officials in charge of the National Hockey League were authentic demons for having the audacity to schedule these mismatched contests between the annual All-Star Game and the hockey tournament that is part of Olympic competition.

More Appropriate: When the Leafs left the ice trailing the Wild 1–0, a smattering of boos rained down from the crowd. The NHL was the real culprit for slipping lopsided games like these between the All-Star Game and the Olympics.

SUBJECT

- Is my choice of words appropriate to the seriousness of my subject? If you are seeking a job, you need to impress your audience. If you are making a joke, you need to make sure that your audience will take it in the right spirit.

AUDIENCE

Ask yourself the following:

- What type of language will my audience expect?
- Is my choice of words appropriate for the intended audience?
- Does my choice of words and the tone these words create make me seem too close or too distant from my readers?

In any academic or business writing you do, use a formal level of writing and assume a serious tone. Be aware, however, that the level of language can also seem highly inappropriate if it is too formal.

Sexist language is biased in attributing characteristics and roles to people exclusively on the basis of gender. Sometimes sexist language is very obvious, but often it is less so. Sexist language can be explicit, as in calling an attractive young woman a *hot chick*. It can be patronizing, as in referring to a mature woman as a *girl Friday*. It can reflect stereotypical thinking by unnecessarily drawing attention to a person's gender, as in *a female university president*. And sexist language can be subtle, yet still highly biased, by including only male pronouns when more inclusive language is needed; for example, *an athlete always needs to maintain his composure*.

Sexist language can apply to men as well as women—for instance, if a writer describes *a male kindergarten teacher*.

There are a number of strategies you can use to avoid sexist language.

AVOID SEXIST LANGUAGE

STRATEGIES

Strategies for Avoiding Sexist Language
1. Treat all people equally in your descriptions of them.
2. Avoid stereotypes.
3. Use pairs of pronouns to indicate inclusive gender references.
4. Rewrite the sentence as a plural.
5. Rewrite the sentence so there is no gender problem.
6. Make gender-neutral word choices.

Mr. Delmonico, Mr. Habib, Mr. Dawson, and **Tillie, the secretary,** arrived for the meeting.

Mr. Delmonico, Mr. Habib, Mr. Dawson, and **Ms. Lord** arrived for the meeting.

Stereotyping: Like all men, he hates to cook.

A professor is motivated by **his** students.

A professor is motivated by **his or her** students.

Professors are motivated by **their** students.

A professor is motivated by **students**.

Policemen have a difficult job.

Police officers have a difficult job.

Table 13.3 Avoiding Sexist Language

Inappropriate	Gender-Neutral
alderman	city council member, councillor
anchorman	anchor
businessman	businessperson, entrepreneur
chairman	chairperson, chair
clergyman	member of the clergy, minister
coed	student
craftsman	artisan, craftsperson
fireman	firefighter
forefather	ancestor
foreman	supervisor
freshman	first-year student
housewife	homemaker
mailman	mail carrier, letter carrier, postal worker
male nurse	nurse
mankind	people, humankind, human
manpower	personnel, human resources
newsman	journalist, reporter
policeman	police officer
salesman	salesperson, sales clerk
stewardess	flight attendant
to man	to staff, to operate
weatherman	weather forecaster, meteorologist
waitress	server
workman	worker, labourer, employee

Avoid using words that assume gender. Names of occupations should be gender-neutral. Be inclusive in your language choice and refer to gender only when it is relevant to the context.

13-2) PRECISION IN LANGUAGE

When trying to choose the most precise word to communicate your meaning, you may find a number of language reference books helpful.

USE REFERENCE BOOKS WISELY TO ENSURE PRECISE LANGUAGE

Here are some good reference works to consider:
Roget's Thesaurus
Gage Canadian Thesaurus
Fitzhenry and Whiteside's Canadian Thesaurus

13-2A   CONNOTATIONS

Many words have two levels of meaning: a **denotative** meaning and a **connotative** meaning. The denotative meaning of a word is its common, literal, dictionary meaning. The connotative meaning is the emotional meaning of the word, which includes experiences and associations you make when you see a word in print or hear it spoken.

When considering any word for a piece of writing, you should consider both its denotative and connotative meanings. Sometimes, by using a word with certain connotations, you could imply a meaning you do not intend. Conversely, you can enhance your intended meaning by selecting the word with the most appropriate connotations for your subject, purpose, and audience. Often, reviewing all listed meanings in a dictionary

CONSIDER THE CONNOTATIONS OF ANY WORD THAT YOU USE

eagle: denotation = "a large bird of prey"
eagle: connotations and associations = power, pride, majesty, sharp-eyed

laughed
The young women ~~giggled~~ at all the right parts of the Restoration comedy.

Giggled has an association with immaturity, and since the women were described as young, the sentence implies the women were immature. The intended meaning of the sentence was that the women appreciated the humour of the play, so *laughed* is more appropriate.

has   *had*
Ethel ~~is a victim of~~ rheumatoid arthritis and has ~~suffered from~~ it for ten years.

Better: Ethel was diagnosed with rheumatoid arthritis ten years ago.

Emotional language related to suffering is best avoided when discussing ailments and afflictions, since this kind of language adds an inappropriate slant to the meaning.

Consider the context of words. The word *dissipated*, when applied to crowds, means "scattered." When applied to people, it means "drunk" or "disorderly."

entry will give you a sense of a word's connotations. Take special care when using a thesaurus to be sensitive to the connotations of a word.

There are many types of nouns; however, in general, nouns can be divided into two sets of opposites—general and specific nouns, and abstract and concrete nouns.

TO ENGAGE YOUR AUDIENCE, BE SPECIFIC RATHER THAN GENERAL

General: dog
Specific: St. Bernard, schnauzer, pit bull, cocker spaniel, etc.

General: snack
Specific: potato chips, popcorn, chocolate bar (even better: Mars bar)

Abstract Nouns: love, charity, kindness, humanism, youth, integrity
Lily looked at Phillip with love.

Concrete Nouns: snake, dill, sunset, coffee, caramel, harp
My favourite drink is coffee.

GENERAL AND SPECIFIC NOUNS

Nouns can be very general or very specific. For example, consider *clothes* versus *dress*, *suit*, *jeans*, *sweats*, *shorts*, etc.

ABSTRACT AND CONCRETE NOUNS

Nouns can be abstract or concrete. Abstract nouns refer to concepts, ideas, qualities, and conditions. Concrete nouns name things that are detectable by your senses.

In your own writing, try to select the most effective word for your writing purpose. Of course, in the range of your writing assignments, you will frequently need to describe, explain, and evaluate general and abstract content. At these times, general and abstract language will be most appropriate. But wherever possible, use specific and concrete nouns to make your writing clear and evocative.

General abstract nouns, such as *things, considerations,* and *aspects,* are extremely vague and lacking in colour. Replace them wherever possible.

Toronto's smog
~~Hazy city air~~ made it difficult to breathe as we ~~put the~~
launched the sailboat onto Lake Ontario
~~boat in the water~~.

have several renovations done
We plan to ~~do a number of things~~ to improve our home.

issues to discuss
There are several ~~considerations to be addressed~~ before we allow the new subdivision.

poodle
Lilly brought her ~~dog~~ to the office.

features
There are many ~~aspects~~ of Richards's prose to discuss.

Mustang convertible
My parents bought a new ~~vehicle~~.

hugs and kisses
Who doesn't like to receive ~~love~~?

13-2C   ACTIVE AND PASSIVE VOICE

Active voice is recognized by the normal word order in English: subject-verb-object. Passive voice, by contrast, changes that word order so that the subject, if it appears at all in the sentence, does not appear at the beginning. Often, active voice is preferable because it is more direct and clearer.

Passive voice is easily recognized also. It always

USE THE ACTIVE VOICE TO MAKE YOUR WRITING MORE DIRECT

Passive Voice: The eager young actors **were trained** by the dynamic acting coach.

Active Voice: The dynamic acting coach **trained** the eager young actors.

approached
As she ~~got near to~~ the finish line, the marathon runner
lunged for   *grimaced*   *collapsed*
~~leaned toward~~ the tape, ~~crinkled her face~~, and ~~fell down~~.

Active Voice: José **hammered** the nail.

Passive Voice: The nail **was hammered** by José.

The nail **was hammered**. (This construction may be appropriate if the subject is unknown or unimportant.)

The class selected

^"Canada's Ethnic Diversity" ~~was selected by the class~~ as the theme for the panel discussion.

involves a form of *to be*, followed by a past participle. That is why software programs like Microsoft Word can easily identify it.

Only transitive verbs, those that take an object, can change from active to passive voice.

MISUSED WORDS 13-2D

conscious

Burns is ~~conscience~~ of his own powers of destruction.

censored

The provincial review committee ~~censured~~ the pornographic movie.

cited

In a definitive book on Gorbachev, the author ~~sighted~~ the main reasons for the collapse of the Soviet Union.

abhorrent

It is an ~~abhorrence~~ practice when advertisers target viewers under five years of age.

Be careful to choose the right word.

⊘ I am disinterested in the concert my friends are planning to attend.

✔ I am uninterested in the concert my friends are planning to attend.

Because several words in English are spelled similarly or sound alike, writers can sometimes use the wrong word for their meaning. Also, many writers incorrectly use a noun when the meaning and sentence structure require an adjective. For instance, they might use *abhorrence*, *indulgence*, or *independence* in sentences that require the adjective forms *abhorrent*, *indulgent*, or *independent*, respectively.

STANDARD IDIOMS

An idiom is an expression whose meaning can't be determined by simply knowing the definition of each word within the idiom. Many idioms are very colourful and easy to spot: *kill two birds with one stone, read between the lines, the last straw.*

An idiom always appears in one particular form, one that may not necessarily be taken literally. An example of an idiom is *beside himself* [or *herself*]. *She was beside herself* means "She was in a state of extreme excitement or agitation."

Using idiomatic expressions with prepositions can be tricky. An unidiomatic expression may make better literal sense, but the idiomatic expression is used because it is accepted English usage. If you are in doubt, check a good Canadian dictionary by looking up the word before the preposition.

Table 13.4 Avoiding Unidiomatic Expressions

Unidiomatic	Idiomatic
according with	according to
angry at	angry with
capable to	capable of
comply to	comply with
desirous to	desirous of
different than	different from
go by	go to
intend on doing	intend to do
off of	off
plan on doing	plan to do
preferable than	preferable to
prior than	prior to
recommend her to do	recommend that she do
superior than	superior to
sure and	sure to
try and	try to
type of a	type of
wait on a person	wait for a person
wait on line	wait in line
with reference in	with reference to

EXAMPLES OF IDIOMATIC EXPRESSIONS

kill two birds with one stone

read between the lines

the last straw

beside oneself

green with envy

not my cup of tea

keep my finger in the pie

in a nutshell

BEWARE OF CLICHÉS IN YOUR WRITING

Table 13.5   Selected Clichés to Avoid in Your Writing

add insult to injury	easier said than done	in the long run
at long last	few and far between	in this day and age
a word to the wise	finishing touches	it stands to reason
cool as a cucumber	first and foremost	narrow escape
cold as ice	good as gold	red-letter day

He is as strong as an ox; unfortunately, that describes his odour, too.

A **cliché** is an overused phrase or expression that has become tired and predictable and, hence, is ineffective for freshly communicating ideas.

You might wish to create a computer file of clichés to avoid.

Clichés, by being so predictable, deprive writing of any sense of surprise. However, in some rare instances, you might inject freshness into a cliché by giving it an unexpected twist.

USE FIGURES OF SPEECH JUDICIOUSLY

remain
She was able to ~~take a firm foothold~~ in the eye of public opinion.

Harry
~~The Grand Canyon of Harry's depression~~ reached the
depth of depression
~~pinnacle~~ when his pet died.

Simile: Orion [Twain's brother] is as *happy as a martyr when the fire won't burn*. (Mark Twain, letter to his mother, Jane Lampton Clemens, 1872)

Metaphor: Mary-Kate was a night owl, but Ashley was an early bird.

Personification: A tropical destination is calling my name.

In figurative language, words carry more than their literal meaning. **Figures of speech** are particular types of figurative language. Common examples of figures of speech are **similes**, **personification**, and **metaphors**. In a simile, a comparison is made between two different ideas or objects, using *like* or *as*. In personification, human traits are assigned to something that is not human. And in a metaphor, a comparison is made between two otherwise dissimilar ideas or objects; here, the comparison does not use *like* or *as*.

Used effectively, figures of speech can add colour and emphasis to your writing and enrich meaning. However, used without care, they can make writing clumsy. A common writing problem is mixing metaphors. In a **mixed** metaphor, two or more incongruous images are mingled.

AVOID MIXED METAPHORS

⊘ Unless we tighten our belts, we will lose our shirts.

⊘ Brilliant sunshine is raining down on us in Edmonton today.

⊘ We will kick off the hockey season tomorrow.

13-3) THE DICTIONARY AND THESAURUS

13-3A THE DICTIONARY

A student at the postsecondary level needs at least one good Canadian dictionary in his or her personal reference library. Canadian dictionaries provide correct spelling and usage in Canada and are not mere adaptations of American or British dictionaries.

Online dictionaries are also available; however, if they are British or American in origin, be aware that they may not always apply Canadian standards of spelling or usage. For American usage, try the Merriam-Webster online dictionary. For British usage, try the Cambridge or Oxford online dictionaries.

Note that online dictionaries may be useful sources of correct pronunciation. You can hear

USE A GOOD CANADIAN DICTIONARY

Canadian Dictionaries
- *ITP Nelson Canadian Dictionary*
- *The Canadian Oxford Dictionary*
- *Gage Canadian Dictionary*
- *Funk & Wagnalls Canadian College Dictionary*

COMMON GRAMMATICAL ABBREVIATIONS FOUND IN THE DICTIONARY

n. noun
pl. plural
sing. singular
v. verb
tr. transitive (as in *transitive verb*)
intr. intransitive (as in *intransitive verb*)
adj. adjective
adv. adverb
pron. pronoun
prep. preposition
conj. conjunction
interj. interjection

magicoven/Shutterstock.com

Figure 13.2   Sample Dictionary Entry from *ITP Nelson Dictionary*

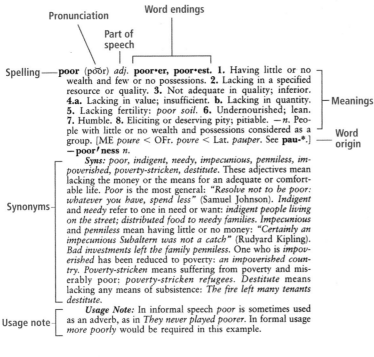

Pronunciation

Word endings

Part of speech

Spelling —— **poor** (pŏŏr) *adj.* **poor•er, poor•est. 1.** Having little or no wealth and few or no possessions. **2.** Lacking in a specified resource or quality. **3.** Not adequate in quality; inferior. **4.a.** Lacking in value; insufficient. **b.** Lacking in quantity. **5.** Lacking fertility: *poor soil.* **6.** Undernourished; lean. **7.** Humble. **8.** Eliciting or deserving pity; pitiable. — *n.* People with little or no wealth and possessions considered as a group. [ME *poure* < OFr. *povre* < Lat. *pauper.* See **pau-*.**] — **poor′ ness** *n.*

Meanings

Word origin

Synonyms —— *Syns: poor, indigent, needy, impecunious, penniless, impoverished, poverty-stricken, destitute.* These adjectives mean lacking the money or the means for an adequate or comfortable life. *Poor* is the most general: "*Resolve not to be poor: whatever you have, spend less*" (Samuel Johnson). *Indigent* and *needy* refer to one in need or want: *indigent people living on the street; distributed food to needy families. Impecunious* and *penniless* mean having little or no money: "*Certainly an impecunious Subaltern was not a catch*" (Rudyard Kipling). *Bad investments left the family penniless.* One who is *impoverished* has been reduced to poverty: *an impoverished country. Poverty-stricken* means suffering from poverty and miserably poor: *poverty-stricken refugees. Destitute* means lacking any means of subsistence: *The fire left many tenants destitute.*

Usage note —— *Usage Note:* In informal speech *poor* is sometimes used as an adverb, as in *They never played poorer.* In formal usage *more poorly* would be required in this example.

Source: From NELSON CANADA. Nelson Canadian Dictionary of the English Language.
© 1997 Nelson Education Ltd. Reproduced by permission. www.cengage.com/permissions.

In square brackets at the end of the entry appears the *etymology*, or information about the origins of the word. According to the etymology for *poor*, the word originated from the Middle English word *poure*, as well as from Old French and Latin. In addition, this dictionary lists synonyms, words with similar meanings, and gives advice on usage.

the word rather than having to puzzle out the phonetic alphabet as in a written source.

SPELLING, WORD DIVISION, PRONUNCIATION

The main entry *(poor* in the sample entry) shows the correct spelling of the word. When there are two spellings of a word (*pickaxe* or *pickax*, for example) both spellings are given, with the preferred Canadian spelling provided first.

If the word is a multi-syllabic word (as in *poor•ly*), the entry shows how to divide the word into syllables. The dot between *poor* and *ly* separates the word's two syllables.

The pronunciation of the word is given just after the main entry. If the word is a multi-syllabic word, accents indicate which syllables are stressed. Other marks help the reader pronounce the word. These marks are explained in a pronunciation key at the beginning of the dictionary.

When a word takes endings to indicate grammatical functions, which are called inflections, the endings are listed in boldface. In the *poor* entry, three inflections are listed: *poor•er, poor•est,* and *poor•ness.*

You may find yourself in a writing situation in which you know a word but want to find a more precise or colourful word with the same or a similar meaning. Or, you may have repeatedly used a word within a paragraph or even a sentence and don't want your writing to sound mechanical. In these cases, a thesaurus can help you find another, similar word.

HOW DO I USE THE THESAURUS?

Suppose you want to find a synonym for *plenty*. Your first step is to find *plenty* in the extensive index at the back of the thesaurus.

Of the possibilities listed in the entry, the closest to the meaning and part of speech you want is *plenty*. Turn to the Abstract Relations section at the front of the thesaurus to the number listed in the index beside *plenty*, under *abundance*.

Before you actually include a word in your manuscript, double-check its meaning in the dictionary.

USE THE THESAURUS TO LOCATE THE BEST WORD

Figure 13.3   Sample Thesaurus Entry for *Plenty*

plenty *n*   abundance, affluence, a fund, a plethora, a profusion, copiousness, enough, fertility, fruitfulness, heap(s), lots, luxury, mass, masses, milk and honey, mountain(s), oodles, opulence, overabundance, pile(s), plenitude, plenteousness, plentifulness, prosperity, quantities, stack(s), ton(s), volume(s), wealth.
antonyms   lack, need, scarcity, want.

Source: From GAGE CANADIAN THESAURUS (TRADE EDITION). © 2005 Nelson Education Ltd. Reproduced by permission. www.cengage.com/permissions.

The *Gage Canadian Thesaurus* is an excellent resource for finding synonyms, or words with a similar meaning. It is available in hardcover, paperback, and software format.

Figure 13.4   Explanation of Terms and Format of a Thesaurus Entry

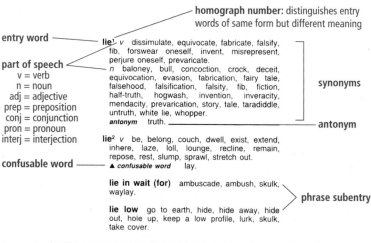

Source: From GAGE CANADIAN THESAURUS (TRADE EDITION). © 2005 Nelson Education Ltd. Reproduced by permission. www.cengage.com/permissions

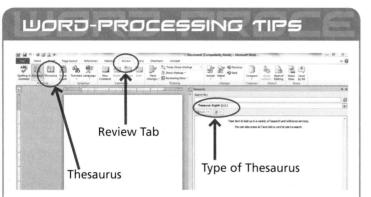

WORD-PROCESSING TIPS

Review Tab

Thesaurus

Type of Thesaurus

The thesaurus in Microsoft Word can be found under the Language heading in the Tools menu. If you do not have access to a printed thesaurus, you may find it somewhat useful. Unlike print sources, though, it does not give you insight into the subtle nuances of word choice and therefore may be less than wholly satisfactory for your writing purposes.

Always strive for simplicity and clarity when writing. If you use the thesaurus to find inflated vocabulary, you'll risk misusing words and make your writing seem pretentious.

QUICK TIP

In Microsoft Word 2010, the thesaurus feature is found in the "Review" ribbon.

No *passion* in the world
is equal to the passion
to alter someone
else's draft.
—H. G. Wells

EL

14

In the 1632 edition of the King James Bible, the omission of the word "not" gave whole new meaning to the seventh commandment, appearing as "Thou shalt commit adultery." The printer of this error was fined £300 for his mistake.

© ajaykampani/iStockphoto.com

Article Source: http://EzineArticles.com/2792064

Spelling and mechanics often make or break a document. Referring to "Robert Bondar" in a fundraising letter when you meant to refer to Canadian astronaut Roberta Bondar may have serious repercussions for your fundraising campaign and will certainly make the reader think twice about your credibility as a writer. Little things mean a lot.

SPELLING 14-1

GET ORGANIZED

How to Improve Your Spelling Habits

❏ Flag difficult words as you go along (*sp.*) and then check them when you edit your final draft.

❏ If you use a spell-checker, remember to query words that are still doubtful to you.

❏ Keep a list of your most common errors.

❏ Turn to a dictionary for best results.

Checking spelling should be one of the final steps in your writing process, and it is an extremely important step. Presenting error-free written work is vital to creating a good impression in academic and business contexts. Spelling errors distract readers and, at their worst, can cause them to lose your meaning; when misspellings suggest entirely different meanings, they can completely confuse readers.

Spell-checkers in word-processing programs can be useful tools for helping you spot *some* potential spelling problems. However, spell-checkers have limitations that allow many spelling errors to be missed. These limitations include the following:

- Many spell-checkers, in their default setting, do not include Canadian spellings. It is, however, often possible to select Canadian spelling. As well, dictionaries such as the *Canadian Oxford Dictionary* are available in CD-ROM and can be installed and used to do the spell-checking.
- Countless words, such as new or marginal words or very specialized vocabularies, are not included. For instance, if you type *tchotchkes* (meaning "cheap, showy trinkets"), the spell-checker may offer you *crotches* as a correction—not what you had in mind at all.

Kalamazoo Gazette/AP

Spell-checking software typically will change *definately* to *defiantly*.

Rumour has it that, in one early spell-checker, a common misspelling of *inconvenience* (*inconvinence*) was corrected to read *incontinence*; well-meaning people who didn't proofread carefully ended up with *Sorry for the incontinence* instead of *Sorry for the inconvenience*. Mistakes of this kind could prove very embarrassing, to say the least.

BE AWARE OF COMMONLY CONFUSED WORDS NOT DISTINGUISHED BY SPELL-CHECKERS

affect and *effect*

➤ What **affect** will that medication have?

to and *too*

➤ He addressed the package **too** Revenue Canada.

do and *to*

➤ I wanted **do** tell you.

allusion and *illusion*

➤ I thought I had included an **allusion** to Shakespeare in my paper, but that was an **illusion**.

STRATEGIES

Remember These Forms:

it's/its: It's my guess that the dog misses its owner.

you're/your: You're going to learn your lesson.

who's/whose: Who's going to know whose book this is?

- Spell-checkers cannot distinguish between commonly confused words that have entirely different meanings.
- They cannot intuit that you have made a simple typographical error (e.g., *form* instead of *from*).
- The majority of proper nouns are not included.

Checking writing drafts for spelling errors demands your complete attention, and a computer spell-checker is just one of many tools and strategies at your disposal.

Good spelling is a challenge in English since sound and letter patterns frequently do not correspond and many spelling rules have exceptions.

Still, you can greatly improve your spelling by concentrating on the following:

- knowing basic spelling rules and their exceptions
- recognizing words that sound alike but have entirely different meanings and spellings
- identifying and remembering commonly misspelled words

Know the major spelling rules.

PATTERNS OF *IE* AND *EI* WORDS

Use *i* before *e* except after *c* or when *ei* sounds like *ay*, as in *weigh*.

DROPPING OR KEEPING A FINAL SILENT *E* WHEN ADDING A SUFFIX

Usually, drop the final silent *e* when adding a suffix that begins with a vowel and keep the final *e* when the suffix begins with a consonant.

ADDING *-ED* OR *-S* TO WORDS ENDING IN *-Y*

When adding *-ed* or *-s* to words ending in *y*, you usually change the *y* to *i* when *y* is preceded by a consonant. However, do not change the *y* when it is preceded by a vowel.

If you need to pluralize a proper name ending in *y* and preceded by a consonant, do not change the *y* to *i* when

REMEMBER *I* BEFORE *E* RULE

i before *e*:	believe, chief, niece, yield, fierce, grieve
e before *i* after *c*:	ceiling, deceive, perceive, receive
ei sounds like *ay*:	eight, vein, neighbour, freight, reign
exceptions:	either, leisure, weird, foreign, seize

BE CAREFUL WHEN ADDING A SUFFIX TO A WORD ENDING IN *-E*

DROP FINAL *E*

love + able = lovable

race + ing = racing

fame + ous = famous

Exceptions: dyeing, changeable, hoeing

KEEP FINAL *E*

achieve + ment = achievement

hope + ful = hopeful

love + ly = lovely

Exceptions: judgment, truly, argument

BE CAREFUL WHEN ADDING *-S* TO A WORD ENDING IN *-Y*

PRECEDED BY A CONSONANT

try + ed = tried

melody + s = melodies

PRECEDED BY A VOWEL

stay + ed = stayed

donkey + s = donkeys

DOUBLE CONSONANTS WHEN ADDING A SUFFIX

bet + ing = betting

fit + ed = fitted

commit + ing = committing

occur + ed = occurred

travel + ed = travelled

ADD -S TO FORM PLURALS

MOST NOUNS

plant + s = plants

fork + s = forks

satellite + s = satellites

NOUNS ENDING IN -S, -SH, -CH, -X, OR -Z

stress + s = stresses

bush + s = bushes

peach + s = peaches

fax + s = faxes

quiz + s = quizzes (Note that the z is doubled, as well.)

The Beatles toured during the 1960s.

Can I have two 5s for a 10?

adding -s. For example, when referring to the Dunwitty family, you would use *the Dunwittys*.

DOUBLING CONSONANTS WHEN ADDING SUFFIXES

Double the final consonant before a suffix starting with a vowel and ending with a consonant preceded by one vowel.

Double the final consonant when the word ends in an accented syllable.

Double the final consonant when the word ends in the consonant *l* (Canadian spelling).

ADDING -S TO FORM PLURALS OF NOUNS

Add -s to make most nouns plural. However, if the noun ends in -s, -sh, -ch, -x, or -z, add -es.

ADDING -S TO MAKE NUMBERS PLURAL

Add -s to make a number plural. Do not use an apostrophe.

CREATING OTHER PLURALS

Usually, add -s to nouns ending in *o* when *o* follows a vowel. However, add -es when *o* follows a consonant.

ADD -*S* IF A NOUN ENDS IN TWO VOWELS AND -*ES* IF IT ENDS IN ONE

O FOLLOWING A VOWEL

studio + s = studios

video + s = videos

O FOLLOWING A CONSONANT

echo + s = echoes

hero + s = heroes

When making a plural of a hyphenated compound word, add -s to the main word of the compound, even if that word does not appear at the end of the compound.

HYPHENATED COMPOUNDS

father-in-law + s = fathers-in-law

Some English words come from other languages, such as French and Latin. These words are usually made plural as they would be made plural in the original language.

WORDS FROM OTHER LANGUAGES

Singular	Plural
criterion	criteria
château	châteaux
datum	data
phenomenon	phenomena

BRITISH AND U.S. VARIATIONS

In your reading, you might notice variations in spellings for certain words. Generally, Canadian spelling follows British usage in its treatment of -*our* words and -*re* words, as well as doubling certain consonants before a suffix beginning with a vowel, but follows American style for -*ize* words. Check

CANADIAN SPELLINGS

colour not *color*

centre not *center*

counsellor not *counselor*

organize not *organise*

apologize not *apologise*

travelled not *traveled*

spelling in a good Canadian dictionary, where the Canadian spelling will be listed first.

Table 14.1   Commonly Confused Words

accept except	a verb meaning "to receive" a preposition meaning "other than" or verb meaning "to exclude"
affect effect	a verb meaning "to cause change" usually a noun meaning "the result of change"
cite site sight	a verb meaning "to quote" a noun meaning "location" a noun meaning "vision"
desert dessert	a verb meaning "to abandon" a noun meaning "sweet course after the main course of a meal"
its it's	possessive pronoun meaning "belonging to it" contraction of *it is*
loose lose	adjective meaning "not well attached" verb meaning "to misplace" or "to part with"
principal principle	noun meaning "the chief person" (as in a school), or adjective meaning "main" noun meaning "a basic truth" or "a rule"
their they're there	possessive pronoun meaning "belonging to them" contraction of *they are* adverb meaning "in that place"
who's whose	contraction of *who is* or *who has* the possessive form of *who*
your you're	possessive form of *you* contraction of *you are*

Words that sound the same but have different meanings and spellings are called **homophones**. Homophones are often the source of spelling problems. As you proofread your work, look carefully for homophones you may have used or spelled incorrectly.

The Glossary of Usage (pages 561–80) contains many homophones, as well as words that sound nearly the same and can cause spelling problems. You will also find definitions there for each word in the sets of words in Table 14.2.

Table 14.2 Homophones and Similar-Sounding Sets of Words in the Glossary of Usage

accept, except	emigrate, immigrate
adapt, adopt	eminent, imminent
adverse, averse	everyone, every one
advice, advise	explicit, implicit
affect, effect	farther, further
aggravate, irritate	ingenious, ingenuous
all ready, already	infer, imply
all together, altogether	its, it's
allude, elude	lead, led
allusion, illusion	licence, license
amoral, immoral	loose, lose
anyone, any one	maybe, may be
awhile, a while	moral, morale
beside, besides	passed, past
capital, capitol	practice, practise
censor, censure	precede, proceed
cite, site	principal, principle
climactic, climatic	respectfully, respectively
coarse, course	sometime, some time, sometimes
complement, compliment	stationary, stationery
conscience, conscious	than, then
continual, continuous	there, their, they're
council, counsel	to, too, two
discreet, discrete	weather, whether
disinterested, uninterested	who's, whose
elicit, illicit	your, you're

Table 14.3   Commonly Misspelled Words

Here is a list of words commonly misspelled by students. Check that they are spelled correctly in your writing drafts.

abbreviate	abhor	absence	absorption
absurd	abysmal	acceptable	accidentally
accommodate	accomplish	accumulate	acquaintance
acquire	address	aggressive	all right
amateur	analyze	annual	apology
apparently	appearance	appropriate	arctic
argument	ascend	association	attendance
attorney	audience	awkward	bachelor
barbarous	basically	beginning	behaviour
believe	beneficial	boundary	brilliant
Britain	bureau	burial	business
cafeteria	calendar	candidate	canister
carburetor	Caribbean	category	cemetery
changeable	choose	chose	column
commission	committee	comparative	competitive
compulsory	concede	conceivable	conference
conqueror	conscience	conscientious	conscious
consensus	courteous	criticism	criticize
curiosity	curriculum	cylindrical	dealt
decision	definitely	descend	description
despair	desperate	diarrhea	dictionary
dilemma	disagree	disappear	disappointment
disastrous	discipline	dissatisfied	dissipate
dominant	dormitory	ecstasy	eighth
eligible	elimination	embarrassment	eminent
entirely	entrance	environment	equipped
equivalent	erroneous	especially	exaggerated
exceptionally	exercise	exhaust	exhilarate
existence	experience	explanation	extraordinary
extremely	fallacy	familiar	fascinate
February	fictitious	foreign	foreseen
forty	frantically	friend	fundamental
further	gauge	genealogy	generally
grammar	guarantee	guard	guerrilla
guidance	harass	height	hereditary
heroine	hindrance	humorous	hungrily

(continued)

hypocrisy	hypothesis	illiterate	imaginary
imagination	imitation	immediately	impromptu
incidentally	incredible	indefinitely	independent
indispensable	inevitable	infinite	ingenious
initiation	inoculate	intelligence	interesting
involve	iridescent	irrelevant	irresistible
jealousy	knowledge	laboratory	legitimate
liaison	license (verb)	lightning	literature
liveliest	loneliness	luxury	magazine
maintenance	manoeuvre	marriage	marshal
mathematics	medieval	miniature	mischievous
misspell	moccasin	mortgage	mysterious
necessary	negotiation	nevertheless	noticeable
obligation	obstacle	occasion	occasionally
occur	occurred	occurrence	omission
opinions	opportunity	optimistic	original
outrageous	pamphlet	parallel	paralyze
particularly	pastime	peer	perform
performance	permanent	permissible	perseverance
perspiration	Philippines	physically	picnicking
playwright	practically	precedence	preference
preferred	prejudice	preparation	prevalent
primitive	privilege	probably	proceed
professor	prominent	pronunciation	psychology
quantity	quiet	quite	quizzes
\recede	receive	recommendation	reference
referred	regard	religious	reminiscent
repetition	resistance	restaurant	rhythm
ridiculous	roommate	sacrifice	sandwich
schedule	secretary	seize	separate
sergeant	several	siege	similar
simultaneous	sincerely	soliloquy	sophomore
specimen	strictly	subtly	succeed
supersede	surprise	syllable	temperament
temperature	tendency	thorough	threshold
tragedy	transferred	tries	truly
typical	unanimous	unnecessarily	until
usually	vacuum	vengeance	villain
weird	whether	written	

USE HYPHENS BETWEEN CERTAIN COMPOUND WORDS

half sister

stepfather

mother-in-law

A **compound word** is made up of two or more words that combine to express one concept. It may be written in one of three ways:

1. As separate words
2. As one word
3. As a hyphenated word

Check in the dictionary to determine whether to write a compound word as separate words, one word, or a hyphenated compound. If a compound word does not appear in the dictionary, treat it as separate words.

The tractor^trailer swerved and almost hit us.

bookshelf

He has an extensive resource library on the ~~book shelf~~ in his dormitory room.

Each time the Davidsons went to the CNE, they made a point of having candy⌇floss.

USE HYPHENS TO JOIN TWO WORDS SERVING AS AN ADJECTIVE BEFORE A NOUN

Vladimir is a well^known tenor in opera circles.

Because the thief was a fourteen^year^old girl, her picture could not be shown on the evening news.

She would go to any type of publicity event in the hope of becoming well⌇known.

To qualify for the league team, Adam had to be seventeen⌇years⌇old.

The family could not decide whether to purchase a one-, two-, or three-day pass to the theme park.

When two or more words function as an adjective before a noun, they are hyphenated.

In most cases, do not use a hyphen when the compound follows the noun.

Hyphens are suspended if the modifying words are in a series.

14-2C   FRACTIONS AND COMPOUND NUMBERS

Use a hyphen with compound numbers from twenty-one through ninety-nine and with fractions.

USE HYPHENS WITH COMPOUND NUMBERS AND FRACTIONS

Faisal dreaded the thought that he would be **sixty-five** on his next birthday.

I use **one-third** of my basement as an office.

14-2D   CERTAIN PREFIXES AND SUFFIXES

Use a hyphen with the prefixes *all-*, *ex-*, *great-*, *quasi-*, and *self-* and with the suffix *-elect*.

Note that U.S. dictionaries suggest that the prefix *non* be used without a hyphen, but Canadian and British style tends to hyphenate *non-,* if not consistently, then at least frequently.

USE HYPHENS WITH MANY PREFIXES

The **ex-premier** always has a difficult time because he is frequently asked his position on controversial issues.

The **mayor-elect** was impatient to begin implementing her agenda.

The truth is **non-existent**.

14-2E   AMBIGUITY AND AWKWARDNESS

A hyphen is used in some words to eliminate awkward double or triple letters—for example, *co-opt*.

Some pairs of words are spelled the same but have entirely different meanings and could cause confusion. In such cases, a hyphen is traditionally used in one of the words to distinguish it from the other.

Examples

co-operative   re-enact   co-author

USE HYPHENS TO AVOID AWKWARD JUXTAPOSITIONS AND CONFUSION

For example, *recount* means "to tell a story," while *re-count* means "to count again."

My uncle used to **recount** terrible stories about life in a concentration camp during the Second World War.

The candidate for council requested a **re-count** after her opponent received only marginally more votes.

USE HYPHENS TO DIVIDE WORDS AT THE END OF A LINE

pro-

If you want to write well, you must follow a systematic ~~proc~~-

cess

~~ess~~ that includes more than one draft.

death

Wounded in the extremely heavy fighting, the officer knew ~~dea~~-

~~th~~ was approaching, and he accepted it with great dignity.

opened

She found the stale air in the room oppressive, so she ~~o~~-

~~pened~~ the window and turned on the fan.

alone

Neighbours of the accused man told reporters that the man lived ~~a~~-

~~lone~~ and was very quiet.

self-

He is not naive in any way; most people consider him a very ~~sel~~-

aware

~~f-aware~~ individual.

base-

The next step, after installing the new carpet, is to nail on the ~~ba~~-

boards

~~seboards~~ where they are required.

Most word-processing programs automatically break between words at the end of a line. However, you will likely encounter some occasions (e.g., when proofreading printed material or handwriting a test) when it will be important to know end-of-line hyphenation rules.

1. Divide words only between syllables or as indicated in your dictionary.
2. Do not divide one-syllable words.
3. Do not divide a word so that only one or two letters remain at the end of the line (unless there is already a hyphen there, as per rule 4).
4. Divide a hyphenated word at the hyphen, and divide a closed compound only between complete words.

Capitalize the first word of every sentence. You will also need to capitalize specific types of words within sentences. Use the following rules as general guidelines for capitalization.

QUICK TIP

Consult your dictionary to determine which words must be capitalized.

14-3A   PROPER VS. COMMON NOUNS

Capitalize proper nouns, and words derived from them, but do not capitalize common nouns.

CAPITALIZE PROPER NOUNS

Proper nouns are the names of specific people, places, and things. Common nouns include all other nouns.

Months, days of the week, and holidays are considered proper nouns. The seasons and numbers of days of the month are not considered proper nouns.

Capitalize the names of school subjects only if they are languages, but capitalize the names of specific courses.

Table 14. 4   Capitalizing Nouns

Proper Nouns	Common Nouns
Zeus	a god
Book of Mormon	a book
Kamloops	a city
Marcel	a man
Aunt Agnes	my aunt
French	a language
Romanticism	a movement
New Democratic Party	a political party
Mars	a planet
the *Formidable*	a ship
Microsoft Word	a software program

Every spring, **Victoria Day** falls on a **Monday** in **May**.

The meeting is held on the second **Tuesday** of **January**, **June**, and **December**.

In his final year, he will need to take microbiology, chemistry, biology, **English**, and **Spanish**.

Professor Woodman teaches **Nineteenth-Century Literature** to all students majoring in English.

Usually, capitalize the following:

- names of religions, religious practitioners, holy books, special religious days, and deities
- geographic place names
- people's names and nicknames
- words of family relationship used as names
- nationalities, tribes, races, and languages
- names of historical events, periods, movements, documents, and treaties
- political parties, organizations, and government departments
- educational institutions, departments, degrees, and specific courses
- names of celestial bodies
- names of ships, planes, and aircraft
- parts of letters, such as the salutation or closing
- names of specific software

14-3B TITLES WITH PROPER NAMES

Capitalize the title of a person when it is part of a proper name.

Do not capitalize the title when it is used alone. *Note:* In some cases, if the title of an important public figure is used alone, the first letter can appear as either a capital letter or a lowercase letter. Conventions vary.

CAPITALIZE TITLES USED WITH PROPER NAMES

Dr. Norman Bethune

Rev. David Rooke

Pat McLauglin, **P.Eng.**

Douglas Fairbanks **Sr.**

Judge Shepperd gave his decision on the appeal.

A **judge** presided over the inquiry.

The **prime minister** [or **Prime Minister**] dodged the protester's pie.

14-3C TITLES OF WORKS

Capitalize the first, last, and all other important words in the titles of works such as books, articles, films, and songs.

IMPORTANT WORDS

These important words should be capitalized in titles and subtitles:

- nouns
- verbs
- adjectives
- adverbs

LESS IMPORTANT WORDS

These less important words should not be capitalized *unless* they are the first or last word of the title or subtitle:

- articles
- prepositions
- coordinating conjunctions

CAPITALIZE MAJOR WORDS IN TITLES OF WORKS

Book Title: *A Feminist Dictionary*

Article Title: "A Turkey with Taste"

Film Title: *From Earth to the Moon*

Song Title: "Do You Know the Way to San Jose?"

"Phantom of the Canadian Opera: Trudeau's Revenge" is Chapter 11 in Peter C. Newman's *The Canadian Revolution*.

Note that capitalization of titles varies depending on style of documentation. Consult the MLA and APA guidelines in this book for specific advice according to each style.

Also use the guidelines above to capitalize chapter titles and other major divisions in a work.

For information on using italics and quotation marks in titles, see 14-6a.

CAPITALIZE THE FIRST WORD OF A SENTENCE

It's Monday morning, time for the weekly editorial meeting at a mass-market publishing house.

The effects of plaque on the heart valves are significant. (**See** Figure 6.)

The effects of plaque on the heart valves are significant (**see** Figure 6).

Capitalize the first word of a sentence.

If a sentence appears within parentheses, capitalize the first word of the sentence. However, do not capitalize the first word if the parentheses are within another sentence.

CAPITALIZE THE FIRST WORD OF A DIRECT QUOTATION (IN GENERAL)

The department chair defended the embattled professor, arguing, "**He** is an outstanding teacher, and the evidence against him is flimsy at best."

In his article "Eco-tourism Boom: How Much Can Wildlife Take?" Bruce Obee says that "**tour** boats ... are a fraction of the traffic."

"She goes by bus," the mother exclaimed with anger, "**and** I'm not very happy about that."

Capitalize the first word of a direct quotation, but do not capitalize it if the quotation is blended into the sentence in which the quotation is introduced.

If you need to interrupt a quoted sentence to include explanatory words, do not capitalize the first word following the interruption.

If you need to quote poetry in an essay, use the capitalization employed by the poet.

Many modern poets do not follow the conventions of capitalization. When quoting their work, copy the text exactly.

Season of mists and mellow fruitfulness,
Close bosom-friend of the maturing sun;
Conspiring with him how to load and bless
With fruit the vines that round the thatch-eves run;…

—John Keats, "To Autumn"

so much depends
upon
a red wheel
barrow

By William Carlos Williams, from THE COLLECTED POEMS: Volume I, 1909–1939, copyright ©1938 by New Directions Publishing Corp. Reprinted by permission of New Directions Publishing Corp.

14-3F FIRST WORD AFTER A COLON

When an independent clause appears after a colon, capitalizing the first word is optional; if the content after the colon is not an independent clause, do not capitalize.

CAPITALIZE A FULL SENTENCE AFTER A COLON (OR NOT)

We were told to bring the following items for the hike: a compass, a sleeping bag, a tent, and enough food to last seven days.

There is one major reason that Phillip doesn't want Kathleen for a friend: **he** [*or* **He**] doesn't trust her.

14-3G ABBREVIATIONS

Capitalize the abbreviations for government departments and agencies, names of organizations and corporations, trade names, and call letters of television and radio stations.

CAPITALIZE CERTAIN ABBREVIATIONS

CSIS   CIA   NATO   CTV   Loblaws Inc.   CHCO-TV   CKNW

In most cases, abbreviations should not be used in formal writing, such as academic essays, unless the abbreviations are very well known; for instance, *CBC* or *UN*. Abbreviations are more widely used in science and technical writing than in writing for the humanities.

Always consider your reader when deciding whether or not to use any abbreviation. Will he or she understand the abbreviation? Otherwise, you run the risk of confusing the reader. If the type of writing that you are doing requires abbreviations, be consistent in your use of them.

- Marshall McLuhan taught at the Univ. of Toronto, in Ont., from 1946 to 1979.
- Marshall McLuhan taught at the University of Toronto in Ontario from 1946 to 1979.

TITLES WITH PROPER NAMES 14-4A

ABBREVIATE TITLES BEFORE OR AFTER PROPER NAMES

professor
The ~~prof.~~ gave an inspiring lecture last Thursday.

- **Dr.** Steven Edwards, M.D.
- **Dr.** Steven Edwards
  OR
- Steven Edwards, M.D.

Abbreviate titles and degrees immediately before and after proper names.

Do not abbreviate a title or degree if it does not accompany a proper name.

Do not use titles and degrees redundantly.

Table 14.5 Abbreviated Titles

Before Proper Names	After Proper Names
Rev. R.W. McLean	Edward Zenker, M.S.W.
Dr. Wendy Wong	Paul Martin Jr.
Asst. Prof. Tom Simpson	Margaret Barcza, M.B.A.
Ms. Germaine Greer	John Bruner, LL.D.
Mrs. Sodha Singh	Eleanor Semple, D.D.
Mr. Wil Loman	Roy Shoicket, M.S.
St. John	Barbara Zapert, Ph.D.

14-4B ORGANIZATIONS, CORPORATIONS, AND COUNTRIES

Use standard abbreviations for names of countries, organizations, and corporations. If you need to use a less familiar abbreviation in your paper, do the following:

1. Write the full name of the organization, followed by the abbreviation in parentheses.
2. For each subsequent reference to the organization, use the abbreviation on its own.

USE ABBREVIATIONS FOR COMMON ORGANIZATIONS, COUNTRIES, ETC.

UK (or U.K.)   FBI   NORAD   RCMP

CIDA   TSN   RCA   IBM

To save money, she got a room at the **YWCA**.

WRITE OUT UNCOMMON ABBREVIATIONS IN FULL THE FIRST TIME YOU USE THEM

Council of Mutual Economic Assistance (COMECON)

Editors' Association of Canada (EAC)

Please consult with a counsellor in the **Centre for Student Development (CSD)** if you need further assistance. Staff at **CSD** may be booked in person, online, or by phone.

14-4C   *B.C., A.D., a.m., p.m., no.*

Use the standard abbreviations *B.C., A.D., a.m., p.m.,* and *no.* only with particular years, times, numbers, or amounts.

The abbreviation *B.C.* ("before Christ") or the acceptable alternative *B.C.E.* ("before the Common Era") always appears after a specific date.

The abbreviation *A.D.* (*Anno Domini*) appears before a specific date. *C.E.,* an acceptable alternative meaning "Common Era," always appears after a specific date.

Use *a.m., p.m.,* or *no.* only with a particular figure.

USE STANDARD ABBREVIATIONS ONLY IN APPROPRIATE CONTEXTS

156 B.C. (or B.C.E.)

A.D. 65
65 C.E.

5:15 a.m.
8:30 p.m.
no. 16 (or No. 16)

afternoon.
We arrived for the dance in the early p.m.

number
It is impossible to estimate the no. of fish in the stream during spawning season.

USE ENGLISH EQUIVALENTS TO LATIN ABBREVIATIONS

Table 14.6   Latin Abbreviations

Abbreviation	Latin	English Meaning
c.	*circa*	approximately
cf.	*confer*	compare
e.g.	*exempli gratia*	for example
et al.	*et alii*	and others
etc.	*et cetera*	and the rest
i.e.	*id est*	that is
N.B.	*nota bene*	note well
P.S.	*postscriptum*	postscript
vs.	*versus*	versus

Since some readers may be unfamiliar with Latin abbreviations, keep use of these abbreviations to a minimum or use the English equivalent.

In informal writing, such as personal emails, it is acceptable to use Latin abbreviations.

In formal writing, use the full English words or phrases.

Jennifer wants to go the Raptors game this Tuesday. It's the Raptors **vs.** the Sonics. After the game let's grab a burger, **etc. N.B.** Dominique and her gang will be there.

DO NOT USE ABBREVIATIONS IN FORMAL WRITING

Abbreviations are generally not appropriate in formal writing.

The Sumerians came down to the bank of the Euphrates and Tigris rivers ~~c.~~ *around* 3500 B.C.E. Many artifacts—~~e.g.,~~ *for example* the headdress of Queen Sub-ad and the bronze mask portrait of King Sargon—provide evidence of their cultural advancement.

Margaret Atwood is a popular author in ~~Can. lit.~~ *Canadian literature* classes because she has written so many outstanding novels.

Metric abbreviations are often permitted in formal writing. However, do not use a number written in words with an abbreviation, as in *twenty cm*.

Abbreviations are acceptable in company or institution names only if the abbreviation is part of the company's or institution's official name.

Table 14.7   Types of Abbreviations to Avoid in Formal Writing

CATEGORY	√ FORMAL	x INFORMAL
Names of Persons	Jennifer	Jen
Holidays	Christmas	Xmas
Days of the Week	Tuesday to Thursday	Tues. to Thurs.
Months	from January to August	from Jan. to Aug.
Provinces and Countries	Saskatchewan	Sask. or SK
Academic Subjects	Biology and English	Bio. and Engl.
Units of Measurement*	6 ounces	6 oz.
Addresses	Madison Avenue	Madison Ave.
Subdivision of Books	chapter, page	ch., p.**

* except metric measurements (*25 kg* or *15 mm*)
** except as part of documentation

Never arbitrarily abbreviate a company's name. For example, if a company's name is *Randolph Architectural Group*, do not shorten it to *Randolph Arch. Gr.*

When corresponding with any company, use the full company name that appears on company stationery, in the firm's advertising, or on its website.

Jack's Windows & Roofing Co., or *Writers Inc. Consulting.*

SPELL OUT SMALL NUMBERS

eight
It has been 8̶ years since we last heard from him. *(just one word)*

356
In a single section of Biology 101 there are ~~three hundred and fifty-six~~ first-year students. *(more than two words)*

Seven hundred and twenty-one
~~721~~ folding chairs are required for the wedding reception. *(at the start of a sentence) You might also consider recasting the sentence if it begins with a figure.*

For the wedding reception, we require **721** folding chairs.

During the Olympic trials, she swam **four 100**-metre heats. *(one word before another number) In some instances, if numbers follow one another, you may wish to write one as a figure.*

Spell out numbers of one or two words, or any number that starts a sentence; use figures for all other numbers and amounts. This style is appropriate for papers without a great deal of statistical information.

Note: In business and technical writing, figures are sometimes preferred for all numbers except one to nine because they provide clarity and brevity. However, usage varies, so it is best to check with your instructor.

USE FIGURES FOR DATES, ADDRESSES, AND EXACT NUMBERS

DATES
January 16, 1952   21 B.C.E.   A.D. 400

TIME
3:51 a.m.   7 p.m.
one o'clock in the morning
midnight
eight-thirty in the evening

ADDRESSES
31 Bloor Street West
75 West Broadway

Figures are acceptable in some writing situations.

Use figures with *a.m.* and *p.m.* If *a.m.* and *p.m.* are not used, write the time in words.

If a paper is heavily statistical use figures and the % sign.

PERCENTAGES, FRACTIONS, DECIMALS

92 percent   1/5   3.75

The poll indicates that the premier has a ~~ninety-three~~ 93 percent approval rating.

STATISTICS, SCORES, SURVEYS

In Canada, 14 babies are born each year for every 1000 people.

Team Canada won the game against Sweden by a score of 3–2.

According to the study, 1 out of every 10 residents was out of work.

MEASUREMENTS AND COUNTS

4.5 metres clearance
19 800 people at the game

DIVISIONS OF BOOKS

Chapter 7, page 381

DIVISIONS OF PLAYS

Act V, Scene ii, lines 10–15

IDENTIFICATION NUMBERS

Highway 427   Room 311   Channel 2   #73321

14-6) ITALICS

Italics is the typeface in which letters slant to the right and appear like handwritten script. Italics is a typeface option on word-processing programs. When writing by hand, use underlining to indicate italics.

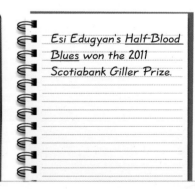

Michael Ondaatje's wonderful novel *The Cat's Table* was shortlisted for the 2011 Scotiabank Giller Prize.

Esi Edugyan's *Half-Blood Blues* won the 2011 Scotiabank Giller Prize.

ITALICIZE NAMES OF LONG WORKS (BOOKS, ETC.)

Table 14. 8   Titles of Works in Italics

PRINT	
Books, Plays, Long Poems	*In the Skin of a Lion*
Journals, Magazines	*Journal of Reading*
Newspapers	*Winnipeg Free Press*
Conference Proceedings	*Women in Physics*
Published Dissertations	*Serial Murder and Leyton's "Proletarian Rebellion"*
Maps, Charts	*Southern Arabian Peninsula*
Comic Strips	*Peanuts*
ART	
Visual Works of Art	*The West Wind*
Musical Compositions, Scores	*Symphony in B Major*
Ballets, Operas	*Don Giovanni*
Performances	*Nothing Sacred*
ELECTRONIC	
Films, Videotapes	*The Sweet Hereafter*
Sound Recordings	*Sgt. Pepper's Lonely Hearts Club Band*
Radio and Television Programs	*Cross Country Checkup, Venture*
Computer Games, Video Games	*Tomb Raider: Chronicles*
ONLINE	
Websites	*The Canada Council for the Arts*
Books, References	*The Martyrology*
Projects, Services, Databases	*Canadian Periodical Index*
Discussion Lists, Newsgroups	*Alliance for Computers and Writing Listserv*
GOVERNMENT PUBLICATIONS	
Acts, Statutes	*The Income Tax Act*
Court Cases	*Norberg v. Wynrib*
Debates	*Debates, Hansard, Congressional Record*
Papers, Hearings, Reports	*Agenda: Jobs and Growth*

Convention requires that you use italics when making reference to certain types of works or materials. These are listed in the table.

Use quotation marks (*not* italics) to identify the titles of the following:

- short stories, essays, and poems (except long poems published independently)
- journal, magazine, or newspaper articles, including titles of reviews, interviews, and editorials
- unpublished material such as theses, dissertations, or papers read at meetings or published in conference proceedings; lectures, speeches, or readings
- manuscripts in collections; published letters
- chapters in a book
- songs
- television episodes

Do not italicize, underline, or place in quotation marks the following:

- names of sacred works, such as the Bible or names of books within it
- laws and treaties

- unpublished letters
- the title of your own essay or report

14-6B NAMES OF SHIPS, PLANES, AND SPACECRAFT

Italicize the names of ships, planes, and spacecraft.

ITALICIZE NAMES OF SHIPS AND AIRCRAFT

Lusitania *Spirit of St. Louis* *Columbia*

During the **Apollo 11** lunar-landing mission, Mission Commander Neil Armstrong became the first person to walk on the moon.

14-6C FOREIGN WORDS

Italicize foreign words that have not become part of the English language. You do not need to italicize words that have become part of the English language, such as café au lait, bon voyage, per se, and habeas corpus.

Remember that English is an evolving language and new words borrowed from other languages are regularly accepted into common English usage. If you are unsure about whether or not to italicize, check in a recent edition of a comprehensive Canadian dictionary.

ITALICIZE FOREIGN WORDS

Their relationship is a classic case of *omnia vincit amor.*

The principle [*sic*] exit was blocked by a ladder.

Something that is true by definition is true *a priori.*

ITALICIZE WORDS AS WORDS, LETTERS AS LETTERS, AND NUMBERS AS NUMBERS

Erika said she could be late, but for her *could* means *will*.

The *W* and the *S* had blown off of the restaurant's sign so that customers couldn't tell what the special was.

When the *–7* went up next to Tiger Woods' name, the whole crowd cheered wildly.

Italicize words, letters, or numbers mentioned as themselves.

It is also acceptable to use quotation marks to set off words mentioned as words.

DO NOT USE ITALICS FOR EMPHASIS TOO OFTEN

Residential development in the Golden Horseshoe of southern Ontario was *rampant*.

I have absolutely no idea what you mean by that.

There is no excuse for sloppy research.

Remember to consult MLA and APA guidelines in this textbook for specific advice on when and what to italicize. Style conventions vary.

Writers occasionally use italics to emphasize important words in their work. Such an emphatic technique is only effective if it is not overused. Allow emphasis to come from the words and structure of the sentence itself, rather than from overuse of italics, underlining, or exclamation marks.

Italics do not add anything to the example sentences. The words *rampant* and *absolutely* are strong enough to stand on their own and do not need any enhancement. The same applies to the phrase *no excuse*.

ELL (English Language Learners)

A writer lives in awe of words for they can be cruel or kind, and they can change their meanings right in front of you. They pick up flavors and odors like butter in a refrigerator.

—John Steinbeck

ELL (English Language Learners)

15

pixinity/Shutterstock.com

This section is written especially for readers whose first language is not English. Some specific features of English are typically problematic and may cause errors in usage; these features are dealt with below.

ARTICLES 15-1

ARTICLES AND DETERMINERS SIGNAL THAT A NOUN FOLLOWS

Articles (a, an, the)
a reason (indefinite article)
an insult (indefinite article)
the point (definite article)

Determiners
Roger's plan (possessive noun)
two suitcases (number)
my pet poodle (pronoun)

The articles in English are *a*, *an*, and *the*. They are determiners, which signal that a noun will follow and that any modifiers appearing before that noun refer to that noun. *A* and *an* are the indefinite articles; *the* is the definite article.

Other determiners that may mark nouns include the following:

- possessive nouns
- numbers
- pronouns

For further information, see Nouns (9-1a); Articles (9-1b); Pronouns (9-1c).

Table 15.1 Guide to Using Articles

Proper Nouns		Common Nouns				
		Count Nouns				Non-count Nouns
the	**Ø (no article needed)**	**Singular**		**Generic**	**Plural**	Ø, some, much, a lot of, a bit of, little, a little, my, your, his, her, this, that
Countries: Netherlands/ Bahamas/ West Indies/ Sudan/ United Arab Emirates/ United Kingdom/ United States	**All other countries** E.g., Ireland/ Jamaica/ Taiwan/ Canada	**General** a/an, one E.g., a bowl, an ant, one girl	**Specific** the, my, your, his, her, our, their, this, that E.g., the bowl, the ant, that girl	**Ø** E.g., bowls, ants, girls	The, two etc., some, several, many, a lot of, few, a few, my, your, his, her, these, those E.g., two bowls, some ants, many girls	**Abstract nouns:** love, happiness
Geographic locations: Nile River/ Great Barrier Reef/Sahara Desert/ Indian Ocean/ Himalayas		**1st mention** I saw a good movie	**2nd mention** the movie was about …			**Consisting of small pieces:** sand, sugar, rice, flour, snow
			Unique the head of our department			**Existing as a solid, liquid, or gas:** silver, water, oxygen, gold

Proper Nouns		Common Nouns			
		Count Nouns			**Non-count Nouns**
the	**Ø** (no article needed)	**Singular**	**Generic**	**Plural**	Ø, some, much, a lot of, a bit of, little, a little, my, your, his, her, this, that
Plural islands, lakes, mountains: Rocky Mountains/ Thousand Islands/Great Lakes	**Singular islands, lakes, mountains:** Mount Alison/Baffin Island/Lake Winnipeg	**Situation** the door of the house **Superlative** the best day of my life			**Academic subjects:** English, Chemistry, Anthropology **Sports:** football, golf, boxing
Educational institutions: University/ College/ School of …	**Educational institutions:** … University/ College/ School	**Definite noun phrase or clause** the book on the library shelf			**Natural phenomena:** wind, hail, fog **Diseases:** rabies, AIDS, cancer***
People: Japanese/ French*	**Languages:** Japanese/ French/ English/**	**Measurement of Non-count Nouns**			
		a bowl of soup	the bowl of soup	bowls of soup	the bowls of soup

Indefinite Article: a cat, **a** Siamese cat

Definite Article: the television, **the** portable television

Beenish's car, **Mom's** birthday

two cats, **102** balloons

each Canadian, **several** items, **a lot of** experience, **those** colours

*Note that if the people name adds -s, like *Americans*, you may omit *the*.

**If part of a noun phrase, then use *the*: e.g., *the English language*.

*** but, *the* flu, *a* cold

If the noun is a singular count noun, use *a* or *an* before the noun. To decide whether the noun is a singular count noun, consult the box on this page.

- Use *a* if a consonant sound follows the article.
- Use *an* if a vowel sound follows the article.

Remember that *h* or *u* may make either vowel or consonant sounds.

Note: A or *an* usually means "one among many" but may simply mean "any."

Note also: Some collective nouns (nouns that name a group of things) are always treated as plural. These include *clergy, military, people, police.* To refer to one member of the group, use a singular noun with these collective nouns, such as *a member of the clergy, a military officer, a man of the people, a police officer.*

H, U as *Consonants*: a horse, a historic trip, a union, a useful tool

H, U as *Vowels*: an hour, an honest man, an ugly face, an umbrella

STRATEGIES

How to Tell If a Noun Is a Singular Count Noun
1. It is a common noun (rather than a proper name).
2. The noun refers to a person, place, or thing that can be counted, such as *one woman, two cities, three bowls.*
3. The noun names something unknown to the reader because it is being used for the first time or because its specific identity is not known even to the writer.

If the answer to all three of these questions is yes, then use *a* or *an* before the noun.

For further information, see Nouns (9-1a).

DO NOT USE INDEFINITE ARTICLES (*A, AN*) WITH NON-COUNT NOUNS

🚫 My professor asked us to do **a research** on the topic of global warming.

✓ My professor asked us to do **research** on the topic of global warming.

🚫 My counsellor gave me **a good advice** on how to conduct my behaviour at the office.

✓ My counsellor gave me **good advice** on how to conduct my behaviour at the office.

DO NOT PLURALIZE NON-COUNT NOUNS

🚫 We use complex **equipments** in our lab.

✓ We use complex **equipment** in our lab.

🚫 **Woods are** expensive building materials.

✓ **Wood is** an expensive building material.

Table 15.2 Non-count Nouns

Groups of Items That Make Up a Whole	baggage, money, silver, research, furniture, mail, clothing, real estate
Abstract Nouns	wealth, awareness, joy, discord, esteem
Liquids	tea, milk, water, beer
Gases	smoke, steam, oxygen, air, fog
Materials	wood, steel, wool, gold
Food	pork, pasta, butter, salmon
Grains or Particles	wheat, dust, rice, dirt
Sports or Games	rugby, hockey, chess, poker
Languages	French, English, Mandarin, Farsi
Fields of Study	chemistry, engineering, nursing
Natural Events	lightning, cold, sunlight, darkness

If the noun is a non-count noun, do not use *a* or *an* before the noun. To decide whether a noun is a non-count noun, ask if it satisfies this statement:

The noun refers to an entity that cannot be counted, such as *philosophy*, *ice*, or *fatigue*.

To express a particular amount of a non-count noun, you can modify it by using another determiner, such as *some, any,* or *more*. Remember these guidelines:

- *A few* or *a little* means "some," whereas *few* and *little* mean "almost none."
- Use *much* with non-count nouns and *many* with count nouns.
- Use *an amount of* with non-count nouns and *a number of* with count nouns.
- Use *less* with non-count nouns (*less money*) and *fewer* with count nouns (*fewer hours*).

You can also add a count noun in front of a non-count noun to make it more specific (*a jug of wine, a piece of jewellery, a game of bridge*).

Note: Some non-count nouns can also be used as count nouns, depending on their meaning. This is usually the case when the noun can be used individually or as part of a larger whole made up of individual parts.

I ate **a bowl of porridge** for breakfast.

I often eat **porridge** for breakfast.

Tim bought me **a coffee** this morning; he knows I love **coffee**.

QUICK TIP

Invest in a dictionary that tells you whether a noun is non-count or count.

15-1C WHEN TO USE *THE*

Use *the* in the following circumstances:

- when the noun has been previously mentioned
- when a modifying word, phrase, or clause after the noun restricts its meaning
- when a superlative (*quickest, smartest, strongest*) makes *the* specific
- when the noun is a unique person, place, or thing that everyone knows
- when the context makes the noun's specific identity clear

USE *THE* WHEN A NOUN HAS BEEN MENTIONED PREVIOUSLY

A woman entered the emergency room of the hospital. **The woman** began to cry.

HOWEVER, USE *A* WITH A NOUN THAT HAS BEEN PREVIOUSLY MENTIONED IF A NEW ADJECTIVE IS USED WITH IT

Rachel wore **a new dress** to the prom. It was **a silk dress**.

USE *THE* WITH NOUNS THAT ARE FOLLOWED BY RESTRICTIVE PHRASES

The program you are about to see has been edited for television.

USE *THE* WITH SUPERLATIVES

Bill Gates is **the richest man** in the world.

USE *THE* WHEN SPECIFIC IDENTITY IS CLEAR

Some people still maintain that **the Earth** is flat.

USE *THE* WHEN SPECIFIC IDENTITY IS CLEAR FROM THE CONTEXT

Feed **the dog** before you leave **the house**.

USE *THE* TO REFER TO A WHOLE GROUP, TYPE, OR SPECIES

The giraffe is the tallest animal on earth.

USE *THE* TO REFER TO A PART OF THE HUMAN BODY

The brain defies human understanding.

- when you refer to an entire group
- when you refer to a human body part

WHEN NOT TO USE *THE*   15-1D

DON'T USE *THE* WHEN REFERRING TO ALL MEMBERS OF A GROUP

Elephants are mammals.

Dogs are great pets.

Award ceremonies are fun to watch on television.

The is not needed when a statement refers to all members of a group rather than the group as a whole. Consider the difference between *The elephant* is a *mammal* and *Elephants* are *mammals*.

DON'T USE *THE* WITH MOST PROPER NOUNS

Proper nouns name specific persons, places, and things and begin with a capital letter. *The* is not used with proper names, except in a few cases.

Articles   **15-1**

| Exceptions: | the Prime Minister of Canada, the province of Manitoba |

- nouns that follow the pattern *the ... of ...*
- plural proper nouns
- collective proper nouns
- some proper names of geographical features, such as large areas, deserts, mountain ranges, peninsulas, oceans, seas, gulfs, canals, and rivers
- names of ships

the Prime Minister of Canada, the province of Manitoba

the Mulroneys, the Toronto Blue Jays, the United States

the Canadian Opera Company, the Royal Canadian Mounted Police, the Supreme Court

the West Coast, the Sahara Desert, the Pyrenees, the Iberian Peninsula, the Pacific Ocean, the St. Lawrence Seaway, the Gulf of Mexico, the Suez Canal, the Ganges

the *Hesperus*, the *Black Pearl*

15-2) VERBS

All writers in English encounter problems with verbs.

For more information on verbs, see Verbs (9-1d); Verbs, Objects, and Complements (9-2b); Verbal Phrases (9-3b); and Subordinate Clauses (9-3e).

15-2A   MAIN VERBS AND HELPING VERBS (*TO BE, DO,* AND *HAVE*)

The verb in a sentence may be one verb or a phrase made up of a main verb and a helping verb. Every main verb (with the exception of *to be*) has five forms that are used to create tenses.

The *-s* form is used with the third-person singular in the present tense.

Base (Simple) Form: work, eat

Past Tense: worked, ate

Past Participle: worked, eaten

Present Participle: working, eating

-s Form: works, eats

Work is an example of
a regular verb; *catch* is an
example of an irregular verb.
(For a list of frequently used
irregular verbs, see 10-4a.)

Table 15.3   Verb Tenses

	Past	**Present**	**Future**
Simple	An action that ended at a specific time in the past.	An action that exists, is usually true, or is repeated.	A plan for future action.
	cleaned	**clean/cleans**	**will clean**
(time indicator)*	e.g., She cleaned her office yesterday.	e.g., She cleans her office every weekend.	e.g., She will clean her office tomorrow.
Progressive *be* + main verb + *ing*	An action that was happening (past progressive) when another action happened (simple past).	An action that is happening now.	An action that will be happening over time, in the future, or when something else happens.
	was/were cleaning	**am/is/are cleaning**	**will be cleaning**
(time indicator)*	e.g., She was cleaning her office when the fire alarm sounded.	e.g., She is cleaning her office now.	e.g., She will be cleaning her office when you go to sleep tonight.

(continued)

	Past	Present	Future
Perfect *have* + main verb	An action that ended before another action or time in the past.	An action that happened at an unspecified time in the past.	An action that will end before another action or time in the future.
	had cleaned	**has/have cleaned**	**will have cleaned**
(time indicator)*	e.g., She had cleaned her office when the fire alarm sounded.	e.g., She has cleaned her office frequently.	e.g., She will have cleaned her office by the time the mail arrives.
Perfect Progressive *have* + *be* + main verb + *ing*	An action that happened over time, in the past, or before another time or action in the past.	An action occurring over time that started in the past and still continues.	An action occurring over time, in the future, before another event in the future.
	had been cleaning	**has/have been cleaning**	**will have been cleaning**
(time indicator)*	e.g., She had been cleaning her office for many years before she hired a housekeeper.	e.g., She has been cleaning her office all morning.	e.g., She will have been cleaning her office all morning by the time the mail arrives.

* Time indicators are words that tell you something about when an action occurs. Here are some examples of words that can indicate the time of an action:

yesterday	simple past
every day	simple present
tomorrow	simple future
while	past progressive
now	present progressive

Time indicators may be used to indicate a number of tenses; for instance, they might indicate that something happened in the past or that it will happen in the future.

Table 15.4 Some Time Indicators and Verb Tenses

	Past	Present	Future
Simple	**Simple Past**	**Simple Present**	**Simple Future**
	yesterday last week/month/ year before for five weeks/days/ etc. one year/month ago	every morning/day always usually frequently sometimes never	tomorrow tonight next week/month/etc. soon in the future
Progressive	**Past Progressive**	**Present Progressive**	**Future Progressive**
	while when	now right now this week/minute/etc.	when after as soon as before
Perfect	**Past Perfect**	**Present Perfect**	**Future Perfect**
	before already by the time until then/last week/ etc. after	until now since ever never many times/weeks/years/etc. for three hours/minutes/etc.	by the time you go (somewhere) by the time you do (something) already
Perfect Progressive	**Past Perfect Progressive**	**Present Perfect Progressive**	**Future Perfect Progressive**
	before for one week/hour/ etc. since	for the past year/month/etc. for the last six months/weeks/etc. up to now for two weeks/hours/etc. since	by the time for three days/weeks by

HELPING VERBS

Helping (auxiliary) verbs always come before main verbs.

Some helping verbs—*to be*, *do*, and *have*—are used to conjugate verbs into their various tenses. *To be*, *do*, and *have* thus change form.

MODALS

Other helping verbs, called modals, usually do not change form to indicate tense or to indicate singular or plural.

- One-word modals do not change form.
- Most two-word modals do change form to indicate tense or to indicate singular or plural.

Modals do not require the word *to* in front of the base verb, except in the case of *need to*, *has to*, and *ought to*. Note that *ought to* is a two-word modal that does not change form.

The snake **has eaten** the frog.

Don't you **find** nature fascinating?

FORMS OF *TO BE, DO*, AND *HAVE*

be, am, is, are, was, were, being, been

do, does, did

have, has, had

Modals include *can, could, may, might, must, shall, should, will,* and *would*.

Examples include *need to* and *has to*.

MODALS AND RELATED EXPRESSIONS

Modals are part of a verb phrase that qualify the verb in some way. Modals are followed by the infinitive or base form of the verb. Some modals can be used with present, past, or future; others are more limited. Also, some modals can be used in negative expressions while others cannot. The chart on the next page summarizes some information about modals.

MODALS ALWAYS PRECEDE VERBS

We **may** attend the party later.

MODALS DO NOT CHANGE FORM, AND MOST DO NOT CHANGE TO INDICATE TENSE

Athletes **must** follow a strict regimen.

MODALS ARE FOLLOWED BY THE BASE FORM OF THE VERB

We **should meet** to discuss this.

Modal	Past	Present	Future	Usage
be able to	*	*	*	Expresses ability or lack of ability *I am/was/will be able/unable to drive a motorcycle to school.*
be supposed to	*	*	*	Expresses expectation *I am/was supposed to/not supposed to speak up in class.***
be to	*	*	*	Expresses strong expectation or lack of it *I am/was to be/am not to be there by midnight.***
can / could		*	*	Expresses ability or possibility or lack of ability or possibility *I can/can't understand./could/couldn't attend the meeting (tomorrow).*
can		*		Expresses permission or lack of permission (informal, speaking only) *You can/can't just make up your own rules.*
could		*		Makes a polite, formal request *Could you help me with the groceries?*
	*	*		Gives suggestions *You could do/have that. Couldn't you do/have done that?*
	*	*		Expresses limited certainty *We could be/have been there.*
	*	*		Expresses impossibility when negative *The suspects couldn't be/have been there.*
had better		*		Suggests advisability *I had better/better not do that.*
have got to		*		Expresses necessity or lack of necessity *You have got/haven't got to do that.*
have to	*	*	*	Expresses necessity or lack of necessity *I have got/had/will have to behave myself.* *I don't have/didn't have/won't have to listen to my parents.*
may		*		Makes a polite, formal request/permission *May I have your assistance? You may have my assistance.*

(continued)

Modal	Past	Present	Future	Usage
		*	*	Expresses limited certainty *I may/may not do that next week.* **
might		*		Makes a formal request *Might I have your vote in the next election?*
		*	*	Expresses limited certainty *I might do that/I might not do that.* **
must		*	*	Expresses strong necessity *I must take the car.* **
		*	*	Expresses prohibition *You must not take the car.* **
		*		Expresses very high certainty *You must be tired after your journey.*
ought to		*	*	Expresses advisability *I ought/ought not to do that.* **
		*	*	Expresses high certainty *I ought to feel better tomorrow.* **
shall		*	*	Makes a polite, formal suggestion/question *Shall I do that?* **
should		*	*	Expresses advisability *I should/should not do that* **
		*	*	Expresses high certainty *I should feel better tomorrow.* **
used to	*			Refers to repeated action in the past *I used/used not to do that regularly.*
will		*	*	Expresses certainty/willingness *I will/I'll/I won't be there* *I will/I'll/I won't do it.*

Modal	Past	Present	Future	Usage
		*	*	Makes a polite, formal request *Will/won't you do that?***
would		*	*	Makes a polite, formal request *Would you do that?***
		*	*	Expresses preference *I would rather/would rather not do that.***
	*			Refers to repeated action in the past. *I would do that years ago.*
		*	*	Expresses advisability—negative *I wouldn't do that (if I were you).***

** present and future form is the same

USE OF *BE* TO FORM THE PROGRESSIVE ASPECT — 15-2B

Present Progressive: Anne **is sitting** in the waiting room while her husband sees the doctor.

Past Progressive: Anne **was sitting** in the waiting room when the doctor rushed from the examining room.

Future Progressive: Anne **will be sitting** in the hospital lounge tomorrow during her husband's surgery.

Present Perfect Progressive: Anne **has been sitting** in the lounge since early this morning.

Past Perfect Progressive: Anne **had been sitting** in the lounge for two hours before the nurse came to tell her about the delay.

Future Perfect Progressive: By the time the surgery is finished, Anne **will have been sitting** in the lounge for seven hours.

The progressive aspect is used to indicate action that is in progress. Create the progressive aspects of the past, present, or future tense by using *am, is, are, was, were, have been, has been, had been, will have been,* or *will be* followed by the present participle of the main verb. (See 10-4f.)

Some verbs are not commonly used in the progressive tense in English. These are considered **static** verbs, which describe a state of being or a mental activity (e.g., *appear, believe, belong, contain, know, seem, think, understand, want*).

There are, however, many exceptions that do normally use the progressive tense, such as *I have been thinking about you.* Keep notes for future reference about the exceptions that you hear and read.

For more information, see Verbal Phrases (9-3b).

USE *-ING* WITH PROGRESSIVE VERBS

❌ Martin Short **is plan** to visit Hamilton, where he was born.

✅ Martin Short **is planning** to visit Hamilton, where he was born.

USE *BE* OR *BEEN* TO FORM PROGRESSIVE TENSES

I **have been worrying** about you. (present perfect progressive)
The teacher **will be watching** you. (future progressive)

NOTE THAT SOME STATIC VERBS HAVE NO PROGRESSIVE FORMS

❌ The canister **is not containing** any sugar.

✅ The canister **does not contain** any sugar.

❌ These shoes **are not belonging** in this closet.

✅ These shoes **do not belong** in this closet.

❌ I **am not believing** you.

✅ I **do not believe** you.

❌ She **is seeming** unhappy.

✅ She **seems** unhappy.

15-2C   USE OF *BE* TO FORM THE PASSIVE VOICE

A verb is in the passive voice when its subject is the receiver of the action, rather than the performer of the action.

The passive voice is formed with one of the forms of the verb *to be* and the main verb's past participle.

The road to hell **is paved** with good intentions.

Passive Voice, Present Tense: Aleksandar Antonijevic and Xiao Nan Yu **are acclaimed** for their recent work with the National Ballet of Canada.

Passive Voice, Past Tense: *Generation X* by Douglas Coupland **has been recognized** as a groundbreaking work of fiction.

Passive Voice, Future Tense: Many Canadians **will be pleased** by the results of the hockey game.

INTRANSITIVE VERBS CANNOT FORM THE PASSIVE VOICE

The accident **happened** last night.
The accident **was** last night.

If a verb is intransitive like those in the examples above, it cannot be used to form the passive voice.

HOW TO USE *BEING*, *BEEN*, OR *BE* TO FORM THE PASSIVE VOICE

He **was being** taken to the hospital after the accident. (Use a form of *to be* with *being* to form the passive.)

I **have been** overwhelmed by work throughout September. (Use a form of *to have* with *been* to form the passive.)

You must **be given** credit for your effort in this endeavour. (Use *be* with a modal verb to form the passive.)

The passive voice can occur in any tense of a transitive verb (that is, a verb that takes an object to complete its meaning). However, if a verb is intransitive, it cannot be used to form the passive voice.

Note: When *be*, *being*, or *been* is used to form the passive voice, it must be preceded by another helping verb. *Been* must be preceded by a form of *have*; *being* must be preceded by a form of *to be*, and *be* must be preceded by a modal verb.

USE OF *DO* TO FORM QUESTIONS AND CREATE EMPHASIS 15-2D

USE *DO* OR *DID* WITH BASE FORMS OF THE VERB

It **does** not **look** like rain.

Did you **look** in the glove compartment?

I **did**n't **believe** it until I saw it.

I **do believe** that you will succeed in your endeavours.

In these examples, *look* and *believe* are base forms of the main verb.

The auxiliary forms of the verb *do* (*do, does, did*) are used to indicate questions, negatives, and emphasis. The verb *do* is always used with base forms of the main verb that do not change.

15-2E USE OF *HAVE* TO FORM THE PERFECT ASPECT

After the helping verbs *have*, *has*, or *had*, use the past participle to form the perfect aspect. (See 10-4f.) Note that past participles frequently end in *-d*, *-en*, *-n*, or *-t*. (See 15-3f.)

Have, *has*, and *had* may also be preceded by modal verbs, such as *will*, used in forming the future perfect.

USE PAST PARTICIPLES IN THE PERFECT FORM OF THE VERB

Though Yuen **has** never **lived** in China, Cantonese is his native language.

We **had** never **paid** any attention to their suggestions before.

By next week, the class **will have done** most of the assignments for the course.

15-2F MODAL VERBS BESIDES *BE, DO,* AND *HAVE*

Use modal auxiliary verbs before main verbs to express the following:

- ability
- necessity
- advisability or expectation
- probability or possibility
- promise or agreement
- preference
- a plan or obligation
- an action now past

USE MODAL AUXILIARY VERBS IN APPROPRIATE CONTEXTS
MODALS

be supposed to	might	used to
can	must	will
could	ought to	would
had better	shall	
may	should	

ABILITY

Can is used to express ability in the present or future tense. *Could* is used to express ability in the past tense.

Popeye **can lift** his own weight, or at least he **could** when he was younger.

I **must insist** that you leave.

I **will have to call** the police if you refuse.

I **needed to clear** the room as quickly as possible.

You **must not** give up.

You **didn't have to get** me anything for my birthday.

I **didn't need to think** about it.

You **should take** my advice.

He **ought to buy** a watch of his own.

It **should snow** tomorrow.

She **should have said** something at the time.

I **ought to have told** you earlier.

You **had better listen** to me this time.

We **may regret** skipping class.

We **could pretend** we overslept.

We **might have missed** something important.

We **must have lost** our minds.

All of us **will be** on our best behaviour.

Would you **be** so kind as to attend?

NECESSITY

Must, have to, and *need to* express the necessity of doing something. *Must* is used in the immediate present and the future tense; therefore, you cannot use an auxiliary verb before *must*. The others are used in all verb tenses.

ADVISABILITY

Should and *ought to* indicate that a certain action is advisable or expected in the present or the future. The past tenses are *should have* and *ought to have*. Note that *had better* implies advice with a warning.

PROBABILITY OR POSSIBILITY

May, might, could, and *must* sometimes express probability or possibility. To form the past tense, add *have* and the past participle of the main verb after the modal. *Could* or *might* are also used for polite requests.

PROMISE OR AGREEMENT

Will and *would* suggest promise or agreement. *Would* may also be used for polite requests.

PREFERENCE

Would rather is used to express preference. To form the past tense, add *have* and the past participle of the main verb after the modal.

He **would rather die** than live with his parents again.

I **would rather have made** the meal myself than have eaten her cooking.

PLAN OR OBLIGATION

Be supposed to indicates that the subject has a plan or an obligation. This modal can be used in the present and in the past tense.

He **was supposed to arrive** at work by 8:30.

It is **supposed to rain** this evening.

AN ACTION NOW PAST

Used to and *would* indicate that a repeated action or habit is now past. Only *used to* can express an action that lasted a length of time in the past.

I **used to smoke**.

I **would light** a cigarette as soon as I woke up in the morning.

I **would live** in the Middle East.

I **used to live** in the Middle East.

15-2G VERBS FOLLOWED BY GERUNDS OR INFINITIVES

A **gerund** is a verb form that ends in *-ing* and is used as a noun.

IDENTIFY GERUNDS AND INFINITIVES AND USE THEM CORRECTLY

My cat likes **sleeping** sixteen hours a day.

George's **moping** began to get on his wife's nerves.

GERUNDS

Smoking is dangerous to your health.

Eating before you go to bed may contribute to weight gain, or so Oprah tells us.

Primož Cigler/Shutterstock

INFINITIVES

My cat likes **to sleep** sixteen hours a day.

When will that child learn **to behave**?

To succeed in sports, you must practise.

To be honest, that dog could use a bath.

VERBS THAT TAKE EITHER GERUNDS OR INFINITIVES

begin	forget*	love	stop*
can't bear	go	prefer	try*
can't stand	hate	remember*	
continue	like	start	

Note that verbs with asterisks above may change meaning depending on usage.

Infinitive: We need **to stop** eating so much junk food.

Gerund: I enjoy **stopping** by antique stores.

Infinitive: Joannie Rochette started **to skate** at three years old.

Gerund: Joannie Rochette started **skating** at three years old.

Gerund: I remember **going** to visit my grandparents when I was little.

Infinitive: Remember **to eat** your vegetables.

An **infinitive** is the base form of the verb preceded by *to*, which marks its use as an infinitive. *To* in front of the base form of a verb is not a preposition but an indication of the infinitive use.

A few verbs, such as *like*, may take either a gerund or an infinitive after them. Other verbs take a gerund but never an infinitive; others may take an infinitive (some with an intervening noun phrase) but not a gerund.

VERBS THAT TAKE EITHER GERUNDS OR INFINITIVES

Some common verbs may take either a gerund or an infinitive, with negligible or no differences in meaning. Here are just a few examples.

Some other verbs (e.g., *forget*, *remember*, *stop*, *try*) can take both gerunds and infinitives, but their meaning changes significantly depending on which is used.

VERBS THAT TAKE ONLY GERUNDS

VERBS THAT TAKE ONLY GERUNDS

acknowledge	detest	miss
admit	discuss	object to
adore	dislike	postpone
advise	dream about	practise
anticipate	enjoy	put off
appreciate	escape	quit
avoid	finish	recall
be left	give up	recommend
can't help	have trouble	resent
complain about	imagine	resist
consider	include	risk
consist of	insist on	suggest
contemplate	keep	tolerate
delay	mention	understand
deny	mind	

Gerund: David and Nate **avoided** *talking* about the funeral.

I **imagine** you *to have* big ambitions.

I **consider** you *to be* a fine person.

We **advise** clients *to seek* a second opinion.

Note that some of these verbs can also take an infinitive if and only if there is an intervening noun or pronoun.

VERBS THAT TAKE ONLY INFINITIVES

afford	decline	plan
agree	demand	prepare
aim	deserve	pretend
appear	expect	promise
arrange	fail	refuse
ask	give permission	say
assent	have	seem
attempt	hesitate	struggle
be able	hope	tend
beg	intend	threaten
care	know how	volunteer
claim	learn	wait
consent	manage	want
dare	mean	wish
decide	offer	would like

Infinitive: My parents **plan *to attend*** the graduation ceremony.

VERBS THAT NEED A NOUN OR PRONOUN TO TAKE THE INFINITIVE

admonish	forbid*	persuade
advise	force	remind
allow	have	request
cause	instruct	teach
challenge	invite	tell
command	hire	urge
convince	oblige	warn
dare	order	
encourage	permit	

*can also take gerund

VERBS THAT TAKE ONLY INFINITIVES

1. Infinitives are used after verbs to indicate desired actions, as well as actions that will not occur or have not yet occurred.

   - I refuse <u>to work</u> overtime.
   - I want <u>to go</u> with you.
   - It is going <u>to rain</u> this weekend.

2. Infinitives are used after nouns expressing ability or circumstance and after nouns that are direct objects.

   - Most birds have the ability <u>to fly</u>.
   - I want you <u>to come</u> with me.

VERBS THAT TAKE INFINITIVES BUT NEED A NOUN OR PRONOUN IN BETWEEN

Some verbs in the active voice usually require an infinitive, but a noun or pronoun must come between the verb and infinitive. The noun or pronoun usually names a person affected by the action in the sentence.

Note: There are a few verbs (*ask, need, would like, expect, want*) that can take an infinitive either directly or with a noun or pronoun in between.

Infinitive: She **encouraged** Paolo *to stay* in school.

Direct Infinitive: She **expected** *to leave* the party early.

Pronoun between Verb and Infinitive: I **expected** her *to decline* the invitation.

"SENSE VERBS" THAT TAKE AN UNMARKED INFINITIVE OR A GERUND WITH A NOUN OR PRONOUN

Some verbs that are sometimes called "sense verbs" take either an **unmarked infinitive** (the base form of the verb without *to*) or a gerund, with a noun or pronoun in between.

Note: The verb *help* may be used with either a marked or an unmarked infinitive.

SENSE VERBS

feel	listen to	notice
have	look at	see
hear	make (meaning "force")	watch
let		

Unmarked Infinitive: We **watched** the goalie *defend* the net.

Gerund: We **watched** the goalie *defending* the net.

Marked Infinitive: He **helps** the homeless *to find* shelter.

Unmarked Infinitive: He **helps** the homeless *find* shelter.

15-2H   PHRASAL VERBS

Phrasal, or two-word, verbs consist of verbs with prepositions or adverbs, known as "particles." Phrasal verbs have a distinctive idiomatic usage that requires careful study since it cannot be understood literally. Look at the verbs in these sentences.

Most phrasal verbs can be separated to allow a noun or pronoun object to come between them. Others cannot be separated.

PHRASAL VERBS: SEPARABLE OR INSEPARABLE?

Matt **will call** *back* later in the evening. (inseparable)

Matt and Khiet **called** *off* the wedding. (inseparable)

Matt **calls** *up* his friends every day to discuss what happened. (inseparable)

INSEPARABLE PHRASAL VERBS

The professor **went** the homework *over* with the class.

The professor **went** *over* the homework with the class.

SEPARABLE PHRASAL VERBS

⊘ The chef **threw** *away* them.

⊘ The chef **threw** <u>them</u> *away*.

⊘ The chef **threw** *away* <u>the leftovers</u>.

⊘ The chef **threw** <u>the leftovers</u> *away*.

Table 15.5 Common Phrasal Verbs

ask out	hand out	shut off
break down	hang on (*intr.*)	speak to*
bring about	hang on to*	speak up (*intr.*)
bring up	hang up	speak with*
burn down	help out	stay away from*
burn up	keep on	stay up*
call back	keep up with*	take care of*
call off	leave out	take off
call up	look after*	take out
clean up	look around*	take over
come across*	look into*	take up
cut up	look out for*	talk about*
do over	look over	talk to*
drop in	look up	talk with*
drop off	make up with*	talk over
figure out	pick out	think about*
fill out	pick up	think over
fill up	play around*	think up
get along with*	point out	throw away
get away with*	put away	throw out
get back	put back	try on
get off	put off	try out
get up (*intr.*)	put on	turn down
give away	put out	turn on
give back	put together	turn out
give in (*intr.*)	put up with*	turn up
give up	quiet down	wake up
go out of	run across*	wear out
go over*	run into	wrap up
grow up (*intr.*)	run out of*	
hand in	see off	

With verbs that can be separated from their particles, a pronoun object must always be placed between them. (A noun object can be placed either before or after the particle.)

COMMON PHRASAL VERBS

Here is a list of common phrasal verbs. If the particle (preposition or adverb) cannot be separated from the verb by a direct object, it is marked with an asterisk (*). Phrasal verbs that do not require a direct object are intransitive (*intr.*). Carefully check meanings of phrasal verbs in the dictionary if you have doubts about their usage.

15-2I OMITTED VERBS

All English sentences must have a verb. In some languages, verbs such as *to be* can be omitted. This is not true of English. Always include the verb.

❌ Dolores very industrious.

✅ Dolores **is** very industrious.

❌ Wayne Gretzky in Manhattan.

✅ Wayne Gretzky **lives** in Manhattan.

❌ Roads in Saskatchewan wide.

✅ Roads in Saskatchewan **are** wide.

15-2J CONDITIONAL SENTENCES

Conditional sentences state a relationship between one set of circumstances and another. Conditional sentences can be used for the following purposes:

- to express a cause-and-effect relationship that is factual
- to predict future possibilities or express plans
- to speculate about unlikely future events
- to speculate about events that didn't happen
- to speculate about things that are hypothetical or contrary to fact

Table 15.6 Conditional and Hypothetical Constructions

Meaning	*If* clause verb form	Main clause verb form
	If event "A" occurs	then event "B" happens*
Generally true	simple present If I **am tired**	simple present I **sleep**
True for the future	simple present If I **am tired** (later)	simple future I **will sleep**
Untrue now and future (hypothetical) **I am not tired now, but this is what I would do if I were tired.**	simple past If I **were** tired	*would* + base form I **would sleep**
Untrue in the past (hypothetical) **I was not tired in the past, but this is what I would have done if I were tired.**	past perfect If I **had been** tired	*would* + present perfect I **would have slept**

* Note that the order of the clauses may be reversed.

Table 15.7 Hypothetical Constructions

Usage	Wish	Clause
Wish + a noun clause	simple present (+ *that*) e.g., I **wish** (that)	simple past I **had** more money.*
Generally true	simple present (+ *that*) e.g., I **wish** (that)	simple past I **made** more money.
Statement referring to the past	simple present e.g., I **wish** (that)	past perfect I **had listened** to my mother.
A promise, certainty, possibility, or ability	simple present e.g., I **wish** (that)	modal (*would/could*) + base form (infinitive) I **would be able** to quit. I **could fly** an airplane.

* If the verb *to be* is used, then use the subjective mood, *were,* to indicate uncertainty, e.g., *I wish (that) I were on holiday in Europe.*

Present Conditional Fact: When a leap year **occurs**, there **are** 366 days in the year. [simple present tense]

Past Conditional Fact: Whenever Joe **petted** the cat, he **broke out** in hives. [simple past tense]

If that child **sees** a snake, she **will scream**.

If you **smoke** heavily, you **might develop** lung disease.

If you **insist** on misbehaving, **you will get** a detention.

If you **want** to talk, you **must leave** the room.

CONDITIONALS

If is the most common word used to introduce conditional clauses, though any of the following may also be used:

- Constructions with *if*, such as *even if/only if/if only*
- *Unless* (meaning *except if …*)
- *Whether or not*
- *Providing/provided (that)*
- *In case/in the event (that)*

EXPRESSING FACTUAL RELATIONSHIPS

Such sentences may express scientific truths, or they may simply describe something that usually or habitually happens.

PREDICTING FUTURE POSSIBILITIES OR EXPRESSING PLANS

Normally, use the present tense in the subordinate clause and the future tense in the main clause. Sometimes a modal verb, such as *may, might, can, could,* or *should* is used in the main clause instead of a future tense.

SPECULATING ABOUT UNLIKELY FUTURE EVENTS

The verb in the main clause is usually a modal verb, such as *will, can, could, may, might,* or *should,* followed by the base form of the main verb.

Note: The subjunctive mood is used in the *if* clause; the subjunctive is used when you are describing unlikely events. (See 10-4g.)

If I **won** the lottery, I *could* finally **quit** my job.

If I **had** time, I *might* **travel** round the world.

If I **were** you, I *would* **trade in** that old car.

If I **made** more money, I *would* **buy** a cottage in the wilderness.

SPECULATING ABOUT EVENTS THAT DID NOT HAPPEN

If I **had listened** to my friends, I **would have taken** a vacation last summer.

If my mother **had been** here, she **would have helped** me clean the house.

SPECULATING ABOUT THINGS THAT ARE HYPOTHETICAL OR CONTRARY TO FACT

Note: The subjunctive mood is used in the *if* clause; the subjunctive is used when you are describing a hypothetical case or something contrary to fact.

Hypothetical: If he only **had** a heart, he **would have** friends.

Contrary to Fact: If your story **were** true, you **could sell** it to the *National Enquirer.*

For more information on the types of moods of a verb, see 10-4g.

DIRECT AND INDIRECT SPEECH

When using indirect or reported speech, the tense of the verb changes. Usually indirect speech is introduced by the verb *said*, as in *I said*, *Ethel said*, or *they said*. If the main verb of the reported speech is in the present, it changes to the past tense. If the main verb is already in a past tense, then it moves further back in the past.

Direct Speech	Indirect Speech
simple present She said, "I **go** to the gym regularly."	**simple past** She said (that) she **went** to the gym regularly.
simple past She said, "I **went** to the gym regularly."	**past perfect** She said (that) she **had gone** to the gym regularly.
present perfect She said, "I **have gone** to the gym regularly."	**past perfect** She said (that) she **had gone** to the gym regularly.
present progressive She said, "I **am going** to the gym regularly."	**past progressive** She said (that) she **was going** to the gym regularly.
past progressive She said, "I **was going** to the gym regularly."	**perfect progressive** She said (that) she **had been going** to the gym regularly.

(continued)

An indirect quotation reports what someone said or wrote but with slight changes in verb tense and without quotation marks. Indirect quotations usually occur in subordinate clauses.

When the present tense is used in the main clause, the verb in the subordinate clause is in the same tense as the original quotation.

When the past tense is used in the main clause, the verb in the subordinate clause changes tense from the original quotation. Subordinate clause verbs in the past tense and the present perfect tense change to the past perfect tense; those in the simple present tense change to the simple past tense. The past perfect tense [*had been*] does not change.

Direct Speech	Indirect Speech
future (will) *She said, "I **will go** to the gym regularly."*	**would + base form (infinitive)** *She said (that) she **would go** to the gym regularly.*
future (going to) *She said, "I **am going** to go the gym regularly."*	**present progressive** *She said (that) she **is going** to go to the gym regularly.*
	past progressive *She said (that) she **was going** to go to the gym regularly.*

Direct Question	Indirect Question
auxiliary + verb name *She asked, "**Do you go** to the gym regularly?"* *She said, "**Where do you go** to work out?"*	**simple past** *She asked (me) **if I went** to the gym regularly.** *She asked me **where I went** to work out.*

Direct Command	Indirect Command
imperative *She said, "**Go** to the gym regularly."*	**infinitive** *She said **to go** to the gym regularly.*

*Note than when a Yes/No question is asked in direct speech, then *if* or *whether* is used in reported speech. If a question beginning with a *wh-* word is asked, then use the *wh-* word to introduce the clause. Note that no question mark is used with questions in reported speech.

Note that if another part of the verb *to say* is used instead of *said*, the verb tenses usually remain the same. Look at the following examples:

Direct Speech	Indirect Speech
simple present + simple present She **says**, *"I **go** to the gym regularly."*	**simple present + simple present** She **says** *(that) she **goes** to the gym regularly.*
present perfect + simple present She **has said**, *"I **go** to the gym regularly."*	**present perfect + simple present** She **has said** *(that) she **goes** to the gym regularly.*
past progressive + simple past She **was saying**, *"I **went** to the gym regularly."*	**past progressive + simple past** She **was saying** *(that) she **went** to the gym regularly.*
	past progressive + past perfect She **was saying** *(that) she **had gone** to the gym regularly.*
future + simple present She **will say**, *"I **go** to the gym regularly."*	**future + simple present** She **will say** *(that) she **goes** to the gym regularly.*

(continued)

Sometimes, modal constructions are used in reported speech. If the verb *said* is used, then the past form of the modal or another modal referring to the past is used.

Direct Speech	Indirect Speech
can She said, "I **can go** to the gym regularly."	**could** She said (that) she **could go** to the gym regularly.
may She said, "I **may go** to the gym regularly."	**might** She said (that) she **might go** to the gym regularly.
might She said, "I **might go** to the gym regularly."	**might** She said (that) she **might go** to the gym regularly.
must She said, "I **must go** to the gym regularly."	**had to** She said (that) she **had to go** to the gym regularly.
have to She said, "I **have to go** to the gym regularly."	**had to** She said (that) she **had to go** to the gym regularly.
should She said, "I **should go** to the gym regularly."	**should** She said (that) she **should go** to the gym regularly.
ought to She said, "I **ought to go** to the gym regularly."	**ought to** She said (that) she **ought to go** to the gym regularly.

Indirect Quotation: Sasha Trudeau **says** the Pierre Trudeau fellowships **will change** the country.

Original Quotation: "The Pierre Trudeau fellowships **will change** the country."

Indirect Quotation: Trudeau said that he **had** never **been** president and **wondered** what it would be like.

Original Quotation: "I **have** never **been** president and **wonder** what it would be like."

Indirect Quotation: Trudeau **said** that the state **has** no place in the nation's bedrooms.
Original Quotation: "The state **has** no place in the nation's bedrooms."

When the direct quotation states a general truth, or reports a situation that is still true, use the present tense in the indirect quotation regardless of the verb in the main clause.

Note: In indirect quotations, the pronoun forms of *I* and *we* change to forms of *he, she,* or *they.* Note also that indirect quotations are usually introduced by *that.*

For more information on direct and indirect quotations, see 11-5a; on subordinate clauses, see 9-3e.

MORE ELL ADVICE (15-3

OMITTED SUBJECTS; OMITTED *THERE* OR *IT* 15-3A

⊕ Have a diploma in accounting.

✓ **I** have a diploma in accounting.

⊕ Your daughter is accomplished; seems very gifted.

✓ Your daughter is accomplished; **she** seems very gifted.

⊕ Is a <u>letter</u> in the mailbox.

✓ **There** is a <u>letter</u> in the mailbox.

⊕ As I have explained, are many <u>reasons</u> for my decision.

✓ As I have explained, **there** are many <u>reasons</u> for my decision.

English requires a subject in all sentences except for commands, in which the subject *you* is understood. (See 12-1c.) If your first language does omit subjects in some cases, pay particular attention to this usage in English.

If a subject is not placed in its usual position in front of a verb, it requires an expletive pronoun (*there* or *it*) at the beginning of the clause. *There* used in this way points to the location or existence of something. Note that the verb after *there* agrees with the subject that follows it: *letter is, reasons are.*

The word *it* may also function as an expletive, calling attention to something and introducing it in an impersonal way.

The word *it* is also used as the subject in sentences that

- describe temperature or weather conditions
- state the time
- indicate distance
- state a fact about the environment

Is important to get a good education.

It is important to get a good education.

Is clear that he must arrive on time.

It is clear that he must arrive on time.

It snows less in Canada than people think.

In the summer, **it** can be extremely warm.

It is midnight.

It is a long way from Victoria to St. John's.

It gets busy on the highways on long weekends.

15-3B   REPEATED SUBJECTS

Do not restate a subject as a pronoun before the verb. State the subject only once in the clause.

Note that there is no need for a pronoun even if other words intervene between the subject and the verb.

The **temperature it** reached thirty degrees Celsius.

The **temperature** reached thirty degrees Celsius.

The **professor she** gave a lecture on globalization and the new media.

The **professor** gave a lecture on globalization and the new media.

The **letter** I received today **it** brought good news.

The **letter** I received today brought good news.

BE CAREFUL NOT TO REPEAT OBJECTS AND ADVERBS

➕ He usually works at the desk **that** I am sitting at **it**.

➕ He usually works at the desk I am sitting at **it**.

✅ He usually works at the desk **that** I am sitting at.

✅ He usually works at the desk I am sitting at.

The pronoun *that* replaces *desk* in the adjective clause; hence, *it* is not needed as the object after the preposition *at*. Even when the pronoun *that* is left out, it is still understood.

BE CAREFUL NOT TO REPEAT PRONOUNS

➕ The city where she lives **there** is accessible by bus or train.

✅ The city where she lives is accessible by bus or train.

➕ The school where we attended as children **it** is being torn down.

✅ The school where we attended as children is being torn down.

Adjective clauses begin with relative pronouns: *who, whom, whose, which, that, where(ever),* or *when(ever).* The first word of an adjective clause replaces another word, either the subject, an object, or a pronoun.

Make sure not to restate the word being replaced in the adjective clause. Such repetition occurs in other languages but never in English.

Adverbs in adjective clauses, like objects, do not need to be repeated.

The adverb *there* is not needed in an adjective clause beginning with *where*.

For further information see Subordinate Clauses (9-3e); Pronouns (9-1c); and Subject–Verb Agreement with Relative Pronouns (10-3h).

GENDER IN PRONOUN–ANTECEDENT AGREEMENT 15-3D

➕ Andrew gave the diamond ring to **her** fiancée.

✅ Andrew gave the diamond ring to **his** fiancée.

In English, the gender of a pronoun should match its antecedent (that is, the noun to which it refers) and not a noun that the pronoun may modify.

Note: Nouns in English are neuter unless they specifically refer to males or females. Hence, nouns such as *chair*, *newspaper*, *moon*, and *ring* take the pronoun *it*.

❌ Andrew gave **him** to his fiancée.

✅ Andrew gave **it** to his fiancée.

15-3E PLACEMENT OF ADJECTIVES AND ADVERBS

PLACEMENT OF ADJECTIVES

In English, adjectives normally precede the noun, though they may also follow linking verbs. Table 15.8 shows the proper word order for cumulative adjectives (those not separated by commas); for example, *I ate another five beautiful round ripe black Spanish olives.* Note that some exceptions do occur. (For more information on linking verbs, see 9-2b; on cumulative adjectives, see 11-1e.)

Remember that long lists of adjectives in front of a noun may be awkward. Try to use no more than two or three of them between the determiner and the noun itself.

Table 15.8   Word Order for Cumulative Adjectives

Determiners, if there are any
a, an, another, the, my, your, Canada's, those

Expressions of order, including ordinal numbers, if any
first, second, next, final

Expressions of quantity, including cardinal numbers, if any
one, two, five, each, some, all

Adjectives of opinion, if any
beautiful, fascinating, ugly, dull

Adjectives of size or shape, if any
tiny, huge, tall, rotund, triangular, round

Adjectives of age and condition, if any
new, ancient, ripe, rotten

Adjectives of colour, if any
yellow, purple, magenta, chartreuse, black

Adjectives of nationality, if any
Chinese, Portuguese, German, Spanish

Adjectives of religion, if any
Muslim, Jewish, Protestant, Catholic

Adjectives of material, if any
gold, mahogany, silk, wood

Adjectives that can also be used as nouns, if any
business, English, government

THE NOUN BEING MODIFIED

BE CAREFUL IN THE PLACEMENT OF ADVERBS

Tomorrow afternoon, we're leaving for China.

She opened the door **hesitantly**.

Ansel **always** beats me at checkers.

We have **repeatedly** asked for assistance.

❌ She opened **hesitantly** the door.

✅ **Hesitantly,** she opened the door.

✅ She opened the door **hesitantly**.

✅ She **hesitantly** opened the door.

Here, the adverb *hesitantly* must be placed either at the beginning or the end of the sentence or immediately before the verb. It cannot appear directly after the verb because the verb is followed by the direct object *the door*.

Jules **successfully** crossed the bridge.

She sneezed **violently**.

The voters reacted **angrily** to the tax increase.

Then she searched for her allergy medication.

I saw that film **last year**.

I completed the quiz **yesterday**.

She found it **in her purse**.

The accident occurred **over there**.

PLACEMENT OF ADVERBS

Adverbs and adverbial phrases are flexible in English; they can appear at the beginning, middle, or end of a clause.

An adverb may not be placed between a verb and a direct object, however.

Placement of adverbs in English sentences depends on the type of adverb.

Manner
Adverbs of manner describe how something is done. They usually appear in the middle of the clause or at the end.

Time
Adverbs of time describe when an event takes place or how long it lasts. They usually go at the beginning or end of a clause.

Place
Adverbs of place describe where an event occurs. They usually go at the end of a clause.

Frequency

Adverbs of frequency describe how often an event occurs. They usually appear in the middle of a clause or at the beginning of a clause to modify the whole sentence.

He **always** knows the right thing to say.

Every evening, we meditate for half an hour.

She does her laundry **every Sunday**.

Degree or Emphasis

Adverbs of degree or emphasis answer *how much?* or *to what degree?* and are used with other modifiers. They come immediately before the word they modify.

She is **very** uncomfortable when there are pets around.

Are you **quite** sure about the direction we are going?

Sentence Modifiers

Some adverbs modify an entire sentence, using transitional words or words such as *however*, *therefore*, and *doubtless*. These usually appear at the beginning of a clause.

As a result, she often turns down invitations to visit.

No doubt you will be happy with the accommodations.

15-3F   PRESENT AND PAST PARTICIPLES AS ADJECTIVES

Both present and past participles may be used as adjectives in English.

To decide whether to use the present participle or past participle, ask whether the noun modified is causing or experiencing what is being described.

LEARN TO DISTINGUISH BETWEEN -*ED* AND -*ING* ENDINGS

Present Participles: fascinating, exciting

Past Participles: fascinated, excited

George was bored. (he found his situation dull)

George was boring. (others found him dull)

Oman told us about his **fascinating** project.

The *project*, the noun modified, causes fascination; hence, the present participle, which causes the feeling, is correct.

Your trip sounds very **exciting**.

The *trip*, the noun modified, causes excitement; therefore, the present participle is correct.

The listeners were **fascinated** by Oman's project.

The noun *listeners* experience the fascination; hence, the past participle, which describes something experiencing the feeling, is correct.

She was very **excited** about her trip.

The pronoun *she* experiences the excitement; therefore, the past participle is correct.

For a list of the past tense and past participles of some common irregular verbs, see 10-4a.

PRESENT PARTICIPLES
- always end in *-ing*
- modify a noun or pronoun that is the cause of the action

PAST PARTICIPLES
- usually end in *-ed, -d, -en,* or *-t*, though many other endings are possible
- modify a noun or pronoun that experiences what is being described
- usually refer to living beings

  Note: In English, both the past tense and past participle of regular verbs (such as *talk, work, play, love*) are created by adding *-ed* or *-d* to the base (simple) form of the verb. But this pattern is not followed for all irregular verbs (for example, *ring, rang, rung*).

Although the present and past participles of a verb sound similar, they can mean very different things. *He is annoying* (present participle) means "He is causing an annoyance"—the verb is in the active voice. *He is annoyed* (past participle) means "He is experiencing annoyance"—the verb is in the passive voice.

Table 15.9 Participles That May Cause Confusion

Present Participle	Past Participle
amazing	amazed
amusing	amused
annoying	annoyed
appalling	appalled
astonishing	astonished
boring	bored
confusing	confused
depressing	depressed
disgusting	disgusted
embarrassing	embarrassed
exciting	excited
exhausting	exhausted
fascinating	fascinated
frightening	frightened
frustrating	frustrated
insulting	insulted
interesting	interested
offending	offended
overwhelming	overwhelmed
pleasing	pleased
reassuring	reassured
satisfying	satisfied
shocking	shocked
surprising	surprised
tiring	tired
worrying	worried

TIME

At a specific time: at 9:00 a.m., at midnight, at breakfast

On a specific day or date: on Friday, on June 16

In part of a 24-hour period: in the morning, in the daytime (*but* <u>at</u> night)

In a year or month: in 2003, in June

In a period of time: in two weeks

PLACE

At a specific location: at home, at school

At the edge of something: at the corner

At a target: aim the dart at the board

On a surface: on the wall, on the floor, on the road (*but* <u>in</u> the newspaper)

On a street: the school on my street

In an enclosed place: in the room, in the camera, in the car (*but* <u>on</u> the plane)

In a geographic location: in Winnipeg, in the Northwest Territories

Idiomatic uses of verbs with prepositions must be memorized because no particular rules apply.

Prepositions used with verbs vary widely in meaning. Check in an ELL dictionary for the meanings of verbs in combination with different prepositions. Keep track of their meanings in a notebook as you discover them in different contexts.

Note: Red text indicates terms that, while acceptable in some contexts, should be used with caution or not at all in formal writing (non-standard vocabulary, colloquialisms, jargon, non-inclusive language, and redundancies).

***a*, an.** Use *a* before a word that begins with a consonant sound, even if the word begins with a vowel: *a computer, a desk, a unique individual, a university*. Use *an* before a word that begins with a vowel sound, even if the word begins with a consonant: *an iguana, an oak, an hour, an honour*. Words beginning with the letter *h* often present problems. Generally, if the initial *h* sound is hard, use *a: a hot dog, a heart attack*. However, if the initial *h* is silent, use *an: an honest mistake*. If the *h* is pronounced, Canadian writers generally use *a* with the word: *a history, a hotel*.

accept, except. *Accept* is a verb meaning "to receive" or "take to (oneself)." *He accepted the lottery prize. Except* is very rarely a verb; usually, it is a preposition meaning "to exclude." *Everyone except Jerome received a penalty*.

adapt, adopt. *Adapt* means to "adjust oneself to" or "make suitable," and it is followed by the preposition *to. The lizard will adapt to its surroundings*. The word *adapt* can also mean "revise," in which case it is used with the preposition *for* or *from. They will adapt the novel for the silver screen. Adopt* means "to take or use as one's own." *They plan to adopt the idea for their computer game*.

adverse, averse. *Adverse* means "unfavourable." *Smoking has an adverse effect on your health. Averse* means "opposed" or "having an active distaste"; it can also mean "reluctant," in which case it is followed by the preposition *to. She was averse to fighting of any kind*.

advice, advise. *Advice* is a noun that means "an opinion about what should be done." *Take my advice and sell while you can. Advise* is a verb that means "to offer advice." *The high-priced lawyer will advise us on what course of action to take*.

affect, effect. *Affect* is a verb that most commonly means "to influence." *Water pollution affects the health of fish. Effect* is often a noun meaning "result." *The artist flicked paint on the canvas but could not achieve the effect he wanted. Effect* can also be used as a verb meaning "to bring about or execute." *The cost-cutting moves will effect a turnaround for the business*.

aggravate, irritate. *Aggravate* is a verb that means "to make worse or more severe." *The boy's cold was aggravated by the dry air.* *Irritate*, a verb, means "to make impatient or angry." Note that *aggravate* is often used colloquially to mean *"irritate."* Do not substitute *aggravate* for *irritate* in formal writing. *His constant complaining irritated* [not *aggravated*] *me.*

agree to, agree with. *Agree to* means "to consent to." *The two sides will agree to the proposal. Agree with* means "to be in accord with." *The witness's version of events agrees with theirs.*

ain't. *Ain't* means "am not," "are not," or "is not." It is non-standard English and should not be used in formal writing.

all ready, already. *All ready* means "completely prepared." *The sprinter is all ready for the starter's gun. Already* is an adverb that means "before this time; previously; even now." *They have already seen* The Lion King.

all right, alright. *All right* is always written as two words. *Alright* is non-standard English for *all right* and should not be used in formal writing. *It's all right* [not *alright*] *to eat dinner if Desmond is late.*

all together, altogether. See *altogether, all together.*

allude, elude. *Allude* means "to refer to indirectly or casually." *The poet alludes to several classic poems in her latest work.* Do not use it to mean "to refer to directly." *In his presentation, Freud specifically referred to* [not *alluded to*] *the importance of the subconscious. Elude* means "to evade or escape from, usually with some daring or skill," or "to escape the understanding or grasp of." *I eluded my pursuers, but why they were chasing me eluded me.*

allusion, illusion, delusion. *Allusion* is an "implied or indirect reference." *The prosecuting attorney made an allusion to her criminal past.* The word *illusion* means "an appearance or feeling that misleads because it is not real." *When the bus beside ours backed up, it created the illusion that we were moving.* This should be distinguished from *delusion*, which means "a false and often harmful belief about something that does not exist." *The paranoid reporter had the delusion that every email contained a virus.*

alot, a lot. *A lot* is always written as two words. *We have not had a lot of snow this winter.* Avoid using *a lot* in formal writing.

altogether, all together. *Altogether* means "completely, entirely." *Altogether there were eight novels assigned for the course.* The phrase *all together* means "together in a group." *We found the litter of puppies all together in the garage.*

a.m., p.m. Use these abbreviations only with specific times, when numerals are provided: *10 a.m.* or *1 p.m.* Do not use the abbreviations as substitutes for *morning, afternoon,* or *evening. The mother had to get up early in the morning* [not *the a.m.*] *to take her daughter to the hockey game.*

among, between. See *between, among.*

amoral, immoral. *Amoral* means "not having any morals; neither moral nor immoral." *The cabinet adopted an amoral perspective when they considered tax cuts.* The word *immoral* means "morally wrong or wicked." *It is immoral to steal food from the food bank.*

amount, number. *Amount* is used to refer to things in bulk or mass. These things cannot be counted. *A large amount of litter can be found along the highway. Number* is used to refer to things that can be counted. *He gobbled down a number of bedtime snacks every evening.*

an, a. See *a, an.*

and etc. *Etc. (et cetera)* means "and so forth." Do not use *and etc.* because it is redundant. See also *etc.*

and/or. *And/or* is sometimes used to indicate three possibilities: one, or the other, or both. It is occasionally acceptable in business, technical, or legal writing. Avoid this awkward construction when writing for the humanities.

ante-, anti-. *Ante-* is a prefix that means "before; earlier; in front of." *The reporter waited in an anteroom until the politician could see her.* The prefix *anti-* means "against" or "opposed to." *Thousands of supporters turned out for the antipoverty rally.* Use *anti-* with a hyphen when it is followed by a capital letter *(anti-American)* or a word beginning with i *(anti-intellectual).* Otherwise, consult a dictionary.

anxious, eager. *Anxious* means "nervous," "troubled," or "worried." *The looming, dark clouds made Tim anxious. Eager* means "looking forward" and is often followed by the preposition *to. Stella was eager to receive the Christmas parcel.* Do not use *anxious* to mean "eager." *I'm eager* [not *anxious*] *to spend my gift certificate.*

anyone, any one. *Anyone* is an indefinite pronoun that means "any person at all." *Anyone* is singular. (See 10-3d and 10-5a.) *Can anyone tell me what to do?* In *any one*, the pronoun *one* is preceded by the adjective *any*. Here, the two words refer to any person or thing in a group. *Once the last of the patrons has left, you can jump into any one of the bumper cars.*

anyplace. *Anyplace* is informal for *anywhere*. Do not use *anyplace* in formal writing.

anyways, anywheres. *Anyways* and *anywheres* are non-standard for *anyway* and *anywhere*, respectively. Always use *anyway* and *anywhere* in formal speaking and writing.

as. Substituting *as* for *because*, *since*, and *while* may make a sentence vague or ambiguous. *Since* [not *as*] *we were stopping for gas, we decided to use the restroom.* If *as* were used in this sentence, the cause–effect relationship would be unclear.

as, like. See *like, as*.

averse, adverse. See *adverse, averse*.

awful, awfully. In formal English usage, the adjective *awful* once meant "filled with awe" or "inspiring awe." Now, *awful* is more commonly used to mean "bad" or "terrible." *It was an awful day when I was fired. Awfully* is the adverb form. *He played the piano awfully.* The adverb *awfully* is sometimes used colloquially as an intensifier to mean "extremely" or "very." *He was awfully upset when he opened the bill.* Avoid such colloquial usage in formal writing.

awhile, a while. *Awhile* is an adverb. *Stay awhile, if you wish.* Use the article and noun, *a while,* as the object of a preposition. *We had obviously arrived too early, so we circled the block for a while.*

bad, badly. *Bad* is an adjective. *They felt bad about leaving the party early.* The word *badly* is an adverb. *His infected hand hurt badly.*

being as, being that. Both *being as* and *being that* are non-standard expressions used in place of the subordinate conjunctions *because* or *since*. *Since* [not *Being that*] *vandals had written on the walls, tough security measures were put in place.*

beside, besides. *Beside* is a preposition meaning "by the side of" or "next to." *Grass grows beside the stream. Besides* is an adverb meaning "moreover," or "furthermore." *Jeff did not want to fight; besides, he was injured. Besides* can also be a preposition meaning "in addition to," "except for," or "other than." *Besides me, there is no one working on the project.*

between, among. Use *among* when referring to relationships involving more than two people or things. *You can choose among fifteen sports.* Use *between* when referring to relationships involving two people or things. *When deciding which band is better, you need to take into account the difference in record sales between the two.*

breath, breathe. Use *breath* when you need the noun form. *I will watch every breath you take.* Use *breathe* when you need the verb. *When you get an X-ray at the dentist's office, remember to breathe through your mouth.*

bring, take. Use *bring* when something is being moved toward the speaker. *Please bring the thermometer to me.* Use *take* when something is being moved away. *I ask that you take the pizza to the Simpsons.*

burst, bursted; bust, busted. *Burst* is an irregular verb meaning "to fly apart suddenly with force; explode; break open." *The water-filled balloon burst when it hit the pavement. Bursted* is the non-standard past-tense form of *burst;* use the standard past tense (*burst*) instead. *Bust* and its past-tense form *busted* are slang.

can, may. *Can* means "know how to" or "be able to." *Mai-Ling can play the piano. May* means "be allowed to" or "have permission to." *Ted, you may go now.* The distinction in meaning between *can* and *may* is still made in formal writing. In informal English, *can* is widely used to mean "be able to" and "be allowed to."

capital, capitol. *Capital* refers to a city where the government of a country, province, or state is located. *Edmonton is the capital of Alberta. Capital* can also mean "the amount of money a company or person uses in carrying on a business." A *capitol* is a building in which American lawmakers meet. When referring to the building in which the U.S. Congress meets, capitalize the first letter, as in *Capitol.*

censor, censure. The verb *censor* means "to edit or remove from public view on moral or other grounds." *They will censor the violent movie before it can be seen in theatres.* The verb *censure* means "to express strong disapproval." *The House will censure the minister for giving misleading information.*

cite, site. The verb *cite* means "to quote, especially as an authority." *Doug cited the poet's use of allusion in his essay.* The noun *site* often means "a particular place." *The vacant field will be the site of a new shopping centre.*

climactic, climatic. *Climactic* is an adjective derived from *climax*; *climax* means "the highest point; point of highest interest; the most exciting part." *The scene in which the boy is reunited with his father is the climactic moment of the movie.* The adjective *climatic* means "of or having to do with climate." *In order for a tornado to occur, there must be certain climatic conditions.*

coarse, course. *Coarse* usually means "heavy and rough in texture" or "crude." *Shelley used a coarse sandpaper to finish the table. Course* may refer to a class you are taking. Generally, it means "a line of movement," "a direction taken," "a way, path, or track," or "a playing field." *Seeking help for your drinking problem is the right course of action.*

compare to, compare with. *Compare to* means "to represent as similar." *Shall I compare thee to a summer's day? Compare with* means "to point out how two persons or things are alike and how they differ." *I will compare Millay's poem with Eliot's.*

complement, compliment. The verb *complement* means "to reinforce, add to, or complete something." *The scarf complements his wardrobe.* As a noun, *complement* is something that completes. *Compliment* as a verb means "to say something in praise." *I must compliment you on your fine enunciation.* As a noun, *compliment* means "a remark of praise."

conscience, conscious. *Conscience* is a noun meaning "the sense of moral right and wrong." *His conscience would not let him shoplift the DVD. Conscious* is an adjective that means "aware; knowing." *Nancy Drew was conscious of a shadowy figure sneaking up behind her.*

consensus of opinion. *Consensus* means "general agreement." As a result, the phrase *consensus of opinion* is redundant. *A consensus* [not *consensus of opinion*] *is required before the motion will be passed.*

contact. *Contact* is often used informally as a verb meaning "to communicate with." In formal writing, use a precise verb such as *email, telephone,* or *write. I will telephone* [not *contact*] *you for directions to the plant.*

continual, continuous. *Continual* means "repeated many times; very frequent." *When the roofers were here, there was continual hammering. Continuous* means "without a stop or a break." *During rush hour, there is a continuous line of cars.*

could care less. *Could care less* is non-standard and should not be used in formal writing. Use *couldn't care less* in its place. *Daphne couldn't care less how much the job pays, as long as it gives her satisfaction.*

could of. *Could of* is non-standard for *could have. If not for his injury, Mr. Martin could have* [not *could of*] *become a professional basketball player.*

council, counsel. *Council* is a noun used to describe "a group of people called together to talk things over or give advice"; it also applies to "a group of people elected by citizens to make up laws." *A tribal council will decide the appropriate punishment.* A *councillor* is a member of the *council. Counsel* as a noun means "advice." *The chief gives wise counsel. Counsel* can also mean a lawyer. A *counsellor* is someone who gives advice or guidance.

course, coarse. See *coarse, course.*

criteria, criterion. *Criteria* are rules for making judgments. *Criteria* is the plural form of *criterion. The major criteria for the job are a background in multimedia and a readiness to work overtime.*

data, datum. *Data* are "facts or concepts presented in a form suitable for processing in order to draw conclusions." *Data* is the plural form of *datum*, which is rarely used. Increasingly, *data* is used as a singular noun; however, careful writers use it as a plural. *The new data reveal* [or, increasingly, *reveals*] *that the economy is rebounding.*

defuse, diffuse. *Defuse* means "to take the fuse out" or "to disarm." *The counsellor managed to defuse the volatile family situation. Diffuse* as a verb means "to scatter" or "to spread out," but *diffuse* is more commonly used as an adjective to describe something spread out or, in the context of language, something wordy or verbose. *The smell of cologne diffused after we opened the windows. His speech was diffuse and did not focus on a particular point.*

delusion, illusion. See *allusion, illusion, delusion.*

differ from, differ with. *Differ from* means "to be unlike." *The brothers differ from each other only in their girlfriends. Differ with* means "to disagree with." *I used to differ with my stepmother on what time I should be home on Saturday night.*

different from, different than. In standard English, the preferred form is *different from. The new edition of* Ulysses *is very different from the previous one.* However, *different than* is gaining wider acceptance, especially when *different from* creates an awkward construction. *He is a different person today than* [as opposed to the more awkward *from the person*] *he used to be.*

discreet, discrete. *Discreet* means "prudent and tactful in speech and behaviour." *The mayor was very discreet when talking about the manager's personal life. Discrete* means "separate; distinct." *There are discrete parts of the cell that perform specialized functions.*

disinterested, uninterested. *Disinterested* means "impartial." *The premier appointed a disinterested third party to mediate the dispute. Uninterested* means "lacking in interest," or "bored." *Shelley is uninterested in soap operas.*

don't, doesn't. *Don't* is a contraction for *do not. Don't slam the door.* Do not use *don't* as a contraction for *does not;* the correct contraction is *doesn't. Selma doesn't* [not *don't*] *want to shovel the walk.*

due to. *Due to* means "caused by" or "owing to." It should be used as an adjective phrase following a form of the verb *to be. The inquest ruled that the death was due to driver error.* In formal writing, *due to* should not be used as a preposition meaning "because of." *Classes were cancelled because of* [not *due to*] *the heavy snowstorm.*

each. *Each* is singular. (See 10-3d and 10-5a.)

eager, anxious. See *anxious, eager.*

effect, affect. See *affect, effect.*

e.g. This is the Latin abbreviation for *exempli gratia,* which means "for example." In formal writing, avoid *e.g.* and use phrases such as *for example* or *for instance* instead. *Many fish— for example, salmon and trout—will be affected.*

either. *Either* is singular. (See 10-3d and 10-5a.) For *either . . . or* constructions, see 10-3c.

elicit, illicit. *Elicit* is a verb meaning "to draw forth" or "bring out." *Listening to a great symphony will elicit strong emotions.* The adjective *illicit* means "unlawful." *The neighbours had an illicit growing operation in their basement.*

elude, allude. See *allude, elude.*

emigrate from, immigrate to. *Emigrate* means "to leave one's own country or region and settle in another"; it requires the preposition *from. The Bhuttos emigrated from Pakistan. Immigrate* means "to enter and permanently settle in another country"; it requires the preposition *to. Mr. Bhutto's cousin now plans to immigrate to Canada.*

eminent, immanent, imminent. *Eminent* means "distinguished" or "exalted." *The eminent scientist delivered the lecture. Immanent* is an adjective that means "inherent" or "remaining within." *I believe most Canadians have an immanent goodness. Imminent* is an adjective meaning "likely to happen soon." *Given the troop movements, the general felt that an attack was imminent.*

enthused, enthusiastic. *Enthused* is sometimes informally used as an adjective meaning "having or showing enthusiasm." Use *enthusiastic* instead. *He becomes enthusiastic* [not *enthused*] *about Oilers playoff games.*

-ess. Many readers find the *-ess* suffix demeaning. Write *actor,* not *actress; singer,* not *songstress; poet,* not *poetess.*

etc. *Etc.* is an abbreviation that in English means "and other things." Do not use *etc.* to refer to people. In formal writing, it is preferable to use the expression *and so on* in place of *etc.* See also *and etc.*

eventually, ultimately. *Eventually* often means "an undefined time in the future." *Ultimately* commonly means "the greatest extreme or furthest extent." *Eventually* and *ultimately* are frequently used interchangeably. It is best to use *eventually* when referring to time and *ultimately* when referring to the greatest extent. *Eventually the robber will be found. I find it ultimately the most reasonable alternative.*

everybody, everyone. *Everybody* and *everyone* are both singular. *(*See 10-3d and 10-5a.)

everyone, every one. *Everyone* is an indefinite pronoun meaning "every person." *Everyone wanted to purchase a ticket. Every one* is a pronoun, *one,* modified by an adjective, *every;* the two words mean "each person or thing in a group." *Every one* is frequently followed by *of. Every one of the merchants in Kamloops is participating in this promotion.*

except, accept. See *accept, except.*

except for the fact that. Avoid this wordy, awkward construction. Instead, use *except that. Alex would be a good candidate for office, except that he is unreliable.*

explicit, implicit. *Explicit* means "clearly expressed; directly stated." *The coach gave everyone but Keon explicit orders not to shoot. Implicit* means "meant but not clearly expressed or directly stated." *My mother-in-law's silence was implicit consent to pour her another glass of wine.*

farther, further. In formal English, *farther* is used for physical distance. *On the map, Courtenay is farther than Ladysmith. Further* is used to mean "more" or "to a greater extent." *He took the teasing further than would be appropriate under any circumstances.*

female, male. *Female* and *male* are considered jargon if substituted for "woman" and "man." *Sixteen men* [not *males*] *and seventeen women* [not *females*] *made the team.*

fewer, less. Use *fewer* only to refer to numbers and things that can be counted. *There are fewer houses up for sale than there were last year at this time.* Use *less* to refer to collective nouns or things that cannot be counted. *Generally, there is less traffic congestion at midday.*

finalize. *Finalize* is a verb meaning "to bring to a conclusion." The word, though often used, is considered jargon by many people. Use a clear, acceptable alternative. *The football coach completed [not finalized] plans for the game.*

flout, flaunt. *Flout* is a verb that means "to treat with contempt." *Magdalena flouted the rules of the road until she became one of the worst drivers in Canada. Flaunt means "to show off." Agnes flaunted her new MP3 player.*

flunk. *Flunk* is colloquial for *fail*, and it should be avoided in formal writing.

folks. *Folks* is informal for "one's family; one's relatives." In academic writing, use a more formal expression than *folks*. *My mother and father [not folks] are organizing the family reunion.*

fun. When used as an adjective, *fun* is colloquial; it should be avoided in formal writing. *The Jawbreaker was an exciting [not fun] ride.*

further, farther. See *farther, further.*

get. *Get* is a common verb with many slang and colloquial uses. Avoid the following uses of *get:* "to become" (*He got cold*); "to obtain revenge" (*Gillian got back at Ted for the rumours he spread*); "to annoy" (*His constant complaining finally got to me*); "to elicit an emotional response" (*The final scene in the movie really got to her*).

good, well. *Good* is an adjective. *Michael is a good skier. Well* is nearly always an adverb. (See 10-6a.) *The racing team skis well.*

hanged, hung. *Hanged* is the past tense and past participle of *hang*, which means "to execute." *The man was convicted of treason and hanged. Hung* is the past tense and past participle of *hang*, which means "to fasten or be fastened to something." *Decorations for the dance hung from the ceiling.*

not hardly. Avoid double negative expressions such as *not hardly* or *can't hardly*. (See 10-6d.) *I can [not can't] hardly find words to express myself.*

has got, have got. Avoid using *have got* or *has got* when *have* or *has* alone will communicate the intended meaning. *I have [not have got] two more books to finish reading to complete the course requirements.*

he. Do not use only *he* when the complete meaning is "he or she." In modern usage, this is not inclusive. See 10-5a and 13-2e for alternative constructions.

he/she, his/her. Use *he or she,* or *his or her* in formal writing. For alternative, more concise constructions, see 10-5a.

hisself. Do not use this non-standard form of *himself*.

hopefully. *Hopefully* is an adverb meaning "in a hopeful manner." *Hopefully* can modify a verb, an adjective, or another adverb. *They waited hopefully for news from the surgeon on how the operation had gone.* In formal writing, do not use *hopefully* as a sentence modifier with the meaning "I hope." *I hope* [not *Hopefully*] *the operation will be a success.*

hung, hanged. See *hanged, hung.*

i.e. The abbreviation *i.e.* stands for the Latin *id est*, which in English means "that is." In formal writing, use the English equivalent *that is*.

if, whether. *If* is used to express conditions. *If there is sufficient snow, we will go skiing at Whistler.* Use *whether* to express alternatives. *The couple was not sure whether to take the holiday in St. Lucia or in Aruba.*

illicit, elicit. See *elicit, illicit.*

illusion, allusion. See *allusion, illusion, delusion.*

immanent, imminent, eminent. See *eminent, immanent, imminent.*

immigrate to, emigrate from. See *emigrate from, immigrate to.*

immoral, amoral. See *amoral, immoral.*

implement. *Implement* means "to carry out." It is often unnecessary and pretentious. *The president carried out* [not *implemented*] *the board's recommendations.*

implicit, explicit. See *explicit, implicit.*

imply, infer. *Imply* means "to express indirectly." *Angie's grin implied that she knew Jo had a crush on Bono. Infer* means "to conclude by reasoning." *You could infer that the man was poor by his tattered clothes.*

in, into. *In* generally indicates a location or condition. *She is hiding in the house. Into* indicates a direction, a movement, or a change in condition. *He went into the house to look for her.*

individual. *Individual* is sometimes used as a pretentious substitute for *person*. *The person* [not *individual*] *sitting next to me slept through the entire play.*

ingenious, ingenuous. *Ingenious* means "clever" or "skillful." *The criminal devised an ingenious plan to rob the bank. Ingenuous means "frank" and "simple." His country manner was quite ingenuous.*

in regards to. *In regards to* confuses two phrases: *in regard to* and *as regards*. Use either one of these alternatives instead. *Talk to your counsellor in regard to the application.*

irregardless. *Irregardless* is non-standard English. Use *regardless* instead.

irritate, aggravate. See *aggravate, irritate*.

is when, is where. Do not use *when* or *where* following *is* in definitions. *Photosynthesis is the process by which* [not *is when*] *plant cells make sugar from carbon dioxide and water in the presence of chlorophyll and light.*

it is. *It is* becomes non-standard when used to mean "there is." *There is* [not *It is*] *a glowing disc in the night sky.*

its, it's. *Its* is a possessive pronoun. *The cat will come in its own good time. It's* is a contraction for *it is. It's the perfect time to buy a house.* (See 11-4d.)

kind, kinds. *Kind* is singular and should not be treated as a plural. *This* [not *These*] *kind of painting was popular in that era. Kinds* is plural. *These kinds of paintings were popular in that era.*

kind of, sort of. *Kind of* and *sort of* are colloquial expressions meaning "rather" or "somewhat." Do not use these colloquialisms in formal writing. *I was somewhat* [not *kind of* or *sort of*] *disappointed by the low mark.*

lay, lie. See *lie, lay*.

lead, led. *Lead* is a soft heavy metal. *Led* is the past tense of the verb *lead. His accurate directions led me to the correct address.*

learn, teach. *Learn* means "to gain knowledge of or a skill by instruction, study, or experience." *I learned how to play chess. Teach* means "to impart knowledge or a skill." *I will teach* [not *learn*] *my little cousin to play the game.*

leave, let. *Leave* means "to go away." *Let* means "to allow or permit." Do not use *leave* with the non-standard meaning "to permit." *Let* [not *leave*] *me help you trim the fruit trees.*

led, lead. See *lead, led.*

less, fewer. See *fewer, less.*

liable. *Liable* means "legally responsible." Avoid using it to mean "likely." *Jeff will likely* [not *is liable to*] *catch many fish on this trip.*

licence, license. *Licence* is a noun meaning "legal permission by law to do something." *Joe's business licence hung prominently on the wall. License* is a verb meaning "to permit or authorize." *A veterinarian is licensed to practise animal medicine.*

lie, lay. *Lie* means "to recline." It is an intransitive verb, which means it does not take a direct object. The principal forms of the verb are *lie, lay,* and *lain. Lie down now.* Lay means "to put" or "to place." It is a transitive verb, which means it always requires a direct object. The principal parts of the verb are *lay, laid,* and *laid. Lay the guests' coats on the bed in the spare room.* (See 10-4b.)

like, as. *Like* is a preposition, and it should be followed by a noun or a noun phrase. *Daniel looks like a million dollars. As* is a subordinating conjunction and should be used to introduce a dependent clause. *As I predicted, he is late again.*

loose, lose. *Loose* is an adjective meaning "not firmly fastened." *He has a loose tooth as a result of biting into the hard candy. Lose* is a verb meaning "to misplace" or "to be defeated." *He predicted that the Stampeders would lose the Grey Cup.*

lots, lots of. *Lots* and *lots of* are colloquial substitutes for *many, much,* and *a great deal.* They should not be used in formal writing.

male, female. See *female, male.*

mankind. *Mankind* is not an inclusive term, as it excludes women. Avoid it in favour of terms such as *humans, humanity, the human race,* or *humankind.*

may, can. See *can, may.*

may of, might of. *May of* and *might of* are non-standard English for *may have* and *might have. Mona might have* [not *might of*] *taken the chicken out of the oven too early.*

maybe, may be. *Maybe* is an adverb meaning "perhaps." *Maybe we should build the outdoor rink tomorrow. May be* is a verb phrase. *Since the temperature will be lower on Tuesday, that may be a better day.*

Glossary of Usage

media, medium. *Media* is the plural of *medium*. *The media are offering too much coverage of sensational stories.*

moral, morale. *Moral* is a noun meaning "an ethical conclusion." *Morale* means "the attitude as regards courage, confidence, and enthusiasm." *Team morale was low after the twentieth defeat.*

most. When used to mean "almost," *most* is colloquial. This usage should be avoided in formal writing. *Almost* [not *Most*] *every student went to the party.*

must of. *Must of* is non-standard English for *must have*. See *may of, might of*.

myself. *Myself* is a reflexive pronoun. *I hurt myself. Myself* can also be an intensive pronoun. *I will go myself.* Do not use *myself* in place of *I* or *me*. *Jeremy and I* [not *myself*] *are going on a trip.* (See also 10-5c.)

neither. *Neither* is most often singular. (See 10-3d and 10-5a.) For *neither . . . nor* constructions, see 10-3c.

none. *None* is usually singular. (See 10-3d and 10-5a.)

nowheres. *Nowheres* is non-standard English for *nowhere*.

number, amount. See *amount, number*.

of. *Of* is a preposition. Do not use it in place of the verb *have* after *could, should, would, may, must,* and *might*. *The Johnsons might have* [not *of*] *left their garage door open.*

off of. Omit *of* from the expression as *off* is sufficient. *The young boy fell off* [not *off of*] *the table.*

OK, O.K., okay. All three forms are acceptable in informal writing and speech. However, avoid these colloquial expressions in formal writing and speech.

parameters. *Parameter* is a mathematical term that means "a quantity that is constant in a particular calculation or case but varies in other cases." It is sometimes used as jargon to mean any limiting or defining element or feature. Avoid such jargon and use precise English instead. *The whole project had very vague guidelines* [not *parameters*].

passed, past. *Passed* is the past tense of the verb *pass*, which means "to go by." *Uncle Theo passed by our front window.* Never use *past* as a verb. *Past* can be an adjective that means "gone by; over." *They overcame their past misunderstanding. Past* can also be a noun meaning "the time before the present." *Canada has a rich and glorious past.* Finally, *past* can be a preposition. *Past the exit on the highway, there was a service station.*

people, persons. Use *people* to refer to a group of individuals who are anonymous and uncounted. *The people of South Africa have a long history of apartheid.* Generally, you may use *persons* or *people* when referring to a countable number of individuals. *Only five persons [or people] attended the town meeting.*

percent, per cent, percentage. Always use *percent* (also spelled *per cent*) with specific numbers. *The survey revealed that 48 percent of Canadians want their country to become a republic.* Percentage means "part of" or "portion," and it is used when no number is provided. *A large percentage of the population favoured the Liberals.*

phenomenon, phenomena. *Phenomenon* means "a fact, event or circumstance that can be observed." *Phenomena* is the plural of *phenomenon*. *There were all sorts of paranormal phenomena taking place in the haunted house.*

plus. *Plus* is a non-standard substitute for *and*. Do not use *plus* to join independent clauses. *He has a driver's license; however* [not *plus*], *it has expired.*

p.m. See *a.m., p.m.*

pore, pour. *Pore* is an intransitive verb meaning "to read or study carefully" or "to ponder." *Ahmed has been poring over his chemistry notes to prepare for his exam. Pour* means "to cause to flow in a stream." *It has been pouring rain for days.*

practice, practise. *Practice* is a noun meaning "an action done several times over to gain a skill." *Practice will improve your dribbling. Practise* is a verb meaning "to do something again and again in order to learn it." *Su Li practises the violin twice a day.* In American spelling, both the noun and verb are spelled *practice*.

precede, proceed. *Precede* means "to go or come before." *A mild gust preceded the hurricane. Proceed* means "to go on after having stopped" or "to move forward." *After a family meeting about finances, we proceeded with the wedding plans.*

principal, principle. The noun *principal* means "a chief person" or "a sum of money that has been borrowed." *After Mr. Toutant's retirement from Dauphin Elementary School, a new principal was appointed.* The noun *principle* means "a fact or belief on which other ideas are based." *The constitution is based on the principles of equality and justice.* Note, too, that *principal* can be an adjective, meaning "main." *The principal reason I didn't vote was my disagreement with all the candidates' platforms.*

proceed, precede. See *precede, proceed.*

quote, quotation. *Quote* is a verb meaning "to repeat the exact words of." *She quoted the precise line from "Leda and the Swan" to illustrate her point. Quotation* is a noun meaning "a passage quoted." Do not use *quote* as a shortened form of *quotation. Using a relevant quotation* [not *quote*] *is often a good way to begin a speech.*

raise, rise. *Raise* means "to move to a higher level; to elevate." It is a transitive verb, which means it requires a direct object. *The stage manager raised the curtain. Rise* means "to go up." It is an intransitive verb, which means it does not require a direct object. *The smoke rises.*

rational, rationale. *Rational* is an adjective meaning "logical, reasonable." *The court ruled that no rational person would have deliberately made that choice. Rationale* is a noun meaning "reasonable explanation." *What is your rationale for proceeding with the experiment?*

real, really. *Real* is an adjective. Occasionally, in informal speech and writing, it is used as an adverb, but this usage should be avoided in formal writing. *Really* is an adverb. *Don was really* [not *real*] *excited.* (See 10-6.) In informal writing and speech, *real* and *really* are used as intensifiers to mean "extremely" or "very"; such usage should be avoided in formal writing and speech.

reason is because. *Reason is because* is a redundant expression. Use *reason is that* instead. *One reason we moved from Moose Jaw is that* [not *is because*] *Mom got a teaching job at a community college.*

reason why. *Reason why* is a redundant expression. In its place use either *reason* or *why. I still do not know why* [not *the reason why*] *she rejected my invitation.*

regretfully, regrettably. *Regretfully* means "full of regret." It describes a person's attitude of regret. *Regretfully, he wrote to apologize. Regrettably* means that circumstances are regrettable. *Regrettably, the circus was rained out today.*

rein, reign. *Rein* refers to the restraint a driver uses to control an animal or any kind of restraint in general. *The equestrian champion reined in his horse forcefully. Reign* means "royal authority." *Shakespeare wrote* Hamlet *during the reign of James I.* Be careful not to confuse them in certain idiomatic phrases, such as "give free rein [not reign] to."

relation, relationship. *Relation* is used to describe the association between two or more things. *The scientist studied the relation between lung cancer and smog. Relationship* is used to describe the association or connection between people. *Peter and Olga had a professional relationship that soon blossomed into a personal one.*

respectfully, respectively. *Respectfully* is an adverb meaning "showing or marked by proper respect." *She respectfully presented her counter-argument in the debate. Respectively* is an adverb meaning "singly in the order designated or mentioned." *Chand, Doug, and Lenore are a plastic surgeon, a bus driver, and a company vice-president respectively.*

rise, raise. See *raise, rise.*

sensual, sensuous. *Sensual* is an adjective meaning "relating to gratification of the physical senses." *The chef obtains sensual pleasure from cooking. Sensuous* is an adjective meaning "pleasing to the senses." *Sensuous* is always favourable and often applies to the appreciation of nature, art, or music. *She obtains a sensuous delight from Mozart's music.*

set, sit. *Set* means "to put in place or put down, or to position." It is a transitive verb, requiring a direct object, and its principal parts are *set, set, set. Ali set the book on the ledge. Sit* means "to be seated." It is an intransitive verb, not requiring a direct object, and its principal parts are *sit, sat, sat. Set* is sometimes a non-standard substitute for *sit.* Avoid this usage in formal writing. *The dog sat* [not *set*] *down.*

shall, will. *Shall* was once used with the first-person singular and plural as the helping verb with future-tense verbs. *I shall visit my grandfather on Wednesday. We shall deliver the results on Thursday.* In modern usage, *will* has replaced *shall. I will see you on Friday.* The word *shall* is still often used in polite questions. *Shall I bring the newspaper to your door?*

she/he, her/his. See *he/she, his/her.*

should of. *Should of* is non-standard for *should have. He should have* [not *should of*] *submitted the essay on time.*

since. *Since* should mainly be used in situations describing time. *We have been waiting for the bus since midnight.* Do not use *since* as a substitute for *because* in cases where there is any chance of confusion. *Since we lost the division, we have been playing our second-string players.* Here *since* could mean "from that point in time" or "because."

sit, set. See *set, sit.*

site, cite. See *cite, site.*

somebody, someone. *Somebody* and *someone* are singular. (See 10-3d and 10-5a.)

something. *Something* is singular. (See 10-3d and 10-5a.)

sometime, some time, sometimes. *Sometime* is an adverb meaning "at an indefinite or unstated time." *Let's meet sometime on Thursday*. In *some time,* the adjective *some* modifies the noun *time. We haven't seen the Jebsons for some time. Sometimes* is an adverb meaning "at times; now and then." *Sometimes I'm not sure what major to pursue.*

sort of, kind of. See *kind of, sort of.*

sneaked, snuck. *Sneaked* is the correct past participle. *Sameer sneaked* [not *snuck*] *into his parents' closet looking for his birthday presents.*

stationary, stationery. *Stationary* means "not moving." *At the club, he rode on a stationary bike. Stationery* refers to paper and other writing products. *I will need to buy stationery at the business supply store.*

suppose to, use to. See *use to, suppose to.*

sure and. *Sure and* is non-standard. Instead, use *sure to. Please be sure to* [not *sure and*] *edit your work carefully.*

take, bring. See *bring, take.*

teach, learn. See *learn, teach.*

than, then. *Than* is a conjunction used to make comparisons. *I would rather have cheesecake than pie. Then* is an adverb used to indicate past or future time. *My husband will do the vacuuming, and then he will wax the floors.*

that, who. See *who, which, that.*

that, which. Most North American writers use *that* for restrictive clauses and *which* for non-restrictive clauses. (See 11-1f.) Note, however, that in some circles *that* and *which* are increasingly treated as grammatically identical. Most grammar-checkers still distinguish between them. Your instructor may or may not observe this distinction.

theirselves. *Theirselves* is non-standard English for *themselves. They amused themselves* [not *theirselves*] *by going to the drive-in.*

them. *Them* is non-standard when it is used in place of *those. Please place those* [not *them*] *flowers on the kitchen table.*

then, than. See *than, then*.

there, their, they're. *There* is an adverb meaning "at or in that place." *I'll call home when I get there. There* can also be an expletive, a phrase at the beginning of a clause. *There are two beautiful dogs in the garage. Their* is a possessive pronoun. *It was their first house. They're* is a contraction for *they are. They're first in line for tickets*.

this kind. See *kind, kinds*.

thru. *Thru* is a colloquial spelling of *through*. Do not use *thru* in formal academic or business writing.

to, too, two. *To* can be a preposition. *They swayed to the rhythm. To* can also be part of an infinitive. *We need to talk. Too* is an adverb. *There are too many people in the city. Two* is a number. *I have two red pens*.

toward, towards. Both versions are acceptable; however, *toward* is preferred in Canadian English.

try and. *Try and* is non-standard English. Instead use *try to. Try to* [not *Try and*] *be polite*.

ultimately, eventually. See *eventually, ultimately*.

uninterested, disinterested. See *disinterested, uninterested*.

unique. Like *straight, round,* and *complete, unique* is an absolute. There are not degrees of uniqueness. Especially in formal writing, avoid expressions such as *more unique* and *most unique*. (See 10-6c.)

usage, use. *Usage* refers to conventions, most often of language. *Placing "ain't" in a sentence is non-standard usage. Use* means "to employ." Do not substitute *usage* when *use* is required. *I do not think surfing the Internet is the proper use* [not *usage*] *of your study time*.

use to, suppose to. *Use to* and *suppose to* are non-standard for *used to* and *supposed to. We used to* [not *use to*] *have roast beef for dinner every Sunday night*.

utilize. *Utilize* means "to put to use." Often, *use* can be substituted, as *utilize* can make writing sound pretentious. *He will use* [not *utilize*] *the best material to tile the bathroom*.

wait for, wait on. *Wait for* means "to await." *The girls are waiting for the commuter train. Wait on* means "to serve." It should not be used as a substitute for *wait for. The owner of the bistro waited on our table. We will wait for* [not *wait on*] *the morning bus*.

ways. *Ways* is colloquial in usage when designating distance. *Edmonton is quite a way* [not *ways*] *from Vancouver.*

weather, whether. *Weather* is a noun describing "the state of the atmosphere at a given time and place." *The weather in central Canada has been unseasonably warm. Whether* is a conjunction that signals a choice between or among alternatives. *Grif did not know whether to stay or to go.*

well, good. See *good, well.*

where. *Where* is non-standard in usage when it is substituted for *that* as a subordinate conjunction. *I read in the newspaper that* [not *where*] *Arundhati Roy will be giving a reading at the university.*

whether, if. See *if, whether.*

which. See *that, which* and *who, which, that.*

while. Do not use *while* as a substitute for "although" or "whereas" if such usage risks ambiguity. *Although* [not *While*] *Jennifer's grades got worse, Jack's got better.* If *while* were used, it could mean "although" or "at the same time."

who, which, that. Use *who* not *which* to refer to persons. Most often, *that* is used to refer to things. *There is the boy who* [not *that*] *took the candies.* However, *that* may be used to refer to a class or group of people. *The team that scores the most points wins.*

who, whom. *Who* is used for subjects and subject complements. *Who is coming to dinner? Whom* is used for objects. *He did not know whom to ask.* (See 10-5d.)

who's, whose. *Who's* is a contraction for *who is. Who's going to the dinner? Whose* is a possessive pronoun. *Whose life is it anyway?*

will, shall. See *shall, will.*

would of. *Would of* is non-standard English for *would have. He would have* [not *would of*] *achieved a perfect score if he had obtained one more strike.*

you. Avoid using *you* in an indefinite sentence to mean "anyone." (See 10-5b.) *Any collector* [not *You*] *could identify it as a fake.*

your, you're. *Your* is a possessive pronoun. *Your bicycle is in the garage. You're* is a contraction for *you are. You're the first person I contacted about the job.*

Index   583

CORRECTION SYMBOLS

#	add a space	*gra*	error in grammar or usage	^	something missing
ab	error in abbreviation	*id*	idiom	*wdy*	problem with wordiness
agr	error in agreement (subject/verb or pronoun/antecedent)	*log*	error in logic	*ww*	wrong word
APA	APA documentation	*MLA*	MLA documentation	*X*	obvious error
apos	error in apostrophe use	*mm*	misplaced modifier	∨	insert apostrophe
arg	faulty argumentation	*P*	error in punctuation	[ ] /	insert brackets
awk	awkward wording	*par*	problem with paragraphing	: /	insert colon
bib	error in bibliographical form	*pass*	overuse or misuse of the passive voice	. /	insert comma
○	close up space	?	unclear, doubtful, or unreadable	– /	insert dash
⌐	correct letter case	*ref*	problem with pronoun reference	℈	delete
CBE	CBE documentation	*rep*	repetition	... /	insert ellipsis
coh	problem with coherence	*rev*	revise or proofread	! /	insert exclamation mark
cs	comma splice	*ro*	run-on sentence	∧	omission
cit	error in citation	*shift*	shift in verb tense or logic	( ) /	insert parentheses
d	problem with diction or usage	*sp*	spelling error	. /	insert period
dev	inadequate paragraph development	*ss*	problem with sentence structure	? /	insert question mark
div	incorrect word division	*stet*	keep as it was (ignore changes)	""/	insert quotation marks
dm	dangling modifier	*sub*	faulty subordination	: /	insert semicolon
doc	error in documentation	*t*	error in verb tense	/ /	insert slash
frag	sentence fragment	*trans*	transition problem	∼	transpose
fs	fused sentence	*ts*	problem with thesis statement		
		//	faulty parallelism		

TABLE OF CONTENTS